"*Black Practical Theology* takes seriously the vivid contours of Black existence in the new millennium and gifts the field of Practical Theology with models for using creativity born of marginality as an aid for human flourishing. I have no doubt that this work, which draws on the wisdom of many, will find a place in seminary classrooms and more broadly in theological education."

—*Stephen G. Ray Jr., Neal A. and Ila F. Fisher Professor of Theology, Garrett-Evangelical Theological Seminary*

"This volume makes a decisive contribution to black practical theology as scholars representing the academy and the church tackle critical social issues, from mass incarceration to GLBT matters, with audacious and instructive skill. *Black Practical Theology* is essential reading for those interested in integrative approaches to theory and practice in religious contexts."

—*Linda E. Thomas, Professor of Theology and Anthropology, Lutheran School of Theology*

"Assembling a veritable global team of scholar-practitioners, Dale P. Andrews and Robert London Smith have provided a groundbreaking text of amazing constructive conversations. It will become and remain a watershed book for the academy, church, and broader interested public."

—*Dwight N. Hopkins, Professor of Theology at the Divinity School, University of Chicago*

BLACK PRACTICAL THEOLOGY

Dale P. Andrews
Robert London Smith Jr.
Editors

BAYLOR UNIVERSITY PRESS

Cover Design by AJB Design, Inc.

Library of Congress Cataloging-in-Publication Data

Black practical theology / Dale P. Andrews, Robert London Smith Jr., editors.
  pages cm
  Includes bibliographical references and index.
  ISBN 978-1-60258-435-8 (pbk. : alk. paper)
  1. Black theology. I. Andrews, Dale P., 1961– II. Smith, Robert London.
  BT82.7.B53 2015
  230.089'96073—dc23
                        2015001630

CONTENTS

VII
Mass Incarceration, Capital Punishment, and the Justice System

VIII
Conclusion

Acknowledgments

We first presented the proposal for this project at the Society for the Study of Black Religion (SSBR). The energy for the project even at its early stages was astounding. The support has not waned since. So we must thank our colleagues for their expressed interests in joining the project as contributors and the welcome our invitations received. Some of the original concepts and design of this project stem from research and projects Dale conducted when serving as the Martin Luther King Jr. Professor of Homiletics and Pastoral Theology at Boston University's School of Theology, with the support of its Center for Practical Theology. Likewise, the School of Divinity, History, and Philosophy at King's College, University of Aberdeen, where Robert is currently an honorary researcher in practical theology, has generously supported his ongoing work. We want to thank our cherished colleagues from each of these schools for their support in resources and spirit. In kind, we are grateful for the support and backing received from Dale's current institution (Vanderbilt University's Divinity School) and Robert's congregation at the Rubislaw Parish Church, where he serves as pastor.

We really need to thank the contributors to this project for their provocative insights and willingness to grapple with the rubrics of practical theology we designed for this work, which for many required forays into previously uncharted methods. These authors are astounding researchers and practitioners alike who have tackled some of the most difficult challenges black churches and communities face in our rather diverse diasporan realities. The issues at the centers of our trialogues are those identified by these church and parachurch practitioners for their communities of faith and communities at large. We would also like to thank Dale's research assistant Desmond Coleman and doctoral student, Terrance Dean, for their critical help in reviewing and coordinating the various essays in this volume. Lastly, but certainly not so in our gratitude, we thank Baylor University Press for its unrestrained interest and commitment to this effort. Ultimately, this volume is indebted to the black churches and organizations that indefatigably work in practices of meaning-making and justice-making in the struggles of life and faith that beset our communities. We hope this volume serves such work.

Dale P. Andrews
Robert London Smith Jr.

I
Introduction

<< 1 >>

PROPHETIC PRAXIS FOR BLACK PRACTICAL THEOLOGY

Dale P. Andrews and Robert London Smith Jr.

The editors of this work come to this project as practical theologians whose scholarship has been shaped by and for black theology and black churches. As such, the trajectories of our research are located within social, religious, and cultural contexts that privilege black experience. The aims and outcomes of our respective inquiries, while different, all seek to deepen, clarify, and explore the issues that shape black consciousness through a theological lens. With this project, we hope to prompt scholarly inquiry into the contours of black practical theology by developing its rationale and defining its terms, theological foci, and methodology. Therefore, a key aim of this project is to bring into dialogue with church and parachurch leaders in black communities select scholars who are working within the constructive, biblical, and ethics disciplines of black theology and those scholars who work within practical theology and its customary subdisciplines. This dialogue, or rather "trialogue," calls for a confluence of the research interests and goals of black theology with the approaches and methods of practical theology.

It is understandable when considering the aims of this work that some may be skeptical about its proposed agenda. The question might legitimately be raised, do we really need black practical theology? There is, after all, black theology, which thankfully has become a well-established academic discipline. It has provided a vital means to artic-ulate black voices in the wider academic encyclopedia and to establish the grounds—academic, moral, and theological—upon which the past, present, and future flourishing of dispossessed peoples can be heard and valued. There is also the discipline of practical theology, which while a relative newcomer in the contemporary academic encyclopedia also has a well-established history. Practical theology focuses on human praxis as a point of departure and the mutual interlocutory relationship between practices and theory and their sources. It is our hope that through the scholarly conversation nurtured in this project some suggestions of the contours of black practical theology might be offered and that the insight, creativity, and intellect that the contributors bring to this work will illumine the value and importance of this collaboration between black theologians, practical theologians, and practitioners.

This project attempts to flesh out and investigate questions emerging from within deliberate black contexts, issues, and religious practices that bring the tools of black theology, vocational theological scholarship, religious practices, and the human sciences into new and creative partnership with the approaches and methods of practical theology. This unique body of work, which we envision as black practical theology, will provide a fresh, creative approach to articulating black liberation and transforming black church praxis in light of contemporary contextual realities.

More than an object of study, black church praxis becomes a cornerstone for this project. Therefore, it is necessary that we clarify how we understand and use the term. Firstly, we take "praxis" to denote a kind of reflexive ecology encompassing religious practices and theology that is informed by theory and guided by values and ultimate purpose(s). Praxis is saturated with meaning, theory, and deliberate, critically reflective agency and actions. In the particular case of this work, we are concerned with the agency and actions/practices of black churches, which should not function in isolation, either episodic or enduring. The critically reflective agency around and fluid throughout practices is informed by such sources as theological tradition(s) or convictions, culture, history, and the human/ social sciences. These sources, reflexive activities, and agencies constitute praxis—or in our analysis, black church praxis. In the same manner, this understanding of "praxis" informs the way we use the term variously throughout the project: ecclesial praxis, informed praxis, spiritual praxis, and so on.

We believe the current needs of doing black practical theology lie in developing methodological approaches that privilege human experiences of the contexts, issues, and events shaping black lives and worldviews for the purpose of engaging critically with theological studies and traditions and the human sciences. Therefore, ecclesial praxis, the dynamics of human situations, the values and meaning that inform human acts, and the influence of historical contexts on church praxis are all important areas of critical concern for practical theology. Implicitly, practical theological approaches argue that universal theories of theology are elusive in general and typically risk hegemonic treatment of difference. The pursuit of understanding what might be universal or transcendent about God must move through understanding also what is historical or immanent about God. Theological worldviews, devotional practices of spiritual discipleship, and faith practices of social justice are the substance of inherited theological traditions and evolving church praxis. How, then, to develop black practical theology struggles in the persistent chasm between the black theological disciplines and religious practices in black churches, which reflect implicit but predominating theological worldviews. This project explores how church and parachurch leaders, black theologians, and other disciplines of black theological scholarship might develop practical theological methodology through and for such discourse.

In our previous work, we have taken on different approaches to shaping black practical theology. Andrews has likened black practical theology to prophetic practical theology. This move emerged from a foundation in prophetic consciousness undergirded with the evolutions of covenantal theology. Smith has sought to discipline modes of black praxis in light of contextual and historical realities that shape black worldviews. We understand both moves as nascent steps in what we hope will be a long and fruitful conversation that continues to develop what black practical theology might look like or do.

Andrews' previous work ventured to span the suggested chasm between black theology and black folk religion. He appealed to a strategic reformulation of the inherited traditions of black ecclesiology that have since bifurcated into pastoral refuge paradigms in black churches and the liberation ethics paradigm of black theology.[1] That project, in reformulating or transforming black ecclesiology, constituted a general exercise of practical theological methodology while not attempting to construct theory for developing black practical methodology itself. Our current project moves such efforts forward with more direct attention to exploring how a methodology for black practical theology might be directly developed and engaged.

One proposal with which this project shares its conception is what Andrews has called "hearer-response criticism." Seizing upon methodologies of reader-response criticism from biblical studies (and literary studies),[2] hearer-response criticism proposes a broad paradigm for black practical theology that is also methodologically inherited from black church praxis historically and still reflects the prophetic campaign of the black theology project of the mid-to-late twentieth century into the present. This effort extends beyond cultural theological hermeneutics but is clearly dependent on these hermeneutics as correctives to Western Enlightenment theology.

Response criticism as a practical theological methodology involves studying the meaning-making processes of faith communities in response both to inherited sacred texts like the Bible and to the folk wisdom gleaned from interpreting the Bible within the particular contexts of history that shape their lives. Faith communities, like those oral traditions forming black churches, interpret and reinterpret Christian traditions that somehow become distorted in the Church's struggle to be faithful to divine revelation. This process reflects methods of praxis that critically move between theology and practice. This praxis, however, involves the interpretation and reinterpretation of changing historical contexts of human struggle and also human resources like the human sciences and scholarship. How these methods may successfully or supportively function together constitute what we typically refer to as methodology. For black practical theology, the inherited practices of oral cultural praxis offer foundations upon which we may begin to construct methodology for the evolving historical struggle of black communities and the increasing difficulty to enact hearer-response criticism between black theology scholarship and the predominating paradigms of ministry in the Black Church. The functional question behind developing a methodology for black practical theology remains: How do we transform or redevelop theological worldviews and religious practices, as well as theological traditions, in the interpretation and reinterpretation of inherited sacred texts and sacred traditions within evolving historical conditions and struggles for meaning-making and justice-making for ourselves and others?

Clearly, the goals of methodology point beyond the system itself. It should not be surprising, therefore, that most practical theological methodologies conclude with strategic agency/actions seeking transformation of our understanding, our practices, and our world. If hearer-response criticism is a viable paradigm for constructing practical theology, then we must include the full range of possible transformation between theological worldviews, religious practices, and inherited theological traditions.

Transforming theological traditions has been one of the more successful campaigns of the black theology project. It continues to challenge prevailing Christian theological constructs that buttress oppressive theological distortions and social conditions. Less effective has been black theology's efforts to transform church practices and black theological worldviews that uncritically perpetuate the theological paradigms sustaining the oppressive traditions, at least theologically, and therefore contribute to the lack of prophetic redress among black churches. This is deeply disturbing to both black theologians and practical theologians alike.

Black practical theology will seek to reinterpret traditions and historical contexts together. Prophetic consciousness does not supersede pastoral nurture as the overriding norm of the in-breaking reign of God, nor does the latter tolerably supplant the former as the norm of discipleship. Black practical theology turns to developing methodology for paradigms of interpretation and reinterpretation extending between inherited traditions, religious practices, theological worldviews, and the human resources of the Enlightenment sciences.

As we have already stated, this volume calls for a critical conversation among scholars to begin shaping what black practical theology might look like and how it could contribute to the existing scholarship in black theology and practical theology, as well as the latter's subdisciplines. Smith's understanding of this nascent conversation is rooted in the premise that for any theology to be practical, it must be shaped by practical concerns. Building on the work of black theology, Smith emphasizes what he refers to as "praxiological intent."[3] Quite simply, praxiological intent describes theology that is made tangible through the practices that faith communities engage in daily and, therefore, describes action that is informed by theological judgments. Therefore, black practical theology very broadly at this early juncture takes its sensibilities and cues from within black experience and engages the practices and theological understanding of black faith communities.

Smith utilizes practical theological methods to develop, in collaboration with the insights and the theological focus of black theology, a particular trajectory of theological inquiry with which to understand and transform modes of black church practice. These transformed modes of church practice constitute an "informed praxis" that embodies how a faith community interprets and responds to the issues and events that impact it. Black practical theology privileges concern for the "whats" and "whys" of black church praxis. Its focus is on questions such as "*Why* are we doing *what* we are doing? What does it truly mean? *Who* we are? And what *should* we be doing?" Answering these questions requires looking at how such black church praxis can be disciplined in light of the historical and contextual realities that shape black worldviews.

Congregational practices, the dynamics of human situations, the human sciences, the values and meaning that inform human acts, and the influence of historical contexts on ecclesial practice all become important areas of critical concern for practical theology praxis and methodology. Attention to contemporary black culture, political issues, the effects of globalization, and the continuing impacts of race, class, gender, willful and cultural abuse, and violence toward and within the black community are all important sources of inquiry and grist for black practical theology.

In response to the historical events and cultural contexts that influenced them, how black church praxis continually forms and re-forms is a central focus of black practical theology. Therefore, an approach that allows the careful and critical consideration of the historical contexts shaping black church praxis is important. Smith's approach built upon the concept of a thematic universe.[4] Briefly, a thematic universe comprises the generative themes that reflect the particular ideas, values, and meanings that exist in tension with their opposites and therefore define a situation or condition shaping people's experiences of reality. Therefore, the concept of a black thematic universe is the set of historical and cultural circumstances defining the situations and conditions that shape the experiences of reality for generations of Africans and Pan-Africans. Because of the focus on the black historical contexts and the use of black cultural, religious, and theological resources to respond relevantly and constructively to their contexts, black faith responses are praxiological in nature. In other words, early black faith communities developed critical awareness of their times, used all their resources to reflect on them, and created praxiological faith responses. It was praxis shaped by black theology—that is, theology made evident in black praxis. This dynamic is one of the strengths of the African American faith community, which has enabled generations of enslaved, persecuted, and marginalized black people to survive and thrive first in the plantations and colonies and then in the cities and states of the modern West.

Along with black theology, Andrews and Smith observe significant struggles among black church practices and paradigms of ministry to redress effectively the historically shifting black thematic universe through the course of the Civil Rights era and now afterward. New situations and conditions arise that draw upon previous ones but also possess distinctions all their own. These conditions, and the circumstances that attend them, comprise diverse contemporary black thematic universes and therefore the demands placed upon black church paradigms of faith, identity, and ministry. This pluralism of contemporary black thematic universes increasingly shapes the experiences of reality of contemporary African Americans and Pan-Africans, who yet still share struggles under dehumanizing marginalization. The generative themes and implicated circumstances involve the phenomenon of globalization within which neocolonialism, mutating racism and sexism, sexual ethics, heterosexism, nationalism, religious violence, capitalism, consumerism, and the impact of information technology exist. In light of the careful observations and insights derived from the analysis of contemporary generative themes and circumstances, and understanding that the church praxis of traditional black ecclesiology and black faith responses are greatly challenged by a once dominant, if inadequate and now fading, historical black thematic universe, a revision of contemporary black church praxis is needed.

Informed praxis is the result of critical awareness of dominant values, sound theological reflection, critical engagement with historical contexts and the human sciences, and a deliberate or strategic teleological focus. It is able, therefore, compellingly to address contemporary issues in a way that does not ignore cultural and religious heritage, Christian traditions and Scripture, and contemporary social contexts. The challenges for today's contemporary black churches are how they will develop their own praxiological responses to diverse contemporary black thematic universes and thus create new modes of informed praxis. The *response criticism* and *praxiological intent* of much early black church praxis enabled churches to rise to such noble and often daunting tasks and, in doing so, provide for the survival and flourishing of black people in spite of the many obstacles—social, legal, and otherwise—to their full humanity and inclusion. The Black Church remains a preeminent institution within the black community. However, in the early decades of the twenty-first century, black churches face exigencies to reevaluate their mission, means, and legacy amid a plethora of new challenges and changes in today's contemporary culture.

In envisioning black practical theology, we seek to bring the interdisciplinary and critical methodological tools of practical theology together with black theology's constructive agenda of articulating black epistemology and theological understanding in their myriad expressions to bear upon the ways contemporary black churches might work to meet these challenges—specifically, a careful investigation into black church praxis. This understanding of black practical theology as a conflation of practical theology and black theology extends our pedagogical frameworks for describing and teaching black theology into paradigms of practical theological methods to transform modes of black praxis within the faith community.

This confluence implies that, as we begin to explore the possibilities of what black practical theology might look like and mean, methodology is a critically important consideration. Methodology addresses questions of how we go about understanding those issues and practices within the black faith community and the cultural environment that shape black worldviews such that we might be able to help shape effective responses. Such a methodological approach begins with the critical consideration of praxis; that is, it is concerned with understanding the myriad influences on individuals and church practices, such as the various expressions of contemporary black life, and aims at the formation of faith and the transformation of praxis and agency in light of those contextual realities, beliefs, contemporary events, and issues that impact black experience. Existential and theological considerations engage in interpretive and reinterpretive *response criticism* with *praxiological intent*—a process that is mutually critical and continually reflexive. A methodology for black practical theology would value this sort of model and the kind of hermeneutic approach it seeks to develop.

Any such effort to build methodology must flow from some defining understanding of its constructive paradigm. Hence, we offer the following descriptive outline or definition of black practical theology as a sounding board for further conversation and as a way to locate our vision of this integrative discipline:

> Black practical theology is the disciplined critical reflection between religious practices (both individual and ecclesial), theology, and human sciences seeking to study God's engagement or relationship with humanity, and to interpret and reinterpret ongoing and changing historical contexts of human life, human relations, and human struggle. Persons and communities alike exercise this process of reflection constituting modes of spiritual and ecclesial praxis. For each, the goals of transforming or redeveloping thematic worldviews of black life experiences, values, needs, and theological worldviews are held together in the effort to interpret the historical landscape and reinterpret inherited sacred texts and traditions. Black practical theology moves strategically

to develop agency/action toward faith formation and the transformation of religious practices, inherited sacred traditions, or contemporary
worldviews in the work of meaning-making and justice-making, even as
we seek to understand what it means to be persons of faith, a faith community, or the Church. This praxiological intent unfolds reciprocally
with evolving methods or paradigms of response criticism.

At this point, we have hopefully "set the table" for readers such that our
thinking and understanding of the conversations to follow will have some
foundations. These are offered not proscriptively but as a means to begin a
conversation about shaping or reshaping the discipline.

PRAXIOLOGICAL RESPONSE CRITICISM

We locate the starting point of doing practical theology in the experiences,
practices, and worldviews of persons and communities of faith, especially
when change, conflict, crises, neglect, or ignorance arises. This is not a
concrete beginning; instead it is a "breaking-in" point, to borrow a more
eschatological concept. The actual work of practical theology may at times
begin with a critical look at inherited theological doctrines or traditional
folk tenets of faith; however, even this doctrinal or constructive criticism
is a response to unresolved or expanding questions and even crises emerging from faith practices, exigencies of life, or spiritual worldviews.

Praxiological response criticism places the narrativity of theological thinking in a central dialogical position within practical theology.
Perhaps, a central question is, do people uncritically apply doctrines of
the Christian faith, or even think doctrinally? While, for some, uncritical
adoption of doctrines obviously may occur, response criticism unavoid-
ably influences developed practices in the life of faith surrounding those
doctrines. Even if particularly apologetic practices arise that do not refor-
mulate doctrine, the process for developing those practices should at least
involve response criticism with praxiological intent.

The implication, of course, is that there are normative doctrinal values
at stake in theology. How, then, do we determine the functional claims of
doctrine upon our lives? How do we determine their successful or unsuc-
cessful ability to address the spiritual and historical questions in the life
of faith or worldview of people? Perhaps too often faith claims resort to
doctrinal assertion amid the insecurity of the unsure. Even retrench-
ment is a response criticism, albeit perhaps stemming from the fear of
despair or nihilism. Not all appeals to faith doctrines, however, are based
in fear. Some are based in response to theological tenets of hope or even

discipleship defining practices of faith itself. In cases of normative faith claims or values, praxiological response criticism may appeal also to constructive theology's efforts to correlate doctrinal theological thinking with contemporary or historical experience.

Black theology is an excellent example of this role for constructive theology in relation to praxis, response criticism, and praxiological intent. The corrective or reformulation of systematic theology through the epistemology and hermeneutics of black historical experience has been the primary manner in which black theology does at times function as a practical theological paradigm. Its limitations, however, have been its historical reformulations within the inherited traditions of constructive black theology systematics. What happens when the worldviews, faith practices, and ecclesial paradigms themselves, even as critically reformulated, do not sustain a bridge to contemporary challenges of oppression, not to mention the complicit challenges of liberation? These dynamics reflect the need and work of practical theology, both in focus and in methodology.

We are proposing praxiological response criticism here as a paradigm or methodology for doing black practical theology. This criticism emerges from four aspects we find integral to practical theology. First, the role of praxis is primary. The "trialectic" between theology, theory, and practices is already in motion. One might argue that it may have always been so. Conceptually, any theological awakening for humanity already itself is either a gradual pealing or a kerygmatic encounter of the praxis cycle between spiritual practices in the life of faith, theories of human life and nature, and theological paradigms. We do not find it necessary or even possible to establish a consistent beginning point for a linear process of doing practical theology. Instead, we believe that the work of practical theology initiates from the tremors or quakes in the life of faith within the historical contexts and worldviews of contemporary life, which are always unfolding. The doctrines or tenets of faith are not simply relative structures. They are foundations; however, they are foundations whose stability or enduring strengths are exposed by said tremors and quakes, which always require architectural as well as rehabilitative work, both of which may, at times, require reformulation of the foundation itself. Practical theology investigates the epicenters of those tremors and quakes and critiques the stability of the work of formulating the necessarily cogent faith responses to the events of life—a praxis enterprise working with inherited theology and traditions, theories of human and natural sciences in human development and contemporary life, and practices reflecting spiritual worldviews and historical needs.

This praxis orientation to practical theology involves direct attention to both the second aspect (namely, response criticism in the engagement between traditions and historical life), and the third aspect (namely, praxiological intent of doing practical theology that reevaluates the effective exchanges between the elements of praxis). Ultimately, the fourth aspect, common to nearly all practical theological methodologies, moves to the creation of strategies for transformation of lives, practices, or traditions, but usually much of these together. These four aspects constitute what we propose as a methodology for developing or exploring the work of black practical theology.

PROJECT DESIGN

The central design of this project is to bring into critical exchange three groups of scholars and practitioners from the black theological constructive disciplines, practical theology, and pastoral/community ministries in contemporary black life. The methodological structure of the project is a practical theological one in that it begins with critical problems drawn from the contexts of contemporary black life or religious practices among black churches, as identified by the practitioners. Practical theology attempts to break from its historical formation as the applied science in theological curricula; therefore it breaks into or redefines the theological presuppositions and methods of the classical disciplines of theological education, under which the black theology project itself has labored as a form of constructive theology. This project draws on three of the more common foci used in building methodology in practical theology. These foci include building analyses of situations or contexts of religious communities and contemporary life, building critical reflection on religious or spiritual practices within such contexts, and building upon interdisciplinary dialogue and scholarship. The design of this project supports an integrative approach to these major building efforts.

This text is divided into six contributor sections, each of which treats a significant area of concern in black life in black communities. The work of each section is held together by the critical definition and methodology of black practical theology proffered in this introduction. We asked prominent black pastors and parachurch leaders to identify the critical issues or religious practices that they feel impact their congregations and therefore need both black theologians and practical theologians to engage. The six issues to emerge from this exploration are as follows: black youth, inter-generational relations, and ageism; education, class, and poverty; gender, sexual orientation, and race; globalism, immigration, and diasporan communities; health care, HIV/AIDS, and poverty; and mass incarceration, capital punishment, and the justice system. Each contributor section begins with a description of the issue gleaned and outlined from the initial inquiry with the church and parachurch leaders. Through a draft of this introduction, the editors oriented the contributors to the two-prong argument for envisioning the possibilities of black practical theology.

Each contributor section comprises an invited trialogue around the respective issues our church and parachurch leaders have identified. The initial conversation partner of each section invites a scholar from among the traditional subdisciplines of practical theology to engage the identified issue. Contributors were selected for their work in such disciplines as homiletics, Christian education, and pastoral care and counseling. Their task is to bring their work of training clerical leadership or developing clerical practices into critical dialogue with issues shaping black contemporary worldviews and religious practices in black church communities.

The second conversation partner of each contributor section involves our black constructive, biblical, or ethics theological scholars. We asked these contributors to reflect on how these issues/questions from the pastors/ parachurch leaders and our proposed practical theological definitions and methodology might shape doing theology for them and their home disciplines. In doing so, in effect, they also attempt to redress the chasm that exists between the black theology project and black churches, as well as with contemporary black worldviews. These chapters bring critical issues or practices into dialogue with theological traditions, both within the larger doctrinal cannon and within the black theological project.

The third conversation partner of each contributor section is again a prominent black church pastor or parachurch leader with a significant ministry in a black community. This partner's assigned task is more evaluative in nature and includes providing critical feedback to the two other scholars in the trialogue. We supplied these church/parachurch practitioners with the corresponding chapters from the subdisciplines of practical theology and the black constructive/biblical theology. We asked them to provide their own critical responses in light of their particular attention to the needs, issues, or practices in their communities that originally generated this trialogue. As for the viability of the strategies proffered, we also asked these pastors/parachurch leaders to make further recommendations to these scholars and anticipated readers and to modify suggested approaches to fit more effectively within their particular contexts or communal experiences. With such steps, we intend to open opportunities for continuing scholarship.

It is our hope that this process offers a paradigm for praxiological response criticism, thereby constructing methodology for black practical theology. Still more so, we hope that black practical theology will engender partnerships between the traditional black theological and practical theological disciplines, helping to clarify, add nuance to, and direct/redirect movements of interdisciplinary theological research and scholarship in direct dialectic engagement with black church praxis itself. In the end, we seek to cultivate liberating and transformative strategies that speak compellingly and responsively to increasingly diverse black theological worldviews, faith practices, and a world in continual need of divine in-breaking.

II

Black Youth, Intergenerational Relations, and Ageism

A growing issue in black churches concerns the failure to enfranchise, protect, and nurture black youth, and in some particular cases young black men. In many black communities around the world, large numbers of black youth and young men continue to be at risk of being the perpetrators or victims of violence and crime, both of which are characterized by unfulfilled potential, incarceration, or early death. Raising the aspirations and educational attainment of black youth and young black men and women is one way to fight against the damaging impact these risks have in black communities. While a concern for black youth is evident within the larger black community, few black men are actively involved in helping identify and bring about positive solutions. Psychologist Erik Erikson describes such engagement by black men in the lives of black youth and young adults as the work of "generativity." A previous administration in the United Kingdom introduced the Every Child Matters initiative, which identified five requirements for the development of youth: to be safe, to be healthy, to achieve, to contribute to public life, and to attain economic well-being. Given the precarious existence of many black youths and young adults, not only in the United States and Britain but across the world, it is crucial that more black men and women become generative helpers. In what ways can black theologians and practical theologians work with black churches to engage black youth and young adults to break the various cycles of violence and crime?

Similarly, wider intergenerational relations critically challenge black churches and communities. Black churches are in need of an intergenerational approach to ministry so that young people can learn from their elders and elders can learn from, connect with, and relate to young people.

In this era in which so many alternatives—both secular and spiritual—to the traditional church exist, it is imperative that black theologians and practical theologians assist black churches in bridging contemporary generational divides. One example is the apparent disconnect between the so-called saved saints within congregations and the Hip Hop culture of young people who remain children of the church, not to mention those who have left black churches altogether. This disconnect is experienced by both younger and older generations. Perhaps, too, we need to formulate a new civil rights agenda to include the fight against ageism. The contributions of seniors should be reaffirmed and their personal narratives retold whenever we gather to preach and pray or to promote and practice social ministries. What methods, insights, or constructive dialogue might black theologians and practical theologians offer to address such disconnects in meaningful ways?

<< 2 >>

Bridging Civil Rights and Hip Hop Generations

Evelyn L. Parker

Imagine, if you will, a seventy-five-year-old woman sitting in the same pew as a seventeen-year-old boy as they, among others in a black congregation, rock and bob to the sound of "Jesus Walks" by Kanye West. Some might say that such an image is more frequent than not, while others would consider it impossible in the black congregation where they worship and serve. The latter group's resistance to West's rap lyrics—"God show me the way because the devil is trying to bring me down,"[1] layered on top of the ARC Choir singing the traditional gospel "Walk with Me"—reflects some black churches' demonization of rap music and all aspects of Hip Hop culture. Churches of this type, grounding their responses in stereotypes of rap musicians and Hip Hop culture, would charge West with blasphemous conduct as a rapper who has little or no experience of, or respect for, the African American Church. In contrast, the black congregation that works at critically engaging Hip Hop culture and selectively incorporating rap music into worship or other hallowed places of black congregational life might have not only played the sound track of "Jesus Walks" but also showed one of the three videos that West created with his multiplatinum megahit released in 2005.[2] Black congregations of this type may have intentionally committed to intergenerational conversations on the history and current manifestations of Hip Hop culture, music genres of gospel rap/holy Hip Hop, and the possible congregational exchange with these facets in worship and service. However, the overall responses, given by imagined polar-opposite black congregations, highlight a point of contention between youth and adults when it comes to Hip Hop culture.

The struggle of black youth and their adult affiliates to validate Hip Hop while debating with adults who seek to reject Hip Hop as a viable culture elucidates the contemporary generational divide that needs bridging if the Black Church is to be healthy and wholesome and live out its prophetic mission. This chapter views this imagined intergenerational encounter with Kanye West's "Jesus Walks" and the traditional gospel song "Walk with Me" as two metaphors converging to form a new metaphor of *walking together* to bridge the problem of generational divides between youth of the Hip Hop generation and adults of the Civil Rights generation. *Walking together* symbolizes a praxis model of ministry in black congregations that cultivates vital partnerships between youth and adults for prophetic and liberating work on behalf of the black community.

THE PROBLEM

The problem of contemporary generational divides between young people and elders in black churches and communities is primarily one of diverging worldviews. Black youth have a different worldview than do black adults. As such, black youth and adults misunderstand each other. In his book *The Hip Hop Generation*, Bakari Kitwana comprehensively explores the differences between black youth and adult worldviews. He argues that young men and women born between 1965 and 1984, a time of radical sociohistorical change, and who came of age during the eighties and nineties can be considered the first cohort of the Hip Hop generation. The second cohort, who experienced a different sociohistorical context, are those born between 1985 and 2000. These two cohorts account for the generation of African American youth and young adults that African American churches target for their ministries and programs. Ordinarily, these youth and young adults are of middle school/junior high, high school, undergraduate, and graduate-school age. Some African American congregations include ten- and eleven-year-olds in their programs, depending on their size and local practices. Notwithstanding, black congregations target youth we know as belonging to the Hip Hop generation. The first and oldest age cohort was born when Hip Hop was taking flight in the boroughs of New York City.[3] Economic policies of the Reagan administration, known collectively as "trickle-down economics," shaped the first ten years of their lives. Members of the first Hip Hop cohort experienced a continuation of trickle-down economic policies during the George H. W. Bush administration, which carried these youth into their mid-teenage years. By the late 1990s, when members of the first Hip Hop cohort entered the workforce, they were the least likely to be employed because most were low-skilled workers and were highly concentrated in urban communities.[4] The sounds and sights of Hip Hop culture shaped the identities of youth in poor black urban communities and critiqued the economic climate in which they were coming of age. Even middle-class black youth living in the suburbs with parents who seized the opportunity to leave inner-city black neighborhoods during the post–Civil Rights period embraced a worldview shaped by Hip Hop culture. Such was the economic and political climate that shaped the worldview of the first cohort of the Hip Hop generation. Ultimate in the worldview of this cohort is personal financial success. This value stands in opposition to the high value the older Civil Rights generation placed on communal cultural uplift.[5] A consideration of the values, beliefs, and attitudes that constitute the worldview of the first cohort of the Hip Hop generation offers important insight.

Bakari Kitwana argues that six major phenomena of the 1980s and 1990s shaped the worldview of the Hip Hop generation.[6] The first is pop culture and its ability to serve as a surrogate for the values and attitudes offered by black bodies in the entertainment industry. The very values of popular rap artists are deeply influenced by the "multinational corporations that produce, distribute, and shape these images."[7] Second is the phenomenon of globalization, which evolved from the multinational corporations of the 1970s to transnational corporations that operate primarily in the United States, Europe, and Japan. These transnational megacorporations have economic power fueled by biological and digital technology.[8] International trade agreements, which include the North American Free Trade Agreement (NAFTA) and the General Agreement on Tariffs and Trade (GATT), strengthen these corporations. As Kitwana notes, "Young Black Americans born between 1965 and 1984 are the first generation of Black Americans to come of age in the era of globalization."[9] Some Hip Hop generationers—primarily rap artists, college-educated professionals, professional athletes, and high-tech moguls—benefited from trickle-down wealth from transnational corporations.[10] Their values and beliefs— namely, that personal achievement interlocks with wealth—mirrors the values of globalizing economies. Thus, the worldview of the Hip Hop generationers, both rich and poor, is shaped by globalization. Third, the first cohort of the Hip Hop generation has experienced persistent segregation in a theoretically postsegregated society. Black youth have experienced inequality tantamount to the Jim Crow era, when segregation was legal.[11] Fourth, public policy regarding drugs, violence, education, and even style of dress has criminalized black youth and made them the highest incarcerated population of any racial/ethnic group in the United States.[12] Public policy shapes the values and attitudes of black youth who see no alternative beyond incarceration. This problem persists to the point that some poor black youth expect to serve time in prison as a rite of passage, a point I will revisit regarding the second cohort of the Hip Hop generation. Fifth, media represents black youth as soulless brutes.[13] Sixth, the first cohort of the Hip Hop generation's worldview has been shaped by a quality of life that renders black youth poor, unemployable, and at high risk for death by homicide, suicide, and AIDS.[14] Kitwana concludes his litany of phenomena with the following comment about how the lack of church involvement shaped the worldview of black youth who came of age during the 1980s and early 1990s:

> A further indication of what they deem a withering sense of values and social responsibility among the young generation, they say, is the steady drop in youth membership and attendance in the Black church—long a community haven of spiritual centeredness and respectable values. According to the National Opinion Research Center at the University of Chicago, attendance for eighteen to thirty-five-year-olds has dropped 5.6 percent from 1995 to 2000.[15]

Kitwana's description of the worldview of the first cohort is embodied by a number of black rap artists. Two exemplars of this Hip Hop cohort are Kanye West, who was born in 1977, and female rap artist Nicki Minaj, who was born in 1982. It is also evident in the older Shawn "Jay-Z" Corey Carter, a rap artist and successful entrepreneur who was born in 1969.

The second cohort of the Hip Hop generation was born between 1985 and 2000. This cohort honed a worldview similar to the first cohort, given the political climate during the presidential administrations of Bill Clinton and George W. Bush. Public policies that shaped the values and attitudes of the first cohort continue to fortify the prison industrial complex, perpetuate high dropout rates among black youth, and escalate unemployment numbers, particularly among black youth. Black youth born between 1985 and 2000 have seen an increase in the incarceration of black women and girls. This increase is a function of minimum sentencing laws and rigid sentencing guidelines in the federal criminal justice system, among other things.[16] Additionally, popular culture, globalization, media representation of black youth, and quality of life issues continue to shape the worldview of the second cohort in more virulent ways than in generations past. The media representation of young black women and men being arrested for crimes on cop shows as well as black couples engaged in feuds on talk shows are TV mainstays. Transnational organizations, such as the corporation Viacom, have the machinery to create and nourish the appetite for rap music unparalleled by the efforts of multinational corporations in years past. Scholars have raised a critical voice with regard to the power of Viacom to commodify Hip Hop in such a manner that rappers, music producers, clothing designers, videographers, and a host of other practitioners of Hip Hop culture are at the mercy of Viacom's owners. Other transnational corporations have likewise shaped the values and attitudes of the second cohort. However, the effect of the presidential administration of Barack Obama on the second cohort remains to be seen. Many black youth born between 1985 and 1994 voted in the presidential elections of 2008 and 2012, when President Obama was elected to his first and second terms. Perhaps his election was the sociohistorical moment that connected both cohorts of the Hip Hop generation to members of the Civil Rights generation.

African American adults born between 1929 and 1955 constitute the Civil Rights generation. Some scholars argue the children of the Civil Rights generation, born between 1956 and 1964, make up a transitional generation.[17] Admittedly, the generational boundaries are not rigid. Some argue that this age cohort belongs to the first generation of Hip Hop. To be clear, the transitional generation, as offspring of the Civil Rights generation, birthed and/or parented the second generation of Hip Hop children.[18] With the exception of those parents who succumbed to drug addiction and other demoralizing practices, the transitional generation tend to hold the same values and beliefs as their parents from the Civil Rights generation. In cases where parents are unable to care for their children, grandparents from the Civil Rights generation became the primary caregivers of Hip Hop youth. Nevertheless, some transitional parents opted not to enforce the mandatory church attendance that their Civil Rights generation parents enforced uncompromisingly. It was the Civil Rights generation whose bodies literally were sacrificed for the causes of justice, freedom, and equality denied African Americans for centuries. They fought for the desegregation of schools, equal pay, and affirmative action policies that sought economic justice for African Americans. They fought against redlining and struggled for fair housing, including the opportunity to move their families into predominately white suburbs, if they so desired.

As stated earlier, communal uplift and brotherhood/sisterhood stands at the heart of the Civil Rights generation's worldview. Representative of this generation are Civil Rights activist, icon, and former mayor of Atlanta, Andrew Young, born in 1932, and Diane Nash, Student Nonviolent Coordinating Committee member and leader of the Nashville sit-ins, born in 1938. These, and other lesser-known leaders of the Civil Rights generation, "were so busy fighting [for freedom, justice and equality] that they rarely came home to debrief, particularly with their children."[19] As a result, some of their children and grandchildren failed to understand the struggle and the strategic maneuvers needed to negotiate the emergence of Reaganomics.[20] Thus, the worldview of the Civil Rights generation, shaped as it was by the values of communal work and communal gain, collides with the worldview of the Hip Hop generation, which is characterized by individual financial success and personal uplift. When worldviews collide, misunderstandings are inevitable.

The problem of the contemporary generational divide between the Hip Hop generation and the Civil Rights generation is based on misunderstandings and the exchange of misinformation between the two generations. The older generation at times failed to pass along the intellectual, passionate, and personal calling to freedom, equality, and justice for African-descended people. Additionally, they did not always prepare their children for the world they would inherit. Seduced by the promises of a capitalistic society void of visible bearers of injustice of years past, the Hip Hop generation often feel unprepared to fight for justice in the manner of their parents and grandparents. However, in many ways the cares and concerns of the two generations are the same. Emmett G. Price writes,

> Although Hip Hop Culture in the twenty-first century is different from its infant state in the late 1960s and early 1970s, its urgent cries, moans, groans, and hollers remain consistently focused on the same survival, liberation, and equality that the Black Church has fought for over the generations. In fact, although the Hip Hop modus operandi is dramatically and drastically different, perhaps even polemic, Hip Hop and the Black Church are essentially fighting for the same thing and that is what makes this question of the dilemma of the generational divide and the initial and subsequent disengagement of the Black Church so intellectually perplexing.[21]

Proponents of the African American Church, exemplified by the Civil Rights generation, and African American youth, exemplified by the Hip Hop generation, ultimately desire the same things for the black community:

communal uplift and equality. Yet both generations are at an impasse for discourse and understanding and for bridging the generational divide.

While the gap between the Hip Hop generation and the Civil Rights generation is situated primarily in North America, and the United States specifically, Hip Hop culture has shaped the identity of black youth in the United Kingdom as well. British Hip Hop was born during the early 1980s among multiracial and multiethnic urban youth.[22] British Hip Hop was heavily influenced by U.S. Hip Hop, and its concern for social, economic, and political justice in urban communities was the same as that of its Western counterpart.[23] The Windrush generation in Great Britain is somewhat equivalent to the Civil Rights generation in that the former were African-descended colonialized people from the Caribbean who immigrated to the land of their colonizers in the years after World War II.[24] Confronted by acts of racial discrimination during the 1960s, the Windrush generation fashioned a movement to address inequalities and race relations.[25] The efforts of this generation have been largely lost on black youth in Britain and those around the world who continue to be at risk for violence and crime while consuming forms of Hip Hop culture. Thus, what can be done about the problem of the contemporary generational divides?

THE PRACTICES

Several current practices in congregations and communities contribute to the divide between the Hip Hop and Civil Rights generations. While the evidence is anecdotal, these practices include demonization, disrespect, and disengagement on the part of black youth and older adults. Elders often demonize black girls, assuming that they all engage in booty-clapping dances, are scantily clad and sexually promiscuous, and take illegal drugs. In similar fashion, many elders demonize black boys as dirty-mouthed, saggy-pants-wearing, drug-dealing, violent menaces to society. They see the music, videos, clothing, language, and behavior of black youth as distasteful, demonic, and irredeemable. While black youth tend not to demonize their elders within earshot, such demonization does not go unexpressed. When preachers and prominent entertainers like Bill Cosby demonize black youth over pulpits, on the TV or radio, or in other public spaces, black youth will drop out (stop coming) to the communal spaces (church) where they encounter adults. The shame of demonization leads youth to avoid contact with elders, rather than violently "go off" on them.

Additionally, the demonization of youth leads them to disrespect elders, such as by talking back while being chastised and using dismissive gestures such as smacking or clicking sounds, swerving necks, and the "speak to the hand" sign. Disrespect goes beyond such disdainful gestures toward elders. On the flip side, some adults find youth and their culture so repugnant that they dread their very presence. The old adage "youth should be seen and not heard" is now "youth should be not seen and never heard." Youth and adults practice mutual disrespect.

This mutual disrespect among older adults and youth leads to disengagement with each other. Such disengagement is evinced in the low percentages of teen participation in intergenerational events such as worship services, family reunions, and community summits. Communication between the generations is sparse if not nonexistent. On a familial level, when teens and adults disconnect emotionally and intellectually, the household spirals into chaotic mayhem that can be lethal.

Kai Wright describes a town-hall meeting that sought to bring together black youth and adults in an effort to bridge the generational divide and engage youth in politics. The setting was June 2004 in an "old-school Baptist church, with a high wrought-iron fence dutifully shielding the congregants from Newark's [New Jersey] mean streets."[26] Wright recounts the endless parade of male, suited pastoral officials demanding that youth maintain control. A Civil Rights–era poet "broke into a Motown medley while explaining to the youth that their music wasn't 'real' music, wasn't *movement music*."[27] Following that demonizing remark, a prominent Baptist minister sermonized the youth for fifteen minutes just as they were invited to microphones for the Q&A. The MC, Wright recounts, "promptly concluded the session and sent the young questioners back to their seats." Wright confesses he had given up on intentional and authentic intergenerational dialogue. He then transitions from his lament of this failed opportunity for genuine intergenerational dialogue among youth and adults to a discussion of similar generational divides that have occurred throughout the history of African Americans. He notes the tensions between young Zora Neale Hurston and Langston Hughes and their elders during the Harlem Renaissance.[28] Hurston and Hughes refused "to adapt their art to mainstream black political thought of the time," which antagonized their elders. Wright argues that the contemporary generational feud between black youth and their elders, as in times past, now plays out within Hip Hop culture and its young disciples. As mentioned, the current generational feud between the Hip Hop and Civil Rights generations is wrought with demonization, disrespect, and disengagement. However, there are current practices that hold possibilities for resolving the generational disputes and culture wars.

THE POSSIBILITIES

What practices can bring about wholesome intergenerational relations between the Hip Hop and Civil Rights generations? As I suggested at the onset of this chapter, the imagined intergenerational encounter with Kanye West's "Jesus Walks" and the traditional gospel song "Walk with Me" can be seen as the merging of two metaphors into a new metaphor of *walking together.* This encounter or merger provides a framework for critically and theologically reflecting on the practices of ministry with black teenagers and young adults who are either already members of black congregations or the desired constituents of the ministry the Black Church seeks to serve. Specifically, *walking together* offers a way to engage in ministry with respect to concerns about intergenerational relations and ageism in black congregations from a praxiological perspective.

Kanye West's "Jesus Walks" is a metaphorical response to black teens' trials, disappointments, and troubles. It is sung as a lament in the same manner as the metaphorical response heard in "Walk with Me," although many years before the black youth of the Hip Hop generation were born. "Walk with Me" is a response to the same anxieties, needs, and desires that today's black teens face, and black adults of earlier generations experienced, even as both groups understand those challenges through different worldviews, accompanying practices, and attendant misunderstandings. In the words of the refrain of "Walk with Me," "I want Jesus to walk with me. I want Jesus to walk with me. All along my pilgrim journey, I want Jesus to walk with me." The three verses lament, "trials. . . . When the shades of life are falling . . . sorrows. . . . When my heart within is aching . . . troubles. . . . When my life becomes a burden, Lord, I want Jesus to walk with me." The metaphor that emerges when we combine "Jesus Walks" and "Walk with Me"—namely, *walking together*—calls for the Hip Hop and Civil Rights generations to practice three verbs: listen, learn, and lean.[29]

Listening is necessary if youth and adults are to hear each other on verbal and nonverbal levels of expression in formal settings (i.e., town-hall meetings) and informal settings (i.e., one-on-one partnerships). Adults must listen to youth as they struggle to express feelings of hurt, disappointment, anger, and joy even when words fail to express their emotions.

Likewise, youth must listen to adults whose hearts are also heavy with economic and social burdens that words often fail to describe. Had the adults of the Newark town-hall meeting made time to reciprocate the courtesy of listening to the teens, just as the teens had listened to the adult religious leaders, a fundamental step in communication might have been achieved.

The Civil Rights generation was socialized to internalize their pain and share it, at best, with a friend rather than a spouse and least of all a child or grandchild. It was not until graduate school, when my father insisted that he chauffer me to my late-night shift at the Northwestern University Library just three blocks from my apartment, that I learned of a life-threatening incident my dad experienced. He explained that you never know what evil lurks down streets and around corners. When I pressed him about his care to drive me to work, he told me that many nights he feared he would never make it home from work after passing through Ku Klux Klan roadblocks in various regions of Southern Mississippi. He concluded that the Klan roadblocks urged him to start the practice of keeping his Bible on the front seat beside him as he traveled. My dad never unveiled his fear of death in a white supremacist context to his transitional-generation children. Sharing such experiences with his Hip Hop generation grandchildren was unimaginable. The Civil Rights generation must tell their stories of pain and struggle with humility and risk their vulnerable selves with youth. Upon hearing these stories, teens must listen, even pastorally, to the wounded warriors of the Civil Rights generation.

To listen also means to pay attention to nonverbal expressions of both generations, particularly of youth and adults who find it hard to express themselves verbally. When words fail youth, adults must listen with a "third ear." This is the Spirit of God giving voice to the trials and troubles that teens and adults communicate through facial expressions, hand gestures, and body posture. Some have said that the eyes are the windows to the soul. If there is truth in this old adage, then the challenge for youth and adults engaged in the act of listening to each other is to look into each other's eyes and allow the Holy Spirit to reveal what spoken words are incapable of expressing. Additionally, such facial cues as smiles, frowns, and other expressions of anger, frustration, and sadness complement listening to the soul by looking into the eyes. Listen to the slumped body as well as the upright-forward-leaning body to understand what the soul, through the power of God's Spirit, is communicating.

Mutual listening between youth and adults must be done in a disciplined and attentive way. Consider the following six essential actions for engaging in one-on-one or small group mutual listening between teens and adults:

1. *Sanctify the space.* This means prayerfully inviting the Spirit of God to create a physical environment that is holy and will yield sanctified conversation and communication among youth and adults. A sanctified space begins with conversation partners forming a covenant about the dos and don'ts of wholesome conversation. A visible covenant developed by all youth and adults and signed in worship signals the sincerity and commitment of all participants. Each member of the small group or youth/adult couple should understand the importance of holding each other accountable to the covenant. A sanctified space jettisons traditional dress codes and rituals of respect that hinder honest conversation.[30] Sanctifying the space also means the Holy Spirit prepares participants to receive emotions of rage, sadness, fear, and happiness as human offerings that have potential to transform personal and communal problems.[31]

2. *Pray continuously without uttering sound.* Pray with your eyes open invoking the Holy Spirit to select your words and take control of your emotions. Adults should ask the teen if they can pray before or after the conversation. If necessary, gradually grow into praying out loud for and with each other. Do not assume that youth want to hear you pray. Do not assume that teens are comfortable praying aloud with you. The intimacy of praying together takes time.

3. *Practice reflective listening.* A reflective listener tries to reflect back what the speaker says. In doing so the responder repeats the gist of what the speaker has said. The listener discovers if s/he understood what was being said. Because reflective listening helps people feel heard and understood, they are more likely to share openly and honestly. For example, reacting to a comment about the youth choir being a good place for participation, a youth might say, "That's wack." A reflective listening response might be: "The youth choir is NOT your choice for participation?" Note the reflecting statement is a question and engages the use of the slang word "wack." If an adult encounters unfamiliar slang, she or he should always ask for the definition. Likewise, a teen should feel welcome to ask an adult the meaning of words or to explain what is said. Both the adult and the teen should mutually clarify what is spoken. They should not finish each

other's sentences. Attentive listening allows each person to speak without interruptions.

4. Practice appropriate touching. Ask if you can touch a youth on the shoulder or hold her or his hand. Avoid inappropriate touching. Pastors, adult volunteers, and other adults committed to intentional and effective communication with youth should participate in an official background check and Safe Sanctuaries training. The latter offers skills for appropriately interacting with children and teens that assure safety and security.

5. Listen to silence. Long periods of silence are invaluable to genuine listening and good communication. Listening to silence literally means sitting together, not uttering a word, in silence. Adapted from a discernment group process, this practice requires individuals to sit for five to ten minutes in silence to become receptive to the presence of the Holy Spirit.[32]

6. Prepare for potential emergencies. If an emergency occurs, one should always follow-up with pastoral care. Retain a professional pastoral counselor or psychologist, if needed. Prepare to address any immediate problems of child abuse and neglect that are required by law. Prepare to provide for temporal needs of youth that include a place to stay and money if the situation calls for it.

Although not exhaustive, these six practices of listening are essential for adults and youth to help each other create wholesome intergenerational relations. Stories of struggle and survival shared among the young and old can supersede ageism. Friendships are built on shared life stories that defy age barriers. *Walking together* requires the act of listening to each other for both youth and adults.

The act of learning flows out of teens and adults listening to each other. When we share our troubles and triumphs of life's journey, we learn valuable lessons from each other. Youth and adults learn how to overcome challenges, what obstacles to avoid, and what relationships matter. Learning is mutual for both adults and youth. "Environmental tensions such as violence, poverty, domestic and sexual abuse, family disruption, and racism"[33] shape the day-to-day experiences of many youth. Adults learn the level of stress that presses in on young people's lives. Likewise, youth may discover that adults are stressed by similar environmental tensions. These tensions also obscure traditional roles among adults and youth. Shawn Ginwright underscores how researchers have observed the dynamics of exchanged roles; for example, "in welfare-dependent families, welfare reform has shifted traditional adult responsibilities to youth.

Increasingly, youth are expected to assume responsibilities normally held by their parents, such as paying bills, caring for younger siblings, purchasing clothes, and/or finding housing for the family because their parents are required by welfare regulations to work more hours and therefore have less time to complete household responsibilities."[34] While interviewing youth and adult partners from a group of youth service providers in the San Francisco area, Ginwright noted that "some adolescent girls in this community simply did not want additional decision-making power and responsibilities in their youth programs because they were required to make difficult decisions in their homes regarding childcare for siblings, coordinating grocery shopping, or deciding what to prepare for dinner."[35] Through shared stories, youth and adults become aware that their problems are caused by the systemic factors of racism, classism, sexism, and heterosexism. Learning of this nature can help change perceptions adults have about teens and begin to lay a foundation for mutual collaboration in dismantling systems of oppression.

To learn means to search for more information, knowledge, and skills to address the challenges gleaned from story-sharing among teens and adults. It means to participate in and observe schools and youth clubs, as a volunteer, to learn more about the culture that teens must negotiate. When a teen shares stories of being detained in the county juvenile detention center, we must seek knowledge about such institutions from the library and from conversations with lawyers, judges, and probation officers. We must observe and participate in the juvenile justice detention center as trained volunteers. Youth, upon hearing the story of an elder who participated in sit-ins and boycotts during the Civil Rights movement, may be motivated to learn more about the history that the adult partner has lived. Story-sharing between adults and youth can spark a desire in both partners to know more about the social and historical contexts that shape our experiences.

To learn is to share the wisdom we have gained from our experiences, regardless of age. A teen can share wisdom gained through caring for a disabled parent amid the responsibilities of school and a part-time job. An adult who raised his or her younger siblings can share wisdom with a teen who faces a similar responsibility. In contemporary North American society, wisdom is not equivalent to age. Those who have critically reflected on their life experiences and found new, life-giving ways of engaging people and their environment are wise beyond their age.

Learning flows from experience-sharing among youth and adults as well as from responding to the urgency to know more about the causes and effects of intergenerational stress and tension. Learning, like listening, empowers youth and adults to *walk together* for the transformation of systems of oppression.

Leaning is the final action necessary for wholesome intergenerational relations. This means that youth and adults partner to change their immediate social environment as well as the relevant hegemonic oppressive structures on city, state, and national levels. To lean means to mutually support each other, to rely or depend on each other for a common cause. Leaning is a symbol for youth and adults who depend on each other in the struggles against race, class, gender, and sexual oppression that shape the worldview of powerful men and women who develop public policy. Ginwright describes such leaning between youth and adults as "a collective social-change process"[36] whereby urban youth and adults "coalesce around a common agenda directed at self and social transformation."[37] He describes a clear social-political vision that was honed to improve the quality of life for all members of the community.[38] While Ginwright does not provide details of the social-political vision, he emphasizes the personal wellness of adults and youth. This approach can be a starting point for youth and adults to engage in local and state government lobbying for change in policies that affect African American communities.

Adult and youth partnerships that confront systemic problems (which include multiple forms of violence, substance abuse, and unemployment), require both age cohorts to adopt a common worldview—values, assumptions, commitments—that encourages a clear social-political vision.[39] Mutual support or leaning among adults and youth for the purpose of confronting the root causes of social problems requires adults to adopt values, beliefs, and attitudes about the self that are as important as those they hold about the community. Adults of the Civil Rights generation must practice the spiritual disciplines of meditation and forms of prayer that bring about self-exploration and self-healing. Dr. Martin Luther King Jr., according to Stephen Oates in *Let the Trumpet Sound*, engaged in moments of prayer and meditation to renew his spirit and to fortify his courage.[40] Likewise, leaning requires youth to adopt new values, beliefs, and attitudes about the community that are as equally important as those they hold about the self. Youth of the Hip Hop generation value a form of individualism that focuses primarily on money and material possessions rather than on spiritual healing and uplift. Youth should also engage in meditation and prayer, which benefits the healing and well-being of the self. Practices that focus on the welfare of the black community are also part of adopting a worldview or mutually agreed allegiances that are presupposed in everyday actions and deeds. Mutual leaning among youth and adults requires that they adopt each other's worldview as an affirmation of their differences in values, attitudes, and beliefs.

Leaning also involves accountability. In the kind of faith community where intergenerational divides between worldviews are meaningfully addressed, youth and adults become partners in accountability. The Hip Hop generation must become accountable for and "must engage in honest and critical self-interrogation for the promotion of sexist, misogynistic, and homophobic tendencies among too many of its creators, composers, and consumers."[41] The actions of Hip Hop rappers such as Nelly swiping a credit card between the hips of a young woman or Lil Jon belting out expletives saying "the b_ is leaking"[42] are but a few examples of some of the death-dealing and misogynistic aspects of the Hip Hop worldview against which youth must rise up in protest. Leaning, as accountability, starts with effective communication between youth and adults that grows from listening and discussing misogynistic images and rap lyrics. Such listening should inspire youth to learn more about sexism, misogyny, and gender-based intimate violence from prominent black feminists such as bell hooks and womanist scholars such as Cheryl Kirk-Duggan. Adults are called to accountability for sexism and homophobia in the Black Church and community. Youth must hold adults accountable for these practices and for their silence, which perpetuates sexism and homophobia. Youth must raise a prophetic voice and speak the truth in love when adults fail to act justly toward women and same-gender-loving people. Leaning signifies mutual support for accountability as youth and adults work together in our "hegemonic-capitalist-white-supremacist-patriarchal-heterosexist culture."[43]

Why are "saved saints" or adults in black congregations disconnected from the youth of the Hip Hop generation? The two generations have different worldviews, and this difference perpetuates the generational divide. These divergent worldviews often fuel practices in congregations and communities that blind youth and adults to their common interests of fighting for justice, freedom, and equality against oppressive powers and authorities in North America and around the globe. What insights and constructive practices might black practical theologians offer to connect the feuding generations? *Walking together* offers a new metaphor for an intergenerational approach to ministry among adults and youth partners. *Walking together* involves the praxis of listening, learning, and leaning so that black congregations and communities, led by their teens and adults, locked arm-in-arm, can sing together, "All along my pilgrim journey, I want Jesus to walk with me." And as we attempt to walk with each other and sing, the Hip Hop and Civil Rights generations have the assurance that Jesus walks with them.

<< 3 >>

Rejoining Black Youth, Families, and Our Elders

James H. Evans Jr.

Throughout my career as a theologian, I have been drawn to two separate aspects of this discipline. First, I have been drawn to the symmetry of the story of the Christian faith, and it is for this reason that I embraced the systematic coherence in theology. Second, I have been drawn to the creative dimensions of the Christian faith, and it is for this reason that I embraced the constructive mandate in theology. However, never far from my awareness was the fact that theology was and is connected to the lived reality of specific communities. That is, theology, whether systematic or constructive, finds its reason for being in the practical lives of people. I would suggest that all theology is, to some degree, practical theology. I will return to this suggestion at the conclusion of this reflection.

I am honored to be a part of this project on a black practical theology. I have looked forward to being part of the conversation with pastors and ministers around those issues that so significantly affect the life chances of people in our neighborhoods. I appreciate the fact that in this setting I am not expected to formulate theories to be tested in the field of practice but to serve as a partner in a conversation with other thinkers and doers who are concerned about the survival and liberation of our people. The editors of this project have wisely encouraged us to learn from one another. It is my good hope that whatever insight I can share with ministerial practitioners will be exceeded by what I learn from them. Our editors have defined practical theology in the following manner:

> Practical theology attempts to break from its historical formation as the applied science in theological curricula; therefore it breaks into or

redefines the theological presuppositions and methods of the classical disciplines of theological education, under which the black theology project itself has labored as a form of constructive theology. This project draws on three of the more common foci used in building methodology in practical theology. These foci include building analyses of situations or contexts of religious communities and contemporary life, building critical reflection on religious or spiritual practices within such contexts, and building upon interdisciplinary dialogue and scholarship.[1]

It is this definition that will guide my attempts to reflect on the issues and topics that have been assigned to me. My own view of practical theology has not been shaped by any particular social or critical methodology. Rather, it has been shaped by a persistent question. It is the question that W.E.B. Du Bois posed more than one hundred years ago. Speaking to and about himself as a black man in America, he provokes us likewise to ponder how we contend with being a problem for white America.[2] I have come to see practical theology as the branch of theological reflection that takes as its point of departure a particular social problem or set of social problems. I have written elsewhere,

> The content of practical theology is a particular social problem. It is this content which enervates the theological task, and it is the aspect of theological reflection which is most likely to be seen as relevant to the life of the ordinary Christian. The epigraph which heads this chapter neatly summarizes why theology should be practical and problem oriented. Not only is it difficult to convince theologians that social problems are proper issues for their attention, it is also difficult to convince social theorists that there is any relation between social problems and the subject matter of theology. . . . The aim of the practical task of theology is the transformation of society and the individual.[3]

The three issues on which I have been asked to reflect—black youth, intergenerational relations, and ageism—can be viewed in a variety of ways. But for the purposes of this essay, I want to look at them as a set of interrelated social problems. To define them as social problems simply means that significant concern has coalesced around these issues that warrant corrective action. However, they are not separate and distinct social issues but related. These three issues go to the heart of what it means to be part of a community.

In addressing this set of issues placed before us, our editors suggested three critical objectives. First, we have been asked to address the potential chasms that exist between the black theology project and black churches, on the one hand, and contemporary black worldviews, on the other. It is my view that part of the reason for these potential chasms is a failure to see both the broad social and theological implications of the problems that plague black churches and communities and that continually challenge traditional black worldviews. Second, we have been asked to show how these practical theological issues/questions from these pastors/parachurch leaders might shape doing theology for them and their related concentrations. This means that theologians must be ready and prepared to listen, reflect, and enter into conversation with pastors and other church leaders in a manner that makes theology relevant. Theology must reflect the experience of those to whom it speaks. Third, our aim is to bring critical issues or practices into dialogue with theological traditions, both within the larger biblical or doctrinal cannons and within the black theological project. Here, for example, it is quite possible that the theistic focus of black theological discourse might need to be reexamined. We must ask whether theistic ideas of God articulated within a patriarchal culture make it difficult for black youth, especially young black men, to access the deeper meaning inherent within the tradition. If we are able to keep these broad objectives before us, our success in this endeavor is all but assured.

THE ISSUES/MOTIFS

LET NO ONE DESPISE YOUR YOUTH: A BLACK THEOLOGY OF CHILDHOOD

The editors of this volume observe, "A growing issue in black churches concerns the failure to enfranchise, protect, and nurture . . . young black men. . . . Given the precarious existence of many black youths and young adults, not only in the United States and Britain but across the world, it is crucial that more black men become generative helpers. In what ways can black theologians and practical theologians work with black churches to engage black youth and young black men to break the various cycles of violence and crime?"[4]

Historically, black theologians have not given much attention to the topic of children. Within the Roman Catholic theological tradition, as well as other sacramental traditions, the child is a subject of critical reflection. That is, in those traditions one can find a theology of childhood. From Karl Rahner to new voices such as David Jensen, childhood has received sustained and critical theological attention. The same is not true in black theology. This is to say not that theological reflections on children are not found within black religious traditions but that these reflections have not been among the basic affirmations of faith within black religious communities. Together, black pastors, practitioners, and theologians must work to fashion a theological perspective on childhood that will shield them from the variety of exploitations that threaten their very lives. In a global market economy in which children are seen as pliable customers, marketers deliberately target our young people, selling to them merchandise and services that are often not age-appropriate or spiritually edifying. Further, our children are bought and sold, figuratively and literally. We must give new and sustained attention to what the gospel has to say about what is happening to our children.

Of particular concern is the plight of young black men. In our current situation, it appears that the religious tradition has nothing to say to them and that they have nothing to say to the religious tradition. However, I believe that if we approach the experience of being young, black, and male in our communities with appropriate questions we will find, for example, that the creativity of Hip Hop and the creativity of black worship traditions are rooted in the same fertile culture. Much of the theological work that has been done in searching for the spiritual roots of rap and Hip Hop culture has rightly focused on the fact that these forms of cultural expression grow out of, and formed in order to confront, the contradictions of being poor and powerless in rich and powerful nations. Like the blues, much of rap and Hip Hop cultural expression refuses to begin with the answers but stubbornly navigates the absurdity of the questions. In contrast, many urban youth are drawn to a form of contemporary gospel music that, in many instances, is theologically bereft and spiritually shallow. This form of contemporary gospel music is marked by easy answers to life's questions given in the form of slogans and catchphrases. If black churches are going to speak to the reality of young people, then black church leaders must take their questions seriously. If those within rap and Hip Hop culture are going to resist falling into nihilism and fatalism, then they must be prepared at least to listen to the answers that have sustained their forebears for generations. It is the task of black pastors, ministerial practitioners, and black theologians together to chart a path for our young people. It is up to us to make sure that no one is allowed to despise our youth.

FROM GENERATION TO GENERATION: A BLACK THEOLOGY
FOR THE FAMILY

The editors of this volume observe, "Similarly, wider intergenerational relations critically challenge black churches and communities. Black churches are in need of an intergenerational approach to ministry so that young people can learn from their elders and elders can learn from, connect with, and relate to young people. In this era in which so many alternatives—both secular and spiritual—to the traditional church exist, it is imperative that black theologians and practical theologians assist black churches in bridging contemporary generational divides."[5]

It is not just listening and responding to our youth that is required of our churches and leaders. Our young people must be encouraged and shown how to access the life-saving practices that have allowed black families to survive. Contrary to many popular stereotypes, black young men and women are part of larger familial units. However, the very idea of the black family is under attack. Part of this attack is the pernicious theory referred to as "the culture of poverty." This theory asserts that poor families (read black families) transmit debilitating values from one generation to another. Refuting this point of view is not where the efforts of black pastors, ministers, and theologians should be focused. It is more important to identify, promote, and celebrate those life-giving traditions that allow black families to prosper. This should be the primary focus of a theology of the family for the black community. While a full-fledged theological treatment is not yet available, within black theological discourse one can discern several directives.

One of these directives is that the black family must be seen and understood in its uniqueness. Black theologian J. Deotis Roberts observes,

> The black church has as one of its greatest tasks the "liberation" of the family. It will be unfortunate if blacks begin to participate in male-female conflicts in imitation of others on issues not crucial to the welfare of the black family. The problems which confront the relationship between black men and women are serious, but they must be seen for what they are and dealt with in that context. Most black families abide solidly within the black subculture essential to black survival. We will be defeated if we give our attention solely to mainstream problems and by-pass those concerns peculiar to the black condition.[6]

We must resist the tendency to measure black families using metrics not indigenous to our culture. That is, the aspects that make black families different from the families of other cultures must not be deemed abnormal or dysfunctional.

Another of these directives is to discover, articulate, and celebrate the values that have shaped our families throughout our history. Current political and cultural battles over "family values" have posed both veiled

and overt threats to the survival of black families. J. Deotis Roberts puts
it this way:

> Again, we must no longer look for the ideal family—a husband, wife,
> and children—as the only model of black family life. Although we must
> find ways to lift up and celebrate that ideal, we must not look down upon
> other models of family life. In our ministry to black people we must
> welcome and seek to enrich all families. . . . All families should find
> encouragement, empowerment, and enrichment in the black church.[7]

The values that have shaped our families have had more to do with substantive functions than symbolic form. That is, what makes a family in the
black community is that it behaves like a family rather than necessarily
looking like a traditionally defined family. In a season when retrogres-
sive forces are attempting to reinforce white hegemony by appealing to an
undefined set of political commitments called "family values," it is interesting to note that the policies and politics of "family values" do not support
black families. Instead, black families are often described as dysfunctional
social units. It is our responsibility to resist the demonization of the black
family. Our definition of the black family should be the only one that matters. Where love is poured out abundantly, wisdom is shared liberally, support is given unconditionally, truth is shared compassionately, and joy is
pursued with abandon, there is the family. This is the family that ought to
nurture and prepare our youth for life. Black pastors, ministers, and theologians are uniquely positioned to support the health of black families.
Our churches are often reflections of families. Our ministerial practices
provide a strong point of departure for working with black families. One
of the commonalities between our view of church and our view of family
is that both are measured synchronically as well as diachronically. Much
debate over what constitutes a family in contemporary culture assumes
that families are synchronic phenomena. That is, it is what constitutes a
family *today* that matters most. However, this perspective alone gives too
much weight to the influence of current political and cultural battles over
how a family should be configured. To understand the black family, one
also has to view the development of the black family diachronically—that
is, *over time*. Black families, like other families, are very much a product of
social evolution. However, their development is rooted in African values,
and their development can be truly measured only against those values.
Black people have always had families. They have always configured themselves into mutually supportive and loving households and communities.
What black families are today is only a moment in the long history of what

black families have been. Black pastors, ministers, and theologians need to read the works of black family specialists like George and Yvonne Abatso and begin to develop strategies for strengthening our families.[8]

One of the benefits of strengthening black families is the strengthening of the Black Church. I recently had the honor of preaching at the 135th anniversary of the Mt. Moriah Missionary Baptist Church in Kosciusko, Mississippi. This small rural church was established by people who themselves had been enslaved. This church has about one hundred members and has never been any larger than it is now. However, this church has met continuously for well over a hundred years. What makes this church special is that they remember the name of every pastor and deacon in the history of that congregation. But, an additional feature of the life of the congregation is that it has been sustained by generation after generation of the same families. The tight-knit family structure of this community is the backbone of this church. It is imperative for our churches and for our communities that we contribute to strengthening black families.

OUR HELP IN AGES PAST: A BLACK THEOLOGY FROM OUR ELDERS

The editors of this volume observe, "Perhaps, too, we need to formulate a new civil rights agenda to include the fight against ageism. The contributions of seniors should be reaffirmed and their personal narratives retold whenever we gather to preach and pray or to promote and practice social ministries."[9]

We need not only to work on developing a theology of childhood and a theology for the family but also to address a theology from our elders. This needs to be a theology rooted in the Black Church. It cannot overlook the cultural dynamics of growing old in the black community while it attends to the social dynamics of growing old in a culture that continues to worship the pursuit of perpetual youth. It must recognize the physical dynamics of age-related medical conditions and reduced physical capacities, as well as the prospects for continued physical activity through the advance of medical science. Such recognition, however, is not a theology of the elderly or even a theology about the elderly. The wisdom and knowledge held by our elders should become the basis of our theological reflection. Listening to and attending to our elders is part of our African past. Gwendolyn Fortune notes,

> Americans whose ancestors were captured during the period of slavery and their descendants had particular need to attend to their elders, for there were no written records to provide continuity of their cultures. . . .

The elderly continued the traditions from the African homelands as much as could be remembered. Wrinkles and gray hair denoted experience and wisdom. These, and other signs of age, evoked no stigma for the elders. Actually, they gave the aged dignity and assurance of their own worth.[10]

Importantly, those family values that held black families together persisted beyond institutional slavery. For more than a century after the official end of the slavery of Africans in America, elders were revered.

The attitude of respect and honor for the elders continued in the African-American communities of America for more than 100 years after emancipation. Even having dispersed to all parts of the nation, black communities evolved as microcosms of the familiar. The grandmother and grandfather, aged uncle and aunt were gathered around on special occasions: weddings, dinners, reunions. All older people who were not "blood relatives" were offered respect and deference in the community. The visibility of the elders gave a sense of solidity and belonging.[11]

Over time, the forces of modern globalism and institutional racism frayed the sinewy strength that held black families secure.

Dislocations in urban areas hastened the disintegration of former mores. The majority/white culture brought pervasive images and ways of being via film and television, and now the Internet, that severed historical lines of communication and attachment among the scattered remnants of a once cohesive culture. Among the casualties of this history are the loss of contact between generations, and dismissal and disdain for "anyone over thirty."[12]

This "loss of contact between generations" concerns us the most. It is symptomatic of the loss of historical consciousness. During the weeks that I wrote these reflections, I visited the National Civil Rights Museum at the Lorraine Motel in Memphis, Tennessee. This was the place where Martin Luther King Jr. was assassinated. I noted the many visitors from Europe and other places around the world for whom this history was critical. I also noted the relative paucity of people of African descent among the visitors. The question that ran through my mind at that moment was, who will be the custodians of our history? Liberating knowledge is passed down from one generation to the next. Black pastors, ministers, and theologians must take up the mantle of both the patriarch and the prophet. The patriarch assures continuity with the past, while the prophet demands faithfulness to the divine mandate. Elders are those persons who can link our past and our future. In an age when materialism and easy optimism are ready substitutes for human fulfillment and joy, the counsel of our elders can stave off the threat of nihilism, violence, and despair that confronts our communities. It is true, as Fortune has observed, that "awareness, acceptance, and appreciation for the knowledge of the elders, their role and value to contemporary and future generations have eroded."[13] But the question before us is whether or not the resources of our life-sustaining traditions can be marshaled in the liberation struggle of our people.

A question worth considering is whether or not we need a new civil rights movement focused on the plight and possibilities of our elders in the African American community. During the middle decades of the twentieth century in the United States, a movement for the empowerment of black people emerged. This movement was primarily focused on the economic empowerment of people still suffering the aftereffects of chattel slavery. The aim of the movement was not primarily social integration; it was economic empowerment. Leaders of the movement recognized the foundational character of economic independence. The most visible leader of the American Civil Rights movement, Dr. Martin Luther King Jr., began his leadership with an economic analysis of the plight of black people in America. And Dr. King spent his last days engaged in the struggle for the economic empowerment of sanitation workers in Memphis, Tennessee. The Civil Rights movement in America was not focused on improving the social relationships between black people and white people. It was a movement that recognized that any healthy social relationship must be based on justice and dignity for those involved.

It is in this sense that we might consider the call for a new civil rights movement, one that focuses on the plight of the black elderly. A recent study has identified the primary threat to the elderly in black and Latino communities in the United States as one of *economic insecurity*. This study noted that a majority of black and Latino elders live in a state of constant economic insecurity that is fueled by two major factors: health and housing.[14]

These points of vulnerability indicate a place where churches and their leaders might begin to redouble their efforts to fashion effective ministries. Such economic insecurity, according to this study, threatens the viability of future generations. The economic insecurity of elders can contribute to the economic insecurity of future generations. One reason for this effect is that, in many black and Latino communities, elders are taken into the home of their children or other family members rather than placed in other institutional settings. Clearly, the financial burden of caregiving for an elder can affect the economic viability of a family.

A new civil rights movement directed at improving the life chances of the elders among us finds ready support in the biblical narrative. The writings of the prophets, and even the words of Jesus himself, remind us that Christian communities are charged to care for the least, the last, and the lost among them. Christian communities ought to be at the forefront of both private and public efforts to secure the dignity and well-being of our elders. It is unfortunate that the forces of global economic development judge persons on their capacity to generate wealth for themselves or for others. When elders are seen as no longer able to contribute to the generation of capital, they are often treated as expendable. Much of our political rhetoric around the support of programs like Social Security and Medicare are framed within the context of affordability. Once persons have moved beyond their years of peak employability, questions then arise as to whether or not society can afford to support them. In the early years of the American Civil Rights movement, in the mid-twentieth century, many of the most ardent supporters were elders. Their very important, but often unsung, contributions to this movement were based on what they had experienced in the past and what they hoped for in the future. Many of them knew what it was like to be simply discarded once one's usefulness had been seemingly exhausted. These elders were determined that their children and grandchildren would have a brighter future. They were not simply the recipients of the largesse of others but participants in the struggle. This historical and cultural dynamic suggests that any new civil rights movement focused on the plight of the elders among us will not be a movement for them as much as a movement by them. In the book *Our Help in Ages Past: The Black Church's Ministry among the Elderly*, Bobby Joe Saucer argues that the Black Church is positioned to take up this mantle:

> Given the resourcefulness and resiliency of ministries that are reflected in historical records of African-American churches, it is clear that these churches have striven to witness and lead. They can—and will—continue to advocate and champion causes that address the needs of their constituencies. Their histories give ample reason for such hope and optimism. More specifically, the history of advocacy within these churches is a rich and noble one. It ought to be expanded! In that respect, a focus on the aging and elderly can potentially launch a movement that has implications for the advancement of African American communities in

particular and American society as a whole in situations where needs are evident and, sometimes, epidemic.[15]

Our faith traditions teach us that respect for our elders is blessed. But as people of African descent, we still believe that the elders are the guardians and custodians of life-saving wisdom.

A CONCLUDING OBSERVATION

The task before us is made all the more difficult by the influence of a hedonistic, greed-driven, materialist culture. While we can identify pockets of resistance to that culture in many places, it is still resistance while the dominant themes of our culture remain in place. This means that the work of theologians must adapt to the times and to our situation. We must respond to the actual questions posed *to us*. As systematic and sometimes constructive theologians, this charge does not mean that we merely describe the beauty of what God has done among us, or only attempt to sketch on the canvas of human experience God's continual creative activity among us. What it means is that we must use today's materials to express what God has done and is doing in the world. Theology engages not only what we currently experience but also the past practices of Christian congregations. Every theologian must engage tradition. Every theologian must come to terms with the historical witness of the community. The task of the theologian is to engage the past and to make it relevant to the present. This is why a theology that takes seriously the storehouse of wisdom possessed by our elders is crucial at this moment in our history. Twentieth-century theologian Karl Barth is credited with saying that one must do theology with the Bible in one hand and the newspaper in the other. Another way of saying this is that one must do theology with one's eyes on the past and on the present. It is our elders who will hold us accountable and make sure that our work is faithful to the past and relevant to the present. If there is anything that makes all theology practical theology, it is this!

<< 4 >>

RITUALS OF RESISTANCE TO STRENGTHEN INTERGENERATIONAL RELATIONS

Donna E. Allen

I am grateful for the opportunity to work on this project. It has provided me a useful vehicle with which to address a long held unease I have had about how to apply insights from theological resources to the practical work of pastoral ministry. I have benefited greatly from a seminary education as part of my preparation for pastoral ministry. As I began to serve in church leadership before attending seminary, I had great anticipation of the impact that seminary training would have on my understanding of the historical and theoretical underpinnings of Christianity. I was eager to acquire the education that was necessary for me to pursue my ministry as a well-trained professional. A significant part of my seminary education required a translation of Eurocentric classical works into something relevant to my context as an African American faith leader. It was womanist thought that gave me the necessary tools to "unmask, debunk, and disentangle the interlocking forces of racism, sexism, and classism" and eventually heterosexism in the academic resources I studied.[1] Importantly, the spiritual formation attendant with developing the ability to decode and decipher sacred texts proved to be coveted experience for ministry in the African American community. This formative learning experience had many points of relevance for interpreting the lived experience of an oppressed people and for engaging in critical and spiritual reflection that shapes strategies of survival and coalition building.

One of the most pivotal points of growth for me was the ongoing process of defining myself as a faith leader and preacher. I wrestled with critically examining the ways in which my practices may or may not be consistent with the values and morals I espouse. In the particular case of embracing womanist thought as a critical lens through which I do ministry, I am challenged to find ways to shape the praxis of my faith community that are not in direct conflict with my womanist convictions. So, I have approached this project with the intention of reflecting on the works of the scholars with whom I dialogue while holding the tension of a womanist lens in order to discern how the implications of this discourse can be lived out in ministry in my local church setting. I expect to gain a better understanding of the theoretical and theological contours of an intergenerational examination of ministry with a womanist perspective of ageism and sexism in such a way that will deepen my engagement of the topic in the ritual practices of ministry with the people I serve. The guiding questions for me are: How might ritual practices serve effectively as pastoral resources for bridging generational divides of ageism complicated further by church cultures of sexism and classism, not to mention the society's penchant for racism at large? and, How might such practices form or live in the life of my small, inner-city radically inclusive nondenominational black church?[2]

The traditional church leadership model of the pastor as the sole arbiter of all decision making and the one responsible for overseeing every aspect of the church ministry did not fit with my personality or with my values about what it means to be in community. It was seminary that exposed me to womanist thought as a model of leadership that was more in line with my values. As I developed as a pastor, the womanist tenets of collaboration versus competition, communal decision making, and critical engagement with matters of race, gender, class, and sexuality all informed my leadership style. I was most challenged by translating some of the teachings of womanist thought into my theology in the church, in particular a soteriology that takes seriously the historical experience of African American women as surrogates. This dialogue has inspired me to create a worship ritual of resistance as a means of addressing the Black Church's dilemma of black youth, intergenerational relations, and ageism. I reflect on these areas of concern as a faith leader informed by womanist theology.

James Evans reflects on the Black Church and the challenges of black youth, intergenerational relations, and ageism as "a set of interrelated social problems."[3] For Evans, examining these topics as a social problem "simply means that significant concern has coalesced around these issues that warrant corrective action."[4] Therefore, in this project I propose that a "ritual of resistance" can begin to disentangle the interrelated challenges of black youth, intergenerational relations, and ageism in the Black Church. Such a ritual would take place in the lived experience of community formation that occurs during worship in the Black Church and would have a lasting effect on the community beyond the context of a worship experience. I will expound on a ritual of resistance and womanist worship later in this response. As I stated earlier, Evans' approach to these social problems as interrelated is I think key to their eradication, but he also examines each individually and offers helpful insight.

Evans argues that, when it comes to the Black Church and black youth, it is the responsibility of black church leadership to "give new and sustained attention to what the gospel has to say about what is happening to our children."[5] Evans notes that the current absence of meaningful dialogue between the black religious tradition, the gospel, and black youth has created a situation in which black youth appear to have nothing to say to the black religious tradition and vice versa. Evans rightly concludes that appearances are deceiving and that if one can create a climate conducive to dialogue, the two sides would have much to say to one another. As Evans notes, "Our young people must be encouraged and shown how to access the life-saving practices that have allowed black families to survive."[6] Black youth are not empty vessels waiting to be filled to the brim with the wisdom of the Black Church; rather, they have much to say to the church. This includes their critique that the wisdom of the Black Church is not especially relevant to their daily lives. It has been my experience that black youth do not conflate the wisdom of the gospel with the words or work of black churches. The gospel comes to black youth by means other than the Black Church. While I cannot offer here a systematic analysis of the variety of ways black youth come across the gospel, suffice it to say that the Internet, music from both sacred and secular artists, and nonblack church experiences are a few of the ways that black youth encounter the gospel. I cannot begin to suggest which of these places of encounter with the gospel is most influential, but it is reasonable to acknowledge that for black youth the Black Church is not the sole arbiter or interpreter of the gospel. With this in mind we must acknowledge that black youth have an understanding of the gospel as it informs their lives that makes their testimony a theological resource for the Black Church. There are survival stories and spiritual practices that have allowed black youth to persevere and to find meaning in the gospel. Black churches would be richly informed by what young people have to share from these stories and practices. As Evans suggests, the Black Church is called to dialogue with, both through listening and responding to, black youth.

Evans observes another particularly informative issue in the rejection of "the culture of poverty." He writes:

> It is not just listening and responding to our youth that is required of our churches and leaders. . . . Contrary to many popular stereotypes, black young men and women are part of larger familial units. However, the very idea of the black family is under attack. Part of this attack is the pernicious theory referred to as "the culture of poverty." This theory asserts that poor families (read black families) transmit debilitating values from one generation to another. Refuting this point of view is not where the efforts of black pastors, ministers, and theologians should be focused. It is more important to identify, promote, and celebrate those life-giving traditions that allow black families to prosper.[7]

The need to provide black youth with access to life-saving practices is a helpful starting point for addressing, in part, the role of the Black Church in dialogue with black youth. Such a venture can be concretized in worship and can extend beyond the membership roles of the church to become a means of connecting with the broader community as the church performs the familiar work of preserving and creating values and forming culture.

The final social problem Evans examines is the lack of a black theology of elders. Evans is concerned about the social and political stressors affecting elders and notes the deleterious effect of economic insecurity on their quality of life. However, Evans also believes in the wisdom and knowledge of our elders, which is a critical wealth of information that should not be lost with the passing of the elders. What concerns him most is how the intergenerational divide creates a systematic "loss of historical consciousness."[8] Evans laments the loss of cultural memory, which also constitutes a loss of commitment to and strategy for a liberation agenda in the community's work. The passion and plan for civil rights as Christian discipleship or what it means to be black and Christian is not passed on from one generation to the next. This highlights the interrelation between the devaluation of elders and the intergenerational divide and points to the potential for the Black Church to encourage our black youth to value our elders, thereby positioning the two as allies for social justice in a way that will benefit both. In this way, neither will embrace the other in a utilitarian fashion simply for what one may know that the other may not; rather, each understands the challenges and worth of the other and seeks interdependence for the survival of a people. Drawing on Evans' observations and the praxis model of ministry proposed by Evelyn Parker, I have constructed a womanist ritual as an emancipatory praxis to address the interrelated issues of ageism and the intergenerational divide between the Black Church and black youth. This womanist ritual, or any related ritual of resistance, is intended to be a transformative liturgical act for worship in a Christian tradition in the Black Church experience.

In this project, I use "liturgical acts" and "worship" as loosely synonymous terms as they relate to the Black Church experience. Liturgical acts in black church worship are events for creating an experience. Liturgy as a framework for the order of worship is not a static rehearsal of doctrinal expressions to be completed within a prescribed time with emphasis on authenticity through accuracy of repetition, good form, order, and frequency. Rather, liturgy or worship in the Black Church context is often given over to a desire for the improvisational direction of the Holy Spirit, as well as song and dance. The order of worship and its liturgical acts attempt to shape meaning-making and to be written on the hearts of worshippers as they worship. So, the dynamic event that drifts away from what was planned in the ordering of events in *an order of worship* is also an anticipated event, which thereby assures the authenticity of worship. The words "we had church today" espouse the sentiment of a people who experienced God in the dynamic interplay of improvisational sacred moments. Worship is an expected encounter with God, and the expectation is that God will "show up and show out" in a song, testimony, praise dance, sermon, and so on, however God wants to manifest God's self. Worship is cathartic and convicting; it is prophetic and pastoral; it is a communal expression of God is with us—incarnate in our gathered bodies. Worship or liturgical acts that are attentive to the lived experience of people are evocative and invite communal participation. Like the black sermon, worship is a sacred communal experience that helps to define and disseminate values for the community of faith and contributes significantly to social formation. Liturgies that are vital and relevant to the social and cultural context of the community are not merely a collection of ritualistic acts. Rather, they are dynamic enactments or purveyors of divine encounters that inform our values and the ways we live. Worship in the Black Church tradition often violates patriarchy, sexism, ageism, and other demarcations of oppressive denominational trappings, as the Holy Spirit finds its way to touch all gathered. So, when a child shouts and runs the aisles, or dances in place, the ushers move to attend like doulas for the youth as they would for the senior or for the visitor. The choir typically leads in song during worship. Yet, if the community gets caught up in the experience of the song, the choir yields its leading position and follows the community with musicians and directors in tow. The exchange may lead to another verse and another refrain, both of which may be redacted as the moment suggests—and it *ain't over* until the Spirit says it's over.

Acknowledging this exchange does not negate the fact that, even with many places of inclusive access to the worship experience, there are also moments when the language and the leaders betray the inclusive move of God with god-talk not befitting of the gathering, thus creating what Delores Williams refers to as "quasi-womanist fragments" inter-mingled with genuine womanist moments. The language of the sermon or of the lyrics of a song may be patriarchal, androcentric, heterosexist, and so on and may disrupt the inclusive womanist move of God. Even with these intrusions, black worship is a fertile time to create and cele-brate and to enact experience of the liberating power of God such that the rituals expose our places of needed growth and invite us into our best selves. Ritual acts give voice to and operate out of identity. They create an embrace of God with us and in us, transforming all of us. Even though all of our human offerings in worship are imperfect, the power of worship is so all-encompassing that even fragments of womanist worship are trans-formative. It is this understanding of black church worship that leads me to believe that a ritual of resistance, a womanist construct, that is mindful of the theological insights of Evans' examination of the interrelated issues of the Black Church and black youth regarding intergeneration dialogue and ageism can be one effective strategy for transforming these social problems.

Delores Williams writes, "Womanist worship happens when African-American women's experience is obvious in the leadership, liturgy, and god-talk of the church. . . . Women's language, thought, and experiences of survival, struggle, celebration, and liberation inform the sermon as well as the revision of patriarchal scripture lessons. . . . Womanist worship is family worship because it is also seriously inclusive of the experience of black men and black children."[9] Womanist worship is inclusive. It is not heterosexist or homophobic; it is not racist or sexist; it is not patriarchal or androcentric. Womanist worship is gender inclusive and generation inclu-sive. Williams affirms,

> This means that black women's stories and black men's stories and black children's stories about their experience with mother-father God must be used to support the ideas in the African-American sacred text—ideas

appropriated, at their foundation, from the Bible. The community would select the stories to be incorporated.[10]

Williams further observes, "Womanist worship exists as ideal rather than practice in most Christian churches including black churches."[11] She proposes that womanist worship be created through rituals of resistance. Williams suggests that these rituals meet the criteria of inclusiveness with some focus on gender. I would expand the inclusiveness of rituals of resistance to include a longer list of intentional inclusivity. Williams writes,

> We need ritual in the black church celebrating and remembering important female- and male-led events in the black civil rights struggle when the people believed God was in the struggle with them. We need this ritual in the church to reinforce in our children's minds, at an early age, a sense of African-American history and faith.[12]

For Williams these rituals must include a remembrance of "how black women have resisted sexist oppression . . . and how slave women's faith in God helped them survive and hold on to their self-esteem as they were raped by any white man who felt the inclination."[13] Williams desires a remembrance of struggle and survival, which I propose to add to the multiple facets of African American experiences of oppression, including those experiences within the black community—for example, homophobia within the Black Church. The connection between faith and resistance is a critical component of the potential of rituals of resistance for social transformation. Williams writes, "This inseparable relation between faith and resistance in black people's history needs to be the material of ritual composed and enacted in the church right alongside any other rituals that are part of Christian heritage."[14] I propose the following ritual of resistance to address the interrelated social problems of the Black Church and black youth—namely, intergenerational dialogue and ageism. Communion or the Lord's Supper is a commemoration of the last meal Jesus had with his disciples before his crucifixion. The Gospels suggest to us that Jesus shared words of instruction and advice, even correction, with the disciples. I propose that this combination of prophetic and pastoral sharing at a sacred meal become the biblical cornerstone of my ritual of resistance. Mealtime has become a tradition offering a special time in African American culture. Many womanist scholars have noted the power of conversation at the kitchen table among sister girlfriends. Meals evoke intimacy and care. They establish fellowship and can help to create trust and openness to a meaningful connection. The ritual of resistance I am proposing has two components, one outside the context of a worship service and one within it. The component outside of worship is informed by Evelyn Parker's insights about how a black congregation can critically engage Hip Hop culture. The setting of this component is a meal. It could be an informal meal served at the church or in any other location that is conducive to conversation. Senior members of the congregation pair up with youth (who may or may not be church members) to share a meal and conversation; there is at least a twenty-five-year to thirty-year age difference between the two participants. The meal includes a conversation with a facilitator who uses Parker's guidelines for "wholesome intergenerational relations between the Hip Hop and Civil Rights generations."[15]

Parker identifies six actions as essential "for engaging in one-on-one or small group mutual listening between teens and adults."[16] I agree with Parker's observation that these criteria are necessary for cultivating an effective conversation.

Over the course of the meal, among the things shared is the intentional articulation of life practices that each person performs to prosper as a person of faith. This sharing creates a culture of prosperity sharing.[17] The facilitator is responsible for capturing this part of the conversation and editing it with the participants so as to create a script—liturgy—for the second component of the ritual of resistance. The script is merely a truncated aspect of the dialogue that could serve as a transportable prosperity practice to be shared in a worship service as part of the celebration of communion. A few sentences composing a brief litany (or perhaps a poem, graphics, or rap/music) would be shared with the entire congregation. Then, in dialogue, participants would serve each other the elements of communion, marking a remembrance of their transformative experience over a meal. The words of wisdom shared in this intergenerational manner would include what has helped each party to resist oppression and survive as a person of faith. The ritual in both components creates access to important information for social transformation from an intergenerational dialogue. This project does not afford me the opportunity to explore in-depth the reasons the communion meal is such a critical context for this ritual of resistance. Suffice it to note that it affords retelling and reshaping the soteriology of the communion meal in a manner that emphasizes the meal and wisdom Jesus shared with his disciples, which becomes a fitting example of a womanist soteriology. This soteriology weighs the historical experience of African Americans' forced surrogacy, as associated with the exploitation of their bodies, thereby rendering suspect any theology that affirms the exploitation of the body as a saving act of God. This ritual of resistance creates an opportunity to direct some part of the communion meal toward the salvific ministry of Jesus.[18]

A liturgical act is an intriguing and viable space in the life of a faith community to merge academic and theoretical insights with the practices of ministry. This liturgical ritual of resistance is a means for me, as a faith leader informed by womanist theology, to address the Black Church's dilemma of black youth, intergenerational relations, and ageism. I hope that from this dialogue and worship with a ritual of resistance, additional avenues of healing and strategies of address will be fashioned that are transformative to black churches and the black community. Evans' reflection on black churches and the challenges of black youth, intergenerational relations, and ageism as a set of interrelated social problems prompts us to examine these multiple challenges to the Black Church as interrelated phenomena that illumine a frame for this ritual. Parker's six critical components for fostering productive one-on-one or small group mutual listening between teens and adults—namely, sanctify the space, pray continuously without uttering sound, practice reflective listening, practice appropriate touching, listen to silence, and prepare for potential emergencies—create clear criteria for the communal formation of the meaning-making content and experience of the ritual. Clearly, the ritual will not eliminate the challenges the Black Church faces in this area or obliterate the impact of a generational divide in our communities; but in its formation and practice it will offer us some means of resistance to the increasing bilateral destruction incurred by generational neglect and ageism, and that is a worthy move in the right direction.

III

Education, Class, and Poverty

The issue of class reminds us that academic black theology stresses liberation of the poor. In this capitalistic, materialistic, consumerist society in which we live, black churches have been loath to touch the issue of class. In fact, black churches often tend to be elite social clubs that cater to persons based on personal background, education, occupation, and social status. Black churches, especially in the twenty-first century, are not necessarily "beloved communities" where people feel welcome to mingle, engage in fellowship, and participate comfortably together across class lines. And although materialism was one of the "three giant triplets" (in addition to racism and militarism) that Martin Luther King Jr. lifted up, black churches are no more inclined than mainstream society to upset the status quo in order to bring about a more just and equitable society. Many are too satisfied with the trappings of individual success—a decent job, a nice home, a fancy car—to challenge the systems or dominant cultural ideologies/practices of capitalism.

Recent political gridlocks in the United States over our entrenched economic meltdown reflect the classism shaping current debates concerning people's economic stability and survival. For example, on November 3, 2011, all forty-seven Senate Republicans and one Independent voted against President Obama's stimulus plan, which would have helped construction workers, some of the hardest hit after the housing meltdown and economic downturn. It is a travesty when people do not have the resources to provide for themselves and their families. At stake in what is sometimes charged as "class warfare" are questions over economic thriving and communal or social responsibility for liberation from poverty or rights to basic human needs, employment, and education. How might black theologians and practical theologians dialogue with black churches to address these questions?

The disturbingly high black unemployment rate provides a useful indicator of the degree of the disparity and economic distress found within black communities. Although the unemployment rate for Blacks in the United States recently fell from 16.0 percent to 15.1 percent, it remains dramatically higher than the national rate, and despairingly even higher than the rates among the dominant white classes. Similarly, education in the United States has become a sacrificial lamb. In September 2011, House Republicans unveiled a plan to cut education, job training, and National Public Radio (NPR). A large percentage of Americans with poor education grow up functionally illiterate, virtually unable to communicate in the common job market or acquire the skill sets needed for sustaining employment or retooling. What are the systemic implications and theological challenges for black churches redressing unemployment and education issues?

The critical needs of education affect black church leadership directly. The lack of academically (seminary-) trained clergypersons—across black denominations and congregations, and among the "Bishops," "Apostles," and megachurch clergypersons, who have significant congregations and extended followings in their communities—is an issue needing redress. How might we work with black churches to address these justice issues in the convergence of class, poverty, and education?

<< 5 >>

PARTICIPATIVE BLACK THEOLOGY AS A PEDAGOGY OF PRAXIS

Anthony G. Reddie

My work has always existed at the nexus of the systematic and constructive methodologies of black theology and practical theology. Working at the intersection of two major points of departure in the arsenal of contemporary theological studies can lead to acute feelings of displacement. I have often found myself not entirely understood by either branch of this theo-methodological divide. I am often considered too theological for the practical theologians and too concerned with practice and religious performance for systematic and constructive theologians. Yet, I would argue that it is in this complex nexus that issues pertaining to the performative qualities of black theology, suffused by the agency of practical theology, need to be enacted. This creative and interdisciplinary nexus is necessary if the Black Church hopes to regain the theological verve it once possessed in engaging with those on the margins of society.

Before I proceed any further, let me offer a few contextual caveats by way of some opening explanations for this particular chapter. Many scholars perceive the Black Church as the key social, political, educational, and organizational entity in the collective and communitarian experience of diasporan people of African descent.[1] In Britain, the Black Church is often seen as the key location for the intimations of black selfhood and collective solidarity.[2] Within the United States, the Black Church is a normative context out of which the black religious experience has arisen.[3] The critical challenge that confronts the imagining and development of black practical theology has been the attempt to cultivate more microperspectives on the issues pertaining to black life in the African diaspora. This chapter will address the educational challenge that arises from the creative interface between practical theology, as outlined by the pastors who have articulated their perspective of the issues and challenges faced by black faith communities, and black theology, as articulated by the constructive theologians. What I want to outline in this chapter is the need for a creative and liberative black practical theology that combines the prophetic insights of black theology with the praxiological and methodological intent of practical theology in order to address some of the salient issues facing black people in the twenty-first century.

Although a substantial part of my doctoral training and subsequent early work was very much in the discipline of Christian education, I have since moved away from using that nomenclature to describe myself. The term "Christian education" can be defined and understood in a variety of ways. Jeff Astley and Colin Crowder provide a helpful starting point for a definition and rationale for Christian education. The authors describe Christian education as "those processes by which people learn to become Christian and to be more Christian, through learning Christian beliefs, attitudes, values, emotions and dispositions to engage in Christian actions and to be open to Christian experiences."[4] My movement away from this nomenclature has more to do with my own intellectual wrestling with the nature of my calling and vocation than with any failings concerning the nature of Christian education in and of itself. In terms of my own work, I have come to describe myself as a "Participative Black Theologian." In using this term, I am signifying a creative mutuality between the theological concerns of black liberation theology and the acute practical, methodological particularities of practical theology, especially in terms of the latter's attention to the lived experience of ordinary people. I have used the term "participative" in order to denote the creative, collaborative means of undertaking black theological scholarship *with* ordinary black people as opposed to theorizing merely *about them.* The fruits of this work can be found in a number of my publications.[5]

I have undertaken this movement away from Christian education, which is part of the wider family of practiced-based approaches to theology, toward the less clear and scholarly hybrid identity that is "participative black theology" in order to create greater synergy between black theology and practical theology. In this later work, I have sought to utilize the ideas that have emerged from efforts to transform popular education as a means of effecting a prophetic, educative approach to black practical theology, or what I prefer to call "participative black theology."

TRANSFORMATIVE POPULAR EDUCATION

Transformative popular education is a form of scholarly enterprise and a mode of epistemological construction that is "of the people" and is ultimately accountable to ordinary people. It is an activist mode of scholarly engagement that seeks to provide the necessary theoretical tools to inspire ordinary people to engage in radical action for social change and transformation. Transformative popular education is most often identified with nonstatutory and nongovernmental bodies as it emerges from informal and independent social entities, such as churches, vocational groups, and voluntary social agencies. The church has often been an important harbinger for the development of this mode of intellectual inquiry and pedagogy, most often identified as Sunday school,[6] although the radical intent of this work is often questioned.[7]

While this particular approach to education is undoubtedly a scholarly discipline, its aim, like that of black theology, is to go beyond the formal basis of academic theorizing in order to impact the thinking and actions of ordinary people. Some of the most famous exponents of this mode of educational scholarly endeavor include Paulo Freire,[8] bell hooks,[9] Ira Shor,[10] and James Banks.[11] My own engagement with transformative popular education has its roots in my engagement with these individuals. Banks describes transformative popular education as a form of knowledge creation that challenges the dominant theories and models that are understood as enduring, objective, and universal truths.[12]

Transformative popular education proceeds from a critical, challenging, and dialectical inquiry into the very basis of epistemology.[13] Central to the underlying frameworks for this form of education is its challenge to the alleged objectivity of Western scholasticism. Banks asserts, "The assumption within the Western empirical paradigm is that knowledge produced within it is neutral and objective and that its principles are universal."[14] Banks' challenge to the assumed objectivity and centrality of the Western intellectual tradition is central to this form of intellectual inquiry. In this method for engaging with controversial subject matter in the teaching and learning process, adult learners are invited to reflect in a critical and challenging manner on what constitutes truth. Transformative popular education in the context of this work alludes to a critical process of praxiological reflection on how oppressive theories and forms of knowledge are constructed and enacted. It is an invitation to ordinary learners to assess critically the veracity of particular truth claims and the processes that produce seemingly all-powerful, interlocking systems and structures that constrict and inhibit the God-given selfhood of black people.

The point of departure for this mode of scholarly inquiry is the experiential, social location of the learner. The epistemological underpinning of this mode of scholarly inquiry is one that proceeds in a dialectical manner from the critical engagement of adult learners who are encouraged and are equipped to critique the position of allegedly axiomatic truth claims. The latter are often those notions of truth that emerge from the conflation of human self-interests and power, of which revelatory knowledge is a part;[15] the latter is not assumed to be immune from such epistemological corruptions.[16]

For the purposes of this work, I am proposing a contextual appropriation of the central tenets of transformative popular education in order to develop an alternative pedagogical approach to black practical theology. A black theology–inspired notion of a black practical theology—one that utilizes the central tenets of transformative popular education—is essential to critiquing the overarching power of white hegemonic epistemology. The dominant, captive possession of knowledge and truth—arising from the supposedly objective, Western intellectual tradition—fundamentally characterizes the construction of white Eurocentric power and supremacy in which Christian theology and the church have been convenient handmaidens. Emmanuel Eze has demonstrated the potent and corrosive relationship between Enlightenment thought and white Eurocentric knowledge construction and the hierarchical claims for white superiority and supremacy.[17]

The central task of this work is to use the frameworks of transformative knowledge, coupled with black theology, to reevaluate critically the essential meaning of blackness and the underlying value of black people. Perhaps the central import of this task can be perceived best through Gayraud Wilmore, who writes,

> If I had a choice before I was born to be one color or the other, which would I prefer and why? The pejorative connotations continued in the English vocabulary where we continue to speak of "blackmail," "blackguards," "black sheep of the family," or of having one's reputation "blackened." All these and many more found in the dictionaries, are negative images that reflect on Africans and Diasporic descendents. On the other hand, whiteness has been consistently presented to the world as something positive—something connoting goodness, cleanliness, beauty,

holiness, and purity. It would be much fairer to make the case that we are *all* somehow "obsessed" with color than to single out the psychology of black people as unfortunate. As much as we may deplore it, the color symbolism of our language in Great Britain and North America gives the whiteness/blackness dichotomy ontological significance—at least, up to the end of the twentieth century. We must wait and see what happens now in the twenty-first, but not look for any startling changes.[18]

Using black theology as a model for illustrating the illusory dimensions of the white, Euro-American, Western world order, this work seeks to enable ordinary black people to pose critical questions and to gain important epistemological insights. It does so in the hope that what accrues from this educative process is a form of transformative learning. As bell hooks has observed, transformative knowledge can give rise to new, distinctive forms of thinking, which as a corollary can assist in reshaping one's perception of reality that is not conditioned or silenced by the hegemonic, patriarchal constructs of imperialism and androcentric discourse.[19]

What I am proposing and outlining in this essay is an ongoing, emergent model of black practical theology that fuses the critical insights of black theology and transformative popular education as the means to create a more fluid and improvisatory mode of scholarly inquiry, coupled with the pedagogical tools for conscientizing ordinary black people. This work is an attempt to provide an overarching theory and a practical methodology for engaging the existential experiences of ordinary black people.

In the context of this work, black theology becomes a transformative methodology for conscientizing or raising the critical awareness of ordinary black people. As I will demonstrate shortly, this scholarly work draws on experience-based forms of learning, in which the learner is an active participant and from which new epistemological insights emerge. These insights are then linked to the theoretical ideas and themes that have been central to black theology from its inception. The aim, then, is to create a form of scholarly work that seeks to close the semantic breach that has existed between practical theology as it attends to the lived expressions of faith of ordinary black people (often in black churches) and the prophetic insights of black theology. There is, however, a second aim for this work—namely, the development of a participative methodology that can engage with the sheer messiness and improvisational repertoire of ordinary black people as they utilize and engage with religious themes and concepts as means of making sense of the absurdities that can be construed as black life.

The heart of this essay is an analysis of the participative work I have undertaken with a group of ordinary black people. This work has two aims in mind. First, it tries to provide a means of delineating the central characteristics and methodological challenges posed by this form of black practical theology. Second, the work attempts to provide a practical, working example of scholarly enterprise that can address some of the critical issues in black churches in the twenty-first century.

PARTICIPATIVE BLACK THEOLOGY: A WORKING EXAMPLE

As I have outlined previously, this work combines transformative popular education and black theology. It does so in order to provide a means of illustrating the ways in which ordinary black people are challenged to think and act differently. The use of experiential models of learning—in which the adult learner is immersed within a constructed exercise, game, or drama—becomes a means by which he or she is enabled to reflect critically on the immediate experiences and feelings that have accrued from the participative activity itself. Participants are invited to reflect on what they have felt and learned while immersed within the embodied, metaphorical activity that forms the active element in this practical theological process that emerges from what I have now termed "participative black theology."[20]

Central to this mode of scholarly inquiry is the use of games and exercises. This use is deliberate because the performative mode of this form of dramatic action requires that participants become actively engaged with the "other" in a space in which the rules of such dialectical constructs are constantly redefined.[21] Games and exercises also play important pedagogical roles as they seek to force learners out of their often self-referential world of religiously inspired forms of "learned behavior" and the concomitant notion of "top-down" axiomatic truths. Games and exercises encourage adult learners to draw upon the affective aspects of their mutating subjectivities, as opposed to privileging cognition alone.

Immediately following the performance of the exercise or game, I usually spend several minutes with the participants, helping them to reflect upon the events in which they have just taken part. I encourage participants to connect with their feelings for a few moments as they reflect on the implications of the embodied metaphorical exercise for the faith positions and theology they presently hold. Oftentimes, within the central activity, I will build in dynamics that represent the issues of contestation and argument that are often commonplace in all philosophical and religious frameworks that act as meaning-making operations in life. This opportunity for reflection is essential because it provides the necessary bridge between previous beliefs and attitudes, on the one hand, and the possibilities of critical, reflective change that sometimes accrues from performing the activities, on the other.

At the heart of this methodological approach to theological reflection is the demand—indeed, the expectation—that participants enter into the "internal logic" of the activity. By "internal logic" I mean the process by which the participant takes seriously the realized psychosocial vista of the performative activity itself (i.e., they are acted upon by and are active subjective players within the activity of which they are a part). It is essential that each participant imbue his or her position within the activity with a degree of seriousness. This does not mean that the activity is replete with solemnity and mournful countenances. On the contrary, I would argue that comedy and laughter have been central ingredients in all my participative black theology work since its earliest conception in the mid-1990s.[22] This mode of behavior is not unlike that demanded of participants in Groome's[23] or Berryman's[24] educational approaches to practical theology. Namely, I encourage participants to be involved and active players within any praxis-based approach to theological reflection. The use of laughter and comedy is deliberate because history has shown us that the sharpest and most incisive forms of humor often emerge in times of great distress and emotional turmoil.[25]

This approach to assisting people to engage with black theology, through the refracting lens of practical theology in the form of transformative popular education, challenges ordinary black people to engage in the constructive exercises or game. The resultant challenge for ordinary black people, whose participation gives rise to this scholarly nexus between black theology and practical theology, suspends reality as they have experienced it. They are challenged to enter into the basic logic of a "simple game" in which they are invited to interact with others. The premise of the game may appear absurd or ridiculous, but participants are challenged to take their participation in the exercises seriously.

This sense of asking participants to suspend their critical judgments in order to enter the internal logic and dynamic of an activity is central to this approach to teaching and learning about so-called controversial topics. This approach seeks to engage the emotional or affective repertoire of adult learners and not just their cognitive or thinking domains. The process is also critical because, in the final analysis, it is with the emotional or affective self that profound changes in religious consciousness are most likely to accrue. The best theology is never just cognitive or intellectual. It engages not only the emotions but also, perhaps most crucially, the imagination. What would happen if one could see something completely differently? How might one's perception of God be changed if, through an exercise, one were able to witness or glimpse another way of knowing or an alternative mode of being?

As an educator using this method of teaching and learning, perhaps my greatest challenge is to ensure an environment in which participants can safely and effectively ask critical questions of Christianity and of some of the theology that underpins many of the accepted social norms for black life in the twenty-first century.

ENGAGING BLACK POVERTY

One of the persistent challenges that have confronted black people and the Black Church for centuries is economic, material poverty. Black theology has always provided sharp analyses as to who are *the* poor and why. It has recognized that quite often the spiritualized reasons offered for the relative success and failure of different people in the world are nothing but smoke screens for disguising the callous and greedy forces of Western capitalism.[26] The latter has always benefited from the material poverty of the black majority of the world. The demonization of particular groups of people, most often black people of the African continent, masks the rapacious intent of global capitalism that exploits the natural resources of Africa, for example, while condemning Africans for being lazy and corrupt.[27]

Some black theologians have used the insights of social theory to scrutinize Western capitalism and the overall profit motive that diminishes the basic humanity of black poor people.[28] The poor are the pawns in such industrialized and mechanized processes because they do not have an inherent stake in the means of production for which their labor is an essential source. In more recent times, some African theologians have sought to develop a more culturally oriented approach to African theology, which is often seen as the natural inheritor of black theology.[29] This approach analyzes the ways in which the era of colonization sowed the seeds for Africa's present malaise.

The structural and systemic forms of analysis provided by black theologians[30] have proved most adept at offering a macro perspective on black poverty but have been less successful at engaging with the lived realities of such deprivation at the micro level. In the next section of this work, I would like to offer a participative black theological approach for engaging poverty that provides for a critical, dialectical interplay between black theology and transformative popular education.

The heart of this particular piece of work was my engagement with a group of ordinary black people. Through contact with a number of black pastors of black churches in London and Birmingham,[31] I invited twenty black people to assist me in the following exercise. Although I often create my own games and exercises for the participative work I undertake, on this occasion the exercise I used was a very simple, traditional game that has been played for many years. On this occasion I asked the various individuals to attempt the following task: play a very traditional game of musical chairs.[32]

The game works on the premise that one less chair is available than the number of people taking part in the game. Individuals are asked to walk around the chairs, which are placed in a line. When the music stops, each participant must sit on the nearest available chair. One of the usual provisions in the game is that individuals cannot go backward to claim a vacant chair. Rather, all participants can move only in a forward direction around the chairs; so if there is a vacant chair behind an individual, the individual will have run all the way around the chairs in order to sit on that available seat. At every round of the game, one seat is removed. The last person left standing in each round when the music stops is eliminated from the game. This game has been a staple ingredient of children's parties for many years. It depends on the element of surprise, in that none of the participants knows when the music will stop, which results in individuals running to beat their compatriots to the available vacant seats. The game works on the basis of "fairness" (i.e., all people are subject to the same rules of the game).

When we played the game with a group on two occasions, one of the clear insights that emerged as an experiential, metaphorical truth was the realization that although the rules established for game seek to be fair, they still are not equitable. This observation arises from the fact that, in a game such as this, it soon becomes very clear who is going to win. Namely, those who were healthy, young, and, in two cases, had been trained as athletes (a deliberate choice on my part) would be the ones to remain in the final round to win the game. Those who did not possess these advantages were never going to win the game.

This issue became one of the critical points of learning that arose from this simple, experiential exercise of transformative popular education. As the theologian and educator, I was at pains to remind the participants/ learners that there is a world of difference between equality and equity. In terms of the former, one assumes that all people should be treated the same. In popular parlance this notion is often given expression in the metaphor of the "level playing field" or "the fair race." The race metaphor assumes that all people start from the same place and are subject to the same rules; in effect, all people should be treated in the same manner.

Using the metaphor of the race as my primary example, I asked what happens if governing the race only *appears* to be fair? What happens if some people are given a wealth of unearned advantages while others are required to "earn" these advantages without equitable resources, which renders the notion of "fair play" nothing more than an illusion?

At the time I write this essay, the athletic world of sprinting has been electrified by the charismatic presence of Usain Bolt. In the interests of fairness, Bolt and I may well stand together at the starting line of the race, and when the starter fires the pistol, we may well be notionally taking part in a fair race! We are indeed subject to the same rules. The race can be said to be fair, but it cannot in any way be said to be just. It should come as no surprise, therefore, that in such a setup, Bolt will *always win*.

At the risk of overstretching our metaphors, what if some contestants have unearned privileges from birth, such as schooling, education, ethnicity, gender, social networks, and so forth, which lead them always to prosper in the race? Would such a race truly be fair? Equality often works on the naïve assumption that fairness equals treating all people in the same manner, irrespective of the structural or systemic advantages some groups or individuals inevitably possess.

It goes without saying, of course, that black theology would want to question the extent to which fairness and treating all people in the same manner can be identified in the historic or contemporary practice of Christendom or in Euro-American societies, in terms of their social arrangements regarding darker-skinned people.[33] Notwithstanding the illusory promises, the concept of equality here is a flawed one. Black theology, like all "Theologies of Liberation,"[34] argues for equity and not equality. Equity is based not on notions of fairness but on justice.

In a context of justice, one does not treat all people in the same manner, for that is to sanction the status quo in which some people inevitably win and others are condemned to lose. The iniquities of equality can be seen in the pernicious doctrine of free trade, which is, of course, anything but free. Theoretically, even if we wanted to treat all nations equally, the winners of history—namely, nations in the global north—usually triumph over those in the impoverished south. The global north created, and continues to possess, the means for their economic conquest—means that are denied newer, emerging nations. This system may be called many things, perhaps even "free," but it is never just.[35] The system takes no account of those who have exploited the world markets and the resources of others and who possess a critical advantage over those nations that have been subjected to Western nations' dominant neocolonialist exercise of power.

Black theology and black theologians are committed to the cause of equity. Equity, as a concept, requires that for the sake of justice there must always be a commitment to systemic and structural change. This commitment to change arises from acutely observed forms of social, economic, and cultural analysis for the purpose of unmasking the often hidden and covert ways in which equality seeks to preserve the inbuilt power and advantage of the status quo.[36] By this I mean there can be no serious change without people looking closely at the field or the race and noticing that neither is level or fair! In either case, the traditional winners in an unequal world remain untouched by the reality of the losers, for whom the field and the race remain illusory dreams.

Returning to the metaphor of the athletic race, what if the fictional "Usain Bolts" of this world go to the best schools, live in the best houses, have access to the best trainers, and enjoy all the privileges denied an alternative group of people? Judging the mythical Bolt, with his on-the-field advantages over his competitors who have been denied all of these things in training for the so-called fair race, is in fact a wholesale exercise of false consciousness—a gross deception. The race is as good as rigged. That it looks fair should not disguise the fact that its outcome was determined long before each competitor reached the track. Even if one can find the statistical outlier who has not enjoyed the advantages I have just referenced but still manages to "pull themselves up by their boot straps" to give the mythical Bolt a good race, the discovery of the "exceptional exception" does not change the basic template of the race itself. There will always be extraordinary individuals who can defy the odds and succeed. The proprietors of the race attempt to co-opt such individuals to mask the exclusion of the majority who come from disadvantaged backgrounds. And so the mythical Bolts of this world do not need to be extraordinary in order to succeed in this supposedly free, laissez-faire, fair-play construct. It would be stretching credulity to believe that all successful people who populate

Wall Street and the City of London are exceptional individuals or inhabit these spaces solely on merit!

In the construct I have just described, black theology is indeed biased and unfair. The unfairness of its alleged position arises from the reality that life is most obviously unfair. In the world in which racism blights the potential and everyday life experiences of many ordinary black people, are we seriously saying that God should be "fair"? Do we expect God to ignore injustice and treat the perpetrator and the victim as exactly the same? In the words of James Cone, "In a racist society, God is never color-blind. To say God is color-blind is analogous to saying that God is blind to justice, to right and wrong, to good and evil. Certainly this is not the picture of God revealed in the Old and New Testaments. Yahweh takes sides."[37] The so-called unfairness of black theology in general or James Cone's early writing in particular lies in its defiant call for equity, not equality. It calls for justice, not fairness. This approach to undertaking black theology by means of a participative methodology relies on an inductive mode of education, in which equal attention is given to affective and cognitive modes of learning. This popular educational approach seeks to challenge ordinary black people to reflect critically on their experiences in order to reimagine their existential realities. These reflections are then brought into conversation with the macro forms of analysis provided already by black theologians in order to shape transformative learning for those who participate in the exercises or games outlined earlier. This work asks the participants, "How does this feel?" and "What does it mean?" It then moves toward more generic or wider forms of critical reflection and analysis. The process moves forward with real stories and actual encounters and experiences from which one begins to see how smaller examples inform macro, epistemological truths.

CONCLUSION

In using this method for conscientizing, or raising the critical consciousness of ordinary black people, I am not pretending that such simple exercises or games will enable the participants to understand black theology in its entirety. However, I am using this heuristic method to assist participants not only to understand black theology but also to see how the acquisition of new knowledge can transform their lived experience as Christian disciples. This educative approach to black practical theology challenges ordinary black people to enter a metaphorical world or epistemological framework that permits all parties to test their emotions alongside the "other" in a contested space in which all participants are searching for truth. The truth that will set people free is located in the liberative dimensions of the gospel of Jesus Christ, in which righteousness is both a divine gift and something that experience teaches.

Having utilized this inductive approach to black theology in a variety of settings across the United Kingdom and other countries,[38] I believe that it offers an accessible means to raise the critical consciousness of ordinary black people, in addition to explaining and analyzing the central intent of practical theology. This form of transformative learning is a resource that enables participants to experience, in a more direct way, some of the issues, challenges, and factors that have shaped the development and essential meaning of black theology.

This practical theological method for undertaking black theology begins with the experiences of the learner and brings them into dialogue with the existential experience and essential meaning of the diasporan black experience. This method begins with the premise that people in real contexts matter as much as abstract ideas and disembodied theory. It also begins with the real and concrete feelings and experiences of marginalized, ordinary black people as a means of enhancing their critical consciousness and awareness of their agency as subjects in history.

In using the lived experiences of ordinary black people as its critical point of departure, this method draws upon some of the insights of radical black pastoral theologians. The work of black pastoral theologians, while not to be confused with the emerging discipline of practical theology as an intentional theological form,[39] nevertheless has offered black theology a number critical insights. The question of black self-negation that black pastoral theologians[40] have addressed critically informs my own black participative, theological, and educational work. Similarly, one of the architects of black theology, Gayraud Wilmore, outlines dual perspectives for understanding black theology. He argues that black theology can be understood as a scholarly discipline that seeks to provide a rational account of the meaning of God, in light of black suffering and oppression. But it is also a mode of liberative praxis.[41]

In using the term "liberative praxis," I underscore the need to link faith-based forms of theological reflection with committed attempts to bring about liberative change via action and activism. The combination of the two elements is more than the sum of its parts.[42] Praxis—the nexus of theological reflection and action, for the purposes of bringing about liberative change—should be central to the very identity and intent of black theology. Theory alone will not do, and neither will action alone. I believe that the ultimate challenge for black practical theology is providing the critical resources that will increase liberative praxis within the missional scope of the Black Church. One element of this liberative praxis is the educational task of conscientizing ordinary black people.

Using the game of musical chairs highlighted in this essay, I have tried to demonstrate how a participative black theology can enable ordinary black people to become more critical agents as they reflect on their lived experiences. This game assists them in seeing through the illusionary smoke screen that is the laissez-faire, fair-play dictum that dominates many liberal democratic societies in the West, particularly those of the United States and the United Kingdom. This work does not provide all the answers to how best to effect a more critical dialogue between black theology and black practical theology, but it is a critical attempt to that end and, as such, provides a useful point of departure for this ongoing work.

LISTENING TO THE POOR AND NONLITERATE

Madipoane Masenya (ngwan'a Mphahlele)

At one of the women's leadership seminars of my church,[1] an elderly woman raised a concern about Christians' tendency to be inward-looking. She had noticed that Christians can pass by homeless children at the gate of a church while heading into that church (to attend to the needs of those from within).[2] I was puzzled by the response of the regional women's president, who presided over the meeting; she hinted that if God had laid such a burden on the woman, then she was the one who needed to make sure that it was carried out. In a nutshell, she insinuated that it was the woman's ministry to take care of the homeless children and that she did not have to bother all the other women in that regard. I responded by challenging such a notion in my effort to conscientize the group that it was the responsibility of *all* Christians to do something about the needs of *all* those on the margins of our communities, whether they belong to *our* communities of faith or not. Danal Dorr rightly argues, "Who is asked to make an option for the poor? Everybody. It is part of the universal call of the Christian faith, which is addressed to all people."[3]

I had another relevant experience aboard a fifteen-seat minibus en route to a national women's conference in Bloemfontein, in the Free State Province of South Africa. As we were engaging the challenges of languages and communication at the conference, one elderly woman requested that the group pray then and there that English would not be used as the language of communication at the conference! As one of the keynote speakers of the conference, and knowing that I was going to be presenting the teachings in English, I interjected to suggest that we amend the nature of the prayer request because I already knew that in that multiethnic setting the basic language of communication (which is usually accompanied by translation into one or two of the indigenous languages) would be English! However, it became evident to me that our church pews hold members, particularly elderly female members, whose levels of literacy prevent them from accessing sermons that are preached in English only, something that the elite in our pews usually take for granted.

In terms of the first incidence, I was not so puzzled by the response of the regional president. As citizens of a country such as South Africa, a country with a history of glaring inequalities that were based mainly on the shade of one's skin, we have inherited a legacy of theologies and biblical hermeneutics that hardly touch the harsh realities on the ground. As the theologies we consumed were produced by those who benefited from "royalty" (cf. the Hebrew court prophets of eighth-century to sixth-century Judah and Israel), it makes sense that they would not choose to upset the racist, classist, and sexist status quo from which they also benefited.[4] Elsewhere I have argued, "Many women (and other marginalised people sitting in the church pews) are today being exhorted to focus on serious 'heavenly/spiritual' business. In the process, women are persuaded, through the use of the Bible, to call our own oppression, or violence done to our bodies in the name of a god, a 'worldly' matter that needs to be shunned."[5] It is no wonder that the challenges including, but not limited to, socioeconomic class, poverty, and education, which the majority of church members face, remain basically absent from the churches' priority lists.

Unlike the theology propounded by the benefactors of apartheid, prophetic theology challenges the status quo with a view to bringing transformation within our contexts. According to Cochrane, de Gruchy, and Peterson:

> Prophetic theology is critical of other theologies, whether of the state or church, which legitimate or help to perpetuate an unjust social system. Equally, it unambiguously takes the side of the oppressed and serves the cause of justice and liberation. It is theology in the Mosaic tradition of the eighth to sixth century Hebrew prophets who were engaged in radical social analysis and critique, and who were committed to a vision of society which required fundamental social transformation.[6]

The latter critique is the one I will adopt within the text of the present essay as I seek to assist us in our desire to be relevant to our ecclesiastical contexts, which are typified by problematic socioeconomic conditions like low social class, poverty, and illiteracy.[7] This essay is an attempt at breaking the aforementioned silence by suggesting ways in which black practical theologians and biblical scholars, in collaboration with clergypersons, could tackle these critical issues.

ANYTHING NEW UNDER THE SUN?

As a framework within which to engage my suggestions, I offer an overview of the present scenario in the South African postapartheid church, particularly in some black churches. I argue, like Qoheleth, "What has been is what will be, and what has been done is what will be done; there is nothing new under the sun" (Eccl/Qoh 1:9). Although previously marginalized South Africans—that is, the black majority—have acquired political liberation, the economy, which in my view is the pillar of any society, remains in the hands of the historically privileged. It is important to note that a few black elites have managed to join the "gravy train" since 1994, and there is a noticeable new trend of a class of poor white South Africans. However, the majority of the materially poor in South Africa remain those who were previously disadvantaged.

Also, just as the (black) church in apartheid South Africa chose, on the whole, to remain quiet amid the atrocities that typified the South African landscape then, today it remains basically quiet about corruption among political leaders amid high levels of poverty. With postapartheid South Africa being one of the most unequal societies in the world, poverty-related woes—such as the HIV and AIDS pandemic, nonliteracy, and high unemployment rates, even among the educated youth—continue to exist. Indeed, there is nothing new under the sun! The words of G. E. Dames resonate:

> Some of the traditional churches in South Africa demonstrate an inability "to be reborn in consciousness" and to "die as a class." Furthermore, the uncertainty *and* corruption brought about by South Africa's political transition, globalisation and postmodernity, breed fundamentalism and individualism to the extent that a vision for the common public good of all suffers. The dilemma is that deep levels of distress develop among the majority of the poorest in the broader community.[8]

The seeds of hope that were sown with the release of political prisoners in 1990 and the ushering in of democracy in 1994 were/are being frustrated by the slowness of change with regard to the betterment of the lives of the previously marginalized. The postapartheid South African church, pretty much like its predecessor, does not provide a helpful model of a people-oriented, transformation-driven institution. The self-serving political leaders, most of whom appear to care less about the plight of many a poor person, provide no hope for the poor either. Indeed, there seems to be nothing new under the sun.

What does the black South African church look like today? To this question we now turn.

THE BLACK CHURCH IN SOUTH AFRICA TODAY

Any church is a microcosm of the broader society. Indeed, "many ecclesiastical structures reflect or tend to reproduce the structures of the societies to which they belong."[9] Whatever good fortune the broader South African society experiences will also be experienced by the church. Similarly, the church will experience whatever woes plague the broader South African society, whether or not we would like to acknowledge them. The challenge of nonliteracy, as typified by the preceding example of an elderly woman who wished to resist English as a medium of communication, illustrates well the sharedness of plagues between the church and society. In apartheid South Africa, one's socioeconomic class was closely linked to one's race. Most probably, therefore, on account of material poverty the woman's family could not afford to provide her with sufficient education, which, in turn, made it difficult for her to acquire sufficient skills to take advantage of significant employment opportunities. Such restrictions, coupled with the norms of an African patriarchal culture that did not prioritize the education of a girl, could only exacerbate the woman's already vulnerable situation.[10] Hers can be cited as a practical example of the integration of one's social class, nonliteracy or lack of education, and poverty.

In Africa, material poverty has, and continues to have, a feminine face. By material poverty, we mean a situation in which human beings struggle to meet basic needs such as shelter (consider the many informal settlements that are now the order of the day in South Africa), food, and clothing.[11] According to the Commission on the Churches' Participation in Development of the World Council of Churches (WCC), "To be poor is not to be able to satisfy basic human needs: food, housing, health, education, job and social participation. In this sense, as is very often pointed out in the Bible, to be poor, is the same as to be oppressed."[12] As previously noted, the fact that the black South African majority remains poor reveals something of the face of the Black Church, particularly in rural areas. E. M. K. Mathole has conducted a master's study of how selected South African churches responded to poverty. It is clear from his study that in the South African churches, particularly those of mixed race, poverty continues to plague black communities. Says Mathole: "Poverty is prevalent extensively in churches that are located in previously disadvantaged communities. It therefore affects the black . . . members of the church in particular, the majority of whom are still living in the same needy communities."[13]

The level of one's poverty or wealth determines one's socioeconomic class. The reality is that the majority of black folks remain in the lowest socioeconomic classes, in terms of both poverty and unemployment; this is one of the legacies of our political past. T. Mofokeng notes that the arrival of armed colonial Europeans in South Africa determined our ancestors' response and future in the face of that particular incursion: "Their act of forcing a foreign, capitalist economic system upon our forefathers as well as relegating them to a position of cheap labourers determined the nature of the social, political and economic history of South Africa."[14] Such an unfortunate legacy is perpetuated today by neoliberal economic globalization. The latter refers to the present global economic order, which undermines the majority of the people in the world, specifically poor people, and the earth due to economic impoverishment as well as ecological degradation.[15] It follows, then, that the historically poor, like poor African–South African peoples, will grow only more impoverished within the context of globalization. The repercussions of globalization in Africa are, as a whole, usually detrimental to the poor and vulnerable, to women, and to the working class.[16] Therefore, a question important for this essay emerges: In view of the preceding scenario, in which the Black Church continues to be plagued by the woes of an undesirable socioeconomic class, of poverty, and of nonliteracy or the lack of education, how may church leaders on the ground—that is, clergypersons, theologians, and biblical scholars—jointly respond to the situation?

KNOWLEDGE OF OUR IDENTITIES AS A PEOPLE

Knowing who we are (via self-definitions), where we came from (via herstory/history), what typifies us as people of African descent (via our identities), among others, are pertinent to any endeavor on which we seek to embark, whether theological or not. Having inherited the legacies of self-hate, low self-esteem, being defined by others, and aspiring to be who we are not, we now need a concerted effort by both clergy and practical theologians alike to choose deliberately to be who we *truly* are. We do this by shaping the content of our academic offerings, sermons, and Bible studies according not to the needs identified by those from outside (usually under the banner of the world as global village) but to those who are inside, particularly those insiders on the margins of our faith communities. T. Okure reminds us that the professionally trained African women theologians, unlike the so-called ordinary women who are close to life at the grassroots, "can be tempted to subscribe to abstract ways of theologizing in order to find acceptance in the field. Thus, they can lose focus on life, or seek answers to hermeneutical questions put by others, instead of identifying and addressing their own questions."[17] We need to seek *jointly* such identities as a people united by our common ancestry.

In so doing, we are persuaded by the words of the ancestors, "*Tau tša hloka seboka, di šiwa ke nare e hlotša*," literally, "Lions which are not united, are outrun by a limping buffalo." We acknowledge, indeed, with the comrades of the South African political past, that "an injury to one, is an injury to all."

Such connectedness will enable us to transcend the binaries in which we were nurtured, and thereby to appreciate the holistic outlook of our African ancestry. Moreover, this outlook empowers us further to develop gender-conscious frameworks and methodologies that might enable certain sectors of our communities to embrace shared agency. We would, for example, not be threatened when single women sitting in our church pews feel more affirmed by the womanist or *bosadi* (womanhood) frameworks in their search for affirming definitions of womanhood within their marginalized contexts. In our determination to affirm and celebrate our diversity, even as we seek to deal constructively with the challenges some of our church members face, we should shy away from the mentality of "one size fits all," as strategies that might prove effective in one context may not necessarily be effective in another.

WORKING HAND IN GLOVE

As a people committed to being instruments used by God that the people of God might experience life, we must have the courage and humility to choose deliberately to learn from each other as we seek to do justice to the challenges facing the socioeconomically disadvantaged members of our churches. "One hand washes the other," says an African proverb. The needs of those sitting in our pews should inform the content of our sermons and Bible studies as well as the strategies we develop to address such needs. In our HIV and AIDS-stricken contexts, for example, the pews can only benefit from sermons and teachings that destigmatize as well as constructively engage the discourse on HIV and AIDS. In my view, this exigency implies that clergypersons who are (expected to be) in tune with the holistic lives of their church members must not only allow the needs of their faith communities to shape their sermons, counseling, and pastoral ministry as a whole but also share such needs with academics with a view to shaping some of the academic offerings at the seminaries and faculties of theology. If the latter are relevantly equipped, they will come a long way in enabling "graduate-ness,"—that is, graduates who will relevantly plow back into their communities—and in bringing about the transformation of the lives of our communities, particularly the disadvantaged Others.

LISTENING TO THE WOODEN SPOONS
FROM THE (COOKING) POTS

Two Northern Sotho/Sepedi expressions come to mind here. The first, *leho la go tšwa pitšeng*, literally means "a wooden spoon which comes from a (cooking) pot." Such a spoon has experienced what it means to be made by the cook to function ruthlessly in the midst of the heat from fire. Likewise, *sešo se baba mongwai*, which literally translates as "a sore itches to its owner," reminds us that experience is the best teacher.

In seeking strategies to alleviate poverty, for example, both clergy and black practical theologians alike must first and foremost listen to what the poor themselves are suggesting with regard to their situations. Poverty, to them, is like the proverbial itching sore; they can provide only relevant suggestions. We need to allow the poor's proposed strategies to inform our efforts toward redress. In doing so, we might be surprised to learn just how resilient even marginalized agency can be. Here, we should consider the biblical narrative of two widows who refused to be pulled down by their poor socioeconomic condition. We see Ruth, a Moabite childless widow, choosing against all odds to cling (*davaq*) to her elderly mother-in-law, Naomi (Ruth 1:15-17). She chose to leave the comfort zone of Moab, her home country, which probably promised a brighter future, to travel to an unknown country, which was most likely first introduced to her by her now deceased husband as a country of lack. Vulnerable as Ruth was, a sonless widow and a Moabite, she did not hesitate to propose marriage to Boaz, a "man of substance" (Ruth 1:9). She eventually managed to become an agent of transformation in her own life and in the life of Naomi. She accomplished this agency by extending her *botho/ubuntu/hesed* to her mother-in-law, through her gleanings from the fields (Ruth 2) and later through a son whom she bore (Ruth 4:14). In the same way, encouraged by a tenacious, unstoppable daughter-in-law, Naomi sought security for Ruth through marriage rites (Ruth 2:20; 3:1-2). The two women succeeded in navigating their patriarchal context and eventually got what they needed. The agency of Naomi and Ruth is evident in the agency of widows in our church settings today. The responsibility of black practical theologians and biblical scholars is to allow the "wooden spoons from the cooking pots"—that is, the widows themselves—to display their inherent capacity to be agents of transformation in their own lives, by providing suggestions on how they can be affirmed by the church. The following example is a case in point: in a "father-less," poor, single female-parented family context, concrete suggestions from single women, such as the need for fathers in the church to act as role models to their sons, need to be heeded. In their interactions with such sons, the fathers, through modeling, could encourage the youth to pursue education in order to break the cycle of poverty. Such sons are likely to heed the words of their "mentor-fathers," possibly more than those of their mothers.

CHOOSING TO BE ON THE SAME PAGE

In the biblical sciences, as with the discipline of practical theology, a gap exists between what is done by academics in academia and what is done by clergypersons (some of whom are academics, of course). Such a gap perpetuates the myth that the two parties cannot work together. Depending on the commitment of both parties, though, this myth can become problematic: for example, when clergypersons who must undergo theological training purpose to undergo such training, and when academics who take comfort in theologizing from within the comfort of academia deliberately choose to plow back into our faith communities through active involvement in community affairs.

A practical example of a situation wherein practical theologians and clergypersons can work hand in glove is dealing constructively with the challenge of HIV and AIDS. This challenge is connected to the sufferer's socioeconomic class and level of education. The lower the education level of a church member, the poorer he or she is likely to be and the more vulnerable to the challenge of HIV and AIDS. For those who have already contracted the HIV virus, less education will mean less access to health care. On the one hand, practical theologians and activist biblical scholars can engage the challenge of HIV and AIDS by making it an integral part of their academic offerings. On the other hand, clergypersons can deliberately make the discourse on HIV and AIDS an integral part of their sermons and Bible studies. In some cases, depending on the severity of the pandemic, churches can establish drop-in centers (on the churches' property) in which HIV and AIDS orphans can be cared for during specific hours of the day. In that way, both practical theologians and clergypersons can at least be on the same page regarding their concerted effort to challenge the spread of HIV.

If both black practical theologians and clergypersons could choose, against our human tendencies, to serve and not to be served, if we could deliberately gear ourselves toward washing the feet of the neglected in our faith communities, perhaps then we might instill in ourselves, as well as in the members of our churches, the conviction that the plight of the homeless children roaming our streets, even those streets in the neighborhood of our churches, is our plight as well. Perhaps we might succeed not only in sharing our messages with the many nonliterate persons (mostly women) sitting in our church pews but also in transforming our communities. With such an effort, I think we would be headed in the right direction in our call to be the salt of the earth and the light of the world (Matt 5:13-14).

<< 7 >>

DOING THEOLOGY FOR ORDINARY FOLK

Jeremiah A. Wright Jr.

The title of my reflections and responses to the works of Anthony Reddie and Madipoane Masenya in this volume is taken from the story John W. Kinney tells of his first Sunday back home in the pulpit of the Ebenezer Baptist Church of Beaver Dam, Virginia, after receiving his Ph.D. Kinney earned his doctorate in philosophical theology under James Cone (the "Father" of constructive black theology) at Union Theological Seminary in New York City. Kinney commuted from Richmond, Virginia, to New York City the entire time he was studying under Cone. Kinney's family and his church were in Ashland, Virginia, and Beaver Dam, Virginia, respectively; and for four years he was a Ph.D. student during the week and a husband, father, foster parent, and pastor every weekend. John Kinney was and is a scholar in what Dr. Dwight Hopkins calls "the second generation" of black theologians.

The first generation of black theologians tended to be divorced from the local church, cut off from the lives of local worshippers, highly critical of (while simultaneously being separate and apart from) local faith communities, and at times (some would say) downright hostile to the local black congregation.[1] Dwight Hopkins, in his review of the development of the discipline of black theology,[2] argues that the "second generation" of black theologians—unlike the first generation—maintained their ties with the Black Church and stayed active in local black congregations, with some even serving as pastors of local black churches. Hopkins lists such second-generation black theologians as Kelly Brown Douglas, Dennis Wiley, Jacquelyn Grant, John W. Kinney, and himself as scholars who maintained membership in and remain very much a part of local church congregations. Beaverdam, where Kinney served as pastor of the Ebenezer Baptist Church while earning his Ph.D., is a rural community that sits twenty-five miles north of Richmond, Virginia. To understand better how rural it is, one may consider its historical roots, "Beaverdam" is the name elected officials selected when changing its name from "Negro Foot," which it held from the 1920s to the middle of the Civil Rights movement in the 1950s.

Old rural telephone books of the Ashland, Virginia, Beaverdam community still show the addresses of the residents who lived in "Negro Foot," which is the polite name of the rural community in which Ebenezer Baptist Church sits. Originally the community was called "Nigger Foot," a name it earned because the tree that still sits in front of Ebenezer Baptist Church at the fork in the road in Beaverdam was the tree on which the feet of captured runaway African slaves would be hung as a warning and as a deterrent for any other Africans who thought of trying to free themselves from the horrors of chattel slavery. Ebenezer Baptist Church is built on the site where the symbol and the reminder of chattel slavery still sits. These crossroads shape this rural community and congregation, which Kinney, as of this writing, has served for thirty years!

John tells the story of his first Sunday back in the pulpit after graduation. He was free of the four-year commute. No more traveling back and forth every week from Virginia to New York. No more leaving his wife and children during their school year and no more taking them to New York with him when they were out of school! No more juggling class work, research, paper writing, dissertation anxiety, and hours in the library, wrestling with foreign languages, written exams, and oral defenses, with being a husband, a father, and a pastor! No more choices to make between finals and funerals, hours of study and hospital visits. John had finished his academic work and had earned his Ph.D. He had drunk deeply from the wells of James Cone's wisdom and experience, and he was a proud, black man eager and ready to serve both the Black Church and the academic world!

On that first Sunday back in the pulpit with his Ph.D. in hand, John says, he tried to preach in one sermon everything he had learned under James Cone. He told the members of Ebenezer with as much fire as he could muster how we, as a black people, need to get the chains off our minds, how we need to embrace our blackness—both ontologically and theologically—and how we need to affirm our blackness. John said he preached, "Black This! Black That! and Black the Other!" while wearing his dashiki and sporting his genuine Kente cloth from Bonwire, Ghana. After the worship service was over, as members were leaving the sanctuary, they filed past their pastor, shaking his hand, welcoming him back home "for good," congratulating him on his Ph.D., and asking him how his wife and children enjoyed the academic commencement service in New York. Nobody said a word to him about his sermon! No one offered a commentary, no one, that is, with the exception of an octogenarian—one of the "Mothers" of the church—who came up to him on a walker. She put her hand on his solar plexus and pushed rhythmically with each point she made in her powerful statement. She said to him:

> Son! You've got a bubbling fountain of knowledge, insight, and wisdom in here [as she pushed on his chest]. This fountain God has given you is rich. It comes from a deep well way down inside you. I can feel it when you preach! This fountain is going to bless hundreds if not thousands of people. God has blessed you in a powerful way; but if you want me to drink from your fountain, next time, put it in a cup I can recognize!

"A CUP I CAN RECOGNIZE!"

Putting black theology in a cup that ordinary folk can recognize is what the discipline of practical theology is all about. Putting black theology into a format that Anthony Reddie calls "participative black theology" is putting it in a cup that everyday people (à la Sly & the Family Stone) can recognize.

Reddie's methodology of using games and humor to get nonacademic "church folks" to reflect on their lived experience and to trust their affective senses is a most helpful methodology that, in my opinion, most local church pastors—at least those who are serious about closing the gap between theoretical black theology and praxiological black theology—would welcome. Using the methods of transformative popular education as a way of closing that gap while simultaneously teaching critical thinking is putting black theology in a cup everybody can recognize.

Madipoane Masenya's crucial insights about language are really saying the same thing in a different context! Reading about the wishful thinking of the elderly, black, South African woman's prayer on the minibus en route to the national women's conference in Bloemfontein in the Free State Province of South Africa, one can almost see (and hear!) the octogenarian at Ebenezer Baptist Church in Beaverdam. "Let us pray that English [will] not be used as a language of communication at the conference!" That prayer sounds strikingly similar to the request to put in a cup an offering that ordinary black women (from the townships and the rural areas), who have not had the benefit of so-called education, can recognize!

As Masenya points out, millions of "salt of the earth," black South Africans—especially women—are victims of nonliteracy. Yet, they have developed a rich and powerful tradition as an aural-oral culture people that has not been tapped into because nobody is taking the time to put the "literate" content into cups that ordinary folk can recognize.

Several scholars, including Paulo Freire,[3] Donaldo Macedo,[4] Geneva Smitherman,[5] and Smitherman and Samy Alim,[6] echo the theme. The ability to engage in critical thinking is not limited to those persons who have had access to the academy. Persons from everyday life have that ability, and we rob ourselves of the benefits of learning from them, while sharing with them, when we do not acknowledge this fact. Our mutual tasks are to translate what we each have to offer into terms the other can understand, thereby putting both worlds of words into cups each of us can recognize.

In the field of practical theology, these tasks constitute a common theme that connects the works of Reddie and Masenya. I also find it echoed in the writings of Brandee Jasmine Mimitzraiem,[7] and I use these three scholars' positions to segue into the second part of my reflection. The editors conclude their description of our issue under critical consideration for the black community—namely, education, class, and poverty—as follows:

> The critical needs of education affect black church leadership directly. The lack of academically (seminary-) trained clergypersons—across black denominations and congregations, and among the "Bishops," "Apostles," and megachurch clergypersons, who have significant congregations and extended followings in their communities—is an issue needing redress. How might we work with black churches to address these justice issues in the convergence of class, poverty, and education?[8]

My first response to this challenge is theoretical. If we start from Masenya's premise of not only the reality but also the strength of nonliterate aural culture, what I call "aural-oral" culture, then I suggest that building on cultural strengths is an excellent way to address these justice issues. Rather than seeing nonliterate aural culture as deficient, we may recognize it as a strength.

Education as it is presently perceived (and presented) in American culture is not education at all. It is "training" poor folks for service in low-paying jobs at Walmart, K-Mart, Target, or McDonald's at worst, and, in turn, cultivating college graduates for work in corporate America at best.

Teaching to the test, "racing to the top," and preparing students to work under ceilings do not reflect the objectives of true education. Rather, it is a pedagogy that ensures that its clients (consumers) will not engage in critical thinking.

This type of so-called education exacerbates the classism that poisons the air in our congregations and perpetuates social and economic divides. The demon of classism becomes an even more formidable obstacle to what Jesus talked about as the ethic governing the kingdom of God, or what Martin Luther King Jr. understood as the "beloved community" and Howard Thurman wrote about in his search for "common ground." I see a need for us to define education using a new paradigm that transforms what presently passes itself off as education in America.

We value and valorize people on the basis of the current, false paradigm. We welcome literate, so-called educated people into our congregations, and we structure our Christian-education programs accordingly. We do not think of the poor among us as invaluable members of our congregations. We do not positively valorize those who have not had the benefit of the so-called best schools and training that our college-educated members have had. The nonliterate among us, the nonliterate at the gate (wishing they could get in), and the poor who do not fit in our congregations are just as valuable, however, as those among us with a Ph.D., J.D., or M.D. More importantly, while we often contend that they need what we are offering, the real need is not theirs. It is ours. We need to translate what we are offering and put it in cups they can recognize.

Educators such as Janice Hale[9] and educational psychologists such as Asa Hilliard[10] have been saying for almost half a century (as of this writing) that we need to abandon the deficit model and start learning how to build on cultural strengths.[11] The nonliterate, aural-oral culture is just as valid as the literate culture, and we need to understand and embrace this culture as a strength and then build on it. I am suggesting that we should use the nonliterate, aural-oral culture as a methodological approach to closing the educational gap between those clergy who have not had the benefit of academic and/or seminary training and those who have.

Let us take the principles of Macedo's work[12] and Smitherman's work[13] to put seminary education in a cup those clergy thirsty for training can recognize. Let us use the same methodology for teaching not just the clergy but also the members of our congregations. Learning (or relearning) the language of untrained, ordinary, everyday people and using that language to teach what the academy is offering is a win-win proposition as far as I am concerned. Reddie does it with his "game" approach. His musical chairs illustration is classic. I have used that methodology as a pastor, and I have found it to be mutually beneficial. It benefits nonacademically trained persons, and it helps me to keep exploring ways of putting what the academy and I have to offer in cups that others can recognize!

My second response to the challenge from practical theologians is to offer as practical models three different programs that are doing what is required to address the justice issues that attend the convergence of class, poverty, and education:

Program 1: Nurturing the Call. The Seminary Consortium for Urban Pastoral Education (SCUPE) in Chicago has several different programs that seek to make seminary education accessible to church persons (lay and clergy) for whom seminary at one point in their lives seemed to be an out-of-reach dream. Two of SCUPE's programs speak directly to the issues raised by Reddie, Masenya, Dale Andrews, and Robert Smith: the Nurturing the Call program and the Center for African American Theological Studies program, which is discussed in the following section.

Nurturing the Call is a program designed to take persons at whatever academic level they are on when they discern God's call upon their lives for ministry and to raise their ability to perform (successfully) academically at the seminary and graduate-school level.[14] Persons with only a high school education are given courses in theology, Bible studies, church history, sociology, English, homiletics, hermeneutics, Christian education, and so on, and the material is "put in cups they can recognize."

Nurturing the Call brings individuals with the skills to master more mainstream material and instruction to the point where they can function successfully at the seminary level. Not all people who acknowledge a call to ministry on their lives are called to the preaching ministry or pastoral ministry. Some are called to teach in Christian-education departments. Some are called to teach Sunday school or Bible classes. Some are called to serve as deacons, stewards, trustees, or financial officers or to serve in other positions of church and congregational leadership. The Nurturing the Call program is designed to help individuals prepare for ministry in whatever area they declare as God's design for their lives.

The genius of the program is that it starts (academically) at whatever level people are when they say "yes" to the call and then takes them as far as their ability will allow them to go. Some students who have started their training with only a high school diploma have been able to earn baccalaureate and even master of divinity degrees.

Program 2: The Center for African American Theological Studies. The Center for African American Theological Studies (CAATS) is a SCUPE program that is specifically designed for persons who have an interest in the praxiological dimensions of black theology; who are serious about "participative black theology"; who value the affective, aural-oral culture and reflective cognitive investigations of the black religious traditions; and who believe in the efficacy of transformative popular education.

CAATS accepts students who have not graduated from an undergraduate degree program and seeks to develop them academically until they gain admission into and successfully complete an M.Div. program at an ATS accredited seminary. At the time of this writing, CAATS has twenty students who have earned a master of divinity from the Samuel DeWitt Proctor School of Theology at Virginia Union University. Additionally, Payne Theological Seminary and Garrett-Evangelical Theological Seminary have recently become partnering seminaries in the CAATS program. The A.M.E. church discipline within the past decade was revised to require the master of divinity degree for candidates seeking ordination as Itinerant Elders in that denomination. Payne (an A.M.E. seminary) has partnered with CAATS to make this requirement accessible for hundreds of persons in the A.M.E. church who have acknowledged God's call upon their lives for full-time, ordained service to the church of Jesus Christ. Garrett-Evangelical Theological Seminary is a partner in this new approach to seminary education for students committed to the black and Hispanic communities.[15]

Building on cultural strengths, using cups that ordinary folk can recognize, is one of CAATS' strong points, and it offers a model for theological education that Reddie, Masenya, Andrews, and Smith each use to close the gap between academic and practical understandings of black liberation theology. Courses such as "Public Theology and the City," "Desarrollo economico en la comunidad Latina," and "Christology and Culture" start with sociological and existential realities with which the students are familiar and teach the students to look at the worlds they come from and the worlds they serve through new hermeneutical lenses.

The culture of Hip Hop is engaged and exegeted to prepare the students to "serve this present age," and students are equipped to minister to those whom the urban church traditionally and historically has tended to exclude. I was asked to write a description of the CAATS program to be used on its Web page that captures the uniqueness of this approach to theological education:

Building on the Black Church's tradition of self-determination the Center for African American Theological Studies (CAATS) seeks to provide the academic and cultural tools that ministers need to become informed pastors and leaders capable of revitalizing their churches and communities. An African-centered understanding of one's sociological and theological reality empowers leaders to address the individual and systemic forces which prevent Africans throughout the diaspora from achieving the abundant life which God intended. It is vital that we take control of the curricula, the methods, and the environments in which our leaders are trained.[16]

Program 3: The Urban Theological Institute. The Urban Theological Institute (UTI) of the Lutheran Theological Seminary in Philadelphia is the third program I offer for consideration.[17] It, too, starts to work with students who have not had the benefit of a college education. The UTI program takes those whom Masenya would call students from aural culture and trains them to master what might be considered difficult academic material—by putting that material in cups they can recognize! Both SCUPE and the UTI have been doing this practical training for over thirty years. With the premises of Janice Hale's findings concerning learning styles[18] and of the Academic English Mastery Program,[19] UTI students are given the opportunity to develop new skills and are taught how to master difficult theological concepts. Acknowledging and building on the unique learning styles that the students bring to the seminary, the professors accept and affirm the students' cultural and linguistic variations and prepare the students for ministry by giving them "bilingual" skills that will allow them to better serve congregations made up of persons from diverse socioeconomic and educational backgrounds.

The remaining part of my reflection on the chapters by Reddie and Masenya looks at, or suggests, the training and/or studies I would seek if I had the opportunity to return to full-time theological education in practical theology, especially in the critical areas of education, class, and poverty. The course offerings I feel would be most helpful are (a) courses that teach how to translate theological concepts into the language of everyday people, that is, courses that put those concepts in "recognizable cups"; (b) courses that deconstruct the negative images of seminary education and construct an ethic of *ubuntu* where each person in the community is seen as a person of worth; (c) immersion or "exposure" courses similar to those offered in seminaries like the Samuel DeWitt Proctor School of Theology at Virginia Union University, where the students are given sixty dollars (comparable to the two dollars a day on which the poor in our world live) and have to live among the homeless and the "truly disadvantaged" for a full month to see firsthand what life in that world is like; (d) courses that teach critical thinking and how to use critical thinking in teaching parishioners how to create a more just and equitable world; (e) courses that teach seminarians how to reach the Hip Hop generation, the post–Hip Hop generation, and those who were not raised in the church or who are turned off by the church; and (f) courses that "name the demon" as Jesus confronted and named the demons he encountered (for example, see Mark 5), and/or confront the two-ton gorilla sitting in our sanctuaries: classism!

Courses that translate theological concepts into the language of everyday people are necessary because seminarians and theologians tend to use terms and language that other seminary-trained persons can understand, such as "hermeneutics" and a "hermeneutic of suspicion." The average parishioner in an inner-city, urban, or metropolitan church would not automatically understand either of those terms. In view of practical examples like Anthony Reddie's game of musical chairs, which taught the difference between the concepts of "equality" and "equity," one example of such a course might proceed by teaching the seminarian how to demonstrate the difference in the hermeneutic of a right-wing, racist, white supremacist Christian and the hermeneutic of a radical Christian Hip Hop artist such as Lonnie Rashid (better known as Common).

Courses that construct an ethic of *ubuntu*, a Zulu and Xhosa word that means "community," are also essential. Its rich meaning is perhaps best captured in the Zulu saying, *umntu, ngumntu, ngbantu*, which means, "an individual can only be fully human by being in relationship with other human beings, all of whom have their humanity validated by virtue of the *ntu* [the breath of God!] within them."

In a community where *ubuntu* is lived out no one person is seen as better than or less than another. Valorization of a person's humanity is not based on how much education he or she has, and educated persons are not seen as "sellouts" and hopelessly assimilated enemies of the "real people" who have not been to white schools and poisoned by the "white man's teachings." That perception of seminary-trained clergy is unfortunately widespread in far too many minority communities in the United States. In a community where *ubuntu* is practiced, all persons are valued as equal because all have the breath of God in them and all are made in the image of God.

Courses that address the experience of the poor include those that use the works of Macedo,[20] Henry Giroux,[21] Chris Hedges,[22] Obery Hendricks,[23] and Allan Boesak[24] to critique the theologies of the Prosperity Gospel, contemporary gospel music, and the conflation of the teachings of capitalism and God's "favor," wherein greed and narcissism become synonymous with Christianity as seen through the eyes of the West. These would be most helpful in training seminarians to create a world foregrounded by Jesus' teaching us to pray "Thy kingdom come." The kingdom of God and the kingdom of mammon are dichotomous and hopelessly at odds with each other.

Courses that teach the causes of poverty and capitalism's basic assumptions, the origins of racist thinking and racist theology, the structure of the corporate-controlled privatized prison system and the legalization of what Michelle Alexander calls the "New Jim Crow," the difference between education and the corporate-controlled "training" that prepares privileged children for managerial careers and underprivileged children for service jobs at Target, Walmart, and McDonald's, and the difference between the Israel of the Bible and the State of Israel in the twentieth and twenty-first centuries would go a long way in preparing seminarians and their parishioners for creating a more just and equitable world.

Finally, courses that teach seminarians how to reach the Hip Hop generation and to confront classism seem essential when I consider just how theological education, as presently understood, is truly designed to develop or perpetuate the elite! Poor folk cannot afford, or sustain, access to the necessary skills development for college, much less graduate school. Most of our churches, especially those that can "afford" to have a seminary graduate as their pastor, are made up of and designed for so-called middle-class or upper-class individuals.

Our socialized constructs of theological education and church appointments reveal just how much we do not want poor people in our congregations and just how much we do not want to name the demon! We do not see poor people as equals, nor do we desire them as valued members of our congregations! (That is the name of the demon!) We must develop and support courses that train seminarians in both how to break out of this pedagogical methodology and how to lead their congregations in developing critical thinking (like Reddie's game methodology and like Jesus' example!). We also need courses that teach seminarians how to lead their congregations in these new and exciting directions without losing their jobs as pastors in the process. We "talk" or preach liberation of the poor as we mouth the words of black theology. We preach that God is on the side of the have-nots, but we practice celebration of the haves, rather than the liberation of the have-nots. If we truly want ordinary folk to drink from the fountain of black practical theology—that is, in a cup they can recognize—then we must find a way to develop courses and experiences in our seminaries that teach us how to change current paradigms and become true disciples of that poor carpenter from Galilee who was lynched on a tree outside of Jerusalem.

IV

Gender, Sexual Orientation, and Race

Gender equality remains a critical issue within black churches. While black theology condemns patriarchy and its work has helped pave the way for the emergence of womanist theology, many black churches remain sexist institutions in which gender inequality is a vexing problem. For instance, while black and womanist theologians endorse gender-inclusive language, there are no practical resources or guidelines for introducing and instituting such language within the daily life and rituals of black churches. Moreover, a dearth of women pastors and women in other major positions of leadership continues within black congregations and/or denominations, alongside the unrelenting assault of the sexual objectification of women in black churches and communities. These matters, which illustrate a critical disconnect between black theology and black churches, need to be addressed. In what ways might black theologians and practical theologians formulate theological frameworks for black churches to address gender issues that affirm all people?

Sexual orientation is a very emotive issue that many black churches have failed to engage; when they do engage it, they often perpetuate homophobia and heterosexism. Black and womanist theologians remind us that oppression is multidimensional and that *all* of God's children deserve to be free. Black churches could do a better job in helping black people understand that homosexuality, as a sexual orientation, is not a sin and that God loves gay people just as much as God loves straight people. The hatred, animosity, venom, hostility, and violence often visited upon lesbian, gay, bisexual, and transgender persons and their allies/advocates—all "in the name of Jesus"—constitute an acute malady plaguing black churches. How can the liberating message of black theology and the strategies of practical theology treat this malaise? Meaningful

connections between academic theological understandings and definitions of sex, sexuality, and salvation, and what the "people in the pew"
believe about same-gender-loving people are missing. These missing connections result in many people's confusion over, on the one hand, what
they have been taught the Bible says about this matter and, on the other
hand, what the Bible actually says.

Racism remains a critical issue for black churches. In this so-called
postracial society, we sometime assumed that this issue is behind us.
Partly because of the successes of the historic Civil Rights movement in
the United States, it is often assumed that black churches are perpetually
at the forefront in the struggle for racial justice. Unfortunately, this is
not the case, and, if the truth be told, it was not so much the case during
the Civil Rights struggle either. A large number of black churches were
not involved in the Civil Rights movement and did not actively support
Dr. Martin Luther King Jr. All too often, black churches are reactive rather
than proactive institutions when it comes to racism and with the many
other "isms" that negatively affect black communities. How might black
theologians and practical theologians help black churches identify cultural, systemic, or aversive forms of racism and actualize deliberate ways
to resist and redress them?

<< 8 >>

Building Communities of Embodied Beauty

Phillis Isabella Sheppard

Let him kiss me with the kisses of his mouth! . . . Draw me after you,
let us make haste. . . . I am black and beautiful. . . . Do not gaze at me
because I am dark, because the sun has gazed on me. My mother's sons
were angry with me; they made me keeper of the vineyards, but my own
vineyard I have not kept!

Song of Solomon 1:2-6 (NRSV, Catholic Edition)

The poet who wrote the Song of Solomon reveals much about herself
early in the collection of poems. This woman is passionate, sexual, and
assertive. Concerning her sexual desires for her lover, she is neither silent
nor burdened with reticence or embarrassment. She is far too clear and
committed, and in too much of a hurry—"Draw me after you, let us
make haste"! She makes herself transparent to the world. She knows she
is a beautiful black woman. She is also aware that not everyone shares
her conviction that being black is beautiful, and she names the attitude
concerning blackness. She demands that the daughters of Jerusalem not
stare on the basis of their negative ideologies related to color. The black
woman in the Song of Solomon will not remain silent about her passionate
love, her black beautiful self, or the complexity of her family history: "the
sun has gazed on me," "my mother's sons were angry with me," and,
so, they made her the "keeper of the vineyards." Although they are her
mother's sons—that is, her family—she will not remain quiet about the
truth of how they treat her. She is a model of protest.

If black practical theologians and clergy are going to take gender, sexuality, and race seriously, then we, like the woman in the Song of Solomon, are going to need authentic transparent dialogue in and outside of the auspices of that which we call "the Black Church." And, frankly, I think this is easier said than done. In one of her most referenced poems, Pat Parker writes that if she could just bring her whole self, without apology, into all the places she reads her poetry, it would be a revolution. Her view is in aim and content, by extension, a commentary on the views expressed by the black woman poet of the Song of Solomon. Parker writes that if she could share all the parts of her black lesbian self, then we would have a revolution on our hands. Like the woman from the Song of Solomon, Parker reveals that announcing her whole self—namely, her sexual orientation and her commitment to being her real self—would expose her to racism and heterosexism. These black women poets force us to examine the splits, compartmentalizing, and silences that can govern our lives, both in the broader social context and in the church. The splits of which I speak concern our relationship, as black folks, to our blackness, racial ideologies, gender roles and expectations, and sexualities. What do these splits look and sound like? These are challenges that a relevant black practical theology will have to meet. We claim that black religion is important, even crucial, to the lives of African Americans, and we have research to prove it, but we often give short shrift to the ways in which our experiences of gender, sexuality, and race are situated *in* black religious settings and operational theologies. We hear all kinds of messages from pulpits, television, and good, loving religious folk—ordained and not—that support the emotional, psychological, and spiritual abuse of individuals and groups whose identities do not conform to some normative expression.

These messages in the name of religion, salvation, and morality are forms of cultural violence. According to the social sciences, "cultural violence makes direct and structural violence look . . . right. The study of cultural violence highlights the way in which the act of direct violence and the fact of structural violence are legitimized and thus rendered acceptable in society."[1] We are reluctant to see how black religious/black church practices are practices of violence disguised as theological and spiritual truths. In this chapter, I grapple with the question, what in black religion legitimizes theological, social, personal, or interpersonal violence? And furthermore, what is the place of black practical theology and practices in addressing such legitimization? It is hard to turn a direct light on a spiritual, cultural, and social site of formation that is so important to so many of us. A deep analysis of the ways in which black religious experience is part of what ails us is difficult because racism is such a powerful and intractable reality of the black life that all African Americans share; thus, it is a less contentious topic. Because racism is a mechanism not only of social oppression but also of the formation of the self, I contend that it serves as a template for other forms of oppression and socialization. Therefore, we have to examine how religious practices reproduce these dynamics in the homegrown forms of sexism and heterosexism.

Those who have the privilege of doing black practical theology have to hold up a mirror to black religion and black life to offer an honest, authentic, loving reflection because only this will counteract all other demoralizing reflections. We readily bring a discerning and critical analysis to the multiple forms of black hatred and racism that permeate the airwaves and the political sphere. We rage, as we should, about the ways the first African American president of these United States has been depicted and discussed in the most racist of imagery; we lament disproportionate representation of black boys, men, and, more recently, women in the prison industrial complex. We recognize that the constant apologies from Tea Party leaders concerning racist "elements" in their midst are signs of old racism in a new key.

Racism is as alive, and sick, as ever. We see and hear its message among our congregants, children, and those who are constantly paraded in the news media as our new models of success, beauty, and acceptability—only to have them exploited for the gratification of racialized and sexually perverse fantasies masquerading as public entertainment. It was still possible at the time of this writing, in 2013, to watch television for an evening and not see even twenty minutes reflecting healthy, loving, involved, and beautiful black life. More disturbing to me is that we, black America, are often so desperate to see *any* sustained reflection of our lives that we grasp for a sliver of evidence of our worth, all the while subjecting our psyches to wretched distortions. Emilie Townes asks, "How do we grasp a hold [*sic*] of our identity and truly name ourselves instead of constantly looking into some strategically placed funhouse mirror of distortions?"[2] At some point we have to become enraged that we are exposed to such reflections on a daily basis.

In her poem "Good Mirrors Are Not Cheap" (1970), Audre Lorde describes the complex process whereby our sense of self can be malformed: if we stare into a distorted and despised mirror of ourselves without challenging its source, then, though we may hate the image, we little by little begin to identify with it.[3] We begin to believe we are what we see. Becoming the shape of our distortion takes time and regular exposure to an image we loathe. It takes a socialization process that goes largely unquestioned. A woman attending a conference that highlighted the work and vision of Audre Lorde plaintively explained, "We come to conferences—but we don't understand the dynamics of the internalization of suffering, the soul murder we live with day in and day out, and if you feel the oppression, if you feel it, you have this numbing process."[4] Her statement reiterates the view put forward by Gloria Anzaldúa, "The struggle has always been inner, and is played out in the outer terrains. . . . Nothing happens in the 'real world' unless it first happens in the images in our heads."[5]

To reflect on black practical theology, then, is to recognize and to resist the internalization, the soul murder, and the numbing process that seldom fully anesthetizes; it requires that we bring all of our parts to this dialogue. I am on the faculty of a university school of theology. I am a middle-aged, black lesbian with a loving partner and three children of my heart; I am a womanist practical theologian, a psychoanalyst, and a former member of a community of religious women. I have served as a pastoral associate at two different African American Catholic parishes and as a clinician at two different pastoral counseling centers. I take being black very seriously; thus, I take black people and black religious experience seriously. As a womanist practical theologian and as a psychoanalyst, I bring to this topic a concern for the transformation of the symbols, signs, and practices of religion and society that oppress the body, the psyche, and the spirit of black people. Therefore, I bring to this work a commitment to particularity; in other words, I am interested in articulating a practical theology that epistemologically *centralizes* the experiences of those for whom gender-sexism, sexuality-heterosexism, and race-racism are inextricably linked, and in doing this work from a womanist perspective.

PEDAGOGICAL PRACTICES IN PASTORAL SETTINGS

Pastoral ministry, regardless of its context and task, involves communicating and educating individuals and groups concerning our convictions about faith and life. These convictions are embedded in assumptions and theologies of gender, sexuality, and race, some of which are conscious and some of which are totally out of our awareness. And these assumptions are operative in all parties involved.

As a practical theologian, scholar, and practitioner, my passion for teaching and for engaging the religious and the psychological emerges from my conviction that theologically thoughtful and pastorally gifted persons are formed over a lifetime and that, given the short time students spend with me, teaching becomes a matter of faithful urgency. A large part of what I do involves helping students see the link between the intrapsychic and the cultural and recognize the social structures that situate our lives, theology, and pastoral practices; in short, I want them to be able to articulate a practical theology by placing their pastoral and ministry experiences in conversation with theology. Therefore, I understand my role to be one of developing students' capacity for theological reflection and ministry in the various contexts of faith communities and more broadly defined ministry settings. I want my students to understand that practical theology is grounded in communal, conversational, and socially situated contexts of pastoral practices. Practical theology and pastoral practices are relational, and this profound relationality brings the reality and grit of lived experience to bear on what we see, read, hear, and do. At the heart of my teaching is the conviction that human flourishing occurs at the site where the work of transforming the social surrounds, announces, and embodies the hopes of God for a world oriented toward goodness.

These commitments call for a teaching-learning community that facilitates students' engagement with perspectives with which they may be neither familiar nor comfortable. I address diversity related to class, ethnicity, gender, race, religious background, and sexuality in teaching. The occasion to wrestle with conflict is a given when we take up these concerns. Although they are amplified in faith settings, these concerns are not free of resistance in the classroom, and this opportunity to practice engagement should not be wasted. In and out of the classroom, resistance is persistent, pervasive, rigid, and difficult to transform. Working *with* resistance requires time, tenacity, trust, and desire on the part of faculty and students. Nikol Alexander-Floyd cogently states what the last fifteen years have taught me: "Resistance to learning about race and racism is pervasive."[6] Resistance is not limited to race and racism, of course; the same is true for sexism, heterosexism, and homophobia.

Ultimately, resistances are forms of withdrawing oneself from the process of being transformed by pedagogical efforts. Womanist, feminist, and other contextual pedagogical perspectives such as that described by Cheryl Kirk-Duggan inform my understanding:

A *Womanist* pedagogical theory, as the foundation of a constructive praxis, analyzes and critiques individual human and social behavior towards discerning the good, particularly analyzing the ramifications of injustice and malaise due to oppressions, moving towards change, balance, and promise. Such a liberatory pedagogy engages in . . . critical listening to many texts, and it embraces a message of hope and transformation. This hermeneutic assumes the essential goodness of human beings and that nurture for self and community requires a commitment to justice, respect, and mutuality.[7]

These pedagogical practices are relevant whether the teaching context is to enhance congregational ministries such as preaching, Christian education, or pastoral counseling or in theological education settings. The development of black practical theology is formed and developed in the grit of lived experience, the religious practices that shape one's faith and the broader social structures, and the hopes we harbor for a better, more just world. In my primary setting of teaching practical theology, I attempt to direct students' attention in multiple directions with the hope of tethering pastoral concerns, theological reflection, and ecclesial settings. Of course, I want my students to be able to think theologically and to be compassionate and creative in their responses to the concerns that emerge in their ministry contexts, but these things can happen authentically only if gender, sexuality, and race are brought into the dialogue very early in the educational process.

Recently, several experiences reminded me of the needs to articulate a black practical theology and to develop practices that might address the aims of such an endeavor. On the first day of the Introduction to Pastoral Care and Counseling class in a room where the majority of students (about 80 percent) were white and the remaining were Korean, I explained how class, gender, sexuality, and race would be topics to which we would attend in terms of pastoral identity development, as well as pastoral practices in the church and in the broader community. I had the class reflect in small groups on how these topics impacted their understanding of pastoral care, authority, and call. I encountered some reticence, as some students had not given thought to how their racial or class backgrounds informed what they defined as ministry or the appropriate contexts of ministry. After this exercise, I had the students do a community walk in groups. They were to come back prepared to discuss what they had learned about class, race, sexuality, and gender in the neighboring areas. The students, by and large, tried to see, take notice, and make meaning of this experience, but there was resentment.

One student made it clear that to her mind wrestling with these concerns had nothing to do with pastoral care and counseling or with her future pastoral ministry. She received significant support from some of her colleagues in the room. After class, she came to my office and demanded to know whether I would have given this exercise and discussed these topics with any class; in fact, she wondered whether I would have done the same thing had the class consisted of black students. Finally, she said, "Are you teaching this class this way because we [the students] are all white?" I pointed out to her that gender, race, sexuality, and class are personal and social features of any ministry and that we all must attend to the ways in which we embody these realities. I reminded her that the class was not all white since it contained Korean students as well. She reported she had not really noticed them. She had not noticed 20 percent of the class and had effectively rendered them invisible, but I could not be made to disappear; as the professor of the class, my black lesbian self was not invisible, and so I was suspect and dangerous because I insisted she notice and make meaning.

I discovered resistance to noticing! Another student, when confronted with the task of visiting a neighborhood with her small group, reported that they did not want to go to the site assigned because "as a young white woman she wouldn't feel safe," and she wondered if they could, instead, go to a more affluent neighborhood. When I inquired whether "young white women" were particularly at risk in the neighborhood I had assigned, she did not respond. The question was really a simple one. She could easily have discovered whether or not "young white women" were at risk; she could have done her social analysis, but then she would have had to notice her white privilege.

In a class on the theological foundations of justice, a black male student who was already serving as a pastor of a Baptist church stated that he found it difficult to discuss gay and lesbian issues in terms of civil rights because racism and sexism are about human rights. When I asked him if he was suggesting that gays and lesbians are not human, he replied that they are human but "not acting like humans." This pastor could not explain what "not acting like humans" entailed, but he had no trouble with his theology about what it means to be human, which for him meant being heterosexual. It also meant that, up until this class, he did not have to *think* through his theological anthropology in light of his views on lesbians and gays; he did not have to *explain* the pastoral implications of his theology; and he did not have to be *accountable* for the impact of his theology on those for whom he provided pastoral care. We know that his views and his lack of critical reflection and theologizing are not unusual. We have only to follow the headlines: Rev. Eddie Long and his views on homosexuality—"the problem today and the reason why society is like it is, is because men are being feminized and women are becoming masculine. Everyone knows it's dangerous to enter an exit. . . . You can be converted"[8]—juxtaposed with the settlements he made to the young men bringing claims of sexual misconduct against him. Pamela Lightsey names the problem clearly: "As a queer African American womanist scholar and clergy let me begin by thanking the media for covering the stories of the several lawsuits against Bishop Eddie Long for sexual coercion. . . . The possible sexual coercion of teenagers by anyone is horrible and should be our main concern. However, . . . it is not our only concern. How dare anyone deny . . . the anti-homosexual stance Long displayed before the church and the media while at the same time allegedly sexually abusing teenagers."[9] Clearly, the disconnect between Long's stated theology and his operational theology as practiced in his pastoral ministry suggests a lack of theological reflection on his ministry and his pastoral relations. This observation is based not on his alleged sexual misconduct but on the secrecy surrounding his solution to the problem: pay the accusers and demand their silence. Or, more recently in the headlines, we have Rev. Creflo Dollar proclaiming from the pulpit that "all is well in the Dollar household" in spite of his arrest for "simple battery, family violence and cruelty to children" against his fifteen-year-old daughter, which was substantiated by her nineteen-year-old sister, Alexandria. Dollar, furthermore, reportedly referred to the events and charges as "the devil's plan to 'discredit' [his] ministry."[10] With references to Scripture, he is quoted as claiming, "Malicious witnesses testify against me. . . . They accuse me of crimes I know nothing about. . . . May those who rejoice in my discomfort be humiliated and disgraced."[11] What is the black pastoral theology operative here when a pastor tells his congregation and the world that his daughters are "malicious" and agents of the devil? What is the pastoral message to those who need a word about the malice of domestic violence? What does it convey to children who are taught to "tell an adult if someone hurts you" when they hear the power and the privilege of the pulpit used to demand silence? What does it teach about gender, power, sexuality, and relationship? These examples are evidence of systemic problems. The problems are systemic because while these pastors are accused, they give a variety spiritual dissociations that the devil is attacking them and their ministry, as many congregants are offering unquestioning amens; the adults are complicit in their systemic lack of theological reflection on the potential and realized abuse of power.

An area of concern I have previously discussed relates to the unreflective, exclusive use of male God language in black liturgical and prayer contexts. The women I interviewed offered several reactions to their exposure to "Father-God" in worship settings. In summary, three themes stand out: (1) "I didn't notice it";[12] (2) "I expect it";[13] and (3) even though exclusively male language is used, "we read womanist theologians and are progressive in other areas."[14] The other areas included having women on staff and as frequent guest speakers. In one case it involved an accepting and affirming stance, articulated by the senior pastor, of gays and lesbians in the church.[15] God language is important because in the context of prayer, which generally reveals our affective relationship to religion and makes for a convergence between our theology and our inner life, we can hear how we, as black men and women, are situated in relation to all that is sacred in our lives, most notably our convictions about God, Jesus, and the Holy Spirit as well as faithful and faith-filled communities. If, in our intellectual life, our theologies are challenged and transformed and yet in our prayer and liturgical life we remain unchanged, then, in the final analysis, we only remain the same. Black and womanist theologians have demanded that we theologize from our social position and that we see a God who looks like us and is concerned with the struggles of the poorest among us, the most marginalized in church and society, the ones terrified into muteness, and those with the least power. What does such a God look like in prayer, song, and praise? If we believe that worship and the language we use has any deep meaning for our practice of faith, any efficacy to transform lives, and any power to call a society that favors the socially privileged to repentance, then the faith languages we employ must radically reflect that belief. The language of prayer and worship should be just as radical as the theologies of justice, grace, and transformation we summon to fight racism. The women I surveyed were reluctant to change the language of prayer "because it has deep meaning" to them. Yes, it is important to recognize the deep meaning of religious language to individuals and faith communities. However, these struggles also reveal that on some level "deep meaning" is maintained not by a connection to the divine, but rather it is in the "unlike me-ness" that makes God language usable. If this is the case, how can we say we are created in the image of God? What does the inability to transform our images and language for God reveal about how we feel deeply about our own black selves, about black women and black men? And, finally, what might be the relationship between the exclusive use of male imagery for God and the continuing struggle for black women to receive calls to senior pastorate positions?

These are examples of the ways race, gender, sexuality, and abuse take up residence in the psyche, in interpersonal exchanges, *and in pastoral practices.* They reveal how resistance to engaging deep change is normative for those who somehow benefit from being on the side of privilege in some primary area of self-identification. For others, silence is very often the norm when sexism, heterosexism, and racism daily confront them with distorted reflections of themselves.

THEOLOGICAL ANTHROPOLOGY: EMBODIED, DISTORTED, AND A SOURCE OF BODILY AMBIVALENCE

A critical reflection on black practical theology in light of gender, sexuality, and race and their distortions in the public, religious, and psychic domains requires that we also reflect on the ways the beauty of our createdness—our black humanity—is often denied. For this reason, the theological question we must reflect on is one that considers the implications of black theological anthropology. In recent work, I have turned to the Song of Solomon's "I am black and beautiful," and its marginalization, as a place to reflect on black theological anthropology and embodiment.[16] A black theological anthropology that takes embodiment seriously must recognize that black religious experience and black church practices are frequently embedded in legacies of ambivalence toward the black body, black women, sexual desire, and blackness. These legacies can be traced to the earliest roots of organized Christianity.

(A BRIEF) CASE EXAMPLE FROM THE EARLY CHURCH

For an example, we have only to turn to the fourth-century theologian and bishop, St. Augustine and his *Confessions*. In Augustine we witness the struggles of a highly conflicted North African man. He vividly recalled being thrashed repeatedly by his teachers when he did not excel in his studies. Following his parents' unresponsiveness to his pain and humiliation, he prayed and was again disappointed: "And when you did not hear me . . . my elders and even my parents . . . treated me with stripes as a huge joke."[17] Augustine is conflicted because he discovered that he truly loved those whom he also feared bitterly, and in whom he recognized a tendency to use children as the target of their anger and needs. However, ultimately he determines that God ordained his punishment because he deserved it.

Later, as an adult, he links his painful beatings to his knowledge of God's care.[18] He described his life as a long search for love, a pursuit frequently waylaid by lust and anxiety.

Augustine's *Confessions* is assigned in most first-year theology classes. It is a beautiful text and a revealing text. I have read it a number of times. We encounter his retrospective struggle with his body and to reclaim the goodness of the body from a theology that required its complete renunciation. In another text, *City of God*, he admonishes those who teach that the body is evil: "But if any one says that the flesh is the cause of all vices and ill conduct . . . it is certain he has not carefully considered the whole nature of [humanity]."[19] Even though the body is burdensome, the body is not the cause of sin. It must, however, be controlled because of its corruptibility due to "the fall." Therefore, sexual expression, marriage, and procreation are all goods, but goods that occur after, and as a result of, the fall; these goods were not the original plan for creation.[20]

As proof of his lustful nature, Augustine finds companionship and love with an unnamed African woman who is his lover for thirteen years and the mother of his only child, Adeodatus. Pressure from his mother, anxiety about his life, and his desire to marry someone who might advance his career leads Augustine eventually to dismiss her and send her back to Africa. We do not know how she accepts his report, or how she promises that she will henceforth maintain a celibate lifestyle. Clearly her usefulness to Augustine had ended, and yet he retains her in his psyche, in his theology, and in his fantasy that she will forever long for him. Whatever the depth of their relationship, she was expendable as far as he was concerned. She becomes for him the first proof of his submission to the lust that concealed his search to fill some deep longing in the flesh, marked by sexual expression. This unnamed African woman is, therefore, an object acquired and then dismissed. Yet, she is also a catalyst and a site for the struggle embedded in Augustine's attempts to discipline or control his flesh. She is Augustine's problem; she is an extension of his body at its most unruly; she is the sign that points beyond her body toward true connection with God; she is symbol of human fallen-ness. More important is the sense that embodiment, as his body commingled with hers, converges with Augustine's negative views of African women and of all that represents the flesh.

Augustine, it can be said, carries this conflicted view of the body and of women into his theology, as seen in his reading of the Hagar, Sarai, and Abram story:

A gouty doctor of the same city, when he had given in his name for baptism, and had been prohibited the day before his baptism from being baptized that year, by black woolly-haired boys who appeared to him in his dreams, and whom he understood to be devils, and when, though they trod on his feet, and inflicted the acutest pain he had ever yet experienced . . .[21]

And yet, if Hagar and Ishmael, as the apostle teaches us, signified the carnal people of the old covenant . . .[22]

For it is written, that Abraham had two sons; the one by a bond maid, the other by a free woman. But he who was of the bonds woman was born after the flesh; but he of the free woman was by promise . . .[23]

Abram's wife, Sarai, "gives" him an Egyptian bonds woman, Hagar, because Sarai has not borne a child. After Hagar gives birth to Ishmael, Sarai feels diminished by Hagar and so claims that Hagar is disrespectful of her. We know that Hagar is eventually abused by Sarai—with Abraham's permission. In other words, Abraham "dismisses" her because she is no longer of use once the child is born, and he wants to keep peace with Sarai. Augustine's interpretation of this biblical story fits with his views of the natural order of human relations: the natural subjugation of women, the natural condition of enslavement, and the natural association of black with "badness," as well as the association of demonic forces with the "flesh," and the flesh with separation from God.

Thus, his theology ultimately reveals, and produces, a problematic theological anthropology and practical theology that render the body suspect at every turn, with the *African and female body* as the most suspicious and alien. It is clear that such ideas contributed to early European imperialism, the dehumanization of the Africans they encountered, and the industry that resulted in millions of Africans' enslavement. Obviously Augustine is not solely responsible for the dualistic split when it comes to black bodies in Western Christianity. However, while attempting to establish the place of the body in his theology of embodiment, he developed a perspective that advocated strict control of the body, pleasure, sexuality, and women. We have inherited his commitment to a theological anthropology that included the body *as well as* his ambivalence toward the body, and his spiritualizing bodily trauma. The purpose of this brief reflection on Augustine is to suggest that such associations—his psychological mechanisms of projection and splitting, and the attitudes of his historical context—continue to intrude upon the theologies and ideologies behind the attitudes and practices of Christianity related to gender, sexuality, and race. These *kinds of theologies unconsciously* play out in the contemporary context of black religion and are embedded in our current struggles with gender, sexuality, and race.

CASE EXAMPLE FROM A SCHOLARLY CONFERENCE

The kinds of critical questions and interrogations that I am suggesting are imperative from a womanist perspective. An exchange during a recent meeting of African American scholars in religion can make my point: a panelist who had presented a paper noted that we seldom see paintings of Jesus nursing at Mary's breast, and she wondered if we were afraid to see Jesus as a human who needed his mother. Yes, I imagined, we could be anxious about a Jesus in need of nursing, but I was struck by an absent consideration; that is, in our contemporary Western context, the breast is seldom (and generally, ambivalently) viewed as a source of nutrition. Rather, the breast is highly sexualized, so much so that to see a woman feeding her infant in public is cause for alarm, embarrassment, and attempts to have her covered, set apart, censored, and shamed—Why?

A missing analysis in this conference response was a conscious treatment of the multifaceted and the psychosocial, not the least of which is the *sexualized* meaning of "the" breast. In hearing such a discussion, I could not help but think that the breast functions as a site for displacement, as a kind of religious sexual fetish. To gaze upon a religious sexual fetish in the public domain cannot be permitted because the public gaze—that is, visceral uncontrolled interest—signals alarm and the threat of public exposure of desire, arousal, and longing. I offer this illustration to demonstrate the kind of psychodynamics that are operative when we analyze black religion. This essay is, of course, not about fetishes or the public display of breasts; rather it is about a black practical theology that considers those areas of black religious experience that are embedded in psychodynamic and social processes and the ways in which a lack of critical engagement with complex meanings of black religious experiences results in practices that severely limit black practical theology and practices of care.

But additionally, what might it mean that a black woman made the statement that those who relate to Jesus as a religious divine figure would find his humanity unpalatable? What historical and socially located psychological phenomena might be operative? Is there something historically that *might* make black women likely to read Jesus at the breast—Jesus' humanity—as threatening, anxiety provoking, resisted, and even split out of awareness?

These questions beg for a psychological dimension to our practical theology and pastoral practices, an awareness that the psychological is operative in all pastoral contexts and therefore is a necessary dimension of black practical theologies. Few scholars have presented a sustained psychological perspective on African American religious experience. And, while I am sure most clergy recognize when someone is in psychological distress, linking psychological awareness to how racism, sexism, heterosexism, and homophobia work to maintain positions of privilege (socially, individually, and theologically) is absent. We need to grapple with the psychological forces that make some aspects of religious experience material for the public to practice, understand, and explicitly express while rendering other aspects of public and private religion suppressed, invisible, and split off from the discourse on black religion. For example, consider the disjuncture between what we say we believe and what we actually do, and the ways in which congregations know what we *do* but only hold us accountable for what we say we believe. If black practical theology is going to have efficacy—a usefulness that overturns practices of religion that exclude some from full engagement with the life of the community, for black religious life—it is going to have to articulate these kinds of dynamics and demonstrate the ways they maintain power relations and are implicated in the structures that govern congregations and denominational life.

THE WORK OF BLACK PRACTICAL THEOLOGY

The work of black practical theology and the related practices, then, must be declarative, restorative, and curative. Barbara Smith, in relation to the work of black feminism, is apropos here: "We are actively committed to struggling against racial, sexual heterosexual, and class oppression, and see as our particular task the development of an integrated analysis and practice based upon the fact that major systems of oppression create the conditions of our lives."[24] Our theological anthropologies have to turn to the black woman of the Bible and say, first, and with conviction, "I am black and beautiful." We have to ask ourselves, how does what we believe about black humanity shape our understanding of gender, sexuality, and race and their relationship to black church worship and pastoral care and its mission, aims, practices, and experiences?

If congregants, clergy, and practical theologians are to grapple with these concerns, then churches have to become beacons and refuges of authentic and open conversations. The process of listening and attending to people's life narratives will reveal that we are complex people who are searching for homes where we can bring all the parts of who we are and, having offered up the truth of our existence, hear that we are indeed:

Created
Black
in the image of God,
and good.

When this is our unmovable starting point, our epistemological given, our confirmation of baptism, the aim of our sanctification, the reality of grace, and the ecclesial basis of our membership, then we will have a revolution, and black churches will be a community of beauty.

<< 9 >>

ENCIRCLING IN OUR WOMANIST STRENGTH

Diana L. Hayes

As we look at Christianity and its churches in the twenty-first century, the major issues of concern for many seem to be those of the flesh rather than those of the spirit. Preachers thunder from their pulpits about the "fallen nature" of humanity but have comparatively little to say about the harsh and harmful economic, social, and political situations in which humanity finds itself today. Where is the balance? Why this (over)emphasis on sexuality, sexual orientation, and gender issues while many equally, if not more, important issues persist and flourish, such as the increasing incarceration of young black men and women, the growing poverty rate in the black community, the ongoing assault on the black middle class, the persistence of racism, sexism, and heterosexism in both church and society, and the growing division in U.S. society that is mirrored in the black community based on class? Why is the Black Church so silent about these issues and so vocal about "alleged" sins of the flesh?

Over fifty years ago, Howard Thurman, today considered a forerunner of black liberation theology, raised a question that we, as Christians, are still apparently unable to satisfactorily answer. He asked:

> Why is it that Christianity seems impotent to deal radically, and therefore effectively, with the issues of discrimination and injustice on the basis of race, religion, or national origin? Is this impotency due to a betrayal of the genius of the religion, or is it due to a basic weakness in the religion itself?[1]

Although he does not mention gender and sexuality or class specifically, I believe that today Thurman would have included these areas where injustice and discrimination are so very prevalent especially within Christianity. Is this yet another failure of our faith, or can we find time and space to dialogue responsibly and civilly in response to Thurman's far from rhetorical questions? I believe the answer can be found in exploring race and gender/sexuality and their accompanying behaviors—namely, racism, sexism, and heterosexism—from the perspective of black and womanist liberation theologies. The themes uncovered and resources revealed therein can help us move toward the development and application of a black practical theology.

BLACK AND WOMANIST THEOLOGIES AS BLACK PRACTICAL THEOLOGY

Black and womanist theologies are liberation theologies; that is, they seek to provide a basis for the liberation of persons of African descent from the myriad forms of oppression and discrimination that still bind them in so many different ways. These theologies are also, in my opinion, practical theologies as they find their origins not in academia, although they have increasingly taken up residence there, but in the Black Church, past and present. As Dale Andrews notes: "Practical theology is an engaging process between theology, theory, and practice, with each one feeding back upon the others."[2]

The purpose of black and womanist liberation theologies is to articulate the issues and concerns affecting black Americans, to identify how they interact with and affect their daily lives of faith, and to present them to a larger, not always receptive, audience. The problem historically has been a failure of praxis—in other words, the failure to engage black and womanist theological understandings in the actual lives and situations of the people in the pews and those who seek to guide them from the pulpit. To cite Andrews again, "Theology swings between living in the world and living in a faith community sometimes quite removed from the world. Practical theology attempts to bridge these chasms."[3] It does so by enfleshing the themes and theories by immersing them in the lives of African Americans going about their daily lives.

Just as these theologies are practical theologies, black practical theology is also a theology of liberation; it seeks to bring together the themes and traditions of black faith in ways that can be applied to the actual lives of people today. There has been a lack of sufficient grounding on the part of the Black Church in theologies that have emerged from within the black community itself. None of these are objective theologies, nor can they be. They all recognize the necessity and the honesty of those doing theology to be a part of the community for whom the theology is being done. Black and womanist theologies are practical theologies, and black practical theology is a liberating theology.

Black liberation and womanist theologies are theologies of, by, and for black people wherever they are. They can be seen to liberate in two ways: first, they liberate those with whom they are engaged, which, in this case, are black communities of faith; and second, they liberate theology itself from a top-down, universalistic, narrow-minded, white mindset. Both are critical aspects of their theologizing. A practical theology is one that lives and breathes with the ordinary people who inhabit our pews on a Sunday morning. It is also subjective rather than objective; it is an indwelling in the midst of the people, inspiring and empowering them not only to get over but also to rise.

Black and womanist theologies use a hermeneutic of suspicion critically not just to analyze contemporary society and its ideologies and the Black Church and its community but also to excavate the living history of persons of African descent. This is the case especially in the United States but also in Africa itself, where the church acts to recover what has been "lost, [has been] stolen, or has strayed." In so doing, these theologies seek to provide a foundation for future application and development, as well as to serve as sources for our further growth as a people that can, hopefully, be mined for practical application.

RACE AND RACISM, GENDER AND SEXISM, SEXUALITY
AND HETEROSEXISM

What do we mean when we speak of race and its societal application, racism? Bryan Massingale, a Catholic moral theologian, provides us with both a commonsense understanding and a more nuanced definition of racism:

> Person A (usually, but not always, white) consciously, deliberately, and intentionally does something negative to person B (usually, but not always, a Black or Latino) because of the color of his or her skin.[4]

The second more complex definition is as follows:

> A set of meanings and values that inform the American way of life. It is a way of understanding and interpreting skin color differences so that white Americans enjoy a privileged social status with access to advantages and benefits to the detriment, disadvantage, and burden of persons

of color. It is the set of cultural assumptions, beliefs, and convictions that justify the existence of a "kinder, gentler" racism, that is, one that advocates interpersonal decency, kindness, and respect for all while it yet protects the white systemic advantage and benefit.[5]

Racism persists in the United States. In the aftermath of the Civil Rights movement, it became more covert, hidden away in pockets of U.S. society. Ironically, with the election of a black president, the United States, rather than becoming a postracial society as many in the media trumpeted, has become even more racially polarized. Today's racism is once again overt, openly displayed in defiance of the law, morality, and basic common sense. Many in the black community who profited materially and educationally in the aftermath of the 1960s feel that racism is no longer a problem until it personally affects them, as inevitably and sadly it does. We are not a postracial society, nor can we be a color-blind society, as that would simply negate the existence of persons of color. Again, citing Massingale,

> Obama's presidency, then, does not mark the end of our racial dysfunction. Rather, it is dramatic proof that we are far from being a "color-blind" society. . . . African Americans must still contend with and negotiate through a complex minefield of entrenched racist obstacles that whites do not have to consider.[6]

Black Americans are still negatively impacted by racism, and many Christian churches are yet complicit in that racism. Having used Scripture (especially the curses on Ham and Cain) and dubious science to support its division of the world into separate races, Christianity stands convicted of having used its resources and people, especially missionaries, to spread a false ideology worldwide, where it haunts and constricts us to the present day. Dale Andrews notes:

> [We can see in Christianity an] evolution from Christian supersessionism and a religious racial caste system over Muslims and Jews into a comparable religious supersessionism of "colorized" racial castes constituting the subjugation of the "Black" or "African" race or an "Indian" race. Western capitalistic exploitation drove the formation of color lines in the social construction of race, which were concurrently legitimated by religious and political sanction.[7]

It would seem obvious, therefore, that the Christian churches, as well as other religious entities that have historically benefited from the social construction of race and the persistence of racism, should participate in acts of healing and repentance that change how they teach, preach, and act toward persons of color in the United States. There is resistance to this, however, because as Andrews affirms, "US culture [and thus its cultural institutions] finds reconciliation difficult when it involves social liability or economic costs to achieve."[8] In other words, when required to give up cultural power, privilege, or resources, repentance and reconciliation become almost impossible. Or, in the words of Reverend Martin Luther King Jr., "We know through painful experience that freedom is never voluntarily given by the oppressor; it must be demanded by the oppressed."[9]

The Black Catholic Bishops of the United States have also indicated the need for a repentance and reconciliation on the part of Christianity and Christians that goes beyond mere apologies for promulgating slavery and denigrating their fellow Christian brothers and sisters. They caution:

> When in recent years, we rejected "token integration" for "self-determination," it was not to choose confrontation in place of cooperation but to insist on collaboration with mutual respect for the dignity and unique gifts of all. Reconciliation can never mean unilateral elevation and another's subordination, unilateral giving and another's constant receiving, unilateral flexibility and another's resistance. True reconciliation arises only when there is mutually perceived equality. This is what is meant by justice.
>
> Without justice, any meaningful reconciliation is impossible. Justice safeguards the rights and delineates the responsibility of all. A people must safeguard their own cultural identity and their own cultural values. Likewise they must respect the cultural values of others. For this reason sincere reconciliation builds on mutual recognition and mutual respect.[10]

What is needed, then, is more than words of repentance and reconciliation, but practical actions that bring reconciliation to life. We must change radically how we—all Americans—think and feel about those who are "different" from us. The Black Church has been complicit in this failure of justice with its notorious "brown paper bag" and other tests that sought to segregate based on skin color, hair texture, language or dialect spoken, social class, and, especially today, sexual orientation. How do we move from bias, discrimination, and exclusiveness to inclusiveness, in order to promote justice for all but in particular for our own?

Another critical issue is the role of women in the church, especially the Black Church, which is seen by many, male and female, as a perfect model of misogyny. Kelly Brown Douglas, a womanist theologian, states simply, "The [Black Church] is characteristically patriarchal."[11] Marcia Riggs, a womanist theologian, notes: "[The Black Church] has developed a normative patriarchal institutional ethos" that has enabled it to become a "protected space" for "sexual-gender transgressions."[12] Historically and today, black women's bodies have been viewed solely as sources of temptation to white and black men alike:

> The patriarchal culture of the black church confers on black men the privilege to disregard black women's sincere commitment to "holy living" and the privilege to ignore the hypocrisy of their own lifestyle. Accordingly, black women are held accountable for any sexual lapses that "holy" black men may experience. The logic of the black church's patriarchy suggests that black womanhood seduces black men into sinfully sexist behavior.[13]

Yet, gender and sexuality are also social constructions, fostered by Western European society in conjunction with first the Catholic and eventually the Protestant Christian churches. Women were seen simply as biological entities whose only purpose in life was procreation. They were, in the words of St. Thomas Aquinas, "ill-formed men." Thus, women, like Blacks and others who are systematically oppressed, are denied their humanity and cocreation with men by God, as are persons who are same-sex loving in today's society:

> Homosexuality, like race, is an invention and construction of the post-Enlightenment. As the eighteenth century created different "species" by racial classification, in the late nineteenth century social scientific classification created sexual categorization in which lines were drawn between those with primary opposite sex sexual desire and those with primary sexual desire for the same sex. This sexual construction laid the foundation for the making of a homosexual class. The term "homosexual" emerged as a separate identity in the late nineteenth century.[14]

Somehow, in their encounter with white Christianity and its distortions, African Americans were able to see beyond the lies and create an understanding of Jesus Christ, God the Creator, and the Holy Spirit that nurtured and sustained rather than degraded them. They rejected the efforts at dehumanization and degradation by white Christians and were able to develop a liberating faith that enabled them not just to survive but also, eventually, to thrive. Ironically, however, there was one area in which this transformation of their identity did not take place: black sexuality. Although they rejected the pseudoscience and false interpretations of Scripture that racists used to label them as soulless pieces of property rather than as human beings created in the image and likeness of God, they somehow imbibed and promulgated the lies and slander that Whites spread regarding black sexuality. While Blacks have freely interpreted the Bible to denounce those parts that promoted and affirmed slavery, they have not done so with those lines of Scripture that have been used to denounce women as immoral sexual beings and homosexuals as perverted sinners.

Instead, Blacks often internalize the United States' racist depictions of a black sexuality that is out of control and in need of Christian salvation. As a consequence, black bodies have been devalued, bought, and controlled in slavery by whites who "felt no compunction about exploiting those bodies for their sexual gratification . . . [subjecting] black women . . . to sexual abuse and black men . . . as progenitors of new slaves through siring."[15]

LAYING THE FOUNDATION

Kelly Brown Douglas has explored the background of this seemingly dualistic black perspective. Why denounce one biblical distortion while accepting another that is equally harmful to our people? She updates the question first raised by Howard Thurman: "Why is Christianity so often implicated in vicious crimes of racial, gender, and sexual hatred? Is there something intrinsic to Christianity that makes its complicity in assailing certain human bodies not simply possible but perhaps highly probable?"[16]

Douglas attempts to answer this question by delving into the Christian faith tradition and its appropriation by the Black Church. She identifies how the Protestant churches, particularly Protestant evangelical churches, appropriate, rather than condemn, faith traditions that contribute to the degradation and denigration of black bodies. As she notes, "The Christian theological tradition has contributed to a certain *collective theological consciousness* that allows for, if not sanctions, unrelenting oppression of various human beings."[17]

The reason this is so, Douglas asserts, is that Christianity in its evolution became reliant upon a tradition that elevated certain beliefs and traditions while devaluing others. The Christian tradition is rooted in a Platonic-Stoic understanding of the world and humanity, which is dualistic in nature and denigrates all that is earthly and material, especially the human body, while elevating the spirit in ways that have led to the oppression of blacks and other persons of color, as well as women of all races and ethnicities:

> Christianity's alliance with Platonic/Stoic thought was the primary troubling alliance that laid the foundation for a terrorizing Christian legacy in relation to black bodies. . . . Platonic and Stoic thought coalesced with

Christianity's theological core to establish an influential Christian tradition, identified as *platonized* Christianity, which advanced antagonis-
tic dualistic paradigms and a demonization of the flesh/body. Platonism
is implicit in the attack against the black body.[18]

This attack has expressed itself in terms of both gender/sexuality and race,
among other "isms." Christianity, in other words, has played a major (albeit
not the only) role in the social construction of race, gender/sexuality, class,
and other societal ideologies, and it continues to do so today.

Douglas denounces this Platonic-Stoic tradition as heretical, saying,
"Christianity's investment with social/political power [is] anti-Christ." She
turns to the Christian understanding of incarnation and the crucifixion/
resurrection event as a stronger source for our understanding of the relationship between body and soul, noting that Jesus never condemned sexuality as intrinsically evil although he did advocate celibacy as the truer
path to God's kingdom. Nor did Jesus condemn the human body, for
to do so would be to condemn "his own incarnate/bodily reality."[19] His
faith community expected the imminent coming of the kingdom of God,
yet even with that expectation he broke away from the patriarchal and
misogynistic ethos of his time. As the kingdom did not come as quickly
as expected, it fell to Jesus' followers to develop a religious faith that could
stand the test of time.

They too, however, were constrained by their own particular historical experiences. Paul was a Jew who had participated in the persecution
of early Christians and was fully a part of patriarchal Jewish society;
Augustine had spent his youth carousing and indulging the flesh and then
became a Manichean with that movement's severe dislike of the body and
anything material. In response to their own contextual experiences, these
men and others negatively influenced the church's understanding of the
relationship between body and spirit, which led to a dualistic perspective
that taught Christians to loath their bodies (as well as any natural acts
of those bodies, especially sexual activity) and glorify their spirits. This
dualism, in turn, provided a foundation for the social construction of race
and gender/sexuality that denied the worthiness and God-createdness of
not only black and other bodies of color but also female bodies. It is indeed
sadly ironic that black Americans freely and emphatically denounce and
ignore Paul's teachings on slavery while adopting with apparently little
resistance his misogynistic statements on women and sexuality.

This dualistic and negative perspective, shaped and honed by the
biases of white culture with its cult of white supremacy, became the core

of Christianity in the United States—especially Protestant Christianity, a Christianity that was then adopted and adapted by black Protestant Christians. Douglas asks, "Why did blacks accept a Christianity that 'demonized the body/flesh in the same way that they are demonized by white culture?'" What did they gain and what did they lose by this appropriation? On the one hand, she notes, this tradition, as transmitted primarily through evangelical Protestantism, "has affirmed black people in their blackness, nurtured a sense of divine worth and equality, and even saved black lives." On the other hand, this tradition "has also alienated black people from their very blackness and own black bodies."[20]

Douglas explains at greater length:

> Platonized Christianity in conjunction with white cultural ideology has compelled black women and men to adopt a *hyper-proper sexuality* to secure a "white" soul, thereby redeeming their black body.... [This] platonized black faith tradition has interacted with patriarchal and heterosexist discourse to suborn denigrating disregard for the bodies of black women and dehumanizing treatment of nonheterosexuals (especially gay black men) within the black church community.[21]

Horace Griffin affirms Douglas' perspective on the adoption of hyperproper sexuality:

> Given the majority culture's racism and sexual attitudes, African Americans soon learned that their very survival depended on distancing themselves from any representation of "sexual perversions." Much of black heterosexuals' anti-homosexual sentiment exists as a means of countering the perception of black sexuality being perverse, in order to survive, and gain respectability and acceptance by the majority.[22]

The Protestant churches are not alone in this adoption, however. Prior to the emergence of Protestant Christianity in the sixteenth century, Catholicism, particularly Roman Catholicism as it became known after the eleventh century, had very ably contributed to the construction of race and gender/sexuality, especially in the aftermath of renewed contact by the Portuguese with the African continent and by the opening of the Americas to exploitation and colonization.

Although the Catholic Church has a long and impressive tradition of social justice teachings grounded in sacred Scripture, these teachings were not fully articulated until the latter part of the nineteenth century. Prior to that time, the Church fully participated in the exploitation and enslavement of men, women, and children of African descent and the restriction of the lives of women of every race and ethnicity.

Beginning with the papal document *Dum Diversas* in 1452, Pope Nicholas V, and those who came after him, legalized the enslavement and exportation of Blacks by Catholic nations. This assent (*Asiento*) was later, in 1493, extended to the Americas. Thus, the Catholic Church has been complicit in the development and extension throughout the world of this dualistic Platonic-Stoic tradition as Douglas has presented. Again, we ask, why do Blacks remain in the Catholic Church, and the answer is the same as for black Protestants. Despite their knowledge of their church as a "white racist institution" that has participated in their oppression, they have found a spiritual home that yet sustains and nurtures them and enables them to grow in faith while challenging the biases and discrimination that persist. The results of this complicity throughout Christianity have been a painful ordeal over centuries for most persons of African descent. Thus, to gain respectability, Blacks adopted a sexual conservatism that at times amounted to a puritanical prudishness.

TOWARD A BLACK PRACTICAL THEOLOGY

So, where do we go from here? Having laid the foundations of the theological tradition within the black community, both positive and negative, and having reviewed, briefly, race/racism and gender/sexuality, how do we address these issues in ways that can bring black and womanist theologians, black pastors, the black community, and its churches, temples, and mosques together to act in solidarity? First, it must be acknowledged that when I talk about the Black Church, I am speaking not just about the historical black churches and denominations that evolved and developed during and after the period of slavery. Persons of African descent are a diverse people of myriad backgrounds and cultures. Today we number not only those who are traditionally referred to as African American (i.e., those tracing their African ancestry to the period of slavery in the United States) but also more recent immigrants from Africa, the Caribbean, and Central and South America. These people have very different cultures, traditions, and languages, but they share one thing in common—their skin color, which has been demonized from the fifteenth century to the present day. How, then, do we bridge the gaps of knowledge and understanding that necessarily affect our encounters with each other?

Historically, we were forced to become one people, as those from the same or similar tribes were deliberately separated. As a result, we created our own self-understanding based on our shared experiences of oppression. Black and womanist theologies drew on these experiences; and we continue to draw on them as we develop the themes not only of liberation (black theology) but also of survival and quality of life (womanist theology). What shared experiences can we draw upon today to continue to develop theologies with practical applications, theologies that nurture and heal, that educate us about from whence we have come while building a foundation for us to move forward into the future?

At the same time, we are not, nor have we ever been, followers of the Protestant Christian faith only. How do we bring in other religious voices including those of black Roman and Orthodox Catholics, Muslims, Jews, Buddhists, Yorubas, and followers of other religions? What contributions can they make to our dialoguing? Are we realistic in thinking that the black circle of community, fraying and seemingly self-destructing around us in the twenty-first century, can once again be an unbroken circle of community and solidarity? Or, do we walk away from each other and develop separate and isolated communities based on class, cultural and language differences, sexual orientation, and so on?

Where, indeed, do we go from here? As I stated above, I believe all womanist and black theologies are black practical theologies, and vice versa. What can we find in common to begin the process of reconnecting our theology to our praxis in ways that are healing and holy for all?

To address these issues in the black community and its life of faith today will require courage and a deep and abiding faith, both aspects of the black community that emerged out of slavery and continue, waxing and waning, to the present day. It is the kind of courage and witness of faith that men like Martin Luther King Jr. and women like Fannie Lou Hamer saw as the foundation of their lives and ministry. They were seeking not for self but for all, attempting to rebuild the beloved community of Jesus Christ that had been torn asunder in the United States by the viciousness of racism, sexism, and classism.

Dale Andrews speaks of a chasm that has developed between black and womanist theologies and black churches. The cause for this chasm is twofold: first, black theologians' lack of connection to and interaction with the black religious community, which causes them to speak and act in ways that are disconnected from and at times disparaging of the needs and concerns of that community; and second, the black community's own assimilation of capitalistic individualism, which has proven extremely divisive as everyone seeks their own individual salvation rather than the salvation of all.[23] As Andrews argues,

A principal disparity emerged between their respective theological interpretations of faith and ministry. On the one hand, the black theological project regarded black churches as spiritually removed or "otherworldly." . . .

On the other hand, even the black churches that embraced the identity politics of blackness for its significance to self-esteem and empowerment did not endorse the entire campaign of black theology. . . . Black churches contested that black theology advanced black power in a neglect of the gospel message of universal Christian love.[24]

Both perspectives have aspects of truth in them. Womanist theology, which is also a theology of liberation, has critiqued black (male) theology for its emphasis on race as the basic form of oppression plaguing black people and their need for liberation from this oppression. While claiming to speak for the Black Church and black community as a whole, early black theologians (all male) spoke only in terms of the historical experience of black men and neglected the voices and experiences of black women, slave and free. At the same time, the Black Church has also claimed to speak for the black community, but once again that voice has, historically, been male and usually ordained. Women were denied ordination or any voice within the church, as well as participation in any meaningful way in the movements of the 1960s. This did not stop them from insisting that their voices be heard and attention be paid to the concerns and needs of black women and girls as well as black men and boys. Womanist theologians have been instrumental in bringing these voices into the forefront of our history, where they belong.

Thus, womanist theology as a practical theology would be an excellent bridge between the academy, where black theology is much in evidence, and the Black Church, where it is absent. This is so especially because many, if not most, women have lived lives of multiple oppressions, crossing racial, class, and gender lines. We can now hear their voices in lecture halls and pulpits, and they bring to the fore the voices and the pain, the dreams and the aspirations, of heterosexual and homosexual black women, men, and children, insisting that unless all are free, none are free.

Womanist theology, like black theology, has dug into the history of persons of African descent to reclaim our pasts so that we can move forward into a better future. It recognizes the restricted lives that black people have been forced to live in the United States and calls for a new form of liberation, one coupled with an understanding of the critical significance of survival and a viable quality of life. Black theology's call for liberation is valid but insufficient and too often premature. As Delores Williams critiques, what is the point of liberation if those liberated are as yet unprepared? She points to the story of Hagar in Scripture as an example of how liberation may, at times, have to be delayed while those seeking liberation are prepared for its realities by learning survival skills that will ensure a quality of life that is nurturing and sustaining rather than destructive. God did not liberate Hagar when she ran away from Sarai but requires her to return to slavery. God does, however, bless Hagar by promising her a bloodline that will endure and announces the birth of her son, Ishmael, and his future: "The promise assures survival, and the birth announcement forecasts the strategy that will be necessary for survival and for obtaining a quality of life."[25] True liberation means the freedom to live one's life to its fullest as one chooses rather than to simply trade one form of oppression for another. What is the point of liberation if it provides only the freedom to die? How do we, as a people, teach each other how to survive in this country and to achieve a viable quality of life that will empower us to seek a true liberation of hearts and minds? We cannot do this if we remain captive to a white Christianity that continues to encourage us to hate and despise one another, to fight one another for a few crumbs while they run off with the whole pie. This must be a liberation of the many, not just the few. As Forrest Harris attests, "Unfortunately, the identification of liberation with the material success of a few, who themselves have become physically and mentally severed from the suffering masses, trivializes the unity essential for liberation praxis."[26]

This is where a black practical theology that builds on the retrieval of black history, spirituality, and culture by black and womanist theologies and transforms these new understandings into actions and practices that sustain the Black Church and rebuild the black community as a source of united power and faith can and should emerge. As Harris argues, such a theology must "bridge . . . 'black folk religion and practical theology' with its liberation goals of civic justice and the moral agency of black churches."[27] For we know from our study of our ancestors that they did not stand alone but saw themselves as part of a "great cloud of witnesses" leading back into the past and moving forward into the future. We do not stand alone. I am because we are, and we are because I am.

We have, indeed, in our efforts to survive and thrive, bought into both the American Dream and the motor that runs it: capitalistic individualism. That is one of the reasons why black theologians and black churches are unable to communicate; they speak different languages or at least different dialects of the same language. We must do once again what our ancestors did when they were forcibly separated at the auctions, husband from wife, parent from child, tribal member from tribal member; we must learn to speak with each other, forging once again a language that unites rather than divides us. Individualism, in and of itself, is not wrong as long as we recognize that we are yet part of a larger community. Even as individuals, our identities are shaped in community. No one makes it by themselves, and we lie if we claim we have. We stand on the shoulders of countless others who lived and loved, fought and died, struggled and survived not so that we could self-destruct, going each our own individual selfish way, but so that we could reconnect and reforge the ties that bound us together as people who, as Audre Lorde stated, "were never meant to survive."[28]

The Black Church was once refuge and sanctuary. Inside its doors, Blacks found friendship and a helping hand, solidarity and community. The church eased our pain and awakened our hope; it prepared and strengthened us, empowering us to go forth and do battle with the "princes and principalities." We must once again build churches that are more than just fancy halls empty of the Spirit of God, churches that in their "prophetic ministry [are] not only confronting injustice in society, but equally witnessing against those forces, powers, and principalities which stifle the church from within, thus thwarting the full emergence of [liberation] in the black community."[29]

It is imperative that we, as a community, fight against the "hegemonic powers" of racism, sexism, classism, heterosexism, and a narcissistic individualism that destroy community and identity. We must, as Harris notes, once again, "collectively define [our] situation and develop sustained coalitions for developing new agendas for social policy formation and assessment in which the institutional presence of the Black Church is essential."[30] For, as he notes, it is vital for the lives of our people and our communities that "Black church sanctuaries . . . become places where the prophetic commitment to justice is made real in what people need physically, socially, spiritually, and aesthetically for wholeness of life. The sanctuary must be inclusive places of love where God calls people to lifelong conversion of deepening relationship with God and of turning toward one's neighbor with all that love requires—justice, peace, inner and outer liberation in the world."[31]

In his recent work *The Cross and the Lynching Tree*, James Cone, the first to articulate contemporary black theology, correlates the lynching tree upon which so many black bodies were forcibly crucified with the cross of Jesus. He asserts, "The lynched black victim experienced the same fate as the crucified Christ and thus became the most potent symbol for understanding the true meaning of the salvation achieved through 'God on the cross.'" [32]

He continues:

> The real scandal of the gospel is this: humanity's salvation is revealed in the cross of the condemned criminal Jesus and humanity's salvation is available only with the crucified people in our midst. Faith that emerged out of the scandal of the cross is not a faith of intellectuals or elites of any sort. This is the faith of abused and scandalized people—the losers and the down and out. It was this faith that gave blacks the strength and courage to hope, to "keep on keeping on," struggling against the odds. [33]

It is this understanding of ourselves, as a people of God who have succeeded against all odds yet still struggle, that we must recover and reclaim. Black theology provides the resources, the history, the collective memory of our people; womanist theology has refined that memory to ensure that it remains subversive, challenging the so-called reality of today for the reality of black existence in the United States. Womanist theologians pave the way, in a sense, because they are not only of the academy but also of the pastorate and the community. They bridge the gaps, enabling the development of a black practical theology that works in the academy and in the church and community of which they are a critical part. As we reclaim our stories from past and present, we can move into a future that takes us beyond mere survival to a quality of life that prepares us for a true liberation of body and spirit. As Cone affirms:

> The lynching tree frees the cross from the false pieties of well-meaning Christians. . . . It reveals the true religious meaning of the cross for American Christians today. The cross needs the lynching tree to remind Americans of the reality of suffering—to keep the cross from becoming a symbol of abstract, sentimental piety. . . . [I would add also as a symbol of white supremacy and terror.]
>
> Yet the lynching tree also needs the cross, without which it becomes simply an abomination. It is the cross that points in the direction of hope, that there is a dimension to life beyond the reach of the oppressor. [34]

The ongoing challenge therefore, for both theology and the Black Church, "is how to define ourselves by the gospel of Jesus' cross" rather than by the biased and dualistic perceptions of white Christianity for the benefit of the countless black Americans, male and female, gay and straight, who are still being lynched today.

<< 10 >>

A Radically Inclusive Vision for the Fellowship of the Black Church

Dennis W. Wiley and Christine Y. Wiley

Early in her essay "Encircling in Our Womanist Strength," Diana Hayes cites one of the most important questions ever to confront the Christian faith. As Howard Thurman poses the question in the preface to his classic, *Jesus and the Disinherited* (1949), "Why is it that Christianity seems impotent to deal radically, and therefore effectively, with the issues of discrimination and injustice on the basis of race, religion and national origin?"[1]

While omitting an explicit reference to gender and sexual orientation, the question's abiding relevance is found in Christianity's general and chronic inability to effect a credible response to "issues of discrimination and injustice," regardless of the specific types of oppression on which such "issues" are based. Furthermore, the fact that class—a major concern that Thurman addresses later in the book—is not named here may imply that he did not intend this list to be exhaustive. We believe with Hayes that Thurman, if alive today, would have included contemporary matters, such as gender and sexual orientation, among those that he treated in his volume. Still, Thurman was ahead of his time by including religion and national origin on his list.

During the era in which his book was published, black churches, and the African American community in general, tended to focus almost exclusively on resisting the *external* oppression of racism that attacked black people from the outside rather than on resisting the various forms of *internal* oppression that divided the race from the inside.[2] It was not until the last three decades of the twentieth century—after the decline of the

Civil Rights movement, the emergence of Black Power, and the advent of black theology—that black theologians, seminaries, and *some* black clergy and churches gradually began to give more serious attention to internalized oppression.

With the emergence of liberation theologies besides black theology, the traditional emphasis on racism had to make room for an increased focus on other types of oppression. These included classism, as prioritized by Latin American liberation theology, as well as sexism and heterosexism, in conjunction with the birth of womanist theology. Because of the integral, pervasive, and devastating way in which racism has historically dominated the African American experience, however, black people have not always found it easy or comfortable to take seriously internalized forms of oppression that negatively impact subgroups within the Black Church and community.

Yet, according to Phillis Sheppard, our other partner in this trialogue, the direct and structural violence of racism *toward* black people is often replicated through the cultural violence *among* black people in religious institutions like the Black Church, where violent practices are "disguised as theological and spiritual truths."[3] This reality compels her to raise questions similar to the one Thurman posed sixty-four years ago: "What in black religion legitimizes theological, social, personal, or interpersonal violence? And furthermore, what is the place of black practical theology and practices in addressing such legitimization?"[4] Hayes reminds us that womanist theologian Kelly Brown Douglas asks the following version of this question: "Why is Christianity so often implicated in vicious crimes of racial, gender, and sexual hatred? Is there something intrinsic to Christianity that makes its complicity in assailing certain human bodies not simply possible but perhaps highly probable?"[5] Along the same lines, black theologian Mark Chapman inquires, "Is Christianity a liberating reality in African-American life or is it an oppressive ideology that hinders black freedom?"[6]

In her essay "Building Communities of Embodied Beauty," Sheppard contends that, since racism is a common reality shared by all African Americans, "it is a less contentious topic" than some forms of internalized oppression that are experienced among African American subgroups.[7] In other words, the vast majority of black people in the United States would doubtless commonly agree that the persistence of racism is a dogged reality that impacts their daily lives. From her unique perspective as a practical theologian specializing in pastoral theology and psychoanalysis, however, Sheppard incisively argues that because racism not only is an instrument of "social oppression" but also affects "the formation of self," it functions as a *"template* for other forms of oppression and socialization," such as sexism and heterosexism.[8] This important "template" insight helps us to understand that external and internal forms of oppression are not necessarily as separate and distinct from each other as we might imagine.

Ironically, the victims of racism may subconsciously mimic its atrocities in their oppressive treatment of other members of their own race. In 1982 Archie Smith, an African American pastoral theologian, made a similar observation when he said, "Oppression is both an external and internal reality, therefore the process of liberation must seek to transform the social and political order and to emancipate the inner life of human subjects from internalized sources of oppression. The reproduction of oppression is inevitable if emancipation of the inner life of the oppressed is not part of the larger process of social change and transformation."[9] This brings us to Thurman's follow-up question, which is really an extension of his first question with the addition of two proposed alternative answers: "Is this impotency [of Christianity] due to a betrayal of the genius of the religion, or is it due to a basic weakness in the religion itself?"[10] While he leaves the question unanswered, Thurman offers a not-so-subtle challenge to the Christian church that is often overlooked in light of the profundity of his original twofold inquiry: "The question is searching, for the dramatic demonstration of the impotency of Christianity in dealing with the issue *is underscored by its apparent inability to cope with it within its own fellowship.*"[11] In other words, the glaring evidence of Christianity's flagrant incapacity to address matters of social justice, regardless of the underlying reason, is the apparent "inability" of the church, whether black or white, to model human equality *"within its own fellowship."* In fact, whether we are talking about race, religion, national origin, class, gender, or sexuality, the church always seems to lag behind, kicking and screaming, while secular society leads the way toward a more just and equitable social order.

Hence, the litmus test in determining whether black and womanist theologies have found practical applications within the context of local black churches is whether those churches actually *practice* what black and womanist theologies teach. The results of administering this test to black theology and the Black Church—with regard to the issues of race, gender, and sexual orientation—will help us identify what needs to be done in the future to foster a more *practical* black theology.

THE ISSUE OF RACE

The issue of race has been a relentless nemesis that has stalked, harassed, and plagued black people ever since Africans were kidnapped from their homeland and transported to the Americas as slaves. W.E.B. Du Bois succinctly summarized its persistence when, at the dawn of a new millennium, he prophesied, "The problem of the Twentieth Century is the problem of the color line."[12] Now, more than a decade into the twenty-first century, this "problem" betrays no signs of abatement.[13]

In fact, despite the signature gains of the Civil Rights movement—namely, the Civil Rights Act of 1964 and the Voting Rights Act of 1965—racism, though often more subtle, has also become more intractable. Unfortunately, the desegregation of public accommodations and the dramatic increase in black elected officials over the past fifty years, including the recent two-time election of the first African American president of the United States of America, have not resulted in a postracial society. To the contrary, American society continues to be sharply divided racially, as evidenced by the Supreme Court's recent decision to strike down a key provision of the Voting Rights Act; the racist rhetoric of right-wing politicians and media pundits; the lack of racial civility, even in the hallowed chambers of the United States Congress; the emergence of the Tea Party movement; the sharp division of the political landscape into "red" and "blue" states; the disappearance of the so-called War on Poverty, which has seemingly morphed into a War on the Poor; inconsistencies in the "welfare to work" program, resulting in a "war" on poor single mothers with children; the cruel farce known as the War on Drugs; harsh and grossly unfair mandatory minimum sentencing; the mass incarceration of black Americans (especially, black men), resulting in a caste system that has been dubbed the "New Jim Crow";[14] racial profiling and senseless murders of African American men and women by police and vigilantes; the increasing economic, educational, housing, and health-care disparities that exist between black and white Americans; and the seemingly fanatical opposition of white reactionaries to the Affordable Care Act.

It is often said that the Black Church is conservative on virtually every issue other than race. Ironically, however, while race has traditionally been at the forefront of its primary concerns, the Black Church's response to racism—especially during the twentieth and early stages of the twenty-first century—has also been conservative. For example, contrary to popular belief, the majority of black churches were not actively engaged in the Civil Rights movement. In fact, Reverend Dr. Joseph H.

Jackson—president from 1953 to 1982 of the National Baptist Convention, USA Inc. (then, the largest black organization in the world)—adamantly opposed Reverend Dr. Martin Luther King Jr. and his nonviolent protest tactics.[15] As a result, the Progressive National Baptist Convention Inc. was born in 1961, in part, to provide a denominational home for King and the movement he led.[16]

Our experience has been that—with notable exceptions, including the struggle for civil rights between 1955 and 1968—black churches over the last fifty or sixty years have generally tended to be conservative, antiactivist institutions proclaiming a gospel of personal salvation, charitable missions, social service, and individual prosperity. Recently, more congregations have ventured into the area of community economic development. Without diminishing the necessity and importance of these priorities, one must nonetheless conclude that seldom have these churches been agents of sustained social action, collective economic empowerment, and organized political advocacy against racial injustice and for socioeconomic transformation. Even the Civil Rights movement failed to challenge the underlying structures of a racist society. Instead, it sought to integrate African Americans into a societal framework that already existed.

In the last years of his life, Martin Luther King Jr. began to challenge American militarism and materialism in addition to racism. Since then, only a few church-initiated organizations, like the Samuel DeWitt Proctor Conference, have been created to pursue a more progressive agenda in tackling the root causes of racial, social, and economic problems that continue to plague the African American community.

The contemporary Black Church's distant and uneasy relationship with black theology is a direct outgrowth of its relatively conservative approach in dealing with matters of race. This approach reflects internal "dialectical tensions" that have characterized the Black Church ever since its inception. One of these tensions is the dialectic between the priestly and the prophetic.[17] If we can envision the two components of this tension occupying opposite ends of an imaginary scale, then the dynamic between them represents the friction between conservatism and radicalism. The potential power of the Black Church resides in its *creative* ability to hold these opposites together. Unfortunately, however, the Black Church, which occupies the conservative end, and black theology, which clings to the radical end, have usually chosen to pull these opposites apart.

For example, the Black Church tends to embrace its priestly role, whereas black theology implores it to claim its prophetic role. To put it another way, although the Black Church customarily "comforts the afflicted," black theology challenges it to "afflict the comfortable." Both roles are essential to the Black Church's holistic history, identity, and mission, but its heavy tilt toward pastoral care and inspirational worship, and away from political agitation and social protest, have often turned it into a "comfort zone" that provides a false sense of shelter, security, insulation, and disconnection from the harsh realities of the outside world. When this occurs, the church as a *refuge* becomes the church as an *escape*, and its members may stubbornly resist what they perceive to be attempts to push them out of their comfort zones to confront the hard, controversial issues, including racism, that impact the society in which they and the Black Church exist.

Hayes and Sheppard help us as practitioners to appreciate the connection, and even the overlap, between this and other dialectical tensions, such as universalism and particularism, that reflect the tug-of-war between Black Church conservatism and black theological radicalism. For instance, earlier in our ministerial career as pastors of a local church in the inner city of a major metropolis, when one of us would preach a prophetic sermon pertaining to our black identity or addressing the reality of racism, it would not be unusual for us to hear, indirectly of course, that some of our parishioners did not want to hear any of that "black stuff" or "social justice stuff" from the pulpit. All they wanted us to do was "preach the gospel" of Jesus Christ—as if "the gospel" is colorblind and has no relevance to racial issues.

Furthermore, we can recall that when our congregation first entertained our current church vision statement, some members wanted to know why it had to begin with the phrase, "Affirming our African heritage. . . . "[18] Since God is a *universal* God and Jesus died to save *all* people, according to these congregants, what difference did color, race, or ethnicity make? It made no difference to them for us to explain that the origin of all humankind can be traced to Africa. They wanted to know, "Can't we discard these divisive categories and simply worship a colorless God in whose image all human beings are created?"

As we contemplated this concern, we could not help but notice that these questions were not raised when Sunday school literature, vacation Bible school material, or stained glass windows were saturated with white images of Jesus and other biblical characters. They were posed only when the color "black" or the continent of Africa was introduced into the conversation. In reality, then, the issue had little to do with portraying the universality of God and everything to do with the inconceivable prospect that the image of God and/or Jesus had anything to do with blackness.

In agreement with Sheppard, we resist the kind of emphasis on universality that would erase the richness of human particularity. Jesus sought to make people whole, not broken or fragmented. Therefore, any environment—religious or secular—that requires individuals to suppress, deny, or compartmentalize any aspect of their authentic, particularized identity in order to gain "universal" acceptance is, in our opinion, not a healthy or *whole*some environment. To the contrary, just the opposite is the case. To build what Martin Luther King Jr. called "the beloved community," we like Sheppard "bring to this work a commitment to particularity; in other words, [we are] interested in articulating a practical theology that epistemologically *centralizes* the experiences of those" who are marginalized.[19]

Another helpful dialectical tension that both Hayes and Sheppard highlight is the tension between individualism and communalism, or what Lincoln and Mamiya call "the communal and the privatistic." Hayes, in particular, speaking from a womanist perspective in which communal solidarity trumps individual self-centeredness, draws a parallel between the forced breakup of African tribes and black families during slavery and the disconnect between the Black Church and black theology. Just as our African ancestors had to "learn to speak each other's tongue" in order to communicate and unite with their brothers and sisters from other tribes and families, Hayes argues that black churches and black theologians must learn to speak the same language, or at least the same dialect, if they would bridge their differences.[20]

Her point is that black churches have become so enamored of the American Dream and "capitalistic individualism" that black theology's prophetic message of racial unification, sociopolitical liberation, and community empowerment is tantamount to a foreign language. She even suggests that womanist theology—because of its community-building emphasis—would provide "an excellent bridge" between black theology and the Black Church.[21] This suggestion bears promising possibilities. When it comes to practical implementation, however, we are not convinced that academic *womanist* theology does not suffer from some of the same shortcomings as academic *black* theology. We will say more about this when we discuss the issue of gender below.

Of course there is much more that could be said about the problem of race as it pertains to the practical implementation of black theology within the Black Church. Since space will not allow a more extended discussion of this issue here, let us consider a few practical suggestions that may prove helpful in resolving it.

PRACTICAL SUGGESTIONS

As stated above, with reference to Howard Thurman's haunting question, the litmus test of the practical application of black theology within the Black Church is whether or not black churches actually practice what black theology teaches. In other words, can one find, see, hear, taste, feel, and experience the actualization of black theology within the context of local black congregations? We contend that if the Black Church is afraid or unwilling to *test* black theology within the practical setting of the local congregation, then it will never be effective in implementing black theology in the broader society. The following suggestions represent a few key ingredients of such a test.

STUDY BEST PRACTICES

One of the best models of the implementation of black theology at the local, congregational level is the Trinity United Church of Christ in Chicago. As soon as one enters the church, pastored by Reverend Dr. Jeremiah A. Wright Jr. for thirty-six years and currently pastored by Reverend Dr. Otis Moss III, one can sense the presence of black theology; it is evident in the décor, the art, the attire, the music, the dance, the liturgy, the preaching, the teaching, the educational literature, the bookstore, the names of the ministries, the outreach programs, the mission, the motto ("unashamedly Black and unapologetically Christian"), and in just about every other facet of the overall church culture. Black theology—and especially the issue of race/racism—is not an afterthought, an addendum, or a "side show" but resides at the very heart of the church's identity.

At the same time, however, the church is also a shining example of the reality that to be *problack* does not mean to be *antiwhite*. On any given Sunday, white people are welcome, present, and involved in worship as members and visitors. Furthermore, the United Church of Christ—a predominantly white denomination—proudly touts Trinity as its largest congregation. Therefore, if one wants to witness black theology-in-action, Trinity UCC is a good place to start. But while Trinity may be the largest and one of the most successful models of *practical* black theology, it is not the only model. Indeed, its phenomenal ministry raises the question of how success is defined when a black church attempts to practice black theology. This question will be considered in conjunction with the next suggestion for helping the Black Church tackle the problem of race.

BEGIN WITH THE EDUCATION OF BLACK PASTORS AND RELIGIOUS EDUCATORS

Black pastors and ecclesiastical leaders are the keys to implementing black theology within black churches. In traditional black churches, little can be accomplished without the approval, endorsement, and unequivocal support of the pastor. Even if the pastor completed seminary, however, it cannot be assumed that she or he will be open to practicing black theology within the context of her or his congregation. This means that the transformation of pastors in this regard must begin with the transformation of seminary officials and educators. If the latter are not committed to producing progressive pastors and church leaders, few if any will be produced.

In addition to seminary-educated ministers who have had either little or no exposure to black theology, many ministers, especially within the Black Church tradition, have never had the opportunity or the resources to complete or even attend seminary. These ministers can also be transformed, however, if they are open and willing to broaden their perspectives. Through continuing education and advanced degree programs—or through creative, nonformal educational offerings in cases where exposure, resources, and opportunities are limited—these pastors and religious leaders can be equipped with the necessary tools to lead congregations in a progressive direction. For just as only progressive theological education can produce progressive clergy, we submit that only progressive clergy can and will produce progressive laity.

REDEFINE SUCCESS

A major problem, however, is that in this age of the megachurch, most megachurch pastors are not progressive proponents of black liberation theology. As noted above, this is primarily because, as Hayes argues, the Black Church and black theology do not speak the same language—at least, not usually. There are some exceptions, however, where they not only do speak the same language but also have virtually united in holy matrimony and are enjoying phenomenal numerical, financial, programmatic, and spiritual success.

In the thirty-six years Jeremiah Wright pastored Trinity UCC, his success in marrying black theology and the Black Church was due largely to the fact that he was raised in a family with a long, rich tradition of progressive black church pastors and educators who emphasized ecclesiastical leadership, academic preparation, and racial pride. He had also been consistently exposed to the pastor/scholar model of ministry all of his life. Consequently, he was able to remain true to his calling to become both a theologian and a progressive practitioner within the Black Church even though he encountered stiff resistance within the academy to his pastor/scholar aspirations.[22]

Notwithstanding the example of Wright and others, the vast majority of black megachurches are the byproducts of a conservative evangelical movement that emphasizes personal salvation instead of sociopolitical liberation, individual prosperity as opposed to collective economic empowerment, a universal "colorblind" deity (usually portrayed, ironically, with European features), and a conservative rather than a progressive interpretation of the Bible. Thus, since it is highly unlikely that nonprogressive seminaries and theological institutions will produce progressive pastors who, in turn, will develop progressive laity—and since it is also highly unlikely that most progressive pastors will achieve megachurch success—it is imperative that progressive seminary professors and religious scholars earnestly adopt, develop, and teach a new definition of pastoral success that offers viable alternatives to the megachurch ideal.

EMPHASIZE THE CONNECTION BETWEEN THE INDIVIDUAL AND THE COMMUNITY

As stated above, both Hayes and Sheppard refer to the contrast between individualism and communalism, but they do so in significantly different ways. Hayes, through her critique of "narcissistic individualism," longs for a time when black people, after learning to speak the same language, will once again form "an unbroken circle of community and solidarity."[23] She also hearkens back to an era in which the Black Church was a place of black "solidarity and community" that prophetically confronted injustice not only within society but also within the Black Church itself.[24] Unfortunately, Hayes does not precisely locate these historical periods of unity and community so that the Black Church of today can learn from the Black Church of yesterday.

Consequently, we are left wondering whether that unified Black Church is the "invisible institution," the independent Black Church before the Civil War, the independent Black Church after the Civil War, or the Black Church of the early twentieth century. Is that Black Church a romanticized figment of our imagination, or did it actually exist? What's more, even if the Black Church unity and community to which Hayes refers did once exist, is it not anachronistic for us to suggest that today's disunity can be measured against yesterday's unity, especially when the issues that divide us today are so different from the ones that threatened to divide us yesterday?

Finally, Hayes' following claim is problematic: "Individualism, in and of itself, is not wrong as long as we recognize that we are yet part of a larger community."[25] Since individualism is defined as "the pursuit of individual rather than common or collective interests,"[26] we believe that it works against community. Perhaps the valid point that Hayes makes here would be better served by the word "individuality," which is defined as "the particular character, or aggregate of qualities, that distinguishes one person or thing from others."[27] In other words, it is possible to celebrate the particularity of individuality without allowing the autonomy of individualism to frustrate the building of community. The narrow emphasis of conservative evangelicals on personal salvation and individual prosperity, as opposed to social justice and cooperative economics, is based not on *individuality* but on *individualism*. This individualistic obsession with "me" and "mine" instead of "we" and "ours" has had a devastating impact on the struggle of African Americans against racism in at least two ways.

First, the sometimes overwhelming challenge of being black in a white racist society often leads the victims of racism to seek refuge and security in an individualized faith that guarantees personal, otherworldly deliverance rather than to suffer the risks and hardships of a prophetic faith that pursues collective, this-worldly liberation. Obery Hendricks discusses this tendency in his illuminating contrast of gospel music and the spirituals.[28] By way of a stinging critique of the former and a sympathetic assessment of the latter, he determines that these two genres of African American Christian music differ sharply in a variety of ways. Whereas the Spiritual is prophetic music that conveys a collective hope for "justice *in* this world," Gospel is praise music that expresses an individualistic hope for "deliverance *from* this world."[29] And while the Spirituals, forged in the crucible of slavery and in the tradition of the biblical prophets, do not shy away from announcing the "bad news" of human suffering and communal injustice, gospel music, which has evolved into a highly commercialized, market-driven form of entertainment and performance, "consciously eschews both prophetic critique" and social activism in its almost exclusive proclamation and celebration of individualized "good news."[30]

Second, individualism has prevented many black people from understanding that racism is a matter not simply of personal prejudice but of systemic oppression. Consequently, African Americans may be racially prejudiced, but they cannot legitimately be labeled "racist." To be racist is to belong to a group with the power, control, and resources to institutionalize racial prejudice through systems and structures that initiate, legislate, and perpetuate discrimination, inequality, and injustice.

For this reason, it is critically important for the victims of racism, or of any type of oppression for that matter, to understand the systemic causes of personal problems. We have discovered that oppressed people who focus on their problems without considering the structural causes are like a doctor who treats the symptoms of a disease but never determines its root. Many well-intentioned black churches—through their worship, counseling, social service, and missionary outreach programs—are excellent at treating the social ills that plague the members of their communities. However, unless these churches identify and attack the root causes of these ills, as identified with the aid of black and womanist theologies, they are like physicians who apply Band-Aids when radical surgery is required.

RACISM AS A "TEMPLATE" FOR SEXISM
AND HETEROSEXISM

Phillis Sheppard, from her psychoanalytical perspective, helps us to understand that the harmful impact of racism does not end with the direct and/or *structural* violence it inflicts upon the black community and black individuals. She points to another type of violence—namely, *cultural* violence—in which the Black Church, in unintentional complicity with white racism, participates in the emotional, psychological, and spiritual abuse of "individuals and groups whose identities do not conform to some normative expression."[31] This type of abuse, which we call *internalized oppression*, includes sexism and heterosexism. Its existence is aided and abetted by the fact that racism, according to Sheppard's previously mentioned insight, has become a "template" for other forms of oppression within the Black Church and community.

For a long time, because of the prevalence and priority of racism as an ever-present threat to the African American community from *without*, other issues of oppression from *within* were suppressed in the interest of projecting racial unity and harmony. In fact, throughout the Civil Rights movement and the early stages of the Black Power movement, it was not uncommon to hear some within the black community contend, especially with reference to women's rights, that it was inappropriate for black people to air their "dirty laundry" in public. Similarly, Bayard Rustin, the gay architect of the March on Washington in 1963, was kept in the background because of his sexual orientation.

Sheppard, who emphasizes the complexity of human identity, recommends "authentic transparent dialogue" concerning these internal issues both inside and outside the Black Church. She also points us to principles of mutual relations that recognize the critical ethics of social and communal responsibility. Furthermore, she not only connects the individual with the community but also helps us "see the link between the intraspsychic and the cultural and recognize the social structures that situate our lives, theology, and pastoral practices." She helps us to understand that this "process of listening and attending to people's life narratives will reveal that we are complex people who are searching for homes where we can bring all the parts of who we are."[32] With the implementation of a genuinely *practical* black theology, there is no reason why at least one of these "homes" cannot one day be the Black Church.

As stated earlier, Sheppard contends that it is not only *possible* but *essential* that the particularity of the individual is affirmed and celebrated if we would achieve genuine community. Therefore, when she asserts that she brings "to this work a commitment to particularity," she means that she is "interested in articulating a practical theology that epistemologically *centralizes* the experiences of those for whom gender-sexism, sexuality-heterosexism, and race-racism are inextricably linked, and in doing this work from a womanist perspective."[33] Essentially, Sheppard is suggesting that particularity ought not be suppressed in the quest for universality. We would add that neither should individuality be sacrificed in the quest for community.

THE ISSUE OF GENDER

One might say that Howard Thurman's challenge to the Christian Church (including the Black Church), in light of his haunting twofold question, is for it to *be* "the beloved community." Even though he never uses this phrase, his message is consistent with the idea that if the Church claims to be "the body of Christ"—that is, the body of the one who taught us to love each other as he loved us—then it ought to be able to demonstrate this unconditional, indiscriminate, and all-inclusive love within the context of its own fellowship. To do so may be risky and costly, but these possible ramifications do not compare with the risks Jesus took and the price he paid because he loved us—*all* of us—so much.

If black women are not to be excluded from that radical, all-inclusive love, then their role in the Black Church must be seriously examined. The Black Church has made slow, if begrudging, progress in embracing women's full equality over the last forty years. As Hayes and Sheppard have clearly pointed out from their Roman Catholic perspective, some locked doors have gradually been opened and some formidable walls have eventually come tumbling down, but there is still much work to be done in order for the Black Church, even when defined broadly, to become a safe, healthy, wholesome, and affirming environment where women are included at every level of leadership, governance, and participation and are able to realize their full, God-given potential.

While contemporary black theology has progressed at a much faster pace than the Black Church regarding women's rights, even it was slow out of the starting blocks. Out of the forty-eight religious leaders who officially endorsed the Black Power "Statement by the National Committee of Negro Churchmen," marking the official beginning of contemporary black theology when it was published as a full-page ad in the *New York Times* on July 31, 1966, only one signatory was a woman.[34] Even more revealing, however, is the fact that James Cone, the "father of black theology," upon reflecting on his very first book, confessed that this 1969 groundbreaking classic was marred by his own patriarchal blindness:

> An example of the weakness of the 1960s black freedom movement, as defined by *Black Theology and Black Power*, was its complete blindness to the problem of sexism, especially in the black church community. When I read my book today, I am embarrassed by its sexist language and patriarchal perspective. There is not even one reference to a woman in the entire book! With black women playing such a dominant role in the African-American liberation struggle, past and present, how could I have been so blind?[35]

In fact, the birth of womanist theology was, in part, a direct response to the sexism and patriarchy of black theology.[36]

Although some women have made great strides during the last half century, it is fair to say from our Protestant (Baptist/United Church of Christ) perspective that within the Black Church in general, women have been, and continue to be, second-class citizens. While usually outnumbering men by leaps and bounds, they have often borne the burden of supporting the church with their labor and finances. Unfortunately, however, this support has not normally translated into major leadership roles for women within ecclesiastical structures.

Governing leadership in the Black Church—bishops, elders, priests, pastors, deacons, trustees, and so on—primarily remains a "men only" club, whereas women with leadership abilities are usually relegated to subordinate positions such as assistant or associate pastor (if they are allowed to preach and be ordained at all), gender-specific roles such as members of the deaconess board (which is separate and apart from the all-male deacon board), president of the women's missionary society, head of the women's auxiliary, and church "mother," or lay offices such as church clerk, president of the usher board or choir, coordinator of the nursery or youth ministry, food services manager, and teacher/director of the Sunday school or vacation Bible school. It is for these reasons that, when women are supposedly complimented by being referred to as the "backbone" of the church, womanist theologian Jacquelyn Grant retorts, "The telling portion of the word backbone is 'back.' It has become apparent to me that most of the ministers who use this term have reference to location rather than function. What they really mean is that women are in the background and should be kept there."[37]

THE ISSUE OF SEXUAL ORIENTATION

The issue of sexual orientation compels us to revisit Thurman's twofold question/challenge once again, but this time in the form of the following paraphrase:

> Why is it that Christianity seems impotent to deal radically, and therefore effectively, with the issues of discrimination and injustice on the basis of sexual orientation? Is this impotency due to a betrayal of the genius of the religion, or is it due to a basic weakness in the religion itself? The question is searching, for the dramatic demonstration of the impotency of Christianity in dealing with the issue is underscored by its apparent inability to cope with homophobia and heterosexism within its own fellowship.

The early church was often referred to as a "fellowship" based on the Greek word "koinonia,"[38] which also means "association, community, communion, joint participation . . . intimacy." It can further mean sharing in common or "a gift jointly contributed, a collection, a contribution, as exhibiting an embodiment and proof of fellowship."[39] In other words, the term signified not superficial or lighthearted conviviality but a community of love, faith, encouragement, and mutual support. Within this "fellowship," therefore, there was not only teaching, eating, and praying but also the generous sharing of resources: "All who believed were together and had all things in common; they would sell their possessions and goods and distribute the proceeds to all, as any had need."[40]

Even today, those who are baptized are often said to be baptized into not only "the body of Christ" but also "the *fellowship* of believers." For there is no such thing as a Christian being "in fellowship" with God and "out of fellowship" with one's brothers and sisters in the faith. That is why, in many churches, after receiving communion, members extend to one another "the right hand of fellowship," symbolizing the oneness, solidarity, and unity they share as members of "the body of Christ."

This idea of fellowship is critical for an accurate understanding of the true Church. If there is no unity and no harmony among believers, there is no fellowship. And if there is no fellowship, there is no Church. Hence, for Thurman, the Church is a spiritual and pedagogical laboratory for testing the power of the Christian faith in helping the human family cope with the issues that divide us. If the Church cannot deal with these issues within its own fellowship, it cannot "radically, and therefore effectively," deal with these issues in the larger society. It is no accident, then, that the legendary church in San Francisco, that Thurman pastored in an attempt to test his ecclesiastical ideas is called "The Church for the Fellowship of All Peoples."

HOMOSEXUALITY AND MARRIAGE EQUALITY

No issue generates more venom, hostility, and divisiveness within the human family in general, and within the Black Church and community in particular, than the issue of homosexuality. And despite the amazing progress that has been made in the last few years concerning support for marriage equality, we do not yet live in a postheterosexist society just as we do not yet live in a postracial society. As a matter of fact,the Black Church's support for marriage equality, while critically important, has tended to be either nonexistent or decidedly lukewarm. While taking nothing away from the courage required or risk taken by progressive African American clergy to express even remotely support for such a controversial issue, we must resist the temptation to jump to the premature conclusion that homophobia and heterosexism have dramatically decreased within, if not suddenly disappeared from, the Black Church and community.[41]

For both politically strategic and ecclesiastically practical reasons, as the 2012 presidential election campaign coincided with several state campaigns for and against ballot referendums on same-sex marriage, a few progressive clergy voices of support for marriage equality began to emerge from the Black Church. However, most of them made an increasingly sharp distinction between same-sex marriage as a *civil right*, which they endorsed, and as a *religious rite*, which they said was an issue each religious entity should decide for itself. This distinction was ironic since, for so long, many African Americans had staunchly resented and resisted equating or comparing *gay* rights with *civil* rights since the latter was often sentimentally and exclusively associated with the iconic Civil Rights movement of the 1950s and 1960s.

However, in light of President Barack Obama's surprise endorsement of marriage equality just six months prior to the election, this critical distinction became essential if black Americans were to maintain their overwhelming support for his reelection while, at the same time, not feel as if their support for him compromised their deep-seated moral and religious convictions against homosexuality. In other words, this sharp distinction between marriage equality as a *civil* or *legal* matter and marriage equality as a *moral* or *theological* matter meant that members of the Black Church and community could say, even though they did not believe in same-sex marriage and should not be forced to condone or participate in it, it is not fair for them to try to prevent others from practicing it based on their own moral beliefs and convictions.

This strategy was politically expedient and ecclesiastically safe for the progressive ministers who adopted it. Its political success was evidenced in both the decisive reelection of President Obama and the unanimous victory of marriage equality in each state where it appeared on the ballot. Its ecclesiastical success was demonstrated by the fact that the ministers who supported it suffered few if any negative repercussions from their respective congregations and denominational officials. In some instances, they were even lauded for their courage in taking an unpopular stand on what had, at least up until then, been a highly controversial and contentious issue.

MORAL AND THEOLOGICAL INTEGRITY

Serious questions about moral and theological integrity surface when we examine this dualistic approach to the issue of Lesbian, Gay, Bisexual, and Transgender (LGBT) equality in the context of Howard Thurman's haunting, daunting, and penetrating challenge. During the era of Jim Crow segregation, for instance, would it have been acceptable for so-called progressive white Christian clergy to say, "We support racial justice *outside* the church, but our theological convictions (or our *parishioners'* theological convictions) about the inferiority of black people will not allow us to endorse racial justice *inside* the church"? Similarly, is it acceptable for contemporary progressive male ministers to say, "We support women's equality *outside* the church, but our theological convictions (or our *parishioners'* theological convictions) about the subordinate role of women will not allow us to endorse women's equality *inside* the church"? Why are such statements unacceptable with regard to race and gender but perfectly acceptable with regard to LGBT justice and equality? With reference to the latter, why is it okay for progressive black pastors to say, "We have no problem with gay folks getting married *outside* the church—just don't bring that 'mess' *inside* the church!"?

Furthermore, what kind of moral message does this duplicity send to the people in the pews? On the one hand, it hinders straight Black Church folk from adopting a principled position, either in favor of or against their gay brothers and sisters, and sticking with it. Instead, it allows them to waffle, to have their cake and eat it too, to straddle the fence, to walk down both sides of the street at the same time, to simultaneously be allies and adversaries, to publicly support marriage equality while privately opposing it. On the other hand, it requires LGBT persons to compartmentalize themselves in ways that Sheppard describes so that even if they are able to find wholeness *outside* the church, they are still not able to bring their whole selves *inside* the church.[42]

Again, if we read Thurman correctly, he does not say, "The dramatic demonstration of the impotency of Christianity in dealing with discrimination and injustice is underscored by its apparent inability to cope with it *beyond* its own fellowship." To the contrary, he says "*within* its own fellowship." Therein lies the critical difference between the Church and other organizations. The Church is called not only to "*seek* the Kingdom of God" but also to *be* "the beloved community." With the risks of that calling in mind, we believe Martin Luther King Jr. would remind progressive pastors, "Cowardice asks the question, 'Is it safe?' Expediency asks the question, 'Is it politic?' and Vanity comes along and asks the question, 'Is it popular?' But Conscience asks the question, 'Is it right?'"[43] The Black Church is called to do not what is safe, politic, or popular but what is right.

WHY WE CAN'T WAIT

We realize that some will counter that change takes time and that the support of *civil* marriage equality is, for some, a major step in the right direction toward support for *religious* marriage equality. Therefore, according to this line of reasoning, patience is required. While we understand this argument, we cannot help but remember a similar argument that moderate white Christian clergy made to King after Bull Connor and his police force had arrested him during a 1963 voting rights demonstration in Birmingham, Alabama. In his book *Why We Can't Wait*, King included his famous "Letter from Birmingham Jail" in which he responded, "Frankly, I have yet to engage in a direct-action campaign that was 'well timed' in the view of those who have not suffered unduly from the disease of segregation. For years now I have heard the word 'Wait!' It rings in the ear of every Negro with piercing familiarity. This 'Wait' has almost always meant 'Never.'" King concluded this portion of his letter with the immortal words, "justice too long delayed is justice denied."[44]

THE BLACK CHURCH AS A PEDAGOGICAL LABORATORY

Dennis' Ph.D. dissertation, "The Concept of the Church in the Works of Howard Thurman," includes a chapter entitled "The Church as a Pedagogical Laboratory." It focuses on Thurman's belief that the church should be both a place of religious instruction and a "laboratory" where religious experience can be tested. Sheppard's chapter in this book offers fresh ideas for helping us understand some of the components that are essential to such a laboratory. For instance, as stated earlier, she calls for "authentic transparent dialogue in and outside of . . . 'the Black Church.' "[45] We have discovered that dialogue, especially between heterosexuals and LGBT persons, is crucial in getting to know the real human beings behind the statistics, stereotypes, and labels that tend to define and objectify our concepts of each other. We can learn so much about each other by simply talking with one another.

This kind of conversation confirms Sheppard's principles of mutual relationality and responsibility.[46] Similar to Hayes' emphasis on the importance of community as opposed to individualism, Sheppard stresses our mutual responsibility for each other and that "relationality brings the reality and grit of lived experience to bear on what we see, read, hear, and do."[47] In other words, being in relationship with others prevents us from seeing or treating each other as objects rather than subjects.

Furthermore, because "religious folk" are often guilty of committing "cultural violence" against those who "do not conform to some normative expression," Sheppard recommends a pedagogical environment "that facilitates students' [early] engagement with perspectives with which they may be neither familiar nor comfortable," especially as these perspectives pertain to racial, class, gender, religious, ethnic, and/or sexual diversity. This heuristic pedagogical space offers learners an opportunity to struggle with conflict. It also generates resistance, concerning which Sheppard is profoundly enlightening:

> In and out of the classroom, resistance is persistent, pervasive, rigid, and difficult to transform. Working *with* resistance requires time, tenacity, trust, and desire on the part of faculty and students. . . . Ultimately, resistances are forms of withdrawing oneself from the process of being transformed by pedagogical efforts.[48]

As we sought to teach the members of our congregation what it means to be a radically inclusive congregation that is open, welcoming, affirming, and loving toward all of God's children, we encountered resistance in a number of ways. Some refused to attend Bible studies or other educational offerings if they knew that diversity would be the topic of discussion. Others would attend conversational sessions, remain silent, and then express their discontent in "the meetings after the meeting." Some would decrease or discontinue their financial support. Some would find an unrelated issue to get angry about as an excuse to leave the church in a huff. Some would honestly share their struggle or dismay. And others would quietly exit the church never to enter again.

On the other hand, those who appeared to experience the greatest spiritual growth and maturity were those who, as uncomfortable as they may have initially been, persevered, remained faithful, and worked through their feelings of discomfort, resentment, and resistance. It has been amazing to see how those in this latter category have proven to be solid rocks of stability in our congregation as we have taught, tested, and lived the inclusive vision that we believe God has given us.

As the Black Church seeks to implement a *practical* black theology, it is hoped that the thoughts and experiences shared in this chapter will inspire black and womanist theologians and practitioners to deal radically, and therefore effectively, with the issues of discrimination and injustice on the basis of race, gender, and sexual orientation so that the power of Christianity will be dramatically demonstrated, first, within its own fellowship and, then, to the ends of the earth!

V

Globalism, Immigration, and Diasporan Communities

Central to the biblical accounts and the Christian story is the role of diasporan people in defining the nature and practice of Christianity. Questions that demonstrate this role include the following: How does a people living as strangers, foreigners, and immigrants identify with Abraham and Sarah, who, determined to survive, defied (the) laws (of foreign lands)? How does a parent who crossed the Caribbean Sea and the Atlantic Ocean chained in slave ships relate to Moses' mother or sister, who resisted the law of the land to save her son or brother? How does a family seeking a better life relate to Naomi and Ruth as these two lives weaved into a common destiny? How does a people separated from its homeland understand the event of Pentecost and read the message of Peter to the Christians scattered throughout the Roman world? All such questions become important as one considers the challenges of identity, tradition, and changing cultural contexts within which black faith is lived. In essence, what does black theology and practical theology have to say to the issues of migration, diversity, difference, and place among people of the diaspora in the Black Church?

This, in turn, brings us to the issue of religion. Unfortunately, the Black Church struggles to become a progressive institution because of its ultra-conservative, bibliolatrous, Christocentric focus. Consequently, religion—and, especially, Christianity—has been both a blessing and a bane for black peoples. While our faith has enabled us to survive the atrocities of racism, our narrow religiosity has stunted our collective spiritual growth. To insist that Jesus Christ is the *only* way that God engages humanity does a grave disservice to the religious expressions of the majority of the people of the world, who are not Christians. (A related issue is what "conservative theology" teaches about Israel; the confusion between the State of Israel, which was founded in 1948, and the Israel of the Bible; the U.S. government's uncritical and unequivocal support of the State of Israel; and its total disregard for the ethnic cleansing of the Palestinians.) Black theology should have helped the Black Church understand by now that our recognition, appreciation, and affirmation of the validity of other religious faiths and said peoples in no way diminishes the validity of our own faith. Black practical theology needs to help the Black Church be more pluralistic and ecumenical, in both its internal and its external relationships.

<< 11 >>

AFRICAN DIASPORAN COMMUNITIES
AND THE BLACK CHURCH

Esther E. Acolatse

The Black Church in America—or in reality the two black churches in America, one African American and the other African—continue to live and function in isolation from each other even as the issue of racially segregated worship continues to be noted and expressed. Often completely off the radar of these discussions about the infamous "most segregated hour" is the other intraracial segregated hour—that of African and African American worship spaces. This intraracial divide is due in large part to the interrelation of African diasporan and African American experience performed in the interstitial space created by a common race but differing ethnic identities. These ethnic identities are circumscribed by colonial and postcolonial narratives for the former and slave and racial narratives for the latter. The experience of the one African race, vis-à-vis the Caucasian race, has produced the bifurcated ethnic experiences under consideration here.

We experience and live out these so-called ethnic differences in the interactions within all spheres and, in particular, the religious sphere. This is despite noted vestiges of African religious traditions in Black Church liturgical practices. Often, ethnic differences (i.e., the level of culture and experience) affect the way we interpret and communicate Scripture and Christian theology as the ways our faith is expressed in worship and pastoral practice. The result is a plethora of ethnic African churches, most of which struggle to be financially self-sustaining and are led by pastors with little or no theological training. These communities gather together in worship because they hunger for a place to call "home" and for a worship experience that affirms who they are as a distinct people of God. These various ethnic African churches continue to exist alongside thriving black American churches, which are often oblivious to these migrant congregations. Somehow the African churches see themselves as unable to fit not only into black American culture but also into the Black Church. The sense of being an outsider that emerges from African migrant experiences within black culture and even within the Black Church produces a kind of double displacement—only a shade distinct from that experienced in, say, Caucasian mainstream churches. To worship together while speaking different tongues characterizes Christian experiences based on ethnic dialects that bypass each other and undermine the gospel, bifurcating our common racial identity and quite frankly our common humanity.

If black churches are to be home or host to the migrant Africans in their midst, and thereby enliven the rest of black culture, they need to develop "care-full" hospitality—that is, a hospitality that is expansive enough to embrace the African other as oneself. This is hospitality without reservation, narrow consciousness, or questioning. It would be a type entrenched in a deep Trinitarian theology with broad Christological and Christopraxiological breadth that allows for sustaining dynamic hospitality and offers sustenance to others within the current racially marginalized landscapes of both world/state and the church. In short, this hospitality would be grounded in a practical theology of encounter. I am suggesting a theological human encounter of the Other as oneself in light of the God who encounters all in Christ and who offers new language that, while sometimes equivocal in its production, is yet univocal in its reception—a truly pentecostal experience.

A PRACTICAL THEOLOGY OF HOSPITALITY
FOR GLOBAL HORIZONS

Two issues will serve as points of departure and avenues for exploring the kind of practical theology I envisage for black churches. The first involves the embrace of our racial past—that is, our African roots. We accomplish this by engaging with the migrant African who lives at the various intersections of two religious experiences: an animistic African religiocultural reality with its suppositions of a world teeming with spiritual beings and a Christian worldview framed with those prior suppositions. What is required for faithful ministry to "host and guest"—an appropriate label in light of this invitation to hospitality—is at least an exploratory theology of religions that allows for engaging in Christian ministry with peoples of differing worldviews and Christian religious experiences: a truly intra- and interreligious, dialogic encounter!

The second issue is closely tied to the first: In light of the above, how can black churches serve as intra- and intercultural hosts and ministries to African migrants not only in the church but also in the culture at large? Might the explorations of the African religiocultural reality and its influence on Christian experience show points of similarity with Black Church traditions? Or, would the Black Church experience and theological traditions be more in line with other mainstream Caucasian denominations such that a practical theology of ministry needs to be woven from encounters with African migrants and their narrative past directly in order for pastoral care, counseling, and other therapeutic interventions to identify some common ground of encounter? It is the nature of hospitality, albeit a conceptually difficult phenomena, as Derrida points out,[1] that the host or hostess allows his or her space to be penetrated. But this concept of hospitality exists only in view of the foreigner, the non-native other. Thus, in reality, the concept of hospitality needs to be reframed for it to apply to the relation of African and African Americans, whether at home or abroad, on African or American soil. In a sense we are asking, in what way can a host and a guest coexist in a hospitable manner and in mutual interpenetration of each other's space and life? And how may the Black Church, as the current host, lead the way?

In the next few pages, I explore several possible avenues for helping facilitate fruitful conversations around these issues. To answer the preceding, pertinent questions and to chart a way forward, I start with some critical thoughts germane to biblical hermeneutics through which the Black Church explores various avenues, some of which are already expressed in texts like the *Africana Bible* and related projects.[2] The place of foreigners in biblical accounts and their role in shaping the life and thought of Israel in the Hebrew Bible,[3] as well as the New Israel in the New Testament of Christian Scriptures,[4] charts the way for taking seriously the role of diasporan people in what God is doing and intends for life in the household of God. Key to the interpretation of biblical accounts and the Christian story is the role of diasporan people in defining the nature and practice of Christianity. Critical questions emerge: How does a people living as strangers, foreigners, or immigrants identify with Abraham and Sarah, who, determined to survive, defied (the) laws (of foreign lands)? How does a parent, who crossed the Caribbean Sea and the Atlantic Ocean . . . , relate to Moses' mother and sister who resisted the law of the land to save her son and brother? How does a family seeking a better life relate to Naomi and Ruth as these two lives were weaved into a common destiny? How does a people separated from its homeland understand the Event of Pentecost and read the message of Peter to the Christians scattered throughout the Roman world? All of these questions become important as one considers the challenges of identity, tradition, and changing cultural contexts within which black faith lives. How might black theologians and practical theologians address the current climate of social and theological justice regarding migration, marginalized cultures/nationalities, diversity, and difference within black Christianity or among black churches?

I find that the issues of religion or diverse religious traditions, the predominance of ultraconservatism, bibliolatry, and exclusive Christocentric focus among black churches largely prevent them from functioning as places of refuge and liberation for all regardless of creed and faith.[5] Consequently, religion, especially Christianity, has been, as our editors describe, "both a blessing and a bane for black peoples."[6] The same faith that offers liberative praxis seems constricted from living fully into the promises of the liberty it procures, for when only some are free, none are fully free. How does the church maintain its particularity in the light of this plurality without forgoing its missional stance, yet at the same time remain hospitable to those *extra ecclesia* among them? How do we insist that Jesus Christ is the *only* way to salvation without doing a grave disservice to the gospel itself and without condemning the religious expressions of the majority of the people of the world, who are not Christians?[7] The larger evangelical world and some mainstream denominations seem to be concerned about the issues enough to engage them in ongoing critical dialogue with Christian mission and life in a pluralist world. Yet, the Black Church remains seemingly unconcerned with this critical dialogue, even with Christian-Muslim dialogue, considering the history of the leadership of the Civil Rights movement and the religious and political conflicts and issues involved.[8] The task of the Black Church, from which ensues black theology, includes the intentional dedication of resources for equipping communities of faith with the means to traverse the barriers that block people from seeing, hearing, and aiding one another and the scriptural mandate in a nutshell. This task requires the integration of the social sciences with historical, theological, and biblical studies for the purpose of understanding the complexities facing the global Church in the twenty-first century. I suggest that such a task requires a practical theological methodology rooted in a Trinitarian doxology with a Christopraxiological openness. Some might charge that black theology should have helped black churches understand by now that the recognition, appreciation, and affirmation of the validity of other religious faiths in no way diminishes the validity of the Christian faith. Much current thinking, however, bifurcates black theology into theory and practice, an anomaly inherited from theological training within its disciplinary guilds.[9] As an important corrective, the reflexive dynamic of text-context-text interchange[10] uproots such linear precedence of theory over practice.[11]

Black theology and practical theology need to help black churches become more pluralistic and ecumenical, in both their internal and external relationships. We cannot do this in a vacuum, however, for the workings of theology are bound by the Church's understanding of its function and purpose. Thus, we need to revisit the question of ecclesiology and pastoral care together. The Church's pastoral role and the theology that emanates from its practices are the two sides of one coin.

Another global challenge concerns the ways in which black prophetic voices espouse or neglect international political and social justice. For instance, conservative theological stances often confuse the theological underpinnings of the Israel of the Bible with the political sovereignty and policies of the current statehood of Israel.[12] Likewise, the U.S. government's uncritical and unequivocal support of the State of Israel exacerbates the disregard for the ethnic, political, and economic oppression of the Palestinians, not to mention the exchange of violence between the two sides as each seeks the annihilation of the other! Some important questions are the following: How can black theologians and practical theologians help black churches form critical black prophetic voices that can articulate the justice issues at stake nationally and internationally and contend with the attendant political and economic marginalization and suffering? How might black theologians and practical theologians address the current climate of social and theological justice regarding migration, marginalized cultures and nationalities, diversity, and difference within black Christianity or among black churches? These global chasms exist between black theology's and black churches' efforts to shape ministries and do theology within their related contemporary black worldviews.

The challenges black churches face globally reflect how the practical theological issues of encounter germinate between African migrants and black American churches and their theological engagement in and by faith communities and religious practices. The struggles to minister prophetically in society relate to the pastoral-care functions of black American churches in relation to African migrants. These encounters carry with them the global challenges of pastoral engagement within diverse communities. My theological turn to hospitality addresses how to bring critical issues of cultural and faith diversities into dialogue with practical theological disciplines and Christian traditions in the work of developing black clerical leadership and black faith communities in their own critical encounters, practices, and global worldviews.

PASTORAL PRACTICES OF HOSPITALITY IN DIALOGUE

I have addressed the possibilities of cross-ethnic and cross-cultural dialogue in an earlier article constructing an interdisciplinary effort out of psychology and theology for pastoral counseling.[13] This interdisciplinary focus is primarily concerned with the lexicon or language systems that vie for voice in the dialogues operating in pastoral counseling. From this work my own focus is on the actual dialogue and perhaps more so on the pluralism, which I believe serves well the methodological needs here for pastoral practices of hospitality in dialogue. Using the insights of Deborah Hunsinger's effort to shape interdisciplinary pastoral counseling, I stress her point that dialogical pastoral practices by necessity require bilingual skills,[14] which I argue plays critically in translating and transforming cross-ethnic and cross-cultural encounters without a careless encroachment that would violate core values of meaning.

This notion of bilingual dialogue raises an obvious question for the pastoral practices of hospitality; basically, how might hospitality function with bilateral integrity? Even Hunsinger's treatment of interdisciplinary skills for pastoral counseling must contend with challenges to the integrity of differences and a primary discipline language, as I have argued.[15] The significance or formation of theology is a profound concern and often results in the breakdown of interdisciplinary or bilingual dialogue. For my treatment, a theological breakdown often occurs in hospitality praxis around the cross-ethnic and cross-cultural black dialogue in our diasporan encounters and engagement.

When diasporan black communities engage one another—in particular, African American communities encountering immigrant African communities—the contexts of cultural locations and theological orientations between hosts and the newly encountered conflate in the challenges of bilingual theological speech and communal formation at stake in the desired transformation of alienation or marginalization. I continue to believe that bilingual dialogue requires that we each work continuously, especially in critical self-reflection, to recognize and respect what I call "primal" speech.[16] Our primal speech emerges from our core formation, even core createdness. Primal speech therefore is theological. Critical to my conceptualization of theological primal speech is the encounter with God and God's revelations or exchange with humanity. The pastoral practices of hospitality emerge from these exchanges in seeking dialogue in our human encounters—both personally intimate and communal.[17]

Primal language for hospitality dialogue privileges the theological core search of the soul for meaningful exchange in understanding revelation amid human encounters. So our encounters and efforts in ministry expand the contexts of interpretation of even Scripture or dogma. Primal theological language functions in affirming one's divine createdness and relationship with God within relationships with one another. This communion may continue to evolve, so primal speech operates in hospitality of dialogue navigating change, challenges, and charges requiring interpretation and transformation of communities or society.

How then might primal speech operate within my appeal to hospitality and dialogue? As I have explained in more detail elsewhere, any attempt to learn a second language must rely upon one's first language to build interpretation into translation.[18] This dynamic becomes a stumbling block often in everyday dialogue as well as church dialogues. We rely heavily on our primary language at the expense of fully translating another's primal language within an ongoing dialogue of translation between these languages. Primary theological language and meanings often operate unreflectively when churches dialogue together or when churches attempt to engage other communities. Primal language expresses innate love, anger, or even lament, as in the Psalms, in the depths of yearning, questioning, or pain that people feel. With translation between our primary and primal languages, the bilingual struggles of interpretation determine how indispensable the exigencies are to address differences or the unfamiliar with politics of respect and bridge-building rooted in hospitality. Primal speech becomes a resource rather than an obstruction to our dialogue when we recognize it as a divine gift, speaking even pretheoretically from our core being or createdness, seeking meaning or understanding. Hospitality in dialogue would therefore operate in these ways not just theologically but functionally empowered as a theological bilingual operation.

CONTOURS OF PRIMAL SPEECH AND PASTORAL
HOSPITALITY

As I envision pastoral hospitality, there are important implications from historical efforts to translate the gospel message as care providers and community leaders inherently demanded bilingual skills. As with my earlier work in pastoral counseling, here too I turn to Lamin Sanneh to demonstrate how we might understand translation and the appropriation of language in bilingual caregiving between communities and within them. Sanneh explains that early Christians could not rely on a single edition of revelation, especially in the expansion of the faith among Gentile communities. The gathering of Scripture entailed the native testimonies of faithful dialogue. Because the historical, cultural contexts juggled many differences, translation operated centrally to speak in the native language of each community. For my application here, the drive to translate can be described as a primal theological or spiritual urge not to be differentiated from the urge of primal language to express meaning or understanding. The urge for early Christians functioned to drive the necessary dialogue of translation to break through ethnic and cultural obstructions operating typically in bilingual exchange.[19]

In much of my counseling encounters I have observed that these same insights aid in pastoral diagnosis and care. For instance, a religious context like most of sub-Saharan Africa, where belief in the spirit world characterizes common life, may adduce demonic or other evil spiritual influences as a norm. In such cases, I have argued there are several linguistic layers that need careful attention in order to address the core of presenting issues in pastoral counseling. For the professional pastoral counselor, the linguistic demands take account of the movements between theology and psychology in tandem but also must account for the other deep layers of the vernacular of persons in care and how they in a sense *read* Scripture.[20] What is being navigated here are the multiple grammars, as it were, of the intricate dance between the primary pastoral disciplines of the field and how they facilitate the kind of pastoral hospitality required for healing encounters, especially as they are brought to bear in cross-ethnic and cross-cultural contexts. Translation is thus, as I have previously expressed, "a complex negotiation of multiple signifiers."[21] Take for instance such a case in pastoral language encounters in pastoral care wherein someone ailing for many years with a debilitating illness seeks healing and care from her pastor with the firm belief that her illness is caused by evil spiritual forces. She reads and hears words from Scripture that indicate she is not wrong. She hears the following passage both in English and in her mother tongue:

[20]Then suddenly a woman who had suffered from hemorrhages for twelve years came up behind him and touched the fringe of his cloak, [21]for she said to herself, "If I only touch his cloak, I will be made well." [22]Jesus turned, and seeing her he said, "Take heart, daughter; your faith has made you well." And instantly the woman was made well. (Matt 9:20-22)

[20]*Ni Naa, yoo ko ni eye láfɔsemɔ hela affi nyɔŋma ke enyɔ lɛ baje esɛɛgbɛ eta etade naamuu lɛ he.* [21]*Ejaakɛ ekɛɛ yɛ eyiŋ akɛ, "Kɛji mina mita etade lɛ he kɛkɛ lɛ, mihe aaawa mi."* [22]*Shi Yesu tsɔ ehe, ni be ni ena lɛ lɛ ekɛɛ, "Biyoo, hã otsui anyɔ omli, ohemɔkɛyeli lɛ ehere oyiwala!" Ni yoo lɛ he wa lɛ nakai ŋmlɛtswaa lɛ nɔ nɔŋŋ.*

Translations require us to slow down and take time to attend to process as well as the individual in need of care. These considerations involve two kinds and two moments of translation in pastoral care. The first regards attending to someone with whom one shares a similar "Christian grammar" doctrinally but from whom one is divided culturally. The second is a situation in which intrareligious differences foreground the caring encounter because certain pertinent scriptures may mark one as belonging to Christ or may contest it still in dominant practices of pastoral care.

An example extending between these two challenges of translation is the scenario described earlier in this section of a woman needing care, who believes the influence of the demonic is implicated in her ailment. Suppose this woman *reads* from the words of the above Scripture passage either that she is not a daughter or that she does not have faith enough to warrant healing. She is therefore distraught and feels she is being oppressed by a demon. What then would be the appropriate approach to care for her? How does the community or a care provider then negotiate the tensions among the various grammars or signifiers in tandem in order to diagnose and appropriately care for this individual? In her mother tongue, the words "ekɛɛ" and Jesus' words "ekɛɛ" co-inhere. It is as if to say that Jesus affirms her own words that she has spoken about herself in faith. In her language faith literally means that she has taken and imbibed these logoi; and such imbibing then sets to work on procuring what she needs for wholeness.

The multiple layers of translation here require the bilingual tools of translation or dialogue between primary languages along with the professional and theological disciplines of care. Even if her mother tongue is not directly in play, the ability to enter into, engage, and translate her cultural context with enough adequacy to aid in her care requires bilingual skills relating spiritual or theological worldviews, which are in essence quite related to primal speech. The pastoral care provider's familiarity and comfort with the languages of her discipline(s) and in large part her agility with theology are very important here. The care provider and one's community of care need to be willing to embrace these bilingual exchanges with which they share many aims and sensibilities, the least being the hope and work toward wholeness and flourishing of individuals.

In the above scenario, taking into consideration the ailing woman's sociocultural context (as she navigates life in a strange land) and at the same time not neglecting the concurrent psychological or emotional diagnoses possible, the work of translation operates at multiple levels. My bilingual analysis allows for a certain paradoxical playfulness on the woman's words and Jesus' words that are caught up in a time in which a postresurrection context may not necessarily be as immediate as the one in which the woman in the biblical story was healed. The concept of time as fluid within the congregants' original contexts, which many persons in the currently new home context of the black community share, allows for facility between pastor and congregants to indwell the moment. This desired moment is created by the hospitality of shared theological grammar with primal speech and the kindred temporal context. It allows the ailing woman's words and Jesus' words of healing to hold both of them. Of course the pastor does not in the moment forget other dialogical partners, as psychological and medical disciplines of care continue to attend also to healing in search of what may be needed.

Primal speech, thus viewed as theology of hospitality praxis, will have within its purview dialogue with psychological or cultural languages and can more effectively engage other theological languages. Hospitality praxis makes room for them within their spheres of thinking, freeing them to express themselves in their own terms and internal grammatical structures. For our various purposes, counseling and cultural hermeneutics will, of course, still need to speak in their own terms as well. Pastoral care of hospitality, however, seeks to be a bilingual translator in providing pastoral diagnosis and care. Theology and Scripture have within them counseling and care dimensions so that by claiming theology as primal speech the congregant is invited to live more fully in a theological vision of life that encompasses the psychic, cultural, and spiritual dimensions together. But as I have argued, we have to allow for the possibility of what

I call "deceptive primal (theological) speech, especially given the history of colonialism and all of its negative and ongoing effects"[22] as well as the positive, even if often ignored, liberating aspects. Part of these liberating moves is to offer the bilingual gift of hearing the gospel message in one's own mother tongue. That is, to be addressed by a God who speaks one's tongue in cross-ethnic or cross-cultural contexts actually sanctifies and equalizes all primal language in our ensuing communal and pastoral care of mutual embrace and dependence.[23] Hence, the contours of primal speech of theology offer pastoral care providers and our communities of engagement practical theological agency in actions of liberating pastoral hospitality.

<< 12 >>

THE AESTHETIC STRUGGLE AND ECCLESIAL VISION

Willie James Jennings

For our struggle is not against enemies of blood and flesh, but against the rulers, against the authorities, against the cosmic powers of this present darkness, against the spiritual forces of evil in the heavenly places.

Ephesians 6:12

Peoples of African descent in the world bear witness to a horror. We have watched the emergence, growth, cultivation, and expansion of a white (Eurocentric) aesthetic regime that seeks to narrate the true, the good, the beautiful, the intelligent, and the noble around white bodies. Since the advent of this colonialist regime, peoples with bodies deemed black *and black-like* have been forced to face a tragic question, why should I love *my* body? This is not a question about the possibilities of black love, or even black self-love. Nor is this a question about the merits or demerits of European legacies of civilizing projects, although the time is ripe for a theological assessment of the history of Western civilizing projects. This question of why love a *black* body registers the centuries-long outcomes of weaving visions of the transcendent and the universal around the imagined sublime contours of white images.

The aesthetic regime, which originated in colonialism, continues to discipline our collective fantasies through a racializing pedagogy. This was a pedagogy not simply of the oppressed but also of an evangelical gesture inviting all who would live in the new world being wrought by the European to see with new eyes, "his eyes." We who have been the inheritors of this racial optic are now, with each new generation of observers, becoming its progenitors, enfolding our lives again and again within its powerful effects. The emergence of the racial optic and its wider racial aesthetic regime is not a new story, yet it remains an amazing one. In this essay, I reflect on the various contours of this racial optic and its implications for ecclesial vision and pastoral intervention, especially intervention into the lives of people who carry the unbearable weight of the racial aesthetic regime.

Some readers might wonder whether I am simply recycling the critiques of European cultural hegemony and the aesthetics of whiteness that emerged in the Black Power/black liberation movement of the 1960s and 1970s or its social analogs in Third World contexts.[1] Those critiques and their intellectual antecedents represented an important moment when the subaltern began speaking truth to power, yet those critiques did not fully capture or conceptualize the wider horizon of racial formation that always bound blackness and the production of its aesthetic values to the machinations and performances of whiteness. This legacy of critique therefore turned its creative powers toward the conceptual reflexes of cultural nationalism, suggesting that the central work for marginalized peoples was to create their own visions of the sublime and the beautiful and to cultivate their own cultural gardens. Cultural nationalist strategies serve as an important mode of intervention. Yet they have labored within the constraints of global practices of production and consumption that carry two ongoing effects. First, those practices draw all cultural work toward commodification and thereby become fragmented cultural commodities disarmed of their power to call into question or redirect ways of life.[2] Second, those practices move along pedagogical directions that constantly present white bodies as global tutors of all matters of human concern.

We need to begin to conceive an intervention that would not only reorient these pedagogical directions and draw cultural work into a shared cosmopolitan project but also press deeply into a redemptive mode of aesthetic life. To aid in this intervention, I will borrow from the wisdom of the great Syrian (Arabic) theologian John of Damascus, whose groundbreaking defense of icons (images) used in worship and popular piety illumine a set of concerns that are also relevant to our moment.[3] What Damascus helps us to grasp is the architecture of a visual and more generally artistic life set within a Christological and redemptive frame. He thereby opens up the possibilities of transforming visual economies, once imagined as idolatrous and hopelessly turned toward death, into spaces of the iconic—that is, artistic spaces where we might participate in the divine life that has come to us in Jesus of Nazareth.

The iconic—rooted in Jesus, who is the life constituting icon of God—breaks open the power of all aesthetic regimes, especially our modern racial aesthetic, which is nothing less than a principality, a spiritual force of evil in heavenly places (τὰ πνευματικὰ τῆς πονηρίας ἐν τοῖς ἐπουρανίοις [Eph 6:12 BGT]). We should therefore follow the advice of Walter Wink and name this concrete power of the racial aesthetic, recognizing the demonic at play in this citadel of optical illusions that bind a racial calculus to human bodies and human gesture in such a way as to damage the way we see God's creation and see ourselves as God's creatures.[4] Naming this spiritual force might enable us not simply to begin thinking beyond race but also to press down deeply into its inner logics, right down into the configuring operations that create the identity-forming boundaries between and around the beautiful and the ugly, the true and the false, the intellectually weak and the intellectually strong, and the good and the evil and then bind those boundaries to our lives. A Christologically informed iconic logic draws us into new strategies for resisting and redirecting artistic currents and visual economies away from death and toward life.

OPRAH AND THE GLOBAL RACIAL UNCONSCIOUS

Oprah Winfrey unarguably has been one of the most significant black female media personalities of the late twentieth and early twenty-first centuries. On one of her famed television specials, she achieved a rarity by getting George Lucas to agree to an in-depth interview. The creative genius behind the *Star Wars* and *Indiana Jones* sagas and many other epic films, which have had such profound effects on our fantasy life, allowed Oprah an unprecedented view into some aspects of his own interior life. Beyond his dazzling home spread out on thousands of acres, with its impressive array of buildings filled with state-of-the-art multimedia technologies, and the awesome influence he wields over the film industry, what captured my attention were two related things that also seemed to capture Oprah Winfrey's attention during the interview: his forays into the racial dynamics of relationships and into the racial dynamics of aesthetics.

At one point during the interview, Oprah mentioned that when she was watching an awards ceremony on television, she saw George Lucas, who is Anglo-American, holding hands with Mellody Hobson, an African American woman who at the time did financial reporting on NBC. As Oprah put it, seeing them together caused her to sit up in her chair, lean forward, and immediately try to determine the status of their relationship—were they together, were they dating? Part of Winfrey's brilliance is that she asks the questions that we want to ask but would be deathly afraid to. So she asked Lucas and Hobson (who was seated next to him at this point in the interview) about the status of their relationship and the journey of love they are on together. Even at this moment in history, the sight of interracial love captures our imaginations with its signifying possibilities. With their romantic relationship as the immediate backdrop, Oprah turned the interview toward Lucas' then new film venture, *Red Tails.* George Lucas had wanted to make this movie about the famed Tuskegee WWII fighter pilots for at least fifteen years. He believed that the real story was powerful and deserved the fullest display that Hollywood could offer. Lucas told another story during the interview that parallels the tale of the Tuskegee airmen. He had taken his *Red Tails* film project to every major studio in Hollywood, and all of them had turned him down. The reasons they gave for rejection were uniform: The general public would not watch a major motion picture populated mostly with black bodies. More precisely, a WWII picture that maps black bodies as the sites of valor, courage, sacrifice, honor, and even faith, where otherwise white bodies are normally positioned, would not garner a large enough audience either in the United States or abroad to justify its expense.

So George Lucas, one of the most powerful men in the history of the North American film industry, had to put up $100 million of his own money for the production, distribution, and advertisement of *Red Tails,* all the while pressing against the idea that a film filled with black people would not draw a wide audience. This may seem counterintuitive given the uses of black bodies (and people of color in general) in selling products and services, as well as the positioning of Afro cultures as carrier cultures for indexing fashion and cultivating consumptive desire.[5] However Lucas' experience with his film is not surprising because it confirms the aesthetic order of things born of the colonialist moment.

The resistance to this particular artistic witness illumines for us the wider racial aesthetic regime that grew out of a Christian theological matrix. This regime remains out of focus for Christian theology. Lucas' confrontation and struggle with the racial aesthetic foreground the visual education that marks Western ways of life. That education frames our perceptual experiences and forms our processes of evaluation around three factors: (1) beauty, (2) intelligence, and (3) nobility. The recent return to aesthetics in theology, philosophy, and other disciplines has yet to reflect seriously on the wider history and realities of the colonial frame of our current aesthetic circuits of production and consumption.[6]

BEAUTY WITHIN THE COLONIAL MATRIX

Elaine Scarry, in *On Beauty and Being Just*, argues that the category of beauty has been pushed out of the intellectual work of the humanities in recent decades because it has suffered from being falsely accused of two political crimes. First, beauty as a perceptual practice is charged with "mak[ing] us inattentive, and therefore eventually indifferent to the project of bringing about arrangements that are just."[7] The second accusation against beauty is its participation in practices of reification. By staring at the thing we deem beautiful, we transform it into an object. Scarry suggests that these arguments against beauty are incoherent because they fail to understand how perceiving beauty is a radical decentering practice that may inculcate in us an attention to fairness and justice. Seeing a beautiful thing in the world "can make us feel adjacent" while simultaneously bringing us into "a state of acute pleasure."[8] Scarry sees this stunning dual operation of beauty's perception as a gift that could constitute a "precondition for enjoying fair relations with others."[9] Seeing beauty enables an aesthetic symmetry that helps us appreciate our "own lateralness." This aesthetic symmetry can inculcate a desire for "*ethical fairness* which requires 'a symmetry of everyone's relation.' "[10]

Scarry's argument channels the logic of a particular kind of class formation in which aspirations for moral and spiritual growth are bound to aesthetic education:

> The beholders of beautiful things themselves become beautiful in their interior lives; if the contents of consciousness are full of the calls of birds, mental pictures of the way dancers move, fragments of jazz pieces for piano and flute, remembered glimpses of ravishing faces, a sentence of incredible tact and delicacy spoken by a friend, then we have been made intensely beautiful.[12]

Still, an interior life made beautiful by beautiful things does not equate to a life animated toward justice. Scarry grasps this. Her point is that having such beauty attend us enlivens and awakens us to the aliveness of all things around us and draws us into the desire for its protection as a kind of contract between the beholder and the beautiful.[13] These class-formed aspirations for moral edification through perceiving beauty reflect a quasitheological anthropology refined and performed from the colonial moment forward. Scarry describes us as always susceptible to being captured by beauty. This universal human condition need not be debated but only accepted as the given of our psychical architecture. This gesture toward metaphysics invites us to see the world in a particular way, one that aligns peoples of multiple places and spaces into an orbit of consumptive tastes that endlessly circle around white bodies. It would not be accurate to call this a simple case of Eurocentrism, because something far more powerful is on display in her text. She is performing a desire to inhabit our bodies and to be inhabited through presenting a mental frame applicable to us all. Here racial and class gestures masquerade as universals. The kind of presentation we find in Scarry's treatment of beauty hearkens back to Immanuel Kant's aesthetic vision, which as Terry Eagleton notes reflects the desire of a ruling class to construct "a kind of universal subjectivity . . . for its ideological solidarity":[14]

> When, for Kant, we find ourselves concurring spontaneously in an aesthetic judgment, able to agree that a certain phenomenon is sublime or beautiful, we exercise a precious form of intersubjectivity, establishing ourselves as a community of feeling subjects linked by a quick sense of our shared capacities. . . . For the alarming truth is that in a social order marked by class division and market competition, it may finally be here, and only here, that human beings belong together in some intimate *Gemeinschaft* [community].[15]

Equally importantly, aesthetic education in Scarry's account is hypostatized and freed from its history of embeddedness in processes not only of gender and racial formation but also of production and consumption. Scarry's speculations lack sight of the wider plantation of operations that constitute the racial aesthetic. Beauty must be seen in relation to truth and goodness as collaborative, mutually energizing technologies. Furthermore, beauty, truth, and goodness must be grasped in a universalizing frame drawn from deep theological waters. Scarry, as we noted earlier, suggests that aesthetic experiences yield a sense of symmetry that greatly aids the creation of a sense of and desire for ethical fairness. Yet, historically, aesthetic experiences, more often from the colonial moment forward, yielded a sense of and desire for *order*: rightly ordered spaces and rightly ordered relations. One could say that perceiving beauty energizes and is energized by fantasy; therefore, fantasy embarked on a strange new career from the threshold of colonial modernity. Fantasy made love to beauty in a marriage bed sanctioned by two powerful, perceptual logics of order—the salvific and the pastoralist.[16] The salvific and the pastoralist in this regard have primarily to do with correctly ordered spaces coordinated with correctly ordered bodies. Missionaries and others imagined built environments that joined cultivated lands to beautiful churches and to docile and submissive slaves. Early European Christians, as they emerged as central New World powers, drew on a scriptural imagination in which they saw themselves as the people of God, having supplanted Israel. As the people of God, they imagined themselves within the biblical drama. Such an imagined position is in fact a fundamental premise of Christian identity. Yet, when the imagined position is no longer as Gentiles but as Israel's replacements as the *authentic* people of God, the world is over-turned. The Scriptures present an overturned world, a strange new world in which God is an actor who draws us toward a new sense of agency born of our involvement with God in a haunting and sometimes over-whelming reciprocity. Yet, supplanting Israelites as the people of God with Europeans overturned that overturned world and returned it to a path oriented toward pride and idolatry. Early European Christians coming to new lands saw themselves as the embodied will of God for the world. They saw themselves as those who could discern the difference between the demonic and the holy and who therefore could refashion the bodies and behaviors of New World peoples toward the path of salvation. They also saw themselves as people who were ordained to set spaces on a path toward order. In the minds of the colonialists, the new worlds were places of chaos that called for order. So the gospel message called not simply for an ordered body and soul but also for the ordering of plants, animals, places, and landscape as befitting an orderly environment. The pastoral (care of bodies) would merge with the pastoralist (control of space) to form the very ground on which the true, the good, and the beautiful would be constituted.

Those who now constituted that ground were also the ground on which aesthetic discernment would grow. This was first a matter of vicar-ious existence. If Israel in Scripture represented or stood for humanity in its awesome glory and horror, then the European would take that place as the site for all the contours of human existence. Early Europeans became the merchants of the universal. They trafficked in both its creation and its presentation. Here, we must hold together the conceptual and the com-mercial and recognize the ways in which early Europeans set in place an economic cosmopolitan sensibility that flowed around their bodies. Not only did they invite the peoples of colony and metropolis to discern the transcendent along Europe's tutoring lines, but they also gave material direction to that discernment. Riding high on the collaborative work of merchant and missionary, Europeans would establish orthodoxy of thought *and* consumptive tastes. Hence, the Bible was translated not only into many tongues and places, along with orthodox Christian thought and its foundational ancient antecedents like Hellenistic philosophy, but also into the value of, for example, a high-quality cigar; a beautiful dress; wonderful music; fine wine, rum, or port; excellent literature; proper shoes; exquisite architecture; a classic man's attire; and so forth. From Brazil to the Netherlands, from Connecticut to Nova Scotia, from the Canary Islands to Mozambique, from Durbin to Peking, from Chile to Ireland, from Germany to Jamaica, from New York to Paris, worlds of peoples were invited (and often forced) to discern the true, the good, and the beautiful wrapped around white bodies.

This effect has been far more significant than serving merely as examples of benign or malignant forms of inculturation. Orthodox thought was joined to orthodox objects—more precisely, to objects that helped to make one materially orthodox, rightly ordered. The point, however, is not the orthodoxy of the objects but the *orthodoxy of the desire* for those objects. A new way of imagining life rode in on the ships coming from the old world to the new worlds, a way of life that presented new paths of growth, of maturity, and of becoming. Becoming what? The precise nature of what one became was not the point. This was not a simple matter of indigenous peoples being assimilated into European modes of existence, because we now understand that European and indigenous ways of life merged in many contexts to create the cultural baroque.[17] That cultural baroque included native objects and practices that combined with and altered a world of imports. Yet all of it was brought into a circle of exchange and baptized into goods and services.

The point of this new becoming was twofold: First, it was an earth-shattering interruption of old ways of becoming. Where peoples envisaged growth into adulthood, or leadership, or movement into maturity, or new forms of spiritual existence that depended on land, space, place, and involvement with animals to enact or make possible that growth or movement, then with the taking of land and animals that very passageway of becoming would either disappear or reappear in a severely attenuated form. What would "becoming" signify if it no longer had a place to be performed? How can one become a hunter if the land that constituted one's connection with ancestor-hunters and thereby enabled one *to imagine oneself becoming a hunter* had been taken, transformed into private property, and barred from trespass under threat of death? In this regard, the ways of the merchant, the missionary, and the soldier would give birth to multiple new vocations for indigenes, supplanting, if not completely destroying, old ways of becoming. Indeed, the most powerful effect of this new arrangement was not the destruction of old ways of becoming but the rendering of them as insignificant, as pointing to nothing of the future but only to a dead past or a frozen present.

Second, as new globally situated forms of becoming were pressed into local sites with compelling new narratives of becoming, a new relation between objects and becoming emerged. Here we must grasp the intimate relation between objects born to give life to consumptive desire and the vocations (*vocatio*) they inspire. Thanks to the collaborative work of missionary and merchant, *a sense of calling* became embedded in objects themselves, drawing peoples to new ways of imagining becoming. This sense of calling was a residual effect of life pressed between the salvific (the pastoral) and the pastoralist. Indigenous peoples living under the influence of settler cultures experienced orthodoxy not only in being pressed to adhere to orthodox Christian beliefs but also, and more decisively, in the comprehensive disciplining work that orthodoxy had on aesthetic frames of reference. These are the longitudinal effects of a theological orthodoxy that worked its way down to policing the body and thereby helped to sustain senses of proper attire, behavior, and discourse. *Orthodox thought seeped into objects of consumption.* The objects of the Euro-merchant did not necessarily present one particular way of life; rather, they presented new, more acceptable directions for fantasy that would bind peoples to disciplines of education, behavior, mood, and manner commensurate with civilizing impulses.

The historical trajectory of this operation informs the racial aesthetic regime in its continuing global consumptive reflexes. Colonialism yielded a historic turn of human powers of creation toward the production of goods and services around a European vortex that is yet to lose its aesthetic pull. The Western world functions inside a racial imaginary that endlessly creates and coordinates images that hold up white bodies as the tutors of desire, the guides for fantasy production, and the sites on which the world is invited to imagine its humanity, and especially its nobility. One of the central strategies peoples have used to combat the visual order of things has been to seek an image exchange through drawing on cultural and racial alternative portfolios. This is an honorable yet short-sighted tactic. *We need the longer view of what is now in place, a tacit (global) agreement regarding the vicarious reality of white bodies to signify humanity for us, to be the ground on which we fantasize.* We have yielded our collective imaginations to white aesthetic supremacy, signaling with every turn of media currents its right of way. I am not saying that white bodies are the only bodies functioning vicariously, nor am I denying the presence of the visually multicultural, nor am I blind to the presence in some parts of the world of episodic and predominantly ethnic representation in advertisements, movies, and so forth. These visual effects are primarily contrapuntal rather than counterhegemonic. They draw on narrative frames that are improvisationally limited and reaffirm the pedagogical position of white bodies as archetypes.

I am also not disregarding the important countervoices that have always pressed against this order of things through alternative arts, critique, and/or the creation of aesthetic spaces that speak a different way of discerning the good, the true, the beautiful, the intelligent, and the noble. These alternatives have always offered, and will continue to offer, hope. More importantly, these alternatives show us that we are indeed always in need of images and that image making is fundamental to our being. The great need for images, or more generally the coupling of the artistic with the urgent need to overturn the racial aesthetic, constitutes a set of conditions reminiscent of the epic iconoclastic crisis of the Eastern Churches in the seventh and eighth centuries.

The struggle over icons (images) between governmental and ecclesial officials who wanted them banned (*iconoclasts*) and those ecclesial officials and laypeople who understood icons to be an integral and necessary part of Christian devotion and identity (*iconodoles*) created what has been known as the iconoclastic crisis.[18] This crisis centered on the control over the devotional life of the Christian populace by seeking to redirect the proper lines of fantasy production away from alleged idolatry and toward orthodoxy. The iconoclasts seemingly had the stronger argument as they equated icon creation with idol production, and icon veneration with idol worship. The iconoclasts interpreted artistic objects through a hermeneutics of idolatry—that is, any object of veneration placed between God and humanity was fundamentally an obstruction that drew attention away from the divine and toward the creature through creaturely elements. Simply put, iconoclasm in that place and time had to do with two concerns: (1) the hatred of all images (e.g., mosaics, frescos, sacred vessels, garments, books, statues, paintings, etc.) that were seen as being worshipped, and (2) the destruction of all practices of veneration that were seen as nothing less than idolatry.[19]

John of Damascus understood that idolatry was not inherent in the creation and use of images. John of Damascus (645–749 C.E.) lived under the shadow of Muslim rule and, for a time, like his father and grandfather before him, probably served as a civil servant for the Muslim caliph (ruler) in Damascus. He later left Damascus and joined the monastery of Mar Saba in Jerusalem; from there, he wrote against the iconoclastic polices of the Byzantine emperor Leo III. The real issue, as he saw it, was the nature of veneration. For John of Damascus, because God had become incarnate, had become flesh, the body and the material realities of the world mattered in a new way. The material realities of the world took on new signifying capacities for the life of faith. So Damascus suggested that we needed to understand the precise nature of veneration, how it *may* lead to idolatry, and how it *does* lead to imitation or (using more contemporary language) mimicry.

Damascus argued that the life of God in flesh clarified for us our need for images that guide us away from death and toward life with God. Damascus recognized that there were artistic currents all around us; the only real question was concerning their *redirection*. Because God had become flesh, God could be imaged through the body of the Son. God could be drawn and painted; and, equally important, those women and men who were with God, who knew God, who loved and served God could be imaged as well. They could be drawn, pictured, painted, and offered up to the faithful as images to help guide their prayers, their hopes, their dreams, their longings, and their concerns. In short, bodies offered up in artistic display, in impressive exercise of spiritual power, or in commanding control of their souls, especially in times of great temptation and suffering, are poised to guide not only our imaginations but also our lives.

Veneration, however, was delicate, complex, and dangerous work because it involved educating all the senses in a particular direction that was nothing short of establishing the foundations of lifelong devotion and Christian formation. The ever-present reality of artistic currents and our need for images is precisely why the rise of the racial aesthetic has fundamentally emerged as *a secular process of veneration in the West.* This process of veneration wove itself deeply into the political, social, and ecclesial unconsciousness of the West. I suggest that we think of this process of veneration in three gestures that constitute this regime: (1) imitation, (2) reflection, and (3) evaluation. Fundamentally, this path of racial veneration is where particular bodies become the sites for imagining the universal and where only particular bodies expose the *maturity to dance in the universal*. Friedrich Schleiermacher, the great German theologian, following the work of Immanuel Kant, argued that it is precisely in a people's ability to grasp the universal (as the Europeans had grasped it) beyond the mundane realities of the particular that we can see and gauge their cultural maturity and their ability to govern themselves.[20]

IMITATION

This path of veneration opens inevitably toward imitation. If, in fact, the early colonial European had seen God, then those who wished to see God must look to the European. Imitation begins fundamentally as a process of looking. The work of racial mimicry that emerges out of this new reality of veneration is not simply a matter of copying something or someone. The process of racial imitation or mimicry enfolds peoples in unrelenting patterns of comparison bound to visions of originals and copies. Imitation in this regard is a power that not only continuously generates white body exemplars of beauty, goodness, and truth but also carries forward housing capacities—patterns of thinking and ways of being—within which peoples may judge their own bodies, manners, and moods. These housing capacities mean that many people(s) have been and continue to be invited to imagine their worlds through white bodies often bound to Western European/Anglo processes of canonizations. Whether something should or should not be canonized is irrelevant to this analysis. What is crucial here is the way these canonization processes operate within and between the arts *and* forms of commerce. Imitation means peoples all over the world have entered into a powerful accomplishment—*they have yielded to the constant work of approximation.*

The joining of worlds—the native particular to the white universal— did not mean the loss of indigenous agency or the denial of people's ability to determine their lives, express themselves, and make choices; it did mean that all peoples influenced by colonialist legacies were bequeathed the struggle with or against white approximation. Even as native peoples mixed and matched early European cultural realities with their own, creating the cultural mestizo, and even as settler cultures changed through encounters with indigenes, the arch of the universal bent toward whiteness as creative powers were by choice and force marshaled toward the flourishing and supremacy of white bodies. The inertia of that force created imagistic echoes of what a flourishing life looks like. The accomplishment is the iconic position that has been established around white bodies that allows them generative centrality.

Imagine a crowded bus in a major city—Mexico City, Accra, Los Angeles, Mumbai, New York, Chicago—a bus filled with a wide variety of people. There hovering above every head is a Tommy Hilfiger advertisement with several models dressed in the company's latest creations.[21] At the heart of that picture are white bodies, a white man and/or a white woman, easily identified as of European descent. Around them are others appropriate to the different cultural contexts. Although these others are not white, they look like the centered white subjects, having the same facial features, the same body shapes, similar poses and postures toward the world, and often shades of skin very close to the models at the center of the image. My concern in this instance is not with the justice of the advertisement, or the power of the company, but with *the currency of approximation that flows through the image.* The point of imitation here is not that everyone looking at the advertisement wants to become the model. The point that flows from the center of the advertisement out to us is surrender. We are invited to read the image like Scripture, a secular *lectio divina* through which we meditate without giving thought to it, without seeking to understand it, but to allow it to bring its multiple meanings to us. Those meanings flow around the objects for consumption suggested by the advertisement. Yet, as is generally understood, these images are more suggesting (fantasizing) ways of life than they are offering commodities. The expectation is that we surrender our fantasy work to the image. This surrender is not a complete one but one that launches and directs fantasy, building from the beginning of the image. We can imagine ourselves wearing some or all of their clothing and looking good to ourselves and to others. Our fantasies can ride on the bodies of these models. The models however are not simply glorified clothes hangers. They become the bearers of possibility for us, of change, of improvement, of uplift, of development, of sheer newness in our looking and our gazing. They become postures with salvific aim.

REFLECTION

The first gesture of veneration is therefore not a simple act of copying. Mimicry opens up agency and a sense of self constituted in the work of approximation. We are invited to imagine our own possibilities for flourishing through gazing at white bodies. It is less a matter of being like the model than of allowing the model to be the site and/or sound of our self-fulfillment. Here, the term "model" refers to far more than the living mannequins of magazines; it refers to an entire universe of archetypes that populate stage, screen, videogame, and Internet and that echo back to the artistic white supremacy of the past. The past speaks to the present and guides the future so that yearly we are presented with the spectacles of aesthetic validation that reward the best performances, which unrelentingly mirror back to us the white universal. These racial images in media help us find ourselves. But who exactly are we—we who are in the work of being found, who are captured in the diligent work of approximation through what we consume?

A cultural and racial indeterminacy emerged with the visibility of the white image presented for approximation. That visibility has bequeathed to untold generations of peoples the curse of authenticity. It is only with the rise of whiteness that peoples the world over were forced to entertain a horrible question: What does it mean to be culturally and racially authentic? This question is not primarily one of alliance with one's people or allegiance to the master narratives of one's folk. This was a question born out of the creation of "the races of men," as Kant and Herder put it, in which each people performed their cultural and racial distinctiveness.[22]

This is a question of the essential racial being. Even if racial essentialism has been thoroughly denounced in philosophy, theology, and cultural studies, the racial essentialist impulse has not gotten the memo of its demise. On the one hand, that impulse has insinuated itself deeper inside its historical partner—culture. On the other hand, that impulse shows itself to be quite powerful in the visual ecologies of Western societies.[23] Much of what had been conceptualized with the idea of race was refined and embedded in ideas of culture and cultural difference.[24] Culture continues to be a notoriously tangled constellation of ideas that fuel as much confusion as clarity and often leave people groping in a darkness self-imposed by looking for what should not have to be found. This is because they are yet to understand that they are who they are without need of definition. Yet the need to define ourselves culturally (and racially) has been thrust on us by a white universal that permeates our bodies with the desire for definition.

This desire for definition makes intelligible a stubborn habit of visual life in the West that drives us to clarify the racial status of one another. *One of the early pedagogical lessons we learn is how to read racial being.* We learn to determine as quickly as possible the status of those we encounter. Are they black, white, Hispanic, Latin, biracial, Asian, mixed, or mutt? And what is the status of their racial/cultural self-knowledge? How do they carry their racial being, strongly or softly, clearly or in a confused manner? Shaming the desire for definition is not the point; rather, it is grasping how it is vivified by the iconic energy of white visibility. That energy has, in effect, turned us into racial iconographers. Cultural authenticity is the curse given to generations to find, name, and enact a fabrication while entering into the painful life-draining dance of naming the inauthentic over against the authentic.

I am not denying cultural difference, different narratives of peoples, or different ways of life, but that difference is not honored through the optics of authenticity and practices of cultural cleansing. Indeed, the ways of all peoples continue to be subject to subversion as they are drawn into processes of fragmentation and commodification, so that difference is reduced to consumable objects and made to circulate throughout the reigning aesthetic order. In this way, the search for cultural authenticity is another symptom of the hijacking and subverting of ancient practices of becoming now set afloat on a sea of indeterminacy flowing out of the ongoing experiences of unabated white visibility.

EVALUATION

The legacy of veneration born of the racial aesthetic also gave rise to a world of evaluation. Alone and staring into a mirror, we are never alone. There with us, moving all around us, are the voices of the many that have helped shape our body image. There at the mirror, the storytellers in our lives exert their true conjuring power in the ways we see our bodies and our lives. The world of racial evaluation not only lives at the mirror but also permeates every aspect of our lives. The point is not that all peoples see racially alike. The point is that all people can see or can easily be taught to see racially. Even in places where race is not spoken about, at least in the open, many live within what Magnus Mörner called a pigmentocracy.[25] Indeed, in many postcolonial sites—from parts of Africa to Latin America to Australia to the United States and beyond—people live under the social and emotional pigmentocracy of white preference.[26] What evaluation means in these contexts is not only a preference for but also a determiner of the possibilities of personhood. What might be the reach of my life, the range of its cultural expansion, and the angles of its possible transformation? These kinds of questions are thwarted, even killed, by racial caste thinking.

Evaluation here means limitation of what one might become and of what one is. Racial consciousness from its beginnings denies the permeability of existence and the relationality of being itself and instead enacts racial narratives where there is no authentic story. Deeply connected to this limitation of life vision is the way all forms of educational evaluation have been baptized into the world of racial evaluation. If white bodies have been positioned as pedagogue for visions of the true, the good, the beautiful, the intelligent, and the powerful, then educators, East and West, have not yet been able to wrestle this pedagogue to the ground and seize control of the apparatuses—that is, the dream maker's tools—that might open up a different world of evaluation.

The reason for this inability is our failure to analyze fully the deep connection between the visual and our evaluations of intelligence. By evaluation here I am not focused on the cancerous obsession with testing that pervades Western educational systems. Instead, I have in view the wider ecology of assessment that is guided by racially conditioned perceptions and has been encoded in learned bodily practices. From the beginnings of the colonial moment, intelligence was narrated racially. Aspects of this ecology can be seen in David Hume's infamous footnote, which has been much analyzed.[27] However, one aspect of his statement continues to escape significant reflection—that is, the visual and racial register of intelligence he connotes:

> I am apt to suspect the negroes and in general all other species of men (for there are four or five different kinds) to be naturally inferior to the white. There never was *a civilized nation of any other complexion than white*, nor even any individual eminent either in action or speculation. No ingenious manufactures amongst them, no arts, no sciences. On the other hand, the most rude and barbarous of the whites, such as the ancient Germans, the present Tartars, have still something eminent about them, in their valour, form of government, or some other particular. Such a uniform and constant difference could not happen in so many countries and ages, if nature had not made an original distinction between these breeds of men.[28]

The European vision that organized the world according to races then connected levels of intelligence to physical characteristics. This visually marked intelligence existed within the development of those sciences that took humanity and its environment as objects of study. Even when scientific theories about humanity changed, corrected themselves as it were, this deep connection between the visual and signs of intelligence merged with the collective imagination of the Western world—in effect, skin color and other characteristics of racially encoded intelligence.[29] In this schema, the appearance of races different from the so-called white race activated a scale of intelligence, with the white race as the interpreter of that scale.

Such ways of thinking, if openly articulated now, would be seen by many people as heretical, yet we are far from overcoming the energy of this visual register to shape social imagination. The issue here is *the image of the educated*, and that image in the West remains bound to its colonialist legacies. What does it mean to be educated? What do the educated look like? The descendants of slaves and the colonized were left with the incredibly difficult task of telling their children what education means, or should mean, for them. Because education in the Western world most often pivoted around white identity, the image of intelligence in the West is built upon a history of dominance, oppression, and suppression of other images. These issues of identity are also bound up in the performances of class distinctions. However, the deeper dilemma is the identity *imagined* by education. Most often Western education imagines cultural invisibility *as an educated person*. The only visible identity has been a white identity; so *a visible nonwhite educated person is still an imagined exception*. That exception may, among other reasons, be attributed to the peculiarity of an individual or to an ethnic trait of a people.[30]

The reality of an image of an educated person is a separate matter from the agreed upon utility and value of education. The issue here is not whether, or to what extent, or even the manner in which, progeny of enslaved or colonized peoples valued (Western) education. The *image of the educated* that flows through the collective imagination of the West, propelled by its aesthetic regime, joins the colonial moment to the present moment. It fantasizes for us and with us the omniscience of white bodies to know, understand, and create all things new. Even a cursory review of the science-fiction representations of the future in movies, television shows, and popular animation reveal the constancy of this imagined omniscience. So, on the one hand, our fantasy life is plagued with the *necessity of imagining racial exception* inside the process of being educated; on the other hand, we are drawn into the elusive search for the comfort of our basic inquisitive existence, which is the precondition for intellectual confidence. That comfort is continuously drained by the onslaught of images that pile onto white bodies all narratives of knowing and knowledge accumulation.

In essence, processes of accumulation animate the white image of the educated. Historically, knowledge accumulation has been the flip side of the accumulation of resources, land, animals, goods, and services. We have inherited images that echo these processes such that we have *naturalized fantasies of accumulation bound to whiteness.* This ongoing naturalization tutors our perceptions of the right order of leadership bound to knowledge, so that for many people, a *naturally ordered* world seems commensurate with a plethora of white authority figures that fully inhabit not only our real world but also our fantasies of the present and the future world. In effect, processes of accumulation circulating around white bodies constitute the conceptual ground for the actual natural theology being performed through our racialized image of the educated in the West. The racial aesthetic haunts our world of evaluation both personally and socially, and we are yet to grasp the deep psychic struggles caused by the phantasmagoria of whiteness within our ecology of assessment. Until we turn and face the racial simulacra (likeness or semblance) of education's image—that is, the false reality that draws strength from and then successfully supplants the authentic reality of education's aim—the emancipatory possibilities of Western education will always be compromised in the corridors of its haunted racial house.

In response to my analysis of these gestures of veneration, it could be argued that the current aesthetic regime will fade in time with a rising tide of multicultural realities in societies and the global ethnic transformation of the professional classes; however, those kinds of arguments, while appealingly hopeful, tend to miss the point of the racial aesthetic in its universalizing character. The iconic reality of this regime means that it organizes fantasy life and draws new generations of peoples, including those of European descent, to traditionalize thinking about the archetypes of truth, goodness, beauty, intelligence, nobility, and so forth. This has been the painful reality of countless multicultural societies wherein a pigmentocracy yet holds and color caste systems permeate economies of beauty, ecologies of assessment, and the dreamscapes of people.[31] What is needed is an intervention that challenges the gestures of racial veneration that are embedded in the Western world.

The way forward for us begins exactly in the opening up of a different world. And here I return to John of Damascus. Damascus argued that the incarnation in which the Son of God fully assumed material form established for us a powerful new vision of the world. Following the logic of the Cappadocians and Irenaeus before them, Damascus understands the divine embrace of creaturely existence witnessed in the incarnation to magnify the sheer goodness of creation. The world is suitable for divine presence and moreover the site for eternal communion with the triune God. This affirmation challenges the tragic religious habit of separating life between the worship of God and the artistic currents of creation. The prohibition against idolatry is aimed not at creation's artistic currents but at the misdirection of these currents away from God and toward the creature. As Damascus famously stated:

> I do not venerate the creation instead of the Creator, but I venerate the Creator, created for my sake, who came down to his creation without being lowered or weakened, that he might glorify my nature and bring about communion with the divine nature.[32]

This statement reflects the fundamental theological justification for icons, for images that may be brought into the inner life of faith. This also shows us what it means to understand the creation as iconic. The creation is meant for communion with God; God wills to reach out to us, embrace us in unrelenting love and care in and through the material. The key here is the direction of movement. God is reaching out to us, looking (as it were) at us in desire of us through the icon. This is the redirecting of the currents of the artistic. Artistic currents in this regard should be understood more generally as the performativity of life itself. The Son of God, by inhabiting matter, extended God's own expressive impulse into creaturely life, drawing us toward overflowing iconographic gestures. These iconographic gestures are found not only in our practices of worship and praise of God but also in all forms of artistic display, not only in arts but also in all our labor, not only in our work but also in our displays of love and care for one another and all the creation, not only in our care of the creation but also in our acts of discipleship that challenge prevailing regimes of oppression. Damascus notes again:

> I do not venerate matter, I venerate the fashioner of matter, who became matter for my sake and accepted to dwell in matter and through matter worked my salvation, and I will not cease from reverencing matter, through which my salvation was worked. I do not reverence it as God. . . . I reverence the rest of matter and hold in respect that through which my salvation came, because it is filled with divine energy and grace.[33]

Idolatry is a confusion built on an absence. Simply put, idols are objects that coordinate ways of life oriented away from the triune God revealed in Jesus Christ. An object is an idol not by its appearance but by its orientation. Idols are constituted not by the particularities of their materiality but by their trajectories, which are aimed at prescribing the universal. Icons counter idols, Damascus suggested, not through concealing matter but through bringing it to express the divine life. This means that the women and men who knew and know God give witness to that God just as artistic renditions of these women and men (i.e., saints) also give witness. When we rehearse God's mighty acts in artistic display, we not only echo those mighty acts but also participate in the action of God toward us now.

We need icons and the artistic to draw us toward life and away from death and to nurture our souls through communion with God. Damascus sees the artistic as participating in redemption:

> I come into the common surgery of the soul, the church; the luster of the painting draws me to vision and delights my sight like a meadow and imperceptibly introduces my soul to the glory of God. I have seen the perseverance of the martyr . . . and as if by fire I am eagerly kindled to zeal, and falling down I venerate God through the martyr and I receive salvation.[34]

So there is an abiding connection between artistic renderings and the movement of God incarnate toward us through the Holy Spirit. To take an iconoclastic position against the artistic denies this salvific movement. The crucial matter that emerges in Damascus' anti-iconoclasm is how gestures of veneration might be turned toward life. Here, drawing from his meditation, we could suggest three points of theological intervention into our current situation.

First, churches need to develop an *artistic* ecclesiology. We must deepen our sense of common church life not simply as containing artistic expression but also as constituting artistic expression. The church is the place of artists. We together are called to help people grasp their embeddedness both in the artistic currents of creaturely existence and through the Holy Spirit in the expressive impulse of God. This means that creativity is our deepest life calling, our truth vocation. Rather than killing or seeking to domesticate the artistic currents in us, churches should enter into the revolutionary power of creativity as its birthright. This is not an exclusive birthright but the inheritance of leading the creation in the praise of God through the material realities of existence.

Creativity, in this regard, is a much wider reality than a capacity deployed in artistic expression. Rather, it is a fundamental way of life that is open to the expressive impulse of the Spirit of God. This is what it means to be iconic. We are open to God speaking to us through the material, especially the artistic, and in turn we are open to being transformed by, and transforming agents of, material realities to reflect the glory of God found in the life of Jesus. Here agency is exposed exactly in the places where artistic currents are being turned toward death contorted through the racial aesthetic. Here we may take hold of what James Scott designates as one of the arts of resistance used by subjugated peoples to take the given objects of desire and/or processes of control and turn their trajectories against themselves.[35] Anne A. Cheng, reflecting on Scarry's *On Beauty*, speculates on the possibilities for women of color to make productive use of economies of beauty:

> Beauty for the woman of color must be seen as a sign of the possibilities and impossibilities of occupying a certain subject position. For the woman of color looking at herself, beauty as a process of identification registers her relationship to the education of beauty and to her history of negotiating that education—a negotiation of distances rather than an act only of internalization or compliance. Beauty as a question, as much as it may exclude her, also grants her access to the intensities of its demands and its possibilities.[36]

Cheng has captured the sight of beauty as a technology of the self that awaits our deep psychical acceptance and our willingness to make ourselves into *workers for beauty*—that is, to follow its regimes of edification. Here we can see, according to Cheng, beauty "as a powerful tool for exercising racial ideology"[37] because the perception of beauty can be resisted and/or turned toward new possibilities of perceiving the beautiful. Yet the same power of agency exposed through beauty's *wish for our conversion* to beauty, a power that yields the possibilities of breaking open the racial and gendered boundaries it helped to establish, could also seduce us into the eternal search for beauty in ourselves, making our mirrors a map to nowhere and no time.

Genuinely new possibilities demand a space where beauty may be collapsed into its opposite—namely, that which is ugly. In such a space where beauty and ugly collapse into each other, they are both broken open by a life that challenges our power to define beauty or ugliness, goodness or evil, the truth or the lie, wisdom or foolishness. Jesus draws us into his life in which we are known no longer (κατὰ σάρκα) according to human standards (2 Cor 5:16) but are now caught up in the redemptive dynamic of his life where worldly optics are overturned in a light through which we are seen before we see. We are seen by God, and now we may look out onto the world through redemptive eyes. So churches hold within themselves possibilities of newness born of the new creation in Christ. We will find and magnify such new possibilities in and through church life, if and only if churches capture the sense of ecclesial space as a space that distances us from the subjugating demands of the racial aesthetic and brings us into the creative reality of God, who makes all things new and gives us the ability to envision that newness: "So if anyone is in Christ, there is a new creation: everything old has passed away; see, everything has become new!" (2 Cor 5:17).

Second, churches need to cultivate *creative critique* of the prevailing racial aesthetic. This cultivation would be part of the development of an artistic ecclesiology that recognized the importance of image and fantasy. Image and fantasy belong to the artistic currents that flow around us. We cannot, nor should we seek to, stop the flow. The questions are as follows: How do we move in these currents? How might we redirect the flow to move toward life and away from death? How might we *fruitfully question* images of the true, the good, the beautiful, the intelligent, and the noble and then dream together toward new images? Here is where churches need artists *and* need to cultivate seriously the artistic within our common life. We must dispel the false distance and boundary between the professional and the amateur in the cultivation of the artistic, realizing that we have (1) a responsibility to exegete the myriad images and sounds that flow through and around us, and (2) the freedom to play in the artistic by resisting, reformulating, redirecting, and/or simply renouncing the narratives suggested by images of sight and sound that would capture us even more deeply inside the racial aesthetic. Slowly, through thoughtful and intentional reflection, a shared aesthetic ecology should emerge in every local church that reveals a flexible, beautifully expansive, artistic sensibility rooted in the incarnate life of God. Such a sensibility shows us not only how to turn artistic expression and energy toward life but also how to draw on the boundless creative impulse of the Spirit of God to resist or redirect the operations of worldly powers toward life abundant.

This second point of intervention can happen only if people in local churches begin to talk together about what they see, feel, and experience within our ever-expanding sensory environments. If so, this movement forward suggests a third point of intervention: images and fantasy must be considered in community. Fantasy is connected to faith; therefore, fantasy is also bound up inside hope (Heb 11). Yet the question that must be answered in community concerns how fantasy might work through love. Here we are at the threshold of a lifelong struggle. The struggle is to move from fantasy that is directly tied to chaos, nothingness, and the objectification of one another within economies of exploitation to fantasy that grows out of direct encounter, reciprocity, and the realities of one flesh in

Christ. How might fantasy facilitate friendship and friendship facilitate fantasy, helping us to hope all things for one another, seek the best for one another, and dream together? When do fantasies get in the way of relationship, and when do they open us to greater depths of relationship? These questions can be answered only in community—*in the exposition of fantasy and image as a community is able.*

Many churches are not yet ready to live in the real intimacy of human life constituted by the body of Jesus. They have not yet grasped that God has become flesh and has now opened our flesh to life eternal in community. This is not to say that private space is unreal space. Rather, it might be better to think of privacy temporally rather than spatially, as that which exists in a "holding station" until it will be expressed in conversation, testimony, prayer, or gestures of love, concern, and service. The power of the racial aesthetic could be overcome exactly in ecclesial spaces where communal exposition of fantasy and image may yield the creation and promotion of an alternative aesthetic for Christian common life. That alternative aesthetic born of the Holy Spirit brings peoples together in shared desire, appreciation, and celebration of one another. Such an alternative aesthetic opens us to a centrally biblical hope echoed in 1 John that says to us that it does not yet appear what we will be, but when the Son of God appears, we will be like him (1 John 3:2). That likeness will encompass not merely an identity but also a way of seeing that will enfold us in true sight of the divine life embracing us.

<< 13 >>

EMBODIED BLACK PRACTICAL THEOLOGY FOR THE CARIBBEAN DIASPORAN CHURCH

Delroy A. Reid-Salmon

The editors open their description of our topic—globalism, immigration, and diasporan communities—with the following questions: "How does a people living as strangers, foreigners, and immigrants identify with Abraham and Sarah, who, determined to survive, defied (the) laws (of foreign lands)? How does a parent who crossed the Caribbean Sea and the Atlantic Ocean chained in slave ships relate to Moses' mother or sister, who resisted the law of the land to save her son or brother? How does a family seeking a better life relate to Naomi and Ruth as these two lives weaved a common destiny? How does a people separated from its homeland understand the event of Pentecost and read the message of Peter to the Christians scattered throughout the Roman world?"[1] These questions suggest that the role diasporan people play in defining the nature and practice of faith communities is critical, given their centrality in the biblical accounts and the Christian story.

In the case of black Christianity, we must ask the question, what does black theology have to say to the issues of migration, diversity and difference, diaspora,[2] and the place of Caribbean people in the Black Church tradition?[3] Another related question concerns the changing character of black Christianity. There is undoubtedly a transformation taking place that suggests that black Christianity is not monolithic and that identifies a distinct character of black theology and the Black Church, respectively, as an intellectual discipline and a community of faith.

THE DOCTRINE: WHAT WE TEACH

These are the questions and concerns that Willie James Jennings and Esther E. Acolatse attempt to address in their respective essays "The Aesthetic Struggle and Ecclesial Vision" and "African Diasporan Communities and the Black Church." Making the claim that the people of the African diaspora are witnesses to horror, Jennings seeks to answer the question, why should I love my black body?[4] Identifying this horror as a racial aesthetic regime, Jennings delineates the contours, ecclesial vision, and pastoral response to this ideology of racial superiority.[5] Jennings addresses the charge that he is simply repeating the general critique of white supremacy by advancing what he calls the "redemptive mode of aesthetic" based on the work of John of Damascus in the orthodox tradition of Christianity.[6] Jennings believes this approach contributes to a Christological structure and design of the aesthetic life. He carefully writes, "A Christologically informed iconic logic draws us into new strategies for resisting and redirecting artistic currents and visual economies away from death and toward life."[7]

This remark sets the stage for Jennings to delineate some distorted aspects of white hegemony—namely, nobility, beauty, and intelligence. Disarming this regime, Jennings engages in a broad trajectory of anti-iconoclasm predicated on the fact that the incarnation of Jesus Christ leads us to regard the corporeal reality with new significance. Jennings summarizes this view as follows: "Bodies offered up in artistic display, in impressive exercise of spiritual power, or in commanding control of their souls, especially in times of great temptation and suffering, are poised to guide not only our imaginations but also our lives."[8] Jennings is arguing that this new understanding of the human body and physical reality leads to the notion of veneration, which he describes as constituted by three factors: imitation, reflection, and evaluation.[9] He carefully shows that these factors are Western values—or as theologian Kelly Brown Douglas calls it, "Platonized Christianity"[10]—that have become the standard or norm for the ideal and good life.

Regarding the assertion that multiculturalism will lead to the inevitable decline of this Western hegemonic power,[11] Jennings argues that such claims fail to take into account the universal character of racial aesthetics.[12] The solution he proposes rests in ecclesial perspectives and pastoral engagement mediated through an understanding of the church as a work of art and in a hermeneutic of creative self-criticism, with these practices being done communally. Ultimately, this approach will lead to self-understanding and to a way of life that is both inclusive and holistically predicated on the incarnation.[13]

In claiming that the incarnation is the basis for loving one's self, Jennings seems to have overlooked the creation story, which affirms the goodness of human beings. According to the creation account, human beings are essentially good. This point is not about the perfection of persons or the denial of the human capacity and proclivity to do evil but rather about the recognition that God made humans to be good and thus are God's good creation (Gen 1:27–2:3). This further attests to the New Testament writings that teach the church is God's new creation and masterpiece (Eph 2:1-10). Therefore, the basis for loving the body lies rather in moving beyond a critique of the "racial aesthetic regime" to embrace a new way of life that suggests an alternative to the normative view of the black being. Should the Black Church contextualize the meaning of the incarnation? Doing so using various principles that may not change the situation but only lead to reliance on self-help techniques ignores the possibility of such a countercultural way of life. The important thing to know is that the Black Church has its own history and self-understanding,[14] its own values and ethics,[15] and, for the purpose of this essay, its own practical theology.[16]

Developing values and interpreting practices that inform and shape communal life is no small matter. In this regard, Jennings helps to identify and clarify practices that can sustain theology as a way of life. One wonders, nevertheless, what difference it would make had he situated pastoral intervention in the context of Black Church traditions and black theology. By rooting his pastoral intervention in the work of John of Damascus, Jennings is relocating the basis of his hermeneutical framework to premodern Christian sources. This approach represents a major shift in the way black theology is being done,[17] with rather different sources. Whereas Jennings' sources are premodern and Christian, traditional sources of black theology are inclusive and interdisciplinary. The former looks to external sources, while the latter looks to internal sources.[18] Both types of black theology are attempting to do the same thing—that is, to address white hegemony—but are using different sources to do so. Jennings, for example, states:

> What Damascus helps us to grasp is the architecture of a visual and more generally artistic life set within a Christological and redemptive frame. He thereby opens up the possibilities of transforming visual economies, once imagined as idolatrous and hopelessly turned toward

death, into spaces of the iconic—that is, artistic spaces where we might participate in the divine life that has come to us in Jesus of Nazareth.[19]

This remark can be understood as a form of apologetics for premodern Christian resources for black theological discourse. At the same time, this effect can be achieved using any other resource from any historical period. Equally important, the Black Church and black theology—and, for that matter, a black practical theology—need to "drink from their own well" in doing their work.[20]

Above all, one could further ask, by not "drinking from his own well," has Jennings deprived the people of their own kind of historical, contextual, and theological resources given the challenges he is seeking to address? Using black historical, contextual, and theological resources would give black church practice historical significance and give examples of how the Black Church and black theology have addressed similar instances. It would also call attention to the reasons for the intervention and more importantly to the relationship between the entire black diasporan Church and black theology. Jennings certainly provides tools for such interventions but does not construct a practical theological framework for utilizing them. In fact, the tools for pastoral intervention—artistic ecclesiology, creative self-critique, and communal conversation—are, by themselves, grossly inadequate for confronting systemic racism (white hegemony) without a black diasporan-centered intellectual framework rooted in its own culture, history, and experience.[21] Such a framework would not only facilitate going back into the past but also help us to explore the experiences that have influenced our present life and thereby to construct an alternative approach of understanding what it means to be human.[22] As such, this intellectual framework enables black theology to deconstruct, critique, and construct. It deconstructs by identifying existential conditions and by unmasking and disarming hegemonic powers. It critiques by pointing out societal sins—injustices—and by calling attention to the underlying and prevailing systemic and structural evils that parade as normative operations for society. Above all, it constructs a vision of life-affirming blackness by offering an alternative way of living and interpreting life from a diasporan perspective in the process of liberation from all forms of oppression,[23] which entails history, values, and accepting its place in church and society.

In reality, using a diasporan-centered intellectual framework helps us to understand and appreciate self, history, and culture as well as to interpret the causes of oppression and the meaning of liberation. Marcus

Garvey's perennial challenge to Africans and the diaspora as put to music in Bob Marley's *Redemption Song*—"emancipate ourselves from mental slavery [as] none but ourselves can free our minds"[24]—eloquently and artistically describes this intellectual framework and contextual hermeneutic. Yet, the resulting challenge lies not just in applying these suggested principles as artistic, ecclesial, and pastoral practices but more appropriately in practicing them.

THE PRACTICE: WHAT WE DO

Esther Acolatse, in writing about African diasporan Christianity, calls attention to the above-mentioned perspective. She begins by making the important observation that African Americans and Africans in America practice their faith as two separate communities. To overcome this unfortunate reality, she calls for a theology of pastoral care applied through what she defines as "'care-full' hospitality."[25] She argues that practicing faith is central to, even definitive of, both communities. For Acolatse, ethnicity and the legacy of slavery play major roles in creating this divide, which leads to churches born out of the need for belonging.[26] Consequently, many African churches in America remain unknown to African American churches.

Acolatse contends that a practical theology that addresses the issues of intrablack ethnic and cultural diversity and the global, social, and political challenges of the black diaspora is an authentic expression of hospitality.[27] In this regard, she proposes a bilingual methodology as the means of practicing theology in the form of hospitality. She argues that this methodology would require knowledge and expertise in both theology and psychology for the good of the church.[28] Rightly acknowledging the limitations of this approach, she hastens to offer theological language as primal speech.[29] Overall, Acolatse believes that theological language holds great value as a means of pastoral care for a diversity of people, both nationally and globally.[30]

The correct way of doing theology is not in isolation and separation from other disciplines and practices. Acolatse exemplifies this point in her interdisciplinary approach that wrestles with the multiple grammars of psychology and theology. She shows us that complex negotiations operate between these grammars and their purposes. Even as she makes this distinction more broadly to consider bilingualism between our primary languages, however, I find that a theological method is missing, which could be problematic for the church in that it could uncritically lead the church down nontheological paths.

Acolatse begins with addressing the issues of cultural and religious diversity and ends with discussing pastoral care within the diasporan community, focusing primarily on the African immigrant and African American communities. I, in turn, would like to ask to what extent the nature of pastoral care can address the relationship between these two communities and their individual quests for meaning. Building on the notion of bilingualism, Acolatse does offer an interdisciplinary methodology for her version of black practical theology. The strength of this methodology lies in its excellent approach to pastoral care and counseling, but I am not sure how applicable it is to the black diasporan community. I am interested in learning more about whose psychology and theology Acolatse employs. As she notes, if the material or theories from these disciplines do not stem from the diasporan community, then she runs the risk of imposing external and alien thought on the community. Such an imposition would only continue the cultural and intellectual imperialism that the black community resists.

Acolatse proposes making the gospel the new contextual clothing in what she defines as primal speech. This primal speech, she contends, is a quest for meaning and can be likened to a new language wherein Christians think, speak and translate theologically all ideas.[31] Acolatse offers this approach to bridge the gap between cultures and pastoral care. I wonder, though, how this bridge functions in the diasporan context. Helpfully, she calls attention to what such an approach can accomplish in breaking down barriers and engendering relationships among a people of diverse social, cultural, and religious differences.[32] It is therefore reasonable to conclude that while Acolatse is to be commended for delineating the benefits of her bilingual methodology,[33] the process of applying the methodology remains in question.

Acolatse understands that while hospitality is a significant answer, it is a very difficult theological practice.[34] It is significant because it is central to the Christian faith; and it is difficult because it involves taking risks and demands critical reflection. Acolatse, however, may not go far enough to advance the reflective application of this practice. She limits its application to interpersonal/cultural/religious relationships and does not include social, systemic, structural, and public policies.[35] This is unfortunate because the issue of hospitality goes beyond hospitality as merely a practice to offering great possibilities for theological discourse. Moreover, hospitality cannot be divorced from other theological practices, such as justice in particular. Hospitality should seek justice while preventing the reinstituting of systemic and structural injustice within the society.

What, then, does this imply? It implies that black practical theology offers more than hospitality in terms of fostering relationships for mutual existence. If we are to move beyond this single expression of hospitality, it is crucial for Continental Africans and the African diaspora to initiate a conversation on the subject of the Middle Passage by attending to the role Continental Africans played in the slave trade. The Middle Passage, as it is commonly understood, is the almost four-hundred-year practice of "that part of the slave trade that brought the brutally captured and inhumanely treated Africans from West Africa to North America, South America, and the Caribbean."[36] In light of this tragic history and traumatic experience, to practice "'care-full' hospitality," as Acolatse calls it, requires a commitment to care and generosity but also an analysis of the causes of the circumstances that contribute to such needs and a plan of action to address their legacies and thereby ensure that these conditions and practices do not reoccur or continue in any form today. For this analysis to happen, it calls for the honest acknowledgment that a predominant factor in the divide between Continental Africans and the African diaspora has roots in the Middle Passage.[37] Unquestionably, then, the authenticity and fruitfulness of hospitality depends on our willingness to address this shameful period and the painful experiences embedded in the fabric of human history in general and black history in particular.

Given the above concerns, it should be obvious that no one study can adequately address the issues and conditions of any person or community. Nonetheless, in reading Acolatse's essay, I arrive at a serious question regarding the nature of black diaspora Christianity.[38] Acolatse argues that Africans living in the United States and African Americans are the predominant groups of people who constitute the black diaspora.[39] And yet, were the theology she proposes to address only these two different black people groups, it would be myopic and insular. It would be worthwhile to consider, for illustrative purposes, expanding our conceptualization of black practical theology. The discussion to follow here, therefore, adopts a descriptive pattern that defines and delineates a strategy for applying the doctrinal and practical components of black practical theology to historical realities.

THE STRATEGY: WHAT WE BECOME

Regarding the doctrinal components of black practical theology, Jennings provides a helpful attempt to address some concerns of people in the black diaspora. He shows theology becoming aware of its ecclesial responsibility. It would be interesting, however, to learn what Jennings has to say about the Church's theological responsibility to ask questions and seek answers. This perspective suggests that theology is not merely a matter of what the church teaches but a matter of what the church does. As such, the church embodies theology.

The idea of an embodying theology connotes that faith or doctrine in action is a way of life. Faith and doctrines are to be lived. They shape practice, and through this practice a deeper and greater understanding about the doctrine is obtained. The idea of an embodied theology also addresses the issues of disconnection, or more appropriately demonstrates the relationship, between doctrine and practice. Additionally, an embodied theology takes the position that doctrine is not a subset of practices that would make beliefs merely functional. Rather, the term "embodied theology" suggests inanimate objects coming alive. Doctrines by themselves have no life and form as living reality and no means of coming alive. Practices are the tools and the clothing of doctrines, their means of becoming reality or putting on "flesh."

Ethicist Katie Cannon brilliantly illustrates this perspective in her important essay "Homecoming in the Hinterland."[40] Using a case-study approach wherein the ministry practices of preaching and teaching translate social and practical acts in witness to divine purposes in history, Cannon argues that "authentic disciples of Jesus Christ demonstrate by application in the physical world the spiritual values to which we adhere. The emphasis is not on doctrinal purity"[41] but on the embodying of theology. In his *Systematic Theology, Volume 1: Ethics*, American Baptist theologian James Wm. McClendon Jr. recognizes and describes what constitutes an embodied faith, which the church in black traditions symbolizes. He proposes a perspective he calls "embodied self, part of creation, organic and natural."[42]

McClendon's definition of embodied faith is helpful because it deals with the natural order; in this regard, embodiment is not spiritualized and dichotomized as sacred, on the one hand, and secular, on the other. Also, this definition locates embodiment in the context of its adherents as it relates to diasporan experience, especially in dealing with the complex task of discerning the theological dimension and meaning of life.

Katie Cannon illustrates these perspectives through the humanitarian work of a Christian medical doctor, arguing that God raises up fellow human beings to embody faith.[43] In a vivid description of this claim, she expresses: "Christians should constantly minister to others as Christ has done. True believers should imitate Christ in concrete expressions that alleviate unjust conditions."[44]

Through this understanding of the church, Cannon insists that if the Christian faith is to be taken seriously, then it must go against the grain of the dominant culture and resist the perspectives, values, and practices that are inconsistent with the gospel of Jesus Christ. McClendon states this perspective powerfully: "True Christianity is never less than embodied religion, a religion of the body, in all its relations, all its presence to God and brother and sister and neighbor, all its world involvement, all its vulnerability to a cross."[45] In this pastoral liberationist view, theology is understood in terms of the role it plays in the life of the oppressed community of faith. It rejects interpretations that deny freedom and do not seek to liberate the oppressed, and it works to dismantle oppressive systems, ideologies, and structures.[46]

Building on the above claims, Acolatse's essay on the practical aspect of black practical theology offers a more revealing account of embodied theology. Again, I wonder what Acolatse's notion of hospitality would be like if she were to include a theological analysis of the cause of migration and the black diaspora? Of course, this approach would need to take into account the fact that the first Africans who came to the Western world brought their religions with them, which enabled them to deal with their indescribable experiences of enslavement.[47]

Notwithstanding this observation, Acolatse's concern deals with the nature and role of black practical theology in the black diaspora. With hospitality as the central factor of black practical theology, what immediately comes to mind is the Emmaus Road story (Luke 24:13-35). In this account, hospitality is the indication of an embodied theology. The story demonstrates the value of strangers, the importance of embracing others, and the opportunity to encounter God to embody God's liberating purpose in the reality of daily living. These factors raise the question of what Acolatse's perspective of black practical theology might look like had she considered other diasporan communities such as those in the Caribbean.

In his study on the Caribbean diasporan church's ministry to non–United States citizens or legal residents, Russell McLeod provides an excellent example of an embodied theology. McLeod advances the view that the church is called to be a community of redemption, care, and compassion. As such, the church has a moral and theological basis to offer services to all persons, including all categories of immigrants.[48] Although it may be contrary to the law for some of these people to be living in the country, it would not be theologically wrong for the church to offer ministry to them. In fact, it would be sinful for the church not to serve these people by providing the resources they need (Mic 6:8; Matt 25:31-46; Jas 1:27; 1 John 3:17-18). The church is accountable to a higher authority (Acts 5:29-32). McLeod illustrates his view through the use of two different approaches, the redemptive and the caring, to doing ministry.

The redemptive approach is exemplified by the Old Testament story of Ruth (Ruth 1–4). The caring approach is illustrated by the New Testament story of the Good Samaritan (Luke 10:25-37). For McLeod the story of Ruth highlights the life of an immigrant or diasporan person and commu-nity and how society should treat such persons.[49] The immigrant's life res-onates with Ruth in many ways. The areas of resonance include the search for a better life, migration, risk taking, identity, hybridity, assimilation, hardships, and resistance, which are some of the characteristic factors of life for diasporan people.[50]

McLeod demonstrates his approach to the church's ministry as "care and compassion" with the story of the Good Samaritan. This account is paradigmatic of the diasporan life in terms of the victim's loss of identity and the nature of care a person should receive as a result of the sufferings experienced. As McLeod states, "The story yields interesting factors that help in understanding what [*immigrants*] aliens deal with in the pursuit of economic betterment."[51] In utilizing these factors, McLeod reminds us of the victims of poverty, objects of unjust public policies and programs, and the actions that strip them of their identities.[52] These persons, McLeod writes, "have found themselves to be victims, exploited, cheated, stolen from and are left wounded and unable to defend or protect themselves."[53]

As it stands, this case-study approach does not provide a blue print for an embodied theology, as it does not interrogate and treat diasporan peo-ple's experiences as text. However, it nevertheless underscores the biblical witnesses' account of diasporan life. Diasporan existence forces theology to grapple with the realities of life and thereby ensures that the desires and aspirations of those on the margins of society take precedence and are given priority over the interest of the dominant society and a system of structural oppression (Ps 137:1-9; Heb 11:8-10; 1 Pet 1:1). What this the-ology further suggests is that the theology of pastoral care through the practice of hospitality, as Acolatse argues, challenges the churches of the black diaspora to be more intentional in creating bridges between the various black churches and communities and in reflecting a way of life that seeks to embody faith. People who seek to build a community of faith counter to the existing social order know that the purpose of such building is to embody what they believe about God, humanity, and themselves.

Drawing on the insights of Jorgen Lisser, Jack Nelson-Pallmeyer, in his *The Politics of Compassion*, comments on American Christians embodying the compassion of Jesus in a way that can easily relate to Christians in the black diaspora. Nelson-Pallmeyer calls for a lifestyle "as an act of faith . . . solidarity . . . sharing . . . celebration . . . [and] provocation leading to dialogue with others about alienation, social injustice and advocacy of legislated changes in present patterns of production and consumption in the direction of a new international economic order."[54] By engaging in these acts, the diasporan church will become more aware of what is central to black practical theology—that is, the in-depth exploration of what it means to embody the contents of the faith. Moreover, these acts express the prophetic character and dimension of black practical theology. At the same time, such exploration avoids the shallow and insular self-understanding and practices of faith that overlook the realities and complexities of life. This kind of black practical theology seeks to break out of the insularity of so-called private religion and the limitations of a nationalistic and ethnic theology.

Above all, an embodied theology is an indication or sign of the church as the conscience of society and evidence of its moral charter. It attests to the biblical admonition to be "the salt of the earth and light of the world" (Matt 5:13-14; Jas 2:26-27). In short, the church lives in the faith it confesses and the works that its faith requires. As Katie Cannon argues, these beliefs and practices should be "life affirming moral acts."[55] At a more profound level, the church as an embodiment of theology is a purposeful endeavor, commited to analyzing hegemonic beliefs and practices in order to reorient human thinking to embrace a worldview that subscribes to and accepts practices that contribute to human well-being.[56]

At the heart of a black practical theology is something that makes sense and relates to daily life predicated on the revelation of God through Jesus Christ. On this basis, an embodied theology is an antithesis to the status quo and indicates that the church does not mimic or accommodate the values of the dominant culture. More concretely, it is reasonable to conclude that an embodied theology is certainly not merely the showing, telling, or applying of theology. Instead, an embodied theology becomes the visible expression and substance of interpretation and living out of the Christian faith—namely, it becomes a practical theology. Understood in this manner, theology enables the church to be what it teaches and practices amid the ambiguities of living between at least two worlds and dealing with two homelands—residential context and national origin. Essentially, black practical theology should enable persons and communities to navigate life against the odds and live in a society that is not naturally hospitable to their becoming who they were called to be as revealed in God's liberating and redemptive purpose in Jesus Christ.

Although theology is not the absolute truth and the truth it does express is limited, it faces the challenge of cultivating the kind of practices that can sustain its embodiment throughout history. The question then becomes, what are the implications for ministry or putting doctrines into practice? A specific, concrete demonstration or embodiment of theology is expected from those called to be the visible expression of the faith. Indeed, an embodied theology is about modeling a way of life that envisions a people and society where virtuous practices—such as equality, freedom and justice, and liberation and the pursuit of liberation—are realized. The extent to which these values constitute a way of life demonstrates the extent to which we model the Christian faith or imitate God.

This understanding of the relationship between doctrine and practice advances the view that the life of faith is not merely about doing, showing, or telling, as implied in the term "practice," but about being. By embodying the Christian faith, the church is not simply a faithful agent of theology but also the theology itself. The church becomes the faith or beliefs that it practices. On this basis, it is safe to conclude that there is no separation between doctrine and practice. Theology, then, is a pursuit of not merely producing knowledge but embodying or living such knowledge. Hence, it is appropriate to argue that black practical theology is an embodied theology. It is what is believed, said, and done in response to God's call to follow Jesus Christ and to be God's people and to serve God's purpose, bearing in mind that we are looking through tinted glass (1 Cor 13:12).

VI

Health Care, HIV/AIDS, and Poverty

The pressing issues that parishioners have to deal with on a daily basis include inadequate health care for the poor, who cannot afford major health-care coverage, childcare, or even maintenance health care. The sermons preached on any given Sunday must contend with the dire balance that is needed between the economics of research, advanced technology, medical care, and pharmaceutical treatment and the profit economics driving their support. What are the political, social, theological, and ethical issues involved with the health-care and insurance industries, and are they at odds? How might black theology and practical theology help black churches to contend between these two worlds?

The impact of poverty on health and health care has been demonstrated over longstanding social conditions and pandemics as well. One of the starkest needs for care in black communities globally is HIV/AIDS. For example, while African Americans represent approximately 13 percent of the U.S. population, the Centers for Disease Control and Prevention report that this group accounts for almost half of the nation's AIDS cases. Many urban areas are experiencing an expanding HIV/AIDS crisis. For example, at the end of 2009 there were 7,156 reported cases of HIV/AIDS in the Memphis area, and African Americans accounted for 81 percent of those cases. While Latinos/as reported only 113 cases, their rate of incidence (27 per 100,000) is twice the national rate. How have black churches tackled the issues of disease, sexual practices, sexuality, and sexual orientation? How might they have further complicated these economic and class struggles in health intervention? What correctives are possible through critical engagement with black practical theology?

<< 14 >>

LIBERATING BLACK-CHURCH PRACTICAL THEOLOGY FROM POVERTY AND PANDEMIC MARGINALIZATION

Emmanuel Y. Amugi Lartey

Practical theologians have focused on the theme of liberation in their theological explorations of the black experience in the United States and throughout the world. This has been so, in part, because of the connections this theme has to the Exodus, God's redemption of the Hebrews from slavery. Negro spirituals like "Go down Moses (Let my people go)," with obvious allusions to the emancipation of Africans enslaved in America, expressed the longings of Blacks for freedom and constitute some of the earliest sources and works of black theology. Liberation is also clearly connected with the work of Christ for the salvation of humankind from sin. This spiritual transformation lies at the heart of much of the evangelical teaching at the core of black preaching, testimony, and Christian experience.

Liberation, in black Christian thought and experience, has a twofold connotation: one is spiritual (that is, salvation from sin and deliverance from a sinful lifestyle), and the other is sociopolitical (that is, emancipation from slavery and its effects on mind, body, and community). These two notions of liberation have clearly shaped and framed the work of black churches and black theologians, including practical theologians. Black practical theologians have pursued the theme of liberation in this twofold sense in much of the work they have sought to do in providing resources for preaching, Christian education, worship, and pastoral care. The challenge has been and continues to be to keep both aspects on the table and to give due attention to both. More recently, several black churches have tended to emphasize the spiritual, more personal, and experiential aspect of liberation to the neglect of the sociopolitical aspect. This has resulted in the classification of churches in terms of their allegiance to one or the other, rather than to both of these essential sides of the same coin. At times it has seemed as if black churches generally have moved toward the spiritual and black theologians toward social justice. There has developed a sense of suspicion between the two, with each seeing the other as "unspiritual," "theologically naïve," "too secular," and other less charitable categories.

A crucial first step in the dialogue between black churches and black theologians needs to be to address and allay the fears of some black church folk that black theologians, and especially black liberation theologians, are liberal polemicists bent on destroying the faith of ordinary black parishioners. There is a need for black practical theologians to explain and embody the breadth and utility of liberation as a theme of the church. Similarly, black church folk need to recognize and reclaim the historic black Christian experience of struggle for social justice as a crucial and spiritually warranted exercise of Christian faith. Black church folk need to see black theologians as allies in the task of liberation for all. Much is to be gained by mutual dialogue between black theologians and black church members. This essay attempts to advance this dialogue by theologically addressing the issues of health care, HIV/AIDS, and poverty and by exploring some practical theological responses through which the Black Church might engage them.

LIBERATION IN GLOBAL PERSPECTIVE

The theme of liberation entered strongly into theological discourse through the articulations of South American theologians in the late 1960s. These theologians, most of them Roman Catholic by tradition, were outraged by the poverty of their own people in the face of the world community's affluence. One such theologian, the Brazilian Leonardo Boff, explicitly stated that the theology of liberation arose out "of an ethical indignation at the poverty and marginalization of the great masses of our continent."[1] In one instance, a priest recounts the pain and guilt he felt one Sunday as a celebrant at the Eucharist having just ignored a desperately poor and hungry woman at the steps to the cathedral begging for food, only to serve his relatively affluent parishioners with the body of Christ (bread). The methods and content of Latin American liberation theology were formulated in this context, with the expressed desire to face and transform the conditions of "poverty and marginalization" identified as tragically endemic on that continent.

In South Africa, the quest of the black masses was for human dignity and rights in their own land. Black South African theologians, aroused by the black consciousness movement, began emphasizing the black community's concerns in terms of culture and politics. African American theologian Dwight Hopkins captures this dynamic, writing, "Being created black by God meant that one had the right to self-identity (i.e. an accent on a cultural theology) and a right to self-determination (i.e. a move toward a political theology)."[2] Black Christians in the United States share in the global experience of people of color, in terms of poverty and the quest for well-being in a society that historically and systematically has legislatively, socially, and culturally sought to keep blacks down. Globally, theologians and church people who have paid attention to the complexities of their own contexts have essentially raised two kinds of questions in the exploration of their existential realities: questions related to social justice and questions related to human dignity.

SOCIOECONOMIC AND POLITICAL QUESTIONS

The black experience worldwide has been closely related to socioeconomic and political questions that arose from the very first encounter of Africans with European adventurers who appeared on African shores in quest of gold and other valuables. Slavery, as well as imperialism and colonialism, was a commercial enterprise geared toward the enrichment of Europeans. The issues of poverty and illness that blacks face today are squarely socioeconomic and political. Because practical theologians worldwide have raised these kinds of questions and have sought ecclesial and theologically grounded responses to them, dialogue between black church people and black practical theologians clearly could provide some important ways of addressing these issues. Leonardo and Clodovis Boff, both South American liberation theologians, write, "Liberation theology was born when faith confronted the injustice done to the poor."[3] It is not coincidental that statistically African Americans—among the globe's poorest of the poor—have the highest HIV/AIDS infection rates in the United States. There are socioeconomically and politically related structures that work to make and keep this true. Teasing out these structures and finding ecclesial responses to them is a task to which black church people and black practical theologians are called. Some such responses are presented in this chapter.

The European ventures into Africa were conducted in a climate full of questions in the European mind around anthropological, social, and cultural matters. The rhetoric that was used to justify slavery revolved around questioning the humanity of the Africans. Much of the enterprise of Western education had to do with the denigration of all things African so that European values, culture, and society would not only thrive but also totally dominate the world. The issues of health care, HIV/AIDS, and poverty that the Black Church faces today have to do with questions of black humanity and black dignity. The health of African Americans suffers because of social disparities that continue to render health-care access, health-care outcomes, and quality of care unequal. Black practical theologians have long wrestled with how theologically, practically, communally, and ecclesially to restore black dignity to a people who daily face the indignities of a human system devised to exploit their labor and personhood. Dialogue on these issues can be very useful and needs to be central to current discussions between black theologians and black church people. As a people we have survived the onslaughts of Eurocentricism by holding steadfastly to our sense of dignity and humanity, even when we were classified as only three-fifths human. Black theologians have helped to expose the falsehoods underlying white supremacy and the ideologies and theologies that promote it. In South Africa it took the concerted efforts of black theologians for apartheid to be formally declared as heresy. The Civil Rights movement was encouraged by a critique of embedded theologies that insisted on the inferiority of Blacks.

The issues of social justice and human dignity remain central to any engagement with health care, HIV/AIDS, and poverty. Relegating the discourse of soteriology to the afterlife remains a form of reductionism to which too many in the Black Church are wedded. To engage HIV/AIDS seriously, we must have not only a theology for after death but also a theology that helps us to live here and now. The significance of eternity for how we treat the hungry, the naked, and the imprisoned is made clear in Matt 25:31-46. Silence, denial, or condemnation are not options in the current critical social and global environment.

ECCLESIOLOGICAL QUESTIONS: WHAT KIND OF BLACK CHURCH?

The Black Church has historically been the main social institution founded by Blacks in the New World to provide social and communal expression to the longings of black people for humanity and salvation. African cultures in antiquity (and to this day) have been premised on communalistic rather than individualistic tendencies. African proverbs such as "It takes a whole village to raise a child," "Knowledge is like a Baobab tree, one person cannot totally encompass the tree by her/himself," and "One head does not constitute a council" all point to the value of community, which is socially transmitted in African cultures. With the growth of individualism in black communities in the United States and in Africa, these communal values have declined. Black practical theologians (e.g., Dale Andrews)[4] have explored the rise of individualism and its theological and social effects on the black community. Consumerism has been a close partner to individualism in the values that blacks have imbibed. Here is fertile ground for conversation between black churches and black practical theologians. For such discussions to be fruitful, we must pay attention to at least four kinds of questions:

WHAT IS THE BLACK CHURCH?

The fundamental concerns of this question relate to what the church is and for what purpose it exists. A practical theological place from which to begin to answer this question boils down to "What do folk say that it is?" Many identify the church with particular buildings or places of worship. Others point to the founding pastor, current pastor, senior pastor, or bishop. The church is either the place to which we go for worship or the person we go to hear. Neither of these responses, however, adequately captures the theological significance of the church. Essentially, the Church is a gathering of people called out by Christ, who is the head of the Church worldwide. The purpose for this calling out is that we might bear witness to the saving acts of God in Christ through our acts of testimony, care, and love. As such, the church is the community of persons called out of the world and sent back into the world to be a sign, witness, and representative of Christ, the Redeemer.

Biblical imagery for the Church is predominantly personal and communal. Biblical images of the Church present it as the "body of Christ" (1 Cor; Eph 4), the "Bride of Christ" (Eph 5), and an army of soldiers (Eph 6). Body-of-Christ imagery in particular directs the Church toward continuing the redemptive acts of the Christ in the world. The gospels make very clear the saving, healing, teaching, and testifying work of Jesus. The Church, as Christ's body present in the world, now must continue the saving, healing, teaching, and witnessing work of Jesus. There is a need to transition from thinking about buildings and leaders to revisioning the Church as a community of people. The Black Church needs to regain its vision of itself as a *community of care* for black people. The Black Church as a community of care extends the work of Jesus Christ into contemporary society. It is necessary, then, for each local congregation to ask itself questions about what it is and what it is for within its location and context. In what ways can this particular body of people bear witness to the saving acts of God in Christ? In what ways can this community of called-out persons embody the care and love of Jesus for the needy in their locality? What saving acts can this community of people called out from and sent back to society perform that will be a contemporary continuation of the redemptive work of Jesus Christ?

WHAT IS A THRIVING BLACK CHURCH?

For many church leaders and members, thriving is understood in numerical and financial terms. A church's budget and the finances at its disposal define a thriving church. Notions of material prosperity are uppermost in this prevalent way of thinking. The challenge of the gospel is for the Church to be defined in terms of community activism; advocacy for the poor, the naked, and the imprisoned; and all the mobilization of resources to help the weak. Responding to health-care needs in the face of poverty, such as HIV/AIDS, is very clearly mandated by the gospel as a central task of the Church. By this token, theologically speaking, a thriving church is one that actively works for the transformation of communities in need— namely, "the sick, the hungry, the naked, and the incarcerated." Matthew 25 renders a vivid picture of the black community in the United States today. Thriving churches must arise and thrive.

WHAT IS A HEALTHY CHURCH?

The task of the Church has traditionally being couched in terms of saving souls. For many, this task fosters a spiritual relationship with God through the personal acceptance of Christ. Beyond that initial acceptance, the Church's educational programs are geared toward spiritual growth or maturity in relationship with Christ. This understanding is premised on a Greco-Roman dichotomy between spirit and body in which the spirit is preferred. Churches on this reckoning see themselves in the business of enhancing spiritual growth. A fuller and more intrinsically biblical understanding of personhood recognizes the unity and wholeness of the human being. In this essentially more Hebraic and also African perception, we are our whole body. Spirit-soul-body is entwined in a holistic person for whom deficiencies in any one part affect the totality of the being. On this understanding, promoting fitness, well-being, and wholeness in bodies, minds, and spirits is the calling of the Church. In light of the devastating facts concerning the health status of the African American community, churches need to review what they are teaching and practicing to promote and enhance the well-being of the constituency. A healthy church comprises healthy people. Health entails the well-being of the whole of our bodies, souls, spirits, and minds and, by extension, our total community. A healthy church promotes health throughout the neighborhood within which it is placed.

HOW MAY THE BLACK CHURCH RESPOND TO POVERTY WITHIN THE BLACK COMMUNITY?

Faced with the crises of the black community, each black church congregation must give priority to the basic question that practical theologians pose: What in real concrete terms can churches do to respond adequately to the situation? Practical theologians begin their methodological cycles with *experience* and end them with *action*, which then constitutes experience for further reflection and refined action. Practical theology is deeply strategic in ethos. It is not sufficient to diagnose and interpret, important as these are for appropriate action. Practical theologians move theologically beyond the aesthetic to the pragmatic.

African Americans in the United States face a stark social and economic environment of inequality. They face greater exposure to poverty, which results in lower health status. To address this fact one must begin by understanding how poverty and socioeconomic inequalities affect where African Americans live, where or whether we work, what we eat or drink, what we breathe, whether or how we exercise, and how we take care of our lives. Regarding what the poor can do as envisaged in liberation theology, the Boff brothers explain:

> The poor can break out of their situation of oppression only by working out a strategy better able to change social conditions: the strategy of liberation. In liberation the oppressed come together, come to understand their situation through the process of conscientization, discover the causes of their oppression, organize themselves into movements, and act in a coordinated fashion. First, they claim everything that the existing system can give: better wages, working conditions, health care, education, housing, and so forth; then they work toward the transformation of present society in the direction of a new society characterized

by widespread participation, a better and more just balance among
social classes and more worthy ways of life.[5]

Martin Luther King Jr. found in Gandhi's philosophy and practice strategies for operationalizing the teaching of Jesus "to love our neighbors."
The "strategy of liberation," as articulated by the Boff brothers, provides
for us in this day and time a way to translate our theological aspirations
into action. Black practical theologians will seek strategies of liberation as
a means of doing just that.

I consider many of the strategies expressed in Tavis Smiley's *The
Covenant with Black America* significant and useful. I concur with Smiley
that, "by working together, we are capable of bringing about positive
change and building healthy, strong, vibrant, and inclusive communities."[6] Black churches can be the focal points of community action for
social change. The Black Church has a theological mandate and calling to
build "healthy, strong, vibrant, and inclusive communities."

Every black church member may be encouraged to embark on personal strategies of liberation in response to the HIV/AIDS, health care,
and poverty crisis in our communities. Such personal action can include
improving our diets (including fruits and vegetables), exercising daily (for
example, walking one mile each day, using stairs instead of elevators in our
apartment buildings, making sure children have healthy diets and daily
activities), and scheduling regular exams with health-care professionals.
Individuals can be encouraged to take action by talking to neighbors or
otherwise increasing the flow of information in our communities about
disease and health risks. Black church members can organize walking
groups in their neighborhoods, coordinate outdoor activities, and insist
that local store owners stock fresh fruit and vegetables. Many churches
hold annual health fairs. Specific disease-focused forums could supple-
ment these events. Every black church needs discussion forums to provide
HIV/AIDS education so that accurate information circulates within our
communities and appropriate action is encouraged. Pastoral care for the
black community needs to have a component of social justice advocacy
in the face of the health-care crisis, HIV/AIDS, and poverty. The care of
persons in this context must address the huge disparities in health care,
health-care access, and health-care outcomes.

HIV/AIDS, POVERTY, AND PRACTICAL THEOLOGY

The pandemic of HIV/AIDS has presented churches throughout the
world with a huge challenge and opportunity. Precisely because of the

intersecting realities—such as wellness and illness, sex and sexuality, morality and immorality, strength and weakness, life and death—that converge around the subject, each of which has theological purchase, this condition raises questions that affect the embedded theologies of the Black Church, particularly those concerning what it preaches and embodies. Here is an opportunity for black preachers to examine the images of God they project in their sermons. What is our real operational understanding of humanity in the image of God? What is sin in the face of the existential realities we confront? What do we teach about sex and sexuality? Is our teaching life-giving, or is it at best life-denying and at worst death-dealing? How do we embody what we preach?

The Black Church has an opportunity to examine the biblical and theological content of what we preach and how we live. Here, dialogue with theologians can be fruitful. Specifically, we need a conversation on biblical hermeneutics around the topics of personhood, sexuality, sin, suffering, poverty, wealth, health, and wellness. This conversation is critical for the Black Church as it seeks to formulate a meaningful response to HIV/AIDS and the challenge of health-care access in the face of disparities and poverty. How are we approaching the Bible? What passages do we select for emphasis? What is neglected? How do we understand and explain texts? Do we tend in a literalistic direction—even where poetic, evocative language is used in the text? Do we realize that Christians have evolved understandings of topics such as marriage and sexual relations that are very different from stipulations in both the Hebrew Bible and the New Testament? For example, the biblical norm of polygamy as evidenced in the families of faithful people—such as those of Abraham, Isaac, David, and Solomon—has been roundly rejected in favor of a Victorian-era monogamous standard for all Christians. As much as I personally support and practice monogamy, I cannot claim that it is the exclusive model suggested in the pages of the Bible. I would have to overlook much of the Bible in order to make such a claim.

Theologians study the Bible in its historical and cultural context to glean what its message was. We then learn from its message for our times, recognizing how different our contemporary situation is from those referred to in the Bible. We attempt to find the timeless truths to which the Bible points that may help us in a principled and responsible search for wholesome, healthy, God-affirming living in the twenty-first century. We also explore questions around the nature of God and humanity and the relations between them historically, and we seek to discern what the

Holy Spirit might be saying to us these days. The theological challenge is to learn from the past, not merely to repeat it or to attempt to imitate what was written for a bygone time. Literalism in biblical interpretation can be not only dangerous but also death-dealing. Moreover, any claim that our current practices are exclusively sanctioned by the Bible always entails a selective reading of the text. The Black Church needs to revisit biblical hermeneutics and Christian formations of theological ethics in our quest for more healthy and wholesome responses to the current crisis.

In this regard, many black churches embrace particular forms of teaching that adumbrate material prosperity as a goal of faith and as evidence of God's blessing. This so-called prosperity gospel smacks of all the values of capitalist economics. It seems to arise out of and fit the cultural context in which it has been generated. Hence, it strongly advocates individual material wealth. The result has largely been seen in wealthy pastors with expensive personal lifestyles. Critics of this teaching point to the absence of time-honored Christian values of thrift, moderation, and simplicity. They also lament a loss of a sense of following Jesus of Nazareth and of the self-giving suffering that is a part of true discipleship. Individual wealth in the face of communal poverty raises the question of whether we are missing a *communal* prosperity gospel. In light of the challenges facing the black community in the United States, should not "prosperity" be defined in holistic and communal terms? Instead of materially wealthy individuals who care little for others, the goals of a "black prosperity gospel" need to grow healthy persons who work for the well-being of their communities and to enhance thriving communities that are inclusive and actively care for the needy among them.

Inclusivity means that all are invited and welcome at the table of the Lord. The gospel of our Lord Jesus Christ is for "whosoever will." A great challenge facing inclusivity in black churches is when it comes to persons whose sexuality differs from the majority. The exclusion of this minority has rendered the Church unable to reach and ineffective at dealing with a population of Blacks who need to be a part of the healthy discourse around HIV/AIDS in the church—and for that matter in the black community. Because of our outdated, outmoded, and exclusivist attitudes, we are often unable truly to advocate for safety in sexual practices. We fail and fear even to broach the subject of sex in the first place. When we do address sexuality, our theologies often need much more careful psychological, sociological, historical, and cultural study. Too often the theology we hear articulated from black pulpits has failed to keep abreast with the scholarship on humanity that helps to inform our quest for a life-giving gospel for today. We are in need of a theological anthropology that recognizes human diversity and plurality as normative. The manifold wisdom of God is manifest in a creation that is full of diversity and variety. Humans created in the image of God come in very many different shades, colors, and manners of being. All need to be embraced and welcomed into the dialogue on poverty, health care, and especially HIV/AIDS.

The nature of pastoral care, and the pastoral theology that undergirds it, in the black community at this time needs to revolve around themes of redemption and not condemnation. And redemption itself also needs to be envisaged in broad holistic terms, embracing the total experience of the entire black community.

FEATURES OF A NEW "BLACK-CHURCH PRACTICAL THEOLOGY"

The time is ripe for the emergence of an authentic black theological voice from the churches that seriously engage the *Sitz im Leben* of the black community today. We desperately need contemporary black theological explorations of sex and sexuality, sin and redemption, life and death, and health and economic empowerment that begin from the actual experience of black people today in our churches and communities. Practical theologians are generally wedded to methodologies that emphasize their starting points in actual concrete experience. Practical theologians begin their explorations and considerations from the lived experience of real people. A new Black-Church practical theology will need to question seriously the received theologies adopted without critique from the communities of oppression, which Blacks have embraced and continue to use even to the point of oppressing ourselves. This tragic irony calls for a critique of the embedded theologies that, far from addressing the issues, may actually exacerbate them.

Such a critique further calls for the development of constructive theologies that are empowering, life-sustaining, and life-giving. It is time to explore the theme of liberation even more rigorously and to extend it to all twenty-first-century captivities, including captivities to outmoded, irrelevant, and in fact death-dealing theologies and practices in black churches and the black community at large. At least five features characterize the new Black-Church practical theology that I am calling for: radical inclusivity, communal prosperity, full liberation, social activism, and transformative redemption.

RADICAL INCLUSIVITY

Black-Church practical theology needs to affirm in statement and action the full humanity and dignity of all persons within the community. The dogma and the practices of black church communities need to eschew the implication that anyone in the community is less than human in any sense. All are created in and bear the image of God. This means that all are to be treated with respect and dignity. A community that has historically been brutalized by practices based on their God-given attributes of skin color, hair texture, and physiological features must not rise up and discriminate against any on grounds of other God-given (i.e., innate, natural) characteristics. People living with HIV/AIDS are an integral part of the black human community. No one should be shunned or denigrated by virtue of their HIV status. All need to be encouraged and taught the importance of testing, health care, taking care of self, safe sexual practices, and living with dignity and integrity. We must seek access for all to the resources that are available for these needs. The Black Church needs to realize its health promoting capacity to live out that reality through educational programs, health-care-promoting activities, personal mentorship, healthy lifestyle groups, exercise groups, and healthy-eating fairs, from which none are excluded.

COMMUNAL PROSPERITY

The prosperity gospel needs to go communal within the Black Church. The resources of the Black Church need to be turned toward job creation and productive endeavors geared to building a prosperous community. Individualism is countergospel and intrinsically destructive to the black community faced with challenges of HIV/AIDS and poverty. Individualism fueled by private ownership, greed, and sole concern for individual wealth has proved to be the bane of the black community. In this context, such individualism is sin and needs to be named as such. The Black Church can be called to return to its historic African roots and values and to utilize these values to promote the health and the wealth of the community. The earliest church, pictured in Acts 4:32-35, can be a real model for the Black Church of today:

> Now the whole group of those who believed were of one heart and soul, and no one claimed private ownership of any possessions, but every-thing they owned was held in common. With great power the apostles gave their testimony to the resurrection of the Lord Jesus and great grace was upon them all. There was not a needy person among them, for

as many as owned lands or houses sold them and brought the proceeds of what was sold. They laid it at the apostles' feet, and it was distributed to each as any had need. (Acts 4:32-35)

Any church wishing to "give testimony to the resurrection of the Lord Jesus" with "great power" needs to examine this text carefully to see what the community was like. For "great grace" to be upon our communities, we need a spirit of sharing and a real desire for communal prosperity. In addition to sharing our existing goods and services, we need to develop a mindset for the creation of communal wealth. I will explain this factor further under "transformative redemption."

FULL LIBERATION

The liberation theology of the new Black-Church practical theology embraces the fullest implications of the term "liberation." It is based on a whole-person, full gospel notion that affirms the interconnectedness and interrelatedness of *body-mind-soul-spirit-community*. A lack of concern for any aspect of this whole is not tolerated in this liberation. As such, churches and congregations plan their programs and activities in such a way as to promote the well-being of black bodies—male, female, and transgender. Exercise, fitness-training, and outdoor pursuits are as integral to the church as Bible study. The church's agenda includes attention to education and sharing information concerning all aspects of healthy living. Discussion and critical study are encouraged and promoted through programs targeted at specific ages and social groupings within the community. Our church calendars need to incorporate fun activities geared toward emotional well-being, along with spiritual direction through worship, prayer, meditation, and counsel. The goal of the church's overall program is the growth of healthy communities made up of healthy people in healthy surroundings.

SOCIAL ACTIVISM

Black-Church practical theology advances the practices of social change as a means of ushering in the Reign of God, which is characterized by justice, peace, and well-being for all of creation. The *shalom* of God is established when the "will of God is done on earth as it is in heaven." The will of God envisions right relationships within, among, and between persons and the divine realm, in all human communities. As such, churches organize to challenge racism, sexism, ageism, ableism, environmental racism, and all those taken-for-granted social ideologies that militate against the well-being of any part of the community. The quest here is to create social, cultural, and environmental conditions wherein all persons may thrive. As such, churches take action in their neighborhoods—including neighborhood cleaning and health education days. In this theology, the Black Church envisions itself as representative of the human community before God and humankind. It therefore petitions not only God through prayer for the well-being of the community but also the powers-that-be in society for the well-being of the community. The church seeks not only to pray but also to be the answer to the prayer, "Thy will be done on earth."

TRANSFORMATIVE REDEMPTION

In the new Black-Church practical theology, redemption is truly an act of buying back the community from destruction, through transforming the community from illness to a state of well-being and health. The Church believes in redemption through Christ. As the body of Christ, the Church is an agent of redemption for human community. Yet, a fallen state of destruction and sin persists in the black community. The state of the black community related to health care, HIV/AIDS, and poverty can be described theologically as a state of sin. It is a state not only of personal sin but also of structural sin and a great deal of being sinned against. The Black Church, as the body of Christ comprising people "called out" by Christ to return as "Salt and Light" into the world, is an agent of transformative redemption in this community. The Black Church then exists that the community "may have life, and have it abundantly" (John 10:10). Because the Black Church and black practical theologians believe in Christ, they "do the works that (Christ) did, and in fact, greater works than those" (John 14:12), in effectively transforming whole communities from a state of destruction and sin to that of well-being and health in a society that historically has seldom been a safe and healthy place for black bodies.

As an African Christian pastor and practical theologian deeply concerned about issues of health care, HIV/AIDS, and poverty, I have sought to advocate for closer ties of mutual respect between black pastors and black theologians. My desire is that through dialogue we develop what I have termed a "Black-Church practical theology" that churches, communities, and academics can all own. Such a theology aims to inspire liberative action on the part of all for the well-being of the black community. The hallmarks of this practical theology are, first, that it leaves no one out (radical inclusivity); second, that it enhances the greatest benefit for the whole community (communal prosperity); third, that it releases health for body, mind, and spirit (full liberation); fourth, that it builds communities in which there is fullness of life for all (social activism); and, finally, that it releases abundant life for all (transformative redemption). We all need to work at this kind of practical theology!

<< 15 >>

BLACK PRACTICAL THEOLOGY OF HEALTH AND HIV/AIDS HEALTH CARE

Edward P. Antonio

In this essay I engage theology, health, and the health-care system in the context of poverty and the black experience. Specifically, I wish to propose and explore the conditions of a black practical theology of health and health care. I argue that such a theology ought to be at the center of both black theology's and the Black Church's understandings not just of liberation but also of salvation, because a fundamental theological connection exists between the content of the Christian message and health and health care. All three—the gospel, health, and health care—are crucial to the kind of black practical theology I am proposing here. They are concerned with bringing about deliverance from physical, psychological, and spiritual adversity; about promoting and affirming life; and about the well-being of individuals and communities.

The trajectory of my argument in this essay is as follows: First, I briefly suggest that a good black practical theology of health and health care must be framed and sustained by the idea of faith seeking understanding. The understanding faith seeks is that of humans, the world, and God. Second, I demonstrate what such understanding looks like in relation to the world. I therefore describe the disparities and inequalities of the health-care system. In describing these disparities and problems, I highlight the crisis of HIV/AIDS in the African American community. My concern here is threefold: (1) to articulate the extent of the crisis; (2) to show the failure of black and womanist theologies, on the one hand, and the Black Church, on the other, to respond effectively to the crisis; and (3) to suggest that in light of this failure the need for a black practical theology of health and health care becomes an urgent matter. Third, I provide a focused and detailed account of the HIV/AIDS virus and its impact on African Americans. Such an account proves necessary for a theology seeking understanding. Fourth, I propose some basic elements needed for the formulation of a black practical theology of health and health care in the age of HIV/AIDS.

BLACK PRACTICAL THEOLOGY SEEKING UNDERSTANDING:
THE WORLD AS IT IS

An effective and plausible black practical theology of health and health care must be driven by a ceaseless quest to understand the world. This understanding is not, however, merely of the world as it ought or could be, or of the world as imagined through a set of moral practices that exhort Christians to take flight from their present reality; rather, it is an understanding of the world as it actually is. For millions of blacks, the world as it actually is consists of widespread systemic injustice, poverty, marginalization, pain, and suffering. It is a world permeated with sin in the grip of brokenness. However, our world is also a place of hope and struggle against the threat of death-dealing systems of injustice.

There are at least three reasons for theology to start with the world as it is. The first is that effective ministry demands a proper, in-depth understanding of the nature, causes, and effects of systems of oppression. Without such an understanding, the pastor, ethicist, and theologian may lack the knowledge necessary to identify the social problem as well as the skills, resources, capacities, tools, strategies, and tactics for intervening in the world on behalf of the good news of the gospel. In turn, this lack of understanding renders pastoral ministry, theology, and ethics irrelevant and disengaged from people's lives. The second reason is that in the brokenness of the world, God so loved us to the point of becoming incarnate in the material reality of its pain and suffering. The third reason for taking the world seriously as a theological starting point is that, in spite of all of its problems, the world remains an essential part of God's creation. In essence, the way in which a theology positions itself in relation to the world can tell us a great deal about its view of the relationship between the incarnation and creation, on the one hand, and its commitment to the creation of a better world—the making of a new heaven and a new earth—on the other.

I have emphasized understanding the world. But the question surely is, what is the nature of such understanding? I cannot give a full answer here, but I suggest that understanding the world is much more than just getting the facts about the world; it is not just propositional information. Understanding is, to be sure, also theological in that what ultimately drives the acquisition of facts, statistics, and propositional information is the requirement to bring to bear, in relevant and applicable ways, the good news of God's liberating activity on a world ravaged by evil and injustice. In the following section, I offer one example of understanding the world, that is, through a focus on facts and statistics.

The statistics are clear. America is characterized by deep disparities and inequalities in health care. These inequalities reflect widespread social injustices in the larger society. There is general agreement on this argument on almost every front. In January 2011, the Centers for Disease Control and Prevention (CDC) published its *CDC Health Disparities and Inequalities Report*, which defines health disparities as "differences in health outcomes between groups that reflect social inequalities."[1] The Healthy People 2020 program defines a health disparity as follows:

> a particular type of health difference that is closely linked with social, economic, and/or environmental disadvantage. Health disparities adversely affect groups of people who have systematically experienced greater obstacles to health based on their racial or ethnic group; religion; socioeconomic status; gender; age; mental health; cognitive, sensory, or physical disability; sexual orientation or gender identity; geographic location; or other characteristics historically linked to discrimination or exclusion.[2]

The communities and populations most severely affected by these disparities are communities of color, especially the African American community. In this paper, I focus on African Americans. For example, the Office of Minority Health in the U.S. Department of Health and Human Services reports that in 2007 more African Americans than Whites died from cancer, diabetes, stroke, asthma, influenza and pneumonia, HIV/AIDS, and homicide.[3] African American adults are twice as likely to be diagnosed with diabetes as non-Hispanic Whites. In 2008 they were 2.2 times as likely to die from diabetes. In the same year, African American men were more likely to report new cases of lung cancer (1.4 times) and prostate cancer (1.5 times) than Whites, and their cancer survival rates in each were lower.

Although in 2008 African American women were 10 percent less likely to be diagnosed with breast cancer than were non-Hispanic Whites, they were about 40 percent more likely to die from it than non-Hispanic Whites. The infant mortality rate (per 1,000 births) among African

Americans is 2.3 times the rate of Whites. African American babies are three times more likely to die from low birth weight and other complications than are white babies. The most alarming statistics relate to HIV/AIDS. In 2009, African Americans constituted 13.6 percent of the U.S. population but accounted for 43 percent of cases of HIV infection. African American men suffer infection at a rate of 7.6 times higher than that of white men and are 10 times as likely to die from HIV/AIDS. African American women have an infection rate of 20 times higher than that of white women and are over 20 times more likely to die from AIDS than their white counterparts. Children in this community are twice as likely to be infected compared to white children. In 2010, African Americans were 8.5 times more likely to be diagnosed with HIV than were Whites.[4] HIV/AIDS is the leading killer of African Americans between the ages of nineteen and forty-four. It has been described as a national crisis.

These statistics are deeply troubling, and they raise many difficult questions: How did this situation come about? How could it have been allowed to exist in one of the most prosperous, technologically advanced countries on the planet? How can such massive social imbalances exist in a democracy that proclaims the equality of all its citizens? There can be no doubt that the legacies of slavery and Jim and Jane Crow, as well as entrenched racism in contemporary America, are to blame. These disparities are not simply about health and access to health care among African Americans. They represent widespread patterns and effects of social and systemic injustices with a long history in this country.

According to the CDC report mentioned earlier, there is a close link between a person's socioeconomic status and his or her health: "This association is continuous and graded across a population and cumulative over the life course."[5] Both the Healthy People 2020 program and the CDC recognize the importance of the social determinants of health. In addition to economic status, these include "[one's] physical environment, discrimination, racism, literacy levels, . . . legislative policies," disability, sexual identity and orientation, ethnicity, gender, quality of education, and access to nutritious food, decent and safe housing,[6] affordable and reliable public transportation, health insurance,[7] clean water, and healthy air.[8]

Black and womanist theologies, as well as African American churches, have been not only aware of this desperate situation but also shaped by it. Black and womanist theologies claim to be theologies of liberation. They envision liberation precisely from the scandal of the injustices so graphically portrayed by the foregoing statistics. Yet, being aware of this scandal and being shaped by it in one's experience of the world (the majority of African Americans have direct experiences with these injustices), as well as in one's expectations for a different social order, does not necessarily make available the power, capacity, and resources to do something about it. This is why, as I shall argue further, empowerment and capacity-building in the struggle for a more just health-care system are important strategies for any black and womanist practical theologies that seek to make effective emancipative interventions in the social order.

Still, even when resources and the capacity for the praxis of liberation are available, theologians, ethicists, and the Church sometimes fail effectively to confront social injustice. This failure can happen for a variety of reasons. Let me name four: first, the Church's attitude toward the world may discourage certain forms of social engagement; second, there may be conflicts between the theological claims of professional theologians and internal church politics; third, theology, ethics, and the Church might fail to become socially engaged because of anxieties about the technical nature of the social problems confronting them; and, fourth, the Church may fail to engage social issues because of a gap between theory and practice or because of categorical and interpretative mistakes.

In this essay, I argue that black and womanist theologies, on the one hand, and the Black Church, on the other, have not been very attentive to the challenge of both the injustices inherent in the health-care system in this country and the devastating consequences of HIV/AIDS in the African American community. I do not mean that they have completely ignored the problem or that they do not care about it. Rather, their attempts to address health care tend to be sporadic and ad hoc and thus fail to rise to the scale, complexity, and death-dealing impact of disparities in the health-care system. I shall explain this remarkable failure in terms of the reasons just stated. There are hardly any books let alone significant articles by black and womanist theologians dealing with the concrete, practical issues of social policy around health care in a systematic, comprehensive, and sustained manner. What exists is, for the most part, the work not of theologians but of ethicists and practitioners of pastoral care and counseling. And even here one struggles to find sustained, let alone widespread, discussion of just how America's health-care system not only has let down a large part (13.6 percent) of its population but also is continuing to do so by letting them die without sustained attention or intervention.

There are, of course, hundreds of books on liberation, race, black bodies, sexuality, identity, racism, sexism, and so on. Some of this literature speaks very powerfully to the social determinants of health. But, again, it does so indirectly and without always naming the material conditions that actually destroy black bodies and thus black humanity. Since health care is not simply a matter of theoretical discussion, academic taste, and disciplinary preference, however systematic and comprehensive, I must also remark on the absence of a theologically inspired, ecclesial social movement nationally advocating for the rights of blacks to adequate access to health care as well as for the overhaul of the whole system. The failure of African American Christianity *specifically* to address the health-care system, as both a site of theological analysis and ecclesial intervention, is spectacularly odd. Is it not precisely at this site that African American existence is literally rendered a matter life and death, and indeed, if the statistics presented earlier are to be believed, a matter more of death than of life? Is it not at this conjuncture that social suffering takes on its most material form as human bodies are socially devalued and then destroyed by diseases whose organic causes are themselves nurtured by oppressive social conditions? In other words, is this not the site where the deep inequalities of health care in this country pose significant threats and challenges not only to the African American community but also to black and womanist theologies, as well as to black churches?

UNDERSTANDING HIV/AIDS: THE DISEASE

I focus on HIV/AIDS in the African American community for reasons to be outlined shortly. But, before doing so, it is important to indicate that the discussion of the threats and challenges in the crisis of health care among African Americans purports "theology is faith seeking understanding." What it seeks to understand is not just God and God's work of redemption but also the context in which believers appropriate and experience the effects of that work. This context is the world as it actually is in all its pain and brokenness, and not some otherworldly place that has no connection to the everyday realities of real human beings. Indeed, insofar as it is possible to understand God, Christians must take seriously the suffering of the world as their starting point for achieving such understanding. I take this to be at the heart of the story of both the incarnation and the passion of Christ.[9] AIDS has become one of the most direct causes of African American suffering and death. It has been described as a national crisis or a state of emergency; it repeats, reproduces, and exacerbates the inequalities of the health-care system; and it stands as powerful indictment of the failure of black and womanist theologies as well as black churches to make effective interventions in this area.

First, HIV/AIDS is the leading killer of African American men, women, and children. Second, as we shall see later, HIV/AIDS is not just a biomedical condition; it is also a powerful social reality with catastrophic consequences for individual sufferers as well as their families, households, and communities. Third, I approach the problem of health care through HIV/AIDS because both the virus and the disease have globally displayed a persistent tendency to target the disadvantaged and people of color. In particular, the disease targets black people, the poor, and especially women in Africa, the United States, and the Americas. My fourth reason for focusing on HIV/AIDS is that the virus attacks the body's immune system, rendering the body both vulnerable to opportunistic infections and incapable of fighting off disease. This compounds the forms and variety of illnesses in both the body of the victim of AIDS and the social body.

For example, an HIV victim may, in a very short space of time, be ravaged by several concurrent illnesses that an otherwise healthy person would fight off. HIV/AIDS represents an astounding crisis threatening not only the integrity of the African American community in moral terms but also its very existence. Sadly, many African American leaders, especially clergy, remain in denial. I shall respond by saying something about what the disease is and how it is transmitted. Understanding the different ways through which the disease is transmitted is important for two reasons. First, we must reject the persistent but mistaken assumption among many people in the Black Church that HIV/AIDS is contracted only through homosexual sex. Second, the variant ways in which the disease spreads are central to my argument that HIV/AIDS is both an existential and a social threat.

HIV (human immunodeficiency virus) is the virus that causes AIDS (acquired immunodeficiency syndrome). HIV attacks the body's CD4 helper cells called "lymphocytes," which are part of the body's immune system. HIV damages and weakens the immune system so that the body is no longer able to fight infections effectively. In other words, it makes the body vulnerable to opportunistic infections.

HIV can be transmitted in several ways: through unprotected sex, from an HIV-positive mother to her unborn child during pregnancy, through breastfeeding, through exposure to contaminated blood and blood products (this is now rare in the United States), and through needle sticks among health professionals. Let me address two of these ways.

The first I will discuss is transmission through unprotected sexual contact (gay and heterosexual). When HIV/AIDS was first diagnosed in the United States in the early 1980s, it was associated with white gay men. One of the key and unfortunate features of this association has been the persistent notion that HIV/AIDS is a white gay disease only. It is true that unprotected sex with an infected gay partner can lead to HIV/AIDS, but this is equally true of unprotected sex with an infected heterosexual partner—that is, in the context of a relationship between a man and a woman. The fact of the matter is that unprotected sex with a person with HIV or other sexually transmitted diseases (whatever his or her sexual orientation or identity) exposes the uninfected partner to the immediate and direct risk of HIV infection.

Many people infected with the HIV virus look healthy and exhibit no signs of illness. This is especially the case with those whose infection is recent. Not everyone who is infected with HIV experiences immediate symptoms, but those who do complain of flu-like symptoms, such as headaches, nausea, fever, fatigue, and so on. The virus can incubate or lie dormant in the body for a period of between six months and ten years (or more in some cases), during which time there may be no symptoms. However, when full-blown AIDS sets in, the infected person may experience rapid and severe weight loss; pneumonia; chronic diarrhea; sores of the mouth and genitalia; extreme fatigue; skin rash; neurological disorders such as cancerous tumors in the brain, inflammation of the brain (encephalitis), cryptococcal meningitis (serious infection of the brain and spinal column), and neurosyphilis, which may cause the degeneration of nerve cells and nerve fibers; and many other disorders and symptoms.[10]

HIV/AIDS does not discriminate in terms of sexual orientation or identity. It is important to remember that, whatever the early associations of the virus, its modes of transmission have undergone a complex evolutionary and historical process. The fact that, in 2010, African Americans were 8.5 times more likely to be diagnosed with HIV than Whites and that HIV/AIDS is currently the leading killer of African Americans between the ages of nineteen and forty-four clearly points to the fact that it can no longer be explained away as simply a gay disease. I emphasize this point for two important reasons. One is that the early linkage between HIV/AIDS and homosexuality created a widespread ethos of stigma and moralistic aversion among many religious groups, including much of the Black Church. Religious opposition to homosexuality interpreted HIV/AIDS as God's punishment, and religious leaders chose not to be involved with victims of the virus. This attitude has persisted in many sectors of society and remains one of the major causes of the Black Church's indifference to HIV. The other reason for its alienating persistence involves reactions to this stigma. Some thinkers in the black community who worried about discrimination and the rights of gay people lamented the character assault borne of the association between HIV/AIDS and homosexuality and suggested their separation. While I shall discuss the theological implications of these challenges of HIV/AIDS in a separate section, both of these postures must be rejected as ideologically dangerous. They both fail to recognize the extent to which HIV/AIDS challenges and disrupts commonsense ways of thinking about sexuality, sexual identity, and sexual orientation.

Another way in which the virus is contracted is through perinatal transmission—that is, from mother to child either through breast feeding or during pregnancy or at birth. This is a major source of new infections in poor communities where antiretroviral drugs or therapies to treat the mother are not readily available. The Centers for Disease Control and Prevention say that perinatal infections account for nearly all AIDS cases among children in the United States.[11] Its evaluation of data from 2004 to 2007 found that perinatal infections in children younger than thirteen demonstrated serious disparities according to race and ethnicity: 69 percent of cases were black, 16 percent Hispanic, and 11 percent white. Clearly, African American children account for the largest percentage of all pediatric infections. We know that where antiretroviral drugs are available, these perinatal infections can be reduced significantly. I want to make two points here. The first is that these perinatal infections demonstrate the necessity of making adequate and meaningful reproductive health care available to African American women. The second point is that if present perinatal infections among Blacks are not reduced or stopped, they will negatively impact the future of the African American community in terms of its capacity to reproduce itself over time, a fact reinforced by the impact of HIV/AIDS at every level of African American society as well as by a related, but also devastating, fact (which I do not have space to discuss here)—namely, the mass incarceration of black men.

There is overwhelming evidence that HIV/AIDS has turned out to be a disease of poverty and social marginalization. I do not mean that it does not affect the rich and powerful; clearly it does. I mean, rather, that it is a disease that tends to target the poor, women, and marginalized groups such as injecting drug users, homosexuals, Blacks, and other people of color. Women, particularly black women, carry the heaviest burden of

HIV/AIDS. This is why womanist theologians who claim to speak for and as black women must, together with other black theologians, take with utmost seriousness the scourge of HIV/AIDS.

The connection between poverty and HIV and AIDS is disturbing. The disease is fueled by systemic poverty as individuals engage in risky behaviors often caused by poverty and often meant to alleviate impoverishment. In turn, it fuels poverty as it deprives families and households of their breadwinners and income through death and expensive treatment regimes. This means that HIV/AIDS is more than just a biological disease; it is also a social disease that has devastating social consequences. Hence HIV/AIDS and poverty reinforce each other. Some of these consequences include pressure on an already broken and unequal health-care system to deal with increasing cases of sick people who are themselves subject to regular social discrimination and a deepening of the economic crisis in African American communities not only by diverting resources in those communities from other areas of need but also by creating larger numbers of unproductive sick people because HIV/AIDS affects the most active and productive sector of the population. HIV/AIDS also diminishes human personhood by making sufferers vulnerable to stigma and ostracism, a major problem that I come back to later; it further lowers life expectancy in communities where life expectancy is already low, decimates families and households through death, and creates a significant number of orphans.

As is clear from the foregoing, the list of the social effects of HIV/AIDS is long, and, to be sure, other impacts can be added to it. I have described this pandemic and its effects at length in this essay for three reasons: (1) it is not only the leading killer among African Americans but also the pace at which it is operating demands the attention of the Black Church and of black and womanist theologies; (2) it can be said without exaggeration that HIV/AIDS threatens the disintegration of the African American community; and (3) this pandemic threatens the relevance of the Black Church and of those who claim to be its theological representatives. Hence, black and womanist theologies, as well as the Black Church, need to make HIV/AIDS an urgent matter of analysis and action.

TOWARD A BLACK PRACTICAL THEOLOGY OF ENGAGEMENT

What, then, given this terrible crisis, must the Black Church—and those of us who claim to speak on its behalf (i.e., black and womanist theologians)—do to stop HIV/AIDS and to serve its victims? What sort of theology and what sort of practical theological programs do black churches need in order to intervene in this culture of death? Indeed, in what ways must the Black Church rethink and re-create itself in new and more relevant ways of being in the age of HIV/AIDS? These are not easy questions to answer, and I do not pretend to answer all of them here. One important place to begin is by recognizing the unique place of the Black Church in American history. It has always provided leadership in the struggle for freedom. For example, it was central to the emergence and work of the Civil Rights movement; it has defined important forms of Black Nationalism; and it is essential to cultural understandings that have shaped the language and symbols of African American history.

As is well known, the African American church historically was, and in some respects remains, the most important place of community building, identity formation, and social and political refuge, a place where justice was and is preached, black dignity affirmed, and human well-being promoted. This inheritance is, of course, why the African American community is still, perhaps, the most churched in America. Here I wish to signal the strategic place that the African American church occupies in the black community. It is "a pillar of the community."[12] No effective social programs, let alone effective black practical theology, can be forged that do not take seriously the historic centrality of the Black Church.

This no doubt is the reason that health professionals concerned with developing efficacious interventions against HIV/AIDS in the African American community have identified the church as an important institution with which to partner in this effort. Moreover, the strategic importance of the African American church in the effort to combat HIV/AIDS derives from the fact that many African Americans infected with HIV/AIDS see it as a potential source of help and comfort. The findings of the research done by Edward V. Morse et al. confirm this argument.[13]

Of course, it is important to recognize theologically that the church is there not simply to serve as an instrument for accomplishing the goals and purposes of the health-care system but rather to serve the poor, the marginalized, the hungry, and the sick. In other words, there is a specifically theological reason for undertaking this work. All this is well and good. Unfortunately, black churches, together with black and womanist theologies, have been apathetic and slow to intervene against HIV/AIDS. I need to be careful here and acknowledge that the Black Church has a plurality of identities and expressions so that it is, of course, misleading to say that all black churches have not been engaged with HIV/AIDS and the health-care crisis.

I also must acknowledge that not all black churches have the personnel and the financial means to fight HIV/AIDS. To be sure, there are churches that boast of health-care ministries and pastors who have been engaged in fighting HIV/AIDS.[14] Indeed, one could point to the fact that 250 black religious and faith leaders were involved in the creation of the HIV manual for black churches recently released by the National Association for the Advancement of Colored People (NAACP) as evidence to counter my claim that the Black Church has been apathetic with regard to HIV/AIDS. However, my point is not to deny these important efforts but to highlight the fact that black churches have not taken this issue as an urgent matter.

Whether a church has the personnel and the financial means to fight HIV infection is not the primary issue. Churches can use their position in the community to spread the message of HIV prevention. The pulpit provides an authoritative place from which to do so. In 2006, Jesse Jackson said, "HIV/AIDS has been allowed to stalk and murder black America like a serial killer because we have been a compliant victim, submitting through inaction. It is now time for us to fight HIV/AIDS like the major civil rights issue it is."[15] In 2012, six years later, Rev. Timothy W. Sloan of St. Luke's Missionary Baptist Church, in Humble, Texas, said, "It's imperative we begin this conversation [about HIV/AIDS]."[16] It is quite simply remarkable that we are still urging *the beginning* of a conversation about HIV/AIDS decades after the virus started destroying the African American community.

The Black Church continues to be reluctant to engage with HIV/AIDS because infection with the virus is associated with sex and homosexuality. Many churches simply do not want to talk about sex and sexuality, especially where homosexuality is involved. Many churches associate infection with sexual promiscuity and sin. This attitude gives rise to stigma and discrimination against those infected by HIV and those suffering from AIDS as well against homosexuals, injecting drug users, men who have sex with other men "on the down low," and many African American women who are disproportionately impacted by the virus.[17] Stigma is one of the greatest obstacles to fighting HIV/AIDS generally and in the African American community especially. Stigma consists of socially sanctioned attitudes, prejudices, and acts or practices of discrimination, exclusion, and disqualification of people whose identities are thought to be deviant or radically defective and thus in some way threaten the social and moral order. It is the medium of ostracism and marginalization of people with HIV/AIDS. Stigma is a way of suspending or even denying the humanity of the stigmatized other.[18]

Now, these are not attitudes and practices we expect those who proclaim the good news of the love of God to participate in. While, to be sure, the responses of the African American church have been complex and varied, some churches have embraced fear, silence, and stigma as responses to HIV/AIDS. Clearly, some pastors have shown tremendous courage and have spoken out about HIV/AIDS. But many pastors fear speaking to their congregations about HIV/AIDS lest they drive away church members and undermine their financial support; others speak about HIV/AIDS in stigmatizing and derisive terms; and yet still others, while less derisive, have been very slow to take on the challenge of the pandemic. Among the questions that these factors raise is, how can the church broadcast love and salvation while ignoring such massive suffering and death in its midst? Furthermore, how can black and womanist theologies proclaim liberation and freedom while being inattentive to the virulent destruction caused by HIV/AIDS? I propose that these questions provide a great opportunity for both the Black Church and black and womanist theologians to rethink their approach to HIV/AIDS as a theological and ethical issue that demands effective practical intervention. This intervention requires a black practical theology that is fully attuned to the world. I will conclude this essay by suggesting some features of such a theology.

I have already suggested that the first feature of such a theology is faith seeking understanding—namely, understanding of the suffering of African Americans and thus understanding of the social, political, and economic causes of such suffering. The statistics and descriptions of HIV/AIDS that I presented above help us grasp what such understanding entails. Without such understanding, it is impossible to be properly engaged with the world. I have argued that there are at least three aspects of the world as it actually is that a black practical theology must put at the center of its understanding: (1) The world is characterized by moral, social, and physical brokenness. It is circumscribed by the tragic and the messiness of sin, filth, and evil. HIV/AIDS represents this brokenness at all three levels. (2) There is real pain, suffering, and death in the world. And (3) the world is a scene of the great drama of salvation in which God intervenes to heal and restore humans to their true, holistic selves.

This is the context in which faith comes to know God as the God of life and human well-being. Understanding the world is important, not

only because the Church exists in the world and often is part of its brokenness but also because the Church is called to serve the world. Often
Christians separate themselves from the reality of the world by pretending that they belong to another world by virtue of their holiness. This act
misunderstands the gospel of Jesus Christ. Jesus did not separate himself
from the world. His incarnation and ministry attest to God's affirmation
of the world (God so loved the world) as does the coming of the Holy Spirit
into the world. The point is that once detached from the world, holiness
amounts to nothing more than moralistic self-glorification supported by
stigmatizing practices and attitudes. Genuine holiness entails engaging
the world as it presents itself to us in all its grubbiness, deficiencies, and
filth. This was the example of Jesus, who did not run away from tax collectors, adulterers, the disabled, prostitutes, the mentally ill, and lepers but
sat down with them, ate with them, and even touched and healed them.
Ignorance and fear of the world undermine the mission of the church and
compromise the integrity of the gospel of Christ. Pastors and theologians
who want to make the world a better place can only do so to the extent
that they take the world seriously. This means that the church, its pastors,
and theologians must *become* genuinely worldly if they want to be true
followers of Jesus.

This brings me to the second feature of a black practical theology of
engagement on which I wish to comment. To *become* worldly is an act of
repentance. A black practical theology of engagement is one that sum-
mons pastors and their congregations to a fundamental reorientation of
personal, social, and ecclesial attitudes toward accepting and affirming
the dignity of the poor, victims of HIV/AIDS who have been turned into
social outcasts, the wretched, and those facing discrimination because of
ethnicity, race, gender, or sexuality. Repentance, as I envisage it, involves
embracing a new paradigm of being Christian and of being the Church.
It is an active refusal to submit to the stigmatizing logic of fear and ignorance. This refusal must permeate every dimension of a person's being or a
community's life so as to become an intrinsic part of the actions and out-
looks that govern everyday interactions. When that happens, a new active
way of being the Church foregrounds the ongoing creation of inclusive
community.

The third feature of an effective black practical theology is how it
affirms human dignity. This affirmation begins by acknowledging that
victims of HIV/AIDS, drug addicts, gays and lesbians, prostitutes, and
beggars are made in the image of God and possess rights like everyone

else. It is for this reason that Jesse Jackson and the NAACP are right in declaring that HIV/AIDS has become the civil rights issue of this era. Indeed, I wish to go beyond Jackson and the NAACP to add that it is first and foremost a human-rights issue. Civil rights without human rights are empty. The important theological point to keep in mind here is this: both human and civil rights are only meaningful to the extent that they are grounded in some notion of human dignity, which derives from our having been made in God's image. The Black Church must remember its long and hard struggle in this arena.

The fourth feature of the kind of theology I am describing here is practical engagement with social and political problems. Instead of standing on the sidelines, or hiding behind moralistic claims or empty academic generalizations about liberation, black pastors, along with black and womanist theologians, must become fully involved in combating HIV/AIDS. For black and womanist theologians, this means writing books and articles that describe, analyze, and engage the empirical realities of human suffering. For all black Christians, it means working collaboratively with organizations (secular and religious) that provide help to victims of HIV/AIDS. Since the work of combating HIV/AIDS is vast and complex, such collaboration is necessary. No single church can do it effectively. HIV/AIDS work involves supporting programs that promote safe sex and encourage HIV testing drives in churches and other venues. There are many different organizations and agencies with which the African American church can partner in this work. These include, among others, the Balm in Gilead,[19] a faith-based not-for-profit agency founded to combat HIV/AIDS in African American communities; the NAACP, which recently published an HIV/AIDS manual, "The Black Church & HIV, The Social Justice Imperative," for use by black pastors; the Centers for Disease Control and Prevention; the National Minority AIDS Council; the AIDS Foundation; and the many HIV/AIDS programs that have been established in some black churches (such as Trinity United Church of Christ in Chicago or Greater Mount Calvary Holy Church in Washington, D.C.) as part of their health-care ministries.

The fifth and final feature of an effective practical black theology is that it will operate out of the framework of what I call "theodicies of care." This approach actually focuses the Church and Christian theology on witnessing to compassion and love instead of focusing on largely useless philosophical and theological explanations that seek to reconcile evil and the goodness of God in the world. Such theodicy assures victims of HIV/AIDS of the presence and commitment of caregivers that embody solidarity in lament, empathy, and love. As I have argued elsewhere, "The question is not whether God's goodness and evil can be reconciled, but rather what people of faith are doing to alleviate and assuage the suffering of others, and where possible, to rid the world of pain."[20] The challenge of human and care-centered theodicy is to ensure that victims of tragedy and those undergoing pain and distress "retain or have restored to them a grounded sense of their humanity and their dignity."[21] The supreme example of this challenge was Christ, who powerfully dramatized and modeled this kind of theodicy.

<< 16 >>

RETHINKING THEOLOGY FOR
IMPOVERISHED CARE

Gina M. Stewart

In his essay for this volume, "Black Practical Theology of Health and HIV/ AIDS Health Care," Edward Antonio makes a compelling case for a practical theology of health and health care. Antonio argues that black theology and black churches should engage both liberation ethics and pastoral care with an understanding that Christian theology and church ministries ought to cultivate how health or health care lie at the center of the physical, spiritual, emotional well-being of persons in community. Antonio explains that an effective and plausible black practical theology of health and health care will be driven by a ceaseless quest to understand the world. This quest, however, seeks to understand not merely the world as it ought or could be—or the world as imagined through a set of moral practices that exhort Christians to take flight from their present reality—but rather the world as it is, particularly as it is shaped by poverty and HIV/AIDS.

One of the greatest tasks in pastoral ministry for practical theology has been the task of "rethinking theology" for doing ministry in the world as it is. In the book *How to Think Theologically*, Howard Stone and James Duke state,

> Never has sound theological reflection on the part of Christians been more necessary than in a post-911 era. When a quarter of a million people die in a single natural disaster, three million people in Africa die each year from AIDS, millions more groan with rampant hunger and poverty and war continues to tear the world apart, we must bring our faith to bear upon the small and big decisions we make each day. How we think theologically makes a difference. It is a way we witness to our faith.[1]

In the early days of my pastorate, I discovered that many of the beliefs that the people in the pew hold about God and about the manner in which God relates to the world, particularly in relation to HIV/AIDS and poverty, are strongly influenced by what Stone and Duke refer to as "embedded/first order theology or the language of witness." As Stone and Duke describe, "These are the theological messages from the church that have been bred into the hearts and minds of the faithful since our entry into the church. And it is embedded theology that rushes to the front line in every battle over the moral and social issues of the day."[2] Embedded theology for many Christians represents the "oughtness" of the Christian faith or the world as it "ought to be."

For example, the church upholds abstinence as the standard for sexual activity, but the staggering statistics of HIV/AIDS–related deaths, force us to consider the "isness" of life and faith. Stone and Duke argue that people turn to deliberate theological reflections most frequently in times of crises. In this deliberate or deliberative turn to theology, we find that our faith emerges from convictions embedded in experience. Stone and Duke refer to this process of reflection as second-order theology. They explain that with this deliberate reflection we begin to question theology that previously went unchallenged. The effort we face, then, is to explore alternatives that might nurture more coherent meaning between faith claims and experience.[3]

Since all Christians think about God, the larger question is, what kind of theology will we do? And not just what kind of theology, but how will that theology shape and inform our praxis? It is precisely this embedded theology that often impedes our ability to shape a liberating practical theology relative to HIV/AIDS. I will never forget the first time our church observed World AIDS Day by inviting all of our members to wear a red ribbon and offer prayer for the lives lost to HIV/AIDS, as well as their families. At the close of the worship service, a woman walked up to me and said, "There will never be a cure for AIDS until all of the homosexuals repent and change their ways." On that day, I was shaken to the core not just by her boldness but also by her unwavering conviction that *all* instances of suffering for people living with HIV/AIDS were the consequences of sin.

The woman's comments were unsettling because her belief that AIDS was divine retribution for homosexual behavior blinded her to the need for compassion for all who suffer. But more importantly, her comments were not true and do not bear out with the experiences of many who are infected or affected by HIV/AIDS. While HIV can be transmitted through anal sex, it is also transmitted perinatally and through vaginal sex (or, more specifically, unprotected sex of any kind, be it vaginal, anal, or oral), contaminated drug injection equipment, and blood transfusions.

My eyes were opened many years ago after reading the book *Burden of a Secret: A Story of Truth and Mercy in the Face of AIDS* by Jimmy Allen, the former head of the Southern Baptist Convention. The book is a personal account of the transfusion-related death of his daughter-in-law and two grandchildren, and the revelation of one son's homosexuality and infection. Allen's story is a heartbreaking account of the ostracism and stigma his family faced by people whose response was largely shaped by ignorance and fear.

The comments made by that visitor to our World AIDS Day were confirmation that our participation in this event was not optional but essential to address the stigma of HIV/AIDS and to empower our congregation to begin to practice a liberating practical theology. The observance of World AIDS Day is just one of the ways that pastors can address the silence, fear, stigma, ignorance, and discrimination toward people living with HIV/AIDS. World AIDS Day observances provide a nonthreatening way to address the stigma of HIV/AIDS. Personal stories by persons infected and affected by HIV/AIDS, video clips, educational resources, and collaborative partnerships serve as catalysts that help to raise awareness, teach the facts, and dispel the myths.

But World AIDS Day observances are not enough, given the tragic impact of HIV/AIDS on communities, persons, and societies around the world. Pastors courageously must find ways to address the theological, anthropological, and ethical dimensions of HIV/AIDS if the church is to act as an advocate and agent of God's love. As Allen states in *Burden of a Secret*, "The AIDS epidemic provides the Church of Jesus Christ with an opportunity to express loving compassion. AIDS is a new, different sort of disease. Consequently, dealing with people who have been affected by the disease may well be the greatest challenge our modern day churches have. Ironically, AIDS may also force many contemporary churches to examine their motives for existence, to rediscover their mission in the world, and to reconnect with the Power to get that mission accomplished."[4]

The woman's comments about AIDS as a punishment for sin visited upon homosexuals revealed her deep theological convictions about sin and suffering, and the HIV/AIDS pandemic raises complex theological issues about the nature of sin and death, suffering, and human sexuality. It is virtually impossible to engage in any discourse about HIV/AIDS without also engaging in some discussion about deeply entrenched beliefs about human sexuality and more specifically about homosexuality and LGBT issues. For many people of faith, like the visitor who attended our church, HIV/AIDS is a gay disease that affects only homosexuals.

Therefore, it is essential that pastors and the church engage in courageous conversations and break the pulpit silence surrounding HIV/AIDS through awareness, education, and prevention. If the crisis of HIV/AIDS is to end, the church must serve as a trusted and courageous partner in the fight to end HIV/AIDS. One of the reasons I appreciate World AIDS Day is that it provides a platform for pastors to develop and preach sermons that critique our theology, stimulate thought, challenge prevailing myths, address fear, and assist pastors in addressing their congregations about HIV/AIDS issues as well as about compassion and *prevention* strategies. We must address the myths. AIDS is a disease that has had a devastating impact upon *all* people, particularly the African American community. HIV does not discriminate. It can affect anyone, regardless of race, sex, age, class, religion, marital status, or sexual orientation. Faith leaders must address its stigma in houses of worship. Below are some ways to destigmatize the disease:

1. Preach practically and prophetically about real-life issues, including HIV/AIDS, to influence theological reflection and encourage God's compassion.
2. Preach about God's love and compassion to transform the church culture to encourage a new way of living as Christ's people in the midst of suffering. Break the conspiracy of silence by engaging in theological and ethical reflection about HIV/AIDS.
3. Replace the myths with facts. In the past, people have had good reason to be afraid of contracting diseases. Despite the fact that HIV/AIDS has been around for more than thirty years, many people still do not know the truth about the disease and how it is treated and detected. Because of the life-changing work of medical science, we have the knowledge to keep us safe and address our fears. Education and awareness are empowering.
4. Establish an HIV/AIDS ministry to offer support and a place of refuge.
5. Base education on real-life experiences—for example, testimonials from persons infected by HIV/AIDS—to counter the misconception that HIV/AIDS is a homosexual disease.

Thus, Antonio's comments about doing black practical theology by seeking to understand the world as it is are so appropriate to offering a life-saving and life-changing ministry.

Regarding such disparaging embedded thinking on HIV/AIDS, an article by the International Center for Research on Women—citing Mbwambo, Kilonzo, and others—states, "The epidemic of fear, stigmatization and discrimination has undermined the ability of individuals, families and societies to protect themselves and provide support and reassurance to those affected. This hinders, in no small way, efforts at stemming the epidemic. It complicates decisions about testing, disclosure of status, and ability to negotiate prevention behaviors, including use of family planning services."[5] Not only has it hindered families and agencies, but it has hindered the church.

In Memphis, Tennessee, where there are more than 1,500 churches, the July 29, 2012, issue of the *Commercial Appeal* reported that the "city had the fifth highest proportion of newly infected patients. Despite making up just 52 percent of Shelby County's population, black residents accounted for 90 percent of the 2,049 new cases of HIV reported between 2006 and 2010, according to Health Department figures. In Tennessee, African Americans count for the majority of new HIV infections, 70 percent of the AIDS cases secondary to drug use, and 80 percent of AIDS cases among females."[6] The even greater tragedy is that HIV is a manageable chronic disease. With proper care and treatment, people can live longer and healthier lives. But this is difficult when both the infected and the affected are paralyzed by fear of the disease, shame, and fear of rejection.

In our lives as preachers and pastors, we are compelled to challenge and encourage African American people of faith to embrace a more practical, meaningful, and substantive approach to HIV/AIDS. As Emmanuel Lartey notes in his essay in this volume, "The Black Church has historically been the main social institution founded by Blacks in the New World to provide social and communal expression to the longings of black people for humanity and salvation."[7]

The growing crisis of HIV/AIDS has evoked a dilemma for the Black Church that demands concrete responses to the challenges presented by HIV/AIDS. I agree with Lartey, who states, "The Black Church needs to regain its vision of itself as a *community of care* for black people. The Black Church as a community of care extends the work of Jesus Christ into contemporary society. It is necessary, then, for each local congregation to ask itself questions about what it is and what it is for within its location and context."[8]

The statistics previously mentioned reflect a longstanding troubling combination of ignorance, denial, hopelessness, apathy, general mistrust of public health and the health care system, and disinvestment in the holistic health of inner-city residents. Although many promising programs and initiatives provide access to screening and free primary medical and support services to people living with HIV/AIDS, the Black Church must continue to step up to the plate to address the impact of poverty and HIV/AIDS.

Although the Black Church has always been a cornerstone in our communities, it has also been a place that has caused deep hurt and pain. Social stigma makes HIV/AIDS even more difficult to face. Stigma is a powerful and discrediting social label that radically and negatively affects the way individuals view themselves and the way others view them. Stigma reduces a person from wholeness to a tainted, discounted, and second-class, marginalized human being. People infected with and affected by HIV/AIDS are stigmatized for a number of reasons, including the following:

1. Ignorance and fear: There is a lot of inaccurate information about how HIV is transmitted, and this misinformation creates irrational behaviors and misperceptions of personal risk. Many people discriminate because of their lack of knowledge. They think that sitting next to, eating with, or interacting with people living with HIV/AIDS will result in their contraction of the virus. Consequently they consciously or unconsciously avoid those infected.

2. Pride and self-righteousness: Some stigmatize people living with HIV/AIDS because they think they are better or holier than they are. Just as in biblical narratives underscoring some attitudes of the Pharisees confronting Jesus, pride and self-righteousness are vicious stumbling blocks to acts of compassion.

3. Theological conservatism and moral baggage: Many hold religious or moral beliefs that lead them to conclude that being infected with HIV/AIDS is the result of moral fault (such as promiscuity or deviant sex) that deserves to be punished. HIV/AIDS infection is often associated with behaviors (such as homosexuality, drug addiction, prostitution, or promiscuity) that are already stigmatized in many churches and society. From the early days of the AIDS epidemic, a series of powerful images reinforced and legitimized stigmatization and interpreted HIV/AIDS as a punishment (e.g.,

for immoral behavior); as a crime (e.g., in relation to innocence and guilt); as a war (e.g., in relation to a virus that must be fought); as a horror, in which infected people are demonized and feared; and as otherness, in which the disease is an affliction of those who are set apart. Most people become infected with HIV through sex, which often carries moral baggage. HIV infection is often thought to be the result of personal irresponsibility. Although this may be true in some instances, it is not always the case.

The effects of the stigma and discrimination that accompany HIV/AIDS, for whatever reason and at whatever level, bring negative consequences and construct a "no win" situation. Both those stigmatizing and the ones being stigmatized lose.

This stigma has produced destructive perceptions and beliefs about HIV/AIDS that often prevent the Black Church and clergypersons from wholeheartedly addressing its challenges for the following reasons. First, sexuality and sexually transmitted diseases are difficult subjects to talk about in churches, especially when many of the persons in the pew still view HIV/AIDS as God's punishment for homosexuality. Although the Black Church has distinguished itself as a liberating and socially conscious instrument of support in our communities, many African American clergy are theologically conservative in their application of Scripture. In some settings, any attempt to address the issue of HIV/AIDS is construed as condoning sin. Advocacy for HIV/AIDS awareness erects an additional barrier due to the church's general stance toward homosexuality. For many in the church, and in wider society, HIV/AIDS is almost inextricably connected to homosexuality; therefore, much of the early advocacy for HIV/AIDS awareness originated in the community of bisexual and homosexual men, which has had the unfortunate effect that many courageous communities of faith are reduced to silence, apathy, or indifference when it comes to openly addressing AIDS.

Second, the Church's painful silence on the issue of human sexuality exacerbates the stigma of HIV/AIDS. The dominant message of the mainstream evangelical church has been one of silence, denial, and "don't ask, don't tell, don't do," unless you are in a heterosexual marriage. As Hos 4:6 so aptly declares, "My people are destroyed for lack of knowledge." Our failures to articulate a theology of sexuality and/or to celebrate sexuality as one of God's good gifts and God's grand design for us have resulted in an alarming increase of unwed mothers giving birth to children with largely absent fathers and soaring rates of HIV/AIDS and sexually transmitted diseases.

Third, practical prevention messages advocating condom use are often perceived as hypocritically condoning the promiscuous sexual behaviors that most churches condemn. Meanwhile, Blacks and African Americans continue to be disproportionately affected by HIV infection. According to the Centers for Disease Control and Prevention, "The estimated rate of new HIV infections among blacks/African Americans (68.9) was 7.9 times as high as the rate in whites (8.7). In 2010, of all of the new HIV infections among blacks/African Americans, 51% were among MSM and 38% were attributed to heterosexual contact. Though the estimated number of new HIV infections among black/African American females decreased, they are still disproportionately affected by HIV infection. In 2010, 87% of black/African American females newly infected with HIV had infections attributed to heterosexual contact."[9]

Finally, although Jesus had compassion on the marginalized and untouchables of his day, such as lepers, HIV/AIDS has uniquely challenged the African American faith community because, as we repeatedly observe in the gospels, compassion can be difficult to muster when our perception of one's suffering is that it is punishment for sin (e.g., John 9:1-3; Mark 2:1-10). We struggle with significant reluctance and outright antipathy to touching the "new untouchables."

Lartey asks, "In what ways can this particular body of people bear witness to the saving acts of God in Christ? In what particular ways can this community of called-out" persons embody the care and love of Jesus for the needy in their locality? What *saving acts* can this community of people called out from and sent back to the society perform that will be a contemporary continuation of the redemptive work of Jesus Christ?"[10] This challenges churches to participate in "saving acts" and advocate for life through prevention as well as education that moves people of faith toward affirming ministry to persons who suffer with HIV/AIDS. One of the high callings of the church is to care for all who suffer.

Churches can respond in concrete ways by participating in the following actions:

1. *Promote HIV testing.* Everyone should know their status and be tested, particularly those who are sexually active and who have multiple sex partners. Free, anonymous, and confidential HIV counseling and testing are available in most communities. Our church periodically offers free confidential HIV testing, and I along with our ministers have participated in testing from the pulpit.

2. *Preach abstinence; teach prevention.* HIV is a preventable disease that cannot be spread through casual contact. Abstinence is the only 100 percent effective way to prevent the sexual transmission of HIV, but since many may not practice abstinence, safety must become the priority. Share prevention messages that are age appropriate and culturally sensitive.

3. *Show compassion.* Embrace those who are disenfranchised and at risk for HIV, including drug users, addicts, the homeless, and people who may be different in their sexual orientation.

4. *Empower people through collaboration and information.* Invite local HIV professionals to help congregations become knowledgeable about HIV and ways to access medication and treatment. Take advantage of collaborative partnerships to provide information and education to persons affected by and infected with HIV/AIDS.

5. *Provide basic and spiritual support to people living with AIDS.* Love is a universal language. God's love is expressed through loving deeds.

6. *Pray for compassion and a cure.*

7. *Put a "face" to HIV/AIDS.* Education and awareness are the strongest weapons in reversing the devastating toll HIV/AIDS is taking on the African American community. The world as it is demands that we rethink and critique our theology. The church needs new answers to new questions that will help us to reshape our practices.

Additionally, pastors must seek to offer members a broader set of interpretive and theological lenses for responding to this morally and ethically troubling crisis that is heightened by complex social challenges. Stigma and shame shroud HIV/AIDS. Stigma is a key factor in the spread of HIV/AIDS. Conservative theological stances in the pulpit and pew enact much of the stigma, particularly regarding issues of human sexuality, sexual health, and responsibility. There is hardly a more anxiety-provoking task for the preacher/pastor than to address controversial or potentially divisive matters of faith from the pulpit. Whether a public crisis erupts in the world around us or we hear congregational murmurings about difficult issues we have long avoided, there are moments when every preacher feels the need to speak a compelling—if not provocative—word related to some challenging aspect of faith.

Many people in our pews on Sunday morning wrestle with strong desires to hear their pastors address a full range of controversial and sensitive subjects. A great number of listeners express deep longing for an authentic word from preachers who are willing to risk and join with others in the difficult task of understanding God's ways amid life's challenges and crises. And yet, we seldom contend with the more difficult issues and sensitive topics from our pulpits. The need to address these urgent issues and questions of our time could not be greater. People of faith can benefit from an authentic word from preachers who are willing to risk and join with others in the difficult task of redressing the conflicted values and practices among our churches in society.

While redressing our duplicity with the stigma that shames those infected and affected, we can cultivate a commitment to provide preventive education that does not condemn persons and risk their withdrawal. The church can play a pivotal role in encouraging responsible behavior, HIV risk-avoidance and reduction, and sound and sober decision making within a framework of ethical and moral principles. Despite significant strides in HIV/AIDS prevention campaigns, many people living with HIV are still unaware of their status.

We must create climates of compassion. Christ Missionary Baptist Church created the Incarnational Witness HIV/AIDS ministry to offer education, assistance, compassion, advocacy, and awareness to help equip members with the necessary resources to address this issue with compassion. In addition to this ministry, we have encouraged and provided our congregants with opportunities to be tested or screened throughout the year.

Each year, we observe World AIDS Day. The scheduling of World AIDS Sunday during the season of Advent provides an opportunity for clergy and congregations to relate the hope of God in Christ to the experience of those infected and affected by HIV/AIDS. Advent is a season that represents expectation, hope, or prophecy (in some traditions). It is a time when the church not only celebrates the hope of the coming Christ but also anticipates and yearns for the healing and deliverance of a fallen and broken world. Observing World AIDS Day during Advent provides a perfect opportunity for the church to show the depths of God's love and the breadth of God's saving grace for all of God's children.

UNDERSTANDING HIV/AIDS: THE DISEASE, ADVOCACY, AND AGENTS OF GOD'S LOVE

Antonio reviewed some alarming statistics in his essay. African Americans suffer rates of illness (e.g., diabetes, various forms of cancer, infant mortalities, and HIV/AIDS) well beyond the predominantly white population and are crippled further by gross inequities of treatment or preventive health care. How, then, may our churches possibly respond?

A striking model for our response is the advocacy found in the Gospel of Mark (5:25-34), which records the story of an unnamed woman living with a chronic condition described as "an issue of blood." The facts of her illness are straightforward; she had suffered for twelve years. She was bleeding to be exact; she had exhausted her HMO plan and could not obtain another referral; her prognosis was not good as her illness persisted. Equally amazing about this story of the woman with a blood-related illness was her effort to touch Jesus. According to the code in Leviticus, a woman with a blood-related illness was "unclean," defiling everyone and everything she touched (Lev 15:19-33). Had Jesus followed this code, he would have denounced the woman for touching him and demanded her punishment. Instead, Jesus had her stand up and openly identify herself; and then he publicly affirmed her: "Daughter, your faith has saved you; go in peace, and be healed from your scourge" (Mark 5:34). Jesus thus rejected the cruel stigma imposed upon this woman. He rejected the fallacy that "an issue of blood" is defiling and instead healed her.

This story is even more powerful when read within the context of the larger story. It is powerful enough that the woman comes up to Jesus from behind and obtains a blessing. She was not on the itinerary to be healed, for Jesus was on his way to Jairus' house to heal his sick daughter. On the surface, it seems that Jairus has the advantage. He is male, ritually pure, and privileged, and he holds a high religious office. The woman with the issue of blood, on the other hand, is female, impure, dishonored, and destitute. Although she has none of the advantages of Jairus, especially as she is an anonymous member of the crowd, Jesus has the power in both of these stories to overcome the defilement (bleeding and death) and to reverse it.

The Jewish laws concerning impurity sought to prevent it from infringing on the realm of God's holiness. Jesus' ministry shows that God's holiness is unaffected by human impurity. Throughout the Gospel of Mark, Jesus' connection with what is unclean does not render him unclean. Quite the reverse, Jesus purges the impurity. He touches a leper and cleanses him. He ventures into tomb areas and drives a legion of demons into a herd of pigs. A hemorrhaging woman touches him, and she is made whole. He touches a dead girl and brings her to life. Jesus does not need to purify himself from the pollution of a person with a flux or from contact with a dead body (Hag 2:13); he overcomes it.

Churches may have difficulty in conveying this important idea in our culture since we do not make such distinctions between clean and unclean. We do, however, treat some diseases as respectable and some as disreputable. For example, we attach no blame to someone who suffers a heart attack; but we may regard someone who has contracted a venereal disease quite differently. Perhaps we can recapture the original impact of this account if we try to think of similar characters with whom we are more familiar. The synagogue ruler would be someone well-bred, well-groomed, well-respected, and well-heeled. The woman would be just the opposite, one who would cause others to wrinkle their noses and curl their lips. She is at the mercy of those who make the rules and the money. She suffers from a disease that others judge to be degrading and that makes her life a misery.

Translating these characters into their modern counterparts allows one to raise telling questions. Should Jesus bother to stop for such a woman when he may endanger the life of one who is more "worthy"? We do not have to search the text further for an otherwise elusive answer—Jesus did stop. In this act, our Lord both defied social custom and chose to risk his own health and acceptability in society in order to place his healing hand on the sick woman and then a dead girl.

Why did Jesus act in this socially and medically unacceptable way? His acts worked out of compassion that did not and does not degrade or discriminate. Throughout his ministry Jesus was moved by compassion and modeled compassion. Compassion combines the emotional capacities of empathy and sympathy for the suffering of others. God's response to the human predicament is compassion. Because of divine love, the plight of God's creatures evokes God's compassion. The Hebrew word *racham* expresses a deep and tender feeling of compassion such as is aroused by the sight of weakness or suffering in those who are dear to us or need our help. Jesus' compassion expressed itself in ministry. As he saw the needs of people around him, Jesus did not stand idly on the sidelines. On the contrary, Jesus engaged in action and advocacy to alleviate the misery of others and minister to their needs. To those who had lost loved ones, Jesus responded by raising the dead (John 11; Luke 7:14). To people lacking guidance, he offered instruction and teaching. And to the sick, Jesus administered healing (Matt 14:14; 4:23; 9:35; 19:2).

These selected texts in Mark pose haunting questions in the midst of our uncertainty and caution about HIV/AIDS. If Jesus were present today, would he not be moved to compassion by and for persons with HIV/AIDS? While we must forthrightly admit that our constructed barriers make a compassionate, Christlike response to such persons difficult, the body of Christ is called with agency to dismantle such barriers by responding compassionately to persons suffering from the effects of this deadly epidemic.

I have found that the following characteristics of Jesus' ministry are critical to addressing poverty and HIV/AIDS:

1. Empathy. Empathy refers to the priestly nature of Jesus' ministry that provided comfort and assurance to anyone suffering and in trouble. This is reflected in his inaugural address in Luke 4:18, where Jesus declares that God has sent him to heal the broken and dejected. As Lartey explains, we need to embrace the dignity of divine creations for every person, all within community. We need to reject the rejection of anyone with regard to our interpersonal practices or our ecclesial ethos and dogma. To do otherwise in the Black Church to anyone "afflicted" with difference or need would be to replicate the historically racist practices of our dominating culture over black bodies, creating theological and social castes out of our appearance and political status.[11]

The ministry of Jesus Christ transcended the social constructions of sex, race, and class. All persons were equally valuable in his sight and presence. Jesus gave voice to the marginalized and extended love to the unlovable. The healing of the sick was central to Jesus' ministry. The gospels repeatedly indicate that Jesus was often "touched" by human needs and responded to them with acts of mercy. As Matt 4:23 reveals, Jesus held together proclamation, teaching, and meeting people in their needs with his healing ministry. In addition to sharing the good news of the kingdom, Jesus responded to our very human needs. The most distinctive aspect of Christianity is that the Divine entered into the human experience totally and completely. With such a mission, Jesus challenged those with material possessions to look after the poor as their duty and witness to the kingdom.

2. Advocacy. Jesus often broke barriers that divided people and challenged systems that perpetuated poverty and injustice. He always upheld the righteousness of God in his personal and social life. It was a dangerous and sacrificial path that continues to bring hope for a better world to God's glory. Teachings from the Hebrew Bible and Christ's ministry in the New Testament clearly represent the linkage between sacred revelation and social responsibility. Where the ravages of poverty, injustice, and oppression are clearly present, the Word of God insists that a faith speaking only to the spiritual needs of the people while failing to enact its compassion through practical help will be viewed as false worship (see Isa 58).

This dialectic between faith and care is desirable for black church praxis. As Raphael Warnock remarked during a lecture at Yale Divinity School, "It's a central theological tension in African American Christianity. The black church has had at each juncture in its history to ask itself the following theological questions: As an instrument of salvation through Jesus Christ, is the mission of the Black Church to save souls or to transform the social order? Or is it both? Authentic piety and true liberation are inextricably linked. . . . The mission of the true church is to save bodies and souls." It is only by acknowledging and living into this truth that black Christianity can "[bear] witness to the beloved community and the coming reign of God."[12]

In her book *Ministry at the Margins*, Cheryl Sanders states, "The kingdom prepared from the foundation of the world is a realm where all are filled and fed and free. One is qualified to enter that kingdom by exercising good stewardship of life itself, by ministering life out of the abundance one receives as a divine trust from God. And the gospel declares that eternal life is the reward of those who cherish life. Those who feed the hungry, give drink to the thirsty, take in the stranger, clothe the naked and visit the sick and incarcerated become identified with the inbreeding of God's kingdom in this world and move with God in the realm of human affairs. To disobey this biblical mandate is to deny service to the kingdom and the King."[13] The gospel invites the Christ follower and the church into solidarity with all who suffer, in that together we might receive, embody, and share the good news of Jesus in ways that enhance life for all.

3. Community. America is no different from most societies in our need for community. In every society, in every time, people have been excluded, discriminated against, and even killed because of their sexual preference, ethnicity, social status, disease status, and personal behavior. Jesus' message witnesses on behalf of the weakest and most vulnerable. Just as Jesus sought out and welcomed the marginalized as the first to share in the reign of God (Luke 14:12-14), the church must follow his example in welcoming those whom the world would reject.

Persons who suffer with HIV/AIDS and live in poverty are among the marginalized in today's society. Poverty is a systemic issue that increases the risk of becoming infected with HIV. Poverty drives women and girls to exchange sex for money, drugs, and personal needs. Limited access to quality preventive health care and the skyrocketing costs of health care in general necessitate advocacy by agents of God's love.

Like the lepers in Jesus' day, people in our world who suffer from HIV/AIDS are often pushed to the margins due to fear of contagion. They are isolated by ignorance, fear, bigotry, and prejudice. Thankfully, there are communities of faith that are rising to the occasion to create environments that not only foster acceptance, love, and compassion but also provide much needed services. Among these communities is the Metropolitan Interdenominational Church in Nashville, Tennessee, which operates the First Response Center. An article in *Colorlines* describes the outreach as

> a primary care clinic that provides HIV/AIDS testing, treatment, prevention services and education. Part of the 350-member church's outreach program, the health center is the brainchild of the Rev. Edwin Sanders and his fellow founding members. Since its inception, it has become a pillar of the predominantly black community in which it's located, and an essential resource for folks who are not able to obtain such services anywhere else. . . . The church's outreach—which provides HIV/AIDS patients with transportation to appointments, delivers prevention information to young adults, makes condoms available and at one time ran a syringe-exchange program—is distinctive.[14]

The clinic was funded by a generous grant from the URSA Institute several years ago. Per Sanders, "There are other congregations with primary care clinics that do other things, but ours is exclusively focused on HIV/AIDS."

Tony Lee, founding pastor of the Community of Hope Church in the Washington, D.C., metropolitan area, does something truly unusual. Four times a year, at the pulpit, he has himself tested for HIV in front of his entire congregation. "Lee's church holds up abstinence as the standard for sexual activity, but the pastor acknowledges that not everyone will live up to that standard. Safety, then, becomes the main priority. 'We have to deal with the fact that within our congregation and region, HIV and AIDS numbers are so high that we can't act like no one there is infected or affected,' Lee says. His church also distributes condoms. . . . According to Lee, the pastor's unorthodox strategy of testing during services has been encouraged and applauded by the community. He and his congregation have worked to raise AIDS awareness beyond the walls of the church through outreach services in clubs, hair salons, and barbershops."[15]

The weekend of December 1–2, 2012, our church, Christ Missionary Baptist Church, hosted our first Annual World AIDS Day Faith and AIDS

Conference. The conference featured a community breakfast, workshops, and a screening of the documentary *The Gospel of Healing.* The goal of the conference was to bring attention to the AIDS epidemic and to encourage a discussion on AIDS education, treatment, and care, particularly among faith leaders and the faith community. The conference featured national faith leaders who are engaged in HIV outreach and who are featured in the documentary (Edwin Sanders, senior pastor of Metropolitan Interdenominational Church; Tony Lee, the senior pastor of Community of Hope A.M.E Church; and Paul Grant, the producer of the documentary). The conference also provided free HIV testing courtesy of Planned Parenthood. On World AIDS Day, I, along with several of the ministers at the church, was tested for HIV.

The Mount Calvary Holy Church in Washington, D.C., copastored by Alfred and Susie Owens, was one of the first churches to begin an HIV ministry back in the 1990s. Initially, the HIV/AIDS ministry provided voluntary caregiver assistance to HIV-infected district residents who did not have adequate support systems. Today, their ministry has expanded its range of services to include spiritual support, counseling, case-management services, community-outreach partnerships, HIV education, and peer-educator training and certification. These are just a few examples of the ways in which communities of faith are working as advocates and agents of God's love.

HIV/AIDS AND POVERTY AND A BLACK PRACTICAL THEOLOGY OF ENGAGEMENT

No discussion of HIV/AIDS and poverty and of a black practical theology of engagement is complete without a discussion of the influence of prosperity theology. The Black Church has historically functioned as an oasis from a plethora of issues facing the black community. The issues here tend to differ from those among churches serving the majority culture. Black churches often advocate for social, political, and economic empowerment. Out of necessity, black churches historically had to minister to the whole person. As J. Deotis Roberts states in *The Prophethood of Black Believers*, "The black church has been sensitive to social justice issues from its inception because it has been ministering to an oppressed people. Therefore, interpretation of the gospel of Jesus Christ in the Black church tradition has been concerned about justice as well as love. Justice and love cannot be separated."[16] The Black Church has had to minister to the whole person because it rarely had the luxury of separating individual salvation from collective salvation. Consequently, black churches have typically focused on a much broader agenda, by addressing issues related to racism, poverty, economics, civil rights, and injustice, as well as issues of personal piety, holiness, ethics, and righteousness. An ethic of empowerment as espoused by black churches rejects a privatized faith that places a distorted emphasis on a highly spiritualized notion of salvation to the exclusion of a political understanding of salvation. Orthopraxy is just as important as orthodoxy. Faith that is not geared toward social praxis, that gives no consideration to the eradication of dehumanizing political and social structures, is a distorted faith.

I believe that the Black Church has functioned as a voice in the wilderness, crying out for equality and justice despite race, social status, or lived experience. The church operated as a twenty-four-hour, full-service institution, effecting change spiritually, intellectually, emotionally, and socially. People from all walks of life recognized that when resources were denied or exhausted, black churches were places where needs were met and issues addressed. The black minister not only preached a transformative message of salvation but also served as a community representative and social activist, preaching a message of social change, equality, and unconditional love.

However, in recent years, we have witnessed a rise in prosperity preaching practices that focus on personal economic thriving while falling away from a social justice agenda. As Robert Harvey asks, "In our contemporary society, [now] that the black church has become so focused on preaching messages regarding the attainment of economic success and personal prosperity, has it begun to lose sight of its foundational calling, rooted in a message of salvation, with the promotion of life, liberty and the pursuit of happiness?"[17] Lartey suggests, "Many black churches embrace particular forms of teaching that adumbrate material prosperity as a goal of faith and as evidence of God's blessing. This so-called prosperity gospel smacks of all the values of capitalist economics. It seems to arise out of and fit the cultural context in which it has been generated. Hence, it strongly advocates individual material wealth."[18] The calling of the Black Church, using the honored text of the Christian tradition, is best summarized by Jesus' reading of the prophecy of Isaiah: "to bring Good News to the poor . . . to proclaim that captives will be released, that the blind will see, that the oppressed will be set free" (Luke 4:18-19). Lartey presses us further to weigh critically any personal lifestyles that distort the sense of self-giving that is so central to discipleship. Lartey wants us to reevaluate the notions of prosperity within the rubrics of communal prosperity and the gospel, which place well-being of others and our communities at the center of faithfulness.[19]

Similarly, Brad Braxton further argues that we must question the types of churches that we do or do not cultivate. Have worship practices of spirituality become commodities that do not extend well beyond the doors or walls of the church? What roles or effects do our churches have in the world?[20]

For several years, I have served as a trustee for the Samuel DeWitt Proctor Conference (SDPC). The mission of SDPC is to nurture, sustain, and mobilize African American faith communities in collaboration with civic, corporate, and philanthropic leaders to address critical needs of human and social justice within local, national, and global communities. SDPC seeks to strengthen the individual and collective capacity of thoughtful leaders and activists in the church, academy, and community through education, advocacy, and activism. I have been convicted and challenged through my involvement with SDPC to embrace a social justice agenda as a means of engaging black practical theology. Movements like the SDPC have been instrumental in nurturing a social justice imperative while providing pastors and congregational leaders with empowering information, provocative lectures and sermons, models, and practical tools. Clergy and leaders who attend the conference are often energized and empowered to return to their various ministry settings with a renewed commitment to social justice.

According to James 2, Christians should "flesh out" a social justice agenda by fighting poverty. In the example, the believer, instead of filling a hungry stomach, sends the poor person away after spouting an empty cliché. Death is the consequence of socially irrelevant faith. Physically, death will overtake the poor, naked, hungry person. But spiritually, death has already overtaken the faith of unengaged believers. James 2 concludes with a clear equivalence; faith that fails to address serious social dilemmas is like a dead body with no spirit. Indeed, apart from the Spirit, congregations will suffocate, and the body of Christ will become a handsomely embalmed corpse. The Spirit's agenda is life, abundant life. The Spirit raised Jesus from the dead, and that same Spirit can enliven the body of Christ to "flesh out" a revolutionary social justice agenda in Jesus' name.

VII

Mass Incarceration, Capital Punishment, and the Justice System

In the United States, approximately 60 percent of black men without a high school diploma and 30 percent of those who do not have a college education are currently incarcerated. These figures reveal that the mass incarceration of black males in the United States is a crippling problem in the black community. In spite of this, our culture invests financially far more in the prison industry than in educational options. Investment in education could address many problems that otherwise lead to custodial sentences. The scholar Michelle Alexander observes that the justice system, with the high levels of incarceration it imposes on black males, constitutes a new kind of Jim Crow culture of injustice in that it now functions more like a caste system than a system to dispense impartial justice. Racial caste has not ended in America; it has been redesigned. We have a punitive rather than a restorative model of justice. The convergence of race and class among those incarcerated raises critical questions of "racial threat theories," which study the punitive policing and prosecution practices of the criminal justice system in predominantly black neighborhoods. Moreover, the resulting felon disenfranchisement overwhelms many black communities and those churches serving inner-city neighborhoods. There are many African American males who have lost or relinquished not only their right to vote but also opportunities for employment and access to school and housing because of criminal histories or perceived criminal behavior.

The policies and administration of capital punishment execute African Americans and persons of color at an alarmingly disproportionate rate. These practices reveal problems with systemic justice and cultural racism. The large number of exposed cases of wrongfully convicted persons rescued from death row and of those wrongfully executed further chal-lenges the ethics of capital punishment. Additional questions concern-ing racial justice amplify the high levels of poverty among those persons charged, convicted, and executed, the vast majority of whom could not afford a lawyer or legal services beyond the court-appointed system.

In the 1990s, the U.S. Government Accountability Office reported dramatic racial disparities in terms of charges and convictions of African Americans versus those of whites that result in the death penalty, par-ticularly if the victim of the crime was white. Amnesty International's figures underscore this discrepancy; it cites race as a major factor in nearly one-third of cases wherein African Americans end up on death row in some areas of the country, particularly when the victim is white. To put the degree of the problem another way, African Americans are nearly three times more likely to receive the death penalty in such cases.[1] How, then, might black theologians and practical theologians help black churches to frame and engage these systemic issues of justice, race, and poverty to restore, rehumanize, and re-member those disenfranchised in the communities they serve?

<< 17 >>

The Incarceration of Black Spirituality and the Disenfranchised

Michael Battle

I was listening to my friend preach in a maximum-security prison unit in Trenton, New Jersey, when an inmate interrupted the sermon to rebuke the other inmates talking in the corner. "Shut up!" he growled, staring at them with wild eyes. The others laughed while he gritted his teeth. This was the same inmate I had seen earlier tapping the top of his head with both hands to the beat of "Blessed Assurance." A black man, ill-clad, wearing white and faded blue, he lived in a different world than the rest of us, and he wanted to get on with "church." But his interruption did not seem to stop the others.

With peculiar gyrations he continued his command to "Shut up," his arms flinging like a symphony conductor. He looked at the majority of black men and screamed at them in the middle of my friend's sermon, "Are you in church or where you at?" A peculiar question, I thought. How could he really expect others to believe this was a real church service in the middle of a maximum-security prison unit? Sure, they had sung hymns, there were ministers in the room, there was a lectern posing as a pulpit, there were musical instruments for praising God, the chairs were lined up for an assembly of people, and those assembled even prayed to God as if God were truly there, but how could he really expect to be "at" church? The rational explanation is that he does not fit in the normal world.

This experience begins my reflection on figuring out where Christian spirituality is really "at." When I teach spirituality, I find it as difficult to fit its discourse into a university graduate school or church setting as into the prisoner's maximum-security unit. His command to "Shut up" and his question "Are you in church or where you at?" provoked me to analyze the nature of a discourse like spirituality that does not seem to fit anywhere. Perhaps I too will be perceived only as a deranged prisoner, but that is a risk I am willing to take as long as the reader gives me the chance to present my vision.

My essential question is, how might black theologians and practical theologians help black churches to frame and engage spiritual discourse within systemic issues of justice and to re-member those disenfranchised in the communities they serve? Futhermore, how might I be spiritual in settings dissimilar to what I have been socialized to think could ever be where God is?

In this chapter, my goal for the reader is to imagine with me how I do indeed fit spirituality within dissimilar settings while sojourning along with me through the hard questions of the prisoner in the maximum-security unit. At the end of the day, I invite the reader to see (for some, perhaps to imagine) with me how the seeming contradictions of spirituality and the penal system indeed form a paradox. My imagination allows me to envision how spirituality creates a lens through which to see systemic issues of justice that are constitutive of an environment of people corporately attentive to surprising realities, even the reality of the presence of God.

My aim is to connect what I do when I teach and serve as a priest to other artisans in the world. I see others as artisans because we each have been trained in specific ways to continue the traditions of discourse through the ways we have learned to interpret reality. For example, how do other professors teach in a university? The astronomy professor keeps her students open to the surprising realities of black holes. Biologists open the vision of premed students to see beyond the lucrative salaries of being a doctor to the mystery of cellular membranes. I argue that theologians teach in similar ways as these other academic professionals who aim to open their students' minds to surprising realities. Our common craft is our ability to open in our students new worldviews that contain surprising realities. Such a craft is extremely important in a world in which simplistic answers by which we learn to objectify reality and thereby seek absolute control over it are the norm. One would think theologians would naturally swim in a worldview that counters such objectification, that we would naturally understand the complexity of a creation able to be mutual with divine infinity. Our problem as theologians, however, is that we have often abused the process of opening students up to surprising realities through our failing to teach theologically.

The African master of Christian spirituality, St. Antony, teaches us to ask the right questions so we have a chance at discovering the right answers. Largely, when dealing with issues of spirituality, this is the crux of the matter. In the African desert tradition of Christian spirituality, there is a story that goes like this:

> A young student came to a monk and asked, "What kind of prayer is not acceptable before God?"
>
> "This is the right question," the monk answered, and kept silent.
>
> But the student did not perceive that his original question had been answered, and so, asked the same question again.
>
> This time the monk answered, "There are two kinds of prayer that are not acceptable to God. First, to ask for revenge; and second, to pray for yourself."
>
> "How can this be?" the young disciple asked the monk. "How can prayer not involve praying for self?"
>
> The monk answered, "If God bears with us, who are sinners and who often offend God, how much more is it right that we should bear each other's burdens and put up with each other. So, it is not good that we should ask for things for ourselves because such prayer is a sign that we do not believe in God—that God already knows what we need."
>
> The disciple then asked, "How should I then pray?"
>
> The monk said, "Pray for repentance. Pray that the lost will be found. Pray for friendliness toward those who wish you harm and love toward those who persecute you. If you do these things, you cannot help but become that very prayer."[1]

Like St. Antony and the deep African Christian tradition of spirituality, the aim of this chapter is to deepen a sense of consciousness and praxis through the lens of spirituality. Like my colleagues in this volume, I follow some of the questions and contours of black practical theology by developing a sense of spirituality that often remains unconscious and even absent in our black churches. Therefore, a key aim of my chapter is to bring spirituality—a discrete discourse within practical theology—into dialogue with church and parachurch leaders in black communities. First, I seek to do this through the inculturation of spirituality, to which I will speak shortly. By inculturating spirituality, I am able to address the incessant problem of racism—the elephant in the room—within both academic and church institutions. Second, I offer a way forward in terms of what I call "mutuality." Before I get too far ahead of myself, let me reflect further on the purpose of this book.

The discipline of practical theology has a well-established history. Practical theology focuses on human praxis as a point of departure when thinking through and reflecting upon the revelation of God. It is my hope that a conversation with spirituality may offer a creative approach to such revelation, especially among this collaboration with black theologians, practical theologians, and practitioners. Therefore, it is necessary that I clarify how I understand and use the term "spirituality." Spirituality (or ascetical theology) is among the traditional subdisciplines of practical theology. My task here is to facilitate a conversation between the discourse of spirituality and the issues shaping black contemporary worldviews and religious practices in black church communities.

THE INCULTURATION OF SPIRITUALITY

Spirituality in the African context must be addressed in order to understand the resilience and character of African Americans and the Black Church. Although there has been in the last two decades a renaissance in African and African American churches through the arts of storytelling, recitation, dance, mime, and the dramatic representations of the gospel, there remains the difficult dynamic of understanding African spirituality apart from the context of suffering that has shaped the patterns and character of people of African descent. St. Paul seems to understand this pattern when he writes to the Church in Rome, "[S]uffering produces endurance, [4]and endurance produces character, and character produces hope, [5]and hope does not disappoint us" (Rom 5:3-5). However, when we try to apply God's process of spiritual character within our human systems, we still struggle with disappointment.

The systematic and oppressive mass incarceration of black males in America is a justice issue that scholars and pastors must address. In the United States, there continues to be an alarming racial imbalance in the prison population. A review of the research provided earlier in this issue's description of black males incarcerated in the post–Civil Rights era reveals that nearly two-thirds do not complete high school and nearly one-third never attain any college education. Comparatively, the percentages of white males incarcerated in those same years remained in the single digits.[2] The effects of such mass incarceration reveal a systemic assault upon the black community.

Michelle Alexander has demonstrated convincingly that the justice system currently operates with a Jim Crow impunity of injustice. In short, our so-called justice system produces a caste class out of blackness.[3] It is a travesty that racial caste is alive and well in the United States; it may segregate differently, but its ruthlessness is undiminished. In those cases wherein renewed segregation appears inadequate to ward off black threat, execution resurges as the justifiable solution, regardless of the repeated exposure of racially skewed data showing dramatically disproportionate prosecution and conviction, and grotesque executions of innocent defendants.[4] Our models of policing and prosecution are as much targeted as they are retributive. For those who might survive our judicial and penal systems, our felony laws governing them after imprisonment perpetuate the sentencing and segregation from full citizenship in terms of employment, housing, or even voting rights. I learned these things first-hand through my prison chaplaincy work in Alexandria, Virginia, and Los Angeles, California. In light of these systemic issues of justice and a seemingly recalcitrant culture that does not seek change, how might black theologians and practical theologians inculturate spirituality that may attend to those disenfranchised in the communities they serve?

The word "spirituality" is Christian in origin. Like many other words in the Christian vocabulary, it has been devalued to the level of anaemia and banality and denotes a religion characterized by inwardness. Despite the anchoritic character of St. Antony and the African desert tradition, much of African Christian spirituality guards against any such inward spirituality. In other words, Christian spirituality is far from a navel-gazing endeavor. Preoccupation with self is precisely what African Christian spirituality is not meant to be. Instead, spirituality is a dynamic concept in which we are all interdependent. The very word derives from *spiritus*, the life-giving force that stems from God and transforms human relationships. Based upon this character of spirituality, certain themes can be established for the Black Church as a whole. These include the following:

The desire for dynamic worship;
The emphasis on communitarian living;
The effective oral memory of past events;
The vital relationship between the living and the dead;
The faithful vigilance in overcoming the human causes of evil.

Through such themes, we should understand that African American spirituality at its heart is derived from the tragedy of suffering, especially that associated with slavery. It is because of the tragic drama of the slave trade that African Americans learned to practice spirituality differently than Europeans. As a result, another spiritual view of human life emerges for the Black Church. For example, how one responds to death in the Black Church is different than in many white worship services. Whereas in Caucasian worship there is an awkward silence about death, which often manifests in ways of hiding the body or in cremating it, in African American contexts, particularly in rural areas, death is a stark reality with which everyone is familiar. Although death is described in terms of "silence" and "immobility," it is nevertheless a new beginning for black Christians. Wandera-Chagenda, an East African poet, laments such senseless death. She speaks passionately in her work "Zero Hour" about the intruding finger of death that is always near, highlighting the uncertainty of our future and raising the specter of violence before finally rendering us motionless in that "zero hour."[5] It is not just a cipher that signifies nothingness but the end of a countdown.

This East African poet invites us back into the desert tradition. As the monk taught the young student, a spiritually mature person is one who learns how to situate self-consciousness within God's life. By doing so, even death is relativized and defanged. Often, this practice involves detachment from, or a consciousness of the death of, the self, which is essential to spiritual growth. Such practice and meditation fashioned a kind of eternity for those early African Christians. In Jesus Christ, it is no longer difficult to die nobly. Herein, one learns how the church may discover resurrection or freedom through a renewed sense of spirituality, one that is based on not only survival but also transformation.

The tradition of African Christian spirituality understands the interdependence between the personal and the communal in Jesus. Jesus' spirituality is the same thing as living in communion with God. Through Jesus' spirituality, humanity is capable of being personally present in the relationships of God. Jesus makes us see that spirituality rises from his death into the essential disposition of the believer—living in God's community. As Wandera-Chagenda's poem reminds us, death can be an experience not only of culmination but also of starting again. This points to one of the most powerful aspects of Christian spirituality: forgiveness.

Only God forgives, but such forgiveness invites creation into this ability always to start again. This is so with Jesus, as his spirituality imparts a new dimension to the believer's life. In other words, it is not only a new way of looking at human life but also a new way of living it. It follows that the concept of Jesus' spirituality can be applied to the church, especially the Black Church, which was shaped by such a checkered past. But how does a church steeped in the religion of colonialism and civil war begin again? One answer is to understand how God has always been with the Church—trying to free her.

Lamin Sanneh's *Translating the Message* is an example of Christian engagement with how Christians can begin again, especially in understanding the abuses of Christian mission. This is very important, and, as I will discuss shortly, the problems in our penal system have not occurred by accident. Sanneh develops the theme of translation, particularly the translation of the Bible into what he calls "vernacular cultures."[6] Christian missionaries had a great impact on indigenous peoples. And while some missionaries respected the vernacular culture through careful Bible translations and learning the indigenous languages, others were less sensitive and pressed Western culture upon those populations they were intended to serve. Whether they knew it or not, Christian missionaries provided the stimuli to "touch off wider and longer-lasting repercussions in the culture."[7] This benign effect of translating the gospel into other cultures produces what Sanneh describes as a "vernacular logic" (i.e., the constant need of the gospel to empower indigenous peoples).

AFRICAN ELEPHANT IN THE ROOM

The problem, however, for Sanneh throughout his work is the recognition of the obvious abuses of colonialism and a lot of missionary work through which much of African and African American Christians have had to negotiate. How can Christians be more responsible in acknowledging this elephant in the room? "Responsibility" is always in danger of being a rather grey word; it can be used repressively and even menacingly. I have learned a lot from Archbishop Rowan Williams with respect to the problem of responsibility for a colonial past. Williams helps us think critically about how the charge "You must act responsibly!" shapes what the world around says to us, to me; it is about restrictions, about properly negotiating our purposes in full awareness of the claims of others.[8]

Williams also makes us go further. Responsibility means not just that we are responsible *to* others and that others have a right to demand certain kinds of behavior from us; we are also responsible *for* each other. Each of us has to answer for someone else's welfare as well as our own, and that means that someone else must answer for us, whose concern is our welfare. This theme is deeply rooted in our Judeo-Christian ethics. From God's question to Cain—"Where is your brother?"—to St. Paul telling us to "bear one another's burdens," this ethical tradition affirms that the most fruitful and peaceful common life depends on our willingness to speak and act for each other.

Reform in our prisons naturally questions whose interests are suffering at any given moment, whose voice is unheard. And, of course, one must deal seriously with the rights of victims. The way in which our legal processes have exacerbated victimization has been a constant refrain, especially where crimes against women and children or otherwise vulnerable people are concerned. This arises in part from a very natural reaction against sentimental attitudes to offenders.

One reason that Williams' insights are valuable is that it is all too easy to work from a notion of crime wholly bound up with the individual responsibility and punishment of the offender as a means of denying those interpersonal, social, and communal claims. But crime has effects that spiral outward from the single act or group of actions at its center and into the lives of many people. The practical question for all of us is how to attend to the mending of all that has been broken in this process? In this pursuit, the new emphasis on the welfare of victims and the creation of groups like Victim Support modify questions about how various aspects of the legal process intimidate victims.

In terms of being more responsible for both the offender and the victim, Williams points out that consumerism dictates the insidious ways in which the legal system functions, as it does so many other areas of our public life. Even in the attempt to do justice from the perspective of the victim, consumerism runs the risk of imagining the victim as perennially passive, someone to whom things, good or evil, are done. The shift toward the concerns of victims began with the recognition that the existing system left victims feeling powerless; yet, the danger now is the creation of a culture in which they remain powerless to change. A system at the mercy of organized lobbying on behalf of the victim cannot serve the real interests of the victim because it can never break free from the role of the victim at just the point where someone might need help shedding that role. Should we not be thinking about policies aimed at restoration and working to facilitate the victim's ability to engage meaningfully with society again?

If some of the language around the needs of victims has these rather ambiguous implications, how do we begin to think about the needs of offenders in a more healthy way? If the problem underlying crime is a breakage in relationship, then the offender has lost the active sense of being answerable for others. That sense is, as I have suggested, inseparable from the assurance of having others who are answerable for you. The most unhelpful, and indeed damaging, way of treating this breakage is surely a system that leaves the offender without any grounds for believing that he or she is the object of anyone's responsibility.

Much of our present system still sends this message to the offender. The statistical likelihood is that an offender will be warehoused in over-crowded conditions and deprived of privacy; that contact with family will be vulnerable to unpredictable moves and varying policies in differ-ent institutions; and that informal personal support (such as the excel-lent work of many prison ministries, for example) will be at best patchy. Families of prisoners, including very disturbingly remanded prisoners, who die in custody thankfully now have the assurance of a transparent investigation into their deaths. The unrelenting message of second-class citizenship, though, endures well beyond the prison walls. Rehabilitation upon reentry into society is as elusive as restoration in matters of employ-ment applications, public housing, and ever mounting debt from actual prison or parole. And, of course, prisoners are still deprived of the vote.

Likewise, the current prison service understandably prides itself on the quality of some of its rehabilitation and detoxification programs. All of these programs address the urgent need to provide stable and reliable services for offenders at every stage of their progress through the system and back into the community. But plenty of challenges and controversies remain over how to deliver on these new aspirations and standards, and much of this work is still embryonic. The risk of fragmentation, wherein services are contracted to private providers, is still a contested aspect of developing patterns in offender management. And the quality of services within prisons poses the uncomfortable question of why so many people with drug problems and (especially) mental health problems are in cus-tody in the first place, and why prison is expected to supply what ought to be available for vulnerable individuals in the community at large. If cer-tain kinds of care and treatment are more available to some people only in custodial conditions, then the message is still that a deficiency in respon-sibility prevails.

If we seriously want to address the problem of reoffending, then we must realize that a penal culture is worse than useless when it gives so little real attention to how offenders change, as evidenced in the system's reinforcing of alienation, deepening of low self-worth, and lack of any sense that offenders or ex-offenders have a stake in the life of a commu-nity. To create another kind of culture in the criminal justice system, one committed to building responsibility, we must first get rid of the tacit assumption that managing the needs of both victims and offenders is a zero-sum game. According to the logic of this game, for the victim to "win," the offender must "lose" as much possible, and vice versa. In the end the game does nothing to promote the wholeness and healing of either party. Still, new models do not spring to life ready-made. The main tools of a policy that will avoid the zero-sum deadlock are models of community justice and of restorative justice—namely, mediation, conferencing, confrontation between offenders and victims, and attempts to achieve some kind of emotional closure by apology or reparation. Restorative-justice models are seen by some as giving offenders a free pass: the chance to avoid appropriate punishment by going through certain motions that are not too difficult to learn, that may or may not be of use to victims, and that in fact may risk further damaging them. Yet, it would be disastrous if such negative perceptions or suspicion stopped us from thinking through these models more carefully. Actually, community-justice and restorative-justice models have a good deal in common. Both take seriously the notion that those most directly involved in a criminal event have the largest stakes in containing and dealing with its consequences.

Models of community and restorative justice need to gain consent from both offenders and victims. That is, they have to define and deliver outcomes that will be attractive enough to hold the confidence of those involved; these include some sort of reparation and closure for the victim and some sort of new means of self-empowerment and opportunity for the offender. These models and outcomes will take time. What victims and offenders believe they need may not in fact be what will most help them. There will be some victims for whom reparation can mean something like revenge; there will be offenders who confuse empowerment with an escape from guilt. Victims (or their advocates) may, as we have seen, want to control the fate of offenders; offenders may want to accumulate merit marks to secure better treatment (i.e., early parole, if they are within the custodial system). Faced with these difficulties, the temptation may be to cut corners.

The whole complex of penal issues would be less likely to be abused and exploited by politicians and commentators if there were wider ownership of an approach that asks how the criminal justice system helps to bring about change. The law encodes our respect for human dignity in general, but this should not be taken to mean that the function of the justice system is only to flatten out a bumpy surface or to restore a disturbed situation to the status quo. It must also be the guarantor of possibilities, clearing the way for individual citizens to exercise their dignity by taking part in the processes of shaping the conditions of their lives.

This does not mean that the law in itself is the agent of moral change—a tempting but dangerous idea as you can see when it gets into the wrong hands. The law cannot prescribe reconciliation, and it cannot effect forgiveness; what happens if a penalty is completed or remitted in some way but does not result in forgiveness but only discharge? Mended relationships need more than this, and what they do need the legal system does not and should not try to provide. But a system that actively works against reconciliation, against the development of those involved in a criminal event in a manner that moves them toward something more adequately and resourcefully human, is in its way just as dangerous.

In conclusion, the crisis in the penal system is bound up with the wider question of whether our social imagination in general is fed by a vision of mutual responsibility. It is unhappily easy for the skeptic to suppose that the religious perspective on these matters is essentially, and even exclusively, about underscoring guilt and penalty. I have been trying to suggest that the most distinctive contribution a religious perspective can bring is to stress our adult responsibility to care for someone else's welfare. If at least that dimension of the religious ethics of our traditions can be revitalized for our society, then perhaps more than our attitudes to penal policy will be regenerated and transformed.

The elephant in the room is the recognition that the church, which has suffered from and participated in the abuse of slavery and its legacies, often remains oblivious to such history and in fact repeats such history. The church's complicity with the abuse of slavery has produced such habits as turning a blind eye to a broken penal system. In other words, one cannot separate so easily spirituality from the culture in which Christianity is understood.

Sanneh wonders whether a negative colonial history can ever allow a concept of reciprocity between Europeans and Africans. Will there ever be anything commonly understood between the two?[9] It seems that in the end he confesses the need for theological analysis—something, evidently, he neglects.[10] Perhaps he neglects to reflect theologically on this problem because he does not see himself as a theologian. Although Sanneh unveils the African elephant in the room only inadvertently, he does invite a better understanding of how the discourse of Christian spirituality can nurture particularity among people of African descent while increasing the spiritual maturity of the global church. He does this through distinguishing the "vernacular logic" of Christianity from the rational spirit of Western Christianity, which falsely dichotomizes the burden of faith and the burden of method, process, and ways of knowing.[11]

By focusing on how Christianity translates differently among cultures, especially African cultures, Sanneh hopes that his work will make some contribution toward envisioning God's mission (the *missio Dei*) beyond the maladaptive forms of Christianity discussed above—namely, when Christianity was used to justify slavery. It is important to note that Sanneh's intentions are noble as he tries to give a benign read to global Christian practices that resulted in the proliferation of the church. This is indeed rare among scholars but perhaps common among folks in the pews.

To say that Christian missionaries were indeed good for black people may come as a shock to those of us from the academy, who are accustomed to hearing about the abuses of missionaries. With this revisionist agenda, Sanneh prepares to outrun ideological opposition to Christian missions, for in his view such opposition is misinformed in the end and inevitably denies any dynamic among and in cultures to use the power of the gospel to critique perversions of Christianity. Herein lies the appeal of this book and of my chapter on spirituality; namely, it is an apologetic against those who see practical theology as less than the "real" discourses of the church. Similarly, Sanneh helps us see the divide between the church and the academy to which I now turn.

CONSISTENCY OF MUTUALITY

When I taught spirituality and Black Church studies in a divinity school, my essential question was, how do I teach spirituality in a university setting? I concluded that I need not be ashamed of teaching methodologies that seek the presence of God. It is in a restless theological knowledge that I make the claim that "being" a theological teacher defines the "doing" of theological teaching. The result of synthesizing ontology and orthopraxy is the pedagogy of mutuality. So, then, what is it that I do when I teach theologically? In a nutshell, when a teacher teaches spirituality, she or he produces (does) mutuality. As theological teachers, our essential product is mutuality. This claim carries the burden of producing mutuality between student and teacher, as well as between individual and community. My challenge to pastors and church leaders is to see their vocation in the same way. This is a challenge, I think, because the dominant paradigm is often (good) shepherd and (dumb) sheep.

Now that I am working more directly within an institutional church structure as an ordained person, I still agree that my vocation is the production of mutuality. This is why I agree with Williams' analysis of how we can be better in our responsibility for others who have become offenders and victims in our penal systems. Like Williams, we need to think clearly and act responsibly in the more "consumerized" penal system. I think we do this through the practice of mutuality.

What do I mean by "mutuality"? Frederick Buechner helps me explain my meaning of mutuality through his definition of vocation as "the place where your deep gladness and the world's deep hunger meet."[12] I understand the vocation of the theological teacher as that "calling to" or goal in which one's long and rigorous training to be a theological teacher is fulfilled when deep gladness and deep hunger meet. Such vocation proposes an authenticity in which the theological teacher creates congruence between words and ideas; this becomes a space in which students feed to their mind and heart's content. But it does not stop there, in that space of feeding, for a theology teacher. Beyond words and ideas is God, who cannot be fully described. Instead of seeing this condition as a problem, theological teachers see an opportunity to tell our stories of how to find this elusive God, still using words and ideas. We invite our students into our worldview in order to help them see the necessity of knowing God as more than mere words and ideas. All of this requires the process of mutuality, the place where deep gladness and deep hunger meet. Ultimately, *we invite students into our vocation.*

Mutuality is necessary to theological teaching to keep it in its proper vocation of facilitating a student's understanding of God as more than words and ideas. The converse also seems true to me—that is, theology is necessary to mutuality to sustain its proper vocation of leading others to places of deep gladness and not to oppressive understandings of God. This path leads me to where we began—namely, that spiritual discourse is a call to maturity beyond self-preoccupation.

Based on my understanding of the vocation of the theological teacher to go continually beyond self-interest into mutuality, we will never naturally fit anywhere. We will keep being pilgrims or nomads, seeking the spaces of congruence in which students may feed and grow to be mutual with us. This nomadic way of being is not without its dangers, as the following definition of being a theologian indicates. The classic folk definition goes like this: a theologian is one who prays, and one who prays is a theologian. The danger here, I think, is that the theology teacher may give in to the oppressive stereotype that theological discourse is a mere cult of devotion, or devotedness, not to anything in particular but just in itself, a mere tautology. From this perspective of tautology, there is nothing new or unusual in the academic discourse of theology and spirituality.

As theological teachers, how do we respond to the challenge that we present mere tautologies? I think we do it in the following way. The theological teacher is one who readily admits ignorance as a virtue of apophatic knowledge. In other words, the theological teacher admits mistakes and therein builds trust with students through the revelation of the teacher's character. The theological teacher must invite his or her students into a dynamic worldview, though fragile, in order for students to accept the possibility that other worldviews exist outside their own. When the theological teacher does this, the vulnerability between teacher and student allows them to study a subject matter that otherwise cannot be fully studied but nevertheless requires devotion. This is so because the subject is God. The revelation of a theological teacher's character honors the theological student, who innately knows that God is known through vulnerability and kenosis (self-emptying). Therefore, to teach well in theological education requires the ability to create mutuality with students in such a way that both teacher and student acknowledge the impossible task of knowing God outside of mutuality.[13]

Herein, I have assumed spirituality as "praxis" to denote a kind of reflexive ecology encompassing religious practices and theology, informed by theory and guided by values and ultimate purpose(s). In the particular case of this work, we are concerned with the agency and actions/practices of black churches, which should not function in isolation. The critically reflective agency around and fluid throughout practices is informed by such sources as theological tradition(s) or convictions, culture, history, and the human and social sciences. These sources, reflexive activities, and agency constitute praxis—or, in our analysis, black church praxis. In the same manner, this understanding of praxis informs my conclusions for why spirituality and the teaching of it should invite mutuality.

Implicitly, I agree that there are dangers to universal theories of theology that are elusive in general and typically risk hegemonic treatment of difference. The pursuit of understanding what might be universal or transcendent about God must move also through understanding what is historical or immanent about God. This is why black practical theology is important. Theological worldviews, devotional practices of spiritual discipleship, and faith practices of social justice are the substance of inherited theological traditions and evolving church praxis. I have sought in this chapter to redevelop a practical theological approach through my notion of mutuality. Such mutuality assists us in our struggles for meaning-making and justice-making for others and ourselves.

If hearer-response criticism is to endure as a viable paradigm for constructing practical theology, as our editors of this project proffer, then we must include the full range of possible transformation between theological worldviews. We must all guard against ineffective efforts to transform church practices and against black theological worldviews that uncritically perpetuate the theological paradigms sustaining the oppressive traditions. The dynamic of guarding against human evil is one of the strengths of the African American faith community, which has enabled generations of enslaved, persecuted, and marginalized black people to survive and then thrive. It is my hope that this chapter and book will help facilitate the development of partnerships between the disciplines of black theology and practical theology so that the genius of Christian spirituality—namely, the promise of resurrection—can help seemingly irreconcilable differences be clarified and redirected into transformative strategies that speak compellingly to diverse theological worldviews.

<< 18 >>

Lifting Our Voices and Liberating Our Bodies in the Era of Massive Racialized Incarceration

Raphael Warnock

Emerging in the historical context of the Civil Rights and Black Power movements, black theology came into its voice as an important theological affirmation of the humanity of the oppressed and as a radical response to racism, "America's original sin" and "its most persistent and intractable evil."[1] Indeed, racism's intractability and stunning resourcefulness as a sociopolitical virus is, in large measure, a tragic consequence of its sacralization through deep contradictions and glaring omissions in the theological reflections of white theologians and the churches they represent.[2] Accordingly, the sickness of chattel slavery mutated in the post-Reconstruction era into Jim Crow segregation and other manifestations of "re-enslavement."[3] Black theology therefore is of utmost importance in redressing this history of political and theological discourse in American Christianity.

Nascent black theologians rightly asked, how could white theologians—in their orthodox, liberal, and neo-orthodox variations—speak credibly about a loving and just God while refusing to address themselves and their work to the doctrine of white supremacy and its social manifestations in slavery and in segregation? How could they be so silent about something so central and so tragically consequential in American life? Martin Luther King Jr., whose movement did more than any other to provide a larger context ripe for the emergence of the black theology movement, had already hinted at this epistemological problem inherent to the religion of the Christians who opposed his movement for freedom and human fulfillment. Writing from a Birmingham jail, he avers, "On sweltering summer days and crisp autumn mornings I have looked at the South's beautiful churches with their lofty spires pointing heavenward. I have beheld the impressive outlines of her massive religious-education buildings. Over and over I have found myself asking: 'What kind of people worship here? *Who is their God?*' "[4]

In his landmark text, *God of the Oppressed*, black theologian James Cone proffers an answer to King's fundamental question. Cone accounts for the failure of theologians and pastors to address the deepest of American contradictions in this way:

> The history of white American theology illustrates the concept of the *social a priori* asserted by Werner Stark and the other sociologists of knowledge. . . . The social environment functions as a "mental grid," deciding what will be considered as relevant data in a given inquiry. For example, because white theologians are not the sons and daughters of black slaves but the descendants of white slave masters, their theological grid automatically excludes from the field of perception the data of Richard Allen, Henry H. Garnet, and Nathaniel Paul, David Walker, and Henry M. Turner. This same axiological grid accounts for the absence of the apocalyptic expectations of the spirituals among the so-called "hope theologians" and the same explanation can be given why the white existentialists do not say anything about absurdity in the blues. . . . [I]t is obvious that because white theologians were not enslaved and lynched and are not ghettoized because of color, they do not think that color is an important point of departure for theological discourse.[5]

Black theology sought to give voice to those on the underside of slavery and segregation. Initially, it was embodied institutionally in the National Committee of Negro Churchmen (NCNC; later known as NCBC), an activist organization of pastors and academic theologians working together to define the parameters of an emerging discourse. This discourse emerged hermeneutically as the people's apologia, a living theology, walking riot-torn streets and standing in the gap between Jerusalem and Athens, ivory towers and ebony trenches.[6]

Yet, when one considers this history, it is all the more remarkable and lamentable that black and womanist theologians who are writing today and who see justice-making as central to the meaning of the gospel have had so very little to say about the theological implications of the sociopolitical virus of racism as it has mutated into mass incarceration, the most obvious form of re-enslavement with devastating consequences for the African American community. To be sure, notwithstanding a burgeoning black middle class in the decades since the Civil Rights movement and extraordinary examples of upward mobility and achievement facilitated by the breaking down of many barriers, the masses of African American people are still imperiled in a complex web of problems that makes the disaggregation of any single issue difficult and some may argue purely academic.

But while recognizing the structural complexity of racism and its inextricable link to and participation with other constituent parts of hegemonic power, including sexism, classism, and militarism, I would argue that today mass incarceration is Jim Crow's most obvious descendant. And as it was with its Jim Crow ancestor, dismantling mass incarceration will represent not only substantive social transformation but also immeasurable transvaluative power in a society still bent on worshipping whiteness.

Succinctly put, America's so-called criminal justice system is the one area of society that is many times more rabidly racist than anything imaginable during the Civil Rights era, with tragic consequences for black families and black communities. Therefore, a critical question guiding this inquiry is, how is it that black churches, the historical conscience of the American churches, and black and womanist theologies, as liberationist theologies, have yet to focus and find their public voice on likely the one social issue most steeped in the heretical doctrine and practices of white supremacy? In some ways, one might well argue that America's current system of disproportionately policing, targeting, sentencing, and stigmatizing scores of black people in its so-called War on Drugs is as dehumanizing and destructive as slavery itself. As we shall see, both slavery and mass incarceration represent in many cases life sentences in kind. Yet, so far, neither black churches nor black theologians have marshaled their institutional and intellectual resources in a way commensurate with the magnitude of this moral and humanitarian crisis. The question is, why not?

In view of Cone's analysis of white theology in an earlier era, I explore in this era the "social environment" of black theology and the "mental grid" of the Black Church that has rendered both mute with "stammering tongues"[7] when it comes to the most stigmatized people of color in America today—black men and women warehoused in our nation's prison industrial complex. Could it be that both the Black Church and black theology are hampered in their respective vocations of meaningful social praxis and relevant critical reflection by their alienation from one another? Does the fact that neither lives close enough to this problem that plagues the poorest of the poor explain why it has failed to enter in a sustained way into their "field of perception" and social praxis? Has privilege, ecclesial and academic, left black pastors and black theologians blind or paralyzed, or both? In view of their own histories and vocations, how should black theology and black churches think about the problem of mass incarceration?

JIM CROW SEGREGATION AND MASS INCARCERATION

Michelle Alexander has persuasively argued that the mass incarceration of tens of thousands of black men for nonviolent drug-related offenses and the lifelong consequences of that incarceration are constituent parts of the New Jim Crow.[8] I agree. There is no clearer example of America's unfinished business with the project of racial justice in a putatively postracial era than the twenty-first-century caste system engendered by its prison industrial complex. Moreover, I submit that there is no more significant scandal belying the moral credibility and witness of American churches than their conspicuous silence as this human catastrophe has unfolded over the last three decades.

The United States of America is unrivaled in the sheer size and magnitude of its prison population, warehousing about a quarter of the world's prisoners while Americans account for only about 5 percent of the world's population. For many years now, prison construction and maintenance, major economic engines for many small towns and rural communities, have had little or nothing to do with actual crime rates. In all of the large American cities, half of the young black men are caught up somewhere in the matrix and control of the criminal justice system or hampered in their social mobility and civic participation by the social stigma of a criminal record.[9] Most of them are charged with nonviolent drug-related offenses and are casualties in America's so-called War on Drugs. Ironically, having been circulated through the criminal justice system and as a result stigmatized as convicted felons, they come out only to be confronted with all of the legalized barriers against which Martin Luther King Jr. and those who battled the old Jim Crow fought. These include discrimination in housing, employment, voting, some professional licenses, public benefits, and student loans.

Legally barred from the doors of reentry to full citizenship, symbolized in the right to vote, and denied access to ladders of opportunity and social upward mobility, those who have served their time in America's prisons or who plead guilty in exchange for little or no actual prison time are often condemned to eternal social damnation. They are part not of a class but of a permanent caste system of political pariahs and economic lepers, condemned, in a very real sense, to check a box on applications for employment and other applications reminiscent of the ancient biblical stigma, "unclean."[10] Given the sheer magnitude and broad implications of this assault on black people's humanity and their ability to sustain viable communities, one might characterize the quietude and lack of mobilization in black churches and among black liberation theologians as something akin to what the latter labeled in the twentieth century "the de-radicalization of the black church."[11]

The truth is black theologians have been no more responsive in the actual content of their critical reflections and work on the prison industrial complex and the mass incarceration sweeping black communities than were conservative, politically disengaged black pastors during the era of lynching and Jim Crow segregation. How does one account for the deradicalization of black theology and the Black Church? Since we do not ourselves face such severely repressive tactics of domination and intimidation like lynching, the question is, why have black pastors and black theologians been so silent and disengaged on this issue? Mass incarceration represents for our generation what slavery and Jim Crow segregation represented for earlier generations, and our silence is deafening.

MASS INCARCERATION AND THEOLOGICAL SILENCE

Neither the Black Church nor black theology has put forth a clear theological voice and moral witness on the subject of mass incarceration and its implications for human rights in the twenty-first century. To be sure, scores of black churches have prison ministries, and some even have reclamation ministries for formerly incarcerated individuals.[12] But there is a vast difference between offering pastoral care and spiritual guidance to the incarcerated or formerly incarcerated and challenging the public policies, laws, and policing practices that lead to the disproportionate incarceration of people of color in the first place. The relative absence of black church praxis and critical black theological speech around the glaring political contradictions of mass incarceration can be attributed to (1) a sharp emphasis upon privatistic piety in black churches; (2) the social and moral stigma attached to crime, the drug trade, and those involved; and (3) the divide between black theology and the Black Church.

The Black Church is—for reasons of history and theology—a church body with a divided mind.[13] Shaped by the evangelical fervor of the Great Awakening and other similar revivalistic movements, its proclamation has posited the theological sensibilities of a profoundly *privatistic piety*, emphasizing the freedom of the individual soul. On the other hand, because it was formed within the context of the American slavocracy and born fighting for freedom, the Black Church has also embodied in its proclamation and demonstrated through its praxis a prominent theme of *political protest* aimed at the biblical view of salvation as deliverance into a "good and broad land,"[14] "a new heaven and a new earth."[15] Put another way, black churches have addressed their ministries to both *the slavery of sin* and *the sin of slavery*. To be sure, in the broad sweep of black church history, both themes are present and prominent, sometimes complementing and at other times competing with one another for dominance as the Black Church wrestles through the dilemmas and double-consciousness of its own identity and sense of mission.

The soteriological imagination of the American churches has tended to be largely individualistic in a way that mirrors the culture itself. Meanwhile, black churches have not been sufficiently self-reflective about the theological meaning of their own distinctive history and liberationist heritage of radical protest. A privatistic piety emphasizing the salvation of individual souls while eschewing the hard political work of transforming the society tends to be the default position, even for socially oppressed black churches. Because the Black Church, too, is largely evangelical, it is not difficult to see how black churches, caught up in the unexamined political presuppositions of the American evangelical ethos, can become self-alienated from their own liberationist legacy. Moreover, with the increasing upward mobility of much of the black middle class in the decades after the Civil Rights movement, increasing alienation from the Black Church's revolutionary sensibilities risks wholesale abandonment of the work of freedom fighting and its relevancy to Christian identity and praxis. Amid the serenity and so-called safety of the sanctuaries of our churches, the focus is on *souls alone* because the endangered black bodies warehoused in America's prison industrial complex, unlike those oppressed during the era of Jim Crow segregation, are both out of sight and out of mind.

This kind of truncated view of salvation has always been dangerous, particularly for oppressed people. Its tragic political implications can be clearly seen in a letter written by George Whitefield, a prominent preacher during the First Great Awakening and a fierce advocate of saving the souls of slaves while keeping their bodies in physical bondage. He gloats, "Near [*sic*] fifty negroes came to give me thanks for what God had done to their souls. . . . I believe masters and mistresses will shortly see that Christianity will not make their negroes worse slaves."[16] To the contrary, African American Christians resisted this truncated view of salvation, embracing instead a view of divine liberation from both the slavery of sin *and* the sin of slavery. Evidenced in the spirituals, the prominence and distinctive hermeneutical deployment of the Exodus motif and subversive survival ethics like "puttin' on ol' massa," along with other elements of the slave tradition, is an oppositional piety. The distance of this piety from that expressed by Whitefield was "wide and deep," representing what Dwight Hopkins calls "the co-constitution of the black self" under the divine aegis of a God who wills human freedom.

African American slaves rightly understood that a narrow, individualistic conception of Christian salvation and personal piety could never provide an effective moral response to slavery. Their descendants, indeed all freedom-loving people, should know that such a distorted personal piety can never adequately address itself to the systemic injustices of America's prison industrial complex, in many ways a postmodern mutation of the same white supremacist logic that gave birth to slavery and Jim Crow segregation. But if this privatistic piety of the churches presents a theological barrier, then it is further complicated by the moral and social stigma attached to inmates, particularly the guilty, and the ethical dilemmas and complexities therein.

STIGMA

Given the investments of corporate and political interests in the colossal public policy failure that is mass incarceration, nothing short of a massive and sustained movement will undo it and move the nation in a different direction. But how do you build an effective social movement, particularly among churchpersons, when the primary subjects of its advocacy are those stigmatized by the label "convicted felon?" It is one thing to stand up for Rosa Parks, whom Martin Luther King Jr. called "one of the most respected people in the Negro community";[17] it is quite another to fight for the basic human dignity of persons whose individual behavior may well be deplorable and who bear some culpability for their condition. Indeed, this is part of the conundrum posed by racial bias in the criminal justice system. In a world where ordinary black people must navigate everyday the racial politics of respectability and bear the burden of being "a credit to the race," those who find themselves caught up in the criminal justice system are seen as not having kept their side of the deal. If many people outside of the African American community view these young black men who track through the courtrooms of every major American city every single day with fear and contempt, then those within their own families and churches also harbor feelings of disappointment, anger, and ambivalence. They are the ultimate outsiders, stigmatized as both "black" and "criminal," two words that have long been interchangeable in the Western imagination.

The historical interchangeability of these two anathemas is ironically and tragically embodied in the fact that even upon release from prison, many of the same discriminations black people suffered during segregation—including discrimination in employment, housing, and voting—are the lifelong lot of convicted felons. No matter how long ago the crime occurred or what heroic efforts they may have put forth in pursuit of redemption, they are reminded each time they are presented with an application for employment or other paths of inclusion into the marketplace of the "black" mark that hangs over their lives.

But in this culture of dehumanization, no group is more stigmatized than those persons on death row. After years of steady decline and presumptive death by many criminologists, the death penalty reemerged as part of a conservative backlash in the years immediately following the Civil Rights movement. In the realities of its enforcement, the death penalty is the final fail-safe of white supremacy. The data clearly show that its use ensures that, in the final analysis, the lives of white people are regarded as more valuable than the lives of black people. That is why the race of the victim, more than anything else, determines the likelihood that the punishment will be death by execution.[18] And if the victim is white and the presumed perpetrator is African American, the symbolic power of condemning that cardinal trespass is every bit as important as ensuring that the actual person who committed the offense is executed.

That these practices of capital punishment today survive as the modern performance of lynching became exceedingly clear to me a few years ago during my public advocacy for death-row inmate Troy Davis. By the time I met Troy Davis and became involved with his case, both as pastor to him and his family and as a public advocate for the sparing of his life, he had been on death row for nearly twenty years, convicted in 1991 for the

1989 slaying of Savannah, Georgia, police officer Mark Allan MacPhail. It was 2008, and we held the first of several rallies for him at Atlanta's historic Ebenezer Baptist Church, where I serve as senior pastor.[19]

Davis' case had already gained national and international attention and brought together unlikely allies in the struggle to save his life. It embodied so clearly all that is wrong with America's deployment of the death penalty that even proponents of the death penalty, like William Sessions, former head of the FBI, and Bob Barr, a conservative Georgia congressman, stood in agreement with liberals like former president Jimmy Carter and Congressman John Lewis *against* the execution of Troy Davis. The trial provided no physical evidence in support of Davis' conviction. No murder weapon, DNA evidence, or surveillance tapes were ever produced; and in a trial based largely on witness testimony, seven of the nine witnesses supporting the prosecution's case had recanted or materially changed their testimony. On three separate occasions, Davis' execution was stayed within minutes of his death. I sat with him in his cell one September night in prayer as he faced the prospect of imminent death by execution. Two days later, I stood in a prison yard with his family and hundreds of others, as Troy Davis was stretched out and strapped to a gurney, bearing an eerie resemblance to a crucifix, and executed by lethal injection in my name, as a citizen of the state of Georgia. In the years that I have fought for Davis and others like him, for the soul of a nation scarred by deep contradictions in the criminal justice system, and for the lives of young black men like Trayvon Martin, who was tragically endangered and murdered by the stigma of blackness as criminality, I have often reminded myself that I preach each week in memory of a death-row inmate convicted on trumped-up charges at the behest of religious authorities and executed by the state without the benefit of due process.

The cross, the Roman Empire's method of execution reserved for subversives, is a symbol of stigma and shame. Yet, the early followers of Jesus embraced the scandal of the cross, calling it the power of God. To tell that story is to tell the story of stigmatized human beings. To embrace the cross is to bear witness to the truth and power of God subverting human assumptions about truth and power, pointing beyond the tragic limits of a given moment toward the promise of the resurrection. It is to see what an imprisoned exile of a persecuted community saw as he captured in Scripture the vision and hope of "a new heaven and a new earth." But because that hard work involves both serious critical reflection and sustained revolutionary praxis, it is a project well served by bridging the yawning chasm between black theology and the Black Church.

Ironically, the explosive and unprecedented growth of America's prison industrial complex, in practice the clearest and arguably the most consequential incarnation of racial oppression in a so-called postracial America, and the growing divide between black theology and the Black Church occurred roughly during the same period. Holding each other in suspicion and increasingly at arm's length over the last thirty years, black theology and the Black Church have not said much to one another; and neither has had much to say about what Michelle Alexander rightly characterizes as the New Jim Crow.

While acknowledging their distinctive roles, I submit that the increasing distance between the Black Church and black theology is not unrelated to the deafening silence of black churches in the public square. Born fighting for freedom, the Black Church is the living, countervailing conscience of American Christian piety. Emerging in the wake of the Civil Rights movement, black theology—as a movement itself—represents the radical side of the Black Church. As a radical *theology*, it is a liberationist faith questioning itself, a principled critic of the church from within the church that asks anew in each *Sitz im Leben* whether the church is living out its liberationist vocation in proclamation and praxis.

But with the demise of the NCBC, an organization of theologians and pastors working together and a significant institutional site for the actual *doing* of black theology in its early days, black theology has become increasingly academic in its focus and the Black Church has become increasingly conservative. The latter has lost its mind; the former has lost its heart. Uncritical black pastors and anti-intellectual black churches have provided the context for the emergence and popularity of a self-absorbed theology of individual prosperity. Far too many black churches give in to the stealthy pietistic rhetoric of conservative evangelicalism, not recognizing the critical distance between the presuppositions of the latter and their own countervailing heritage of liberation. Meanwhile, black theology has lost its heart, the will actually to change the world, as black and womanist scholars gather at the American Academy of Religion, the Society of Biblical Literature, the Society for the Study of Black Religion, and other regular enclaves of the guild, seeking professional acclamation and tenure.

I submit that the institutional life of each is a far cry from their revolutionary origins.

Meanwhile, the black body is once again, quite literally, trapped at the center of what Gunnar Myrdal characterized in 1944 as the "American dilemma."[20] Viewed essentially as a problem, formerly enslaved black bodies, lynched black bodies, and segregated black bodies are now stopped, frisked, searched, handcuffed, incarcerated, executed, paroled, probated, and seemingly released but never emancipated. There is no more important test to the character of the American churches in general, and black churches and black theology in particular, given their self-understanding and liberationist claims, than their response to this human-rights nightmare unfolding on our watch.

If white theologians, pastors, and the churches they serve will not give their voices to the struggle of dismantling the prison industrial complex, then they will prove again that they are every bit as much invested in the logic and privilege of white supremacy as their predecessors from the eras of chattel slavery and Jim Crow segregation. Likewise, if black theologians and black churches will not give themselves over to this newest incarnation of the struggle to save black bodies, then they will lose their souls and reason for being. And if that is true, both black theology and the Black Church deserve to die. That is why it is urgent that black and womanist theologians and black pastors convene a new conversation and commence a new moment of risk-taking dialogue and praxis so that a new militant church preaching "deliverance to the captives" might be born again. Our lives and the soul of the nation depend on it.

<< 19 >>

JESUS ON DEATH ROW
The Case for Abolishing Prisons

Madeline McClenney

Through the preached word we enter this discussion of how the Black Church may engage the criminal justice system. The beauty of praxiological intent wedded to black theology, historical context, and the black religious tradition is that we have the freedom to reflect truths that we live out daily. That prayers and sermons are commensurate in authority with peer-reviewed journals and books written by scholars is the chosen truth that informs this particular reflection. If, then, we begin with a sermon, as I have chosen to do for this paper, it is fitting in our tradition to end this worshipful exposition with a benediction. What follows is a sermon first preached in 1997 at a white Presbyterian church in Durham, North Carolina.[1] It has been minimally updated and reformulated for this discussion of black theological praxis in light of the mass incarceration of black people. At the time this sermon was first proclaimed, incarceration rates were still escalating around the country. Voices of compassion for people with felony records, if there were any, were not reaching the average church. The attitudes of the people in the pews reflected that reality. For those released who had the audacity to attend a house of worship, condemnation, fear, and criminal-record bias stood in the vestibule to greet them. The average black Christian could not see Christ in the average felon. Sadly, fifteen years later, this sermon still preaches. One can only pray that in another fifteen years to proclaim it again, in any form, will be unnecessary.

* * *

A SAVIOR FOR PEOPLE WITH A RECORD

Pilate went out to them and said, "What accusation do you bring against this man?" They answered, "If this man were not a criminal, we would not have handed Him over to you."

John 18:29-30

If there were ever a time when we ought to look closely at the criminal proceeding in the Gospel of John 18, it is now. The court system in America and the criminal "injustice" system are suffering from overload. In 2012, Salecia Johnson, a kindergartner in Georgia, was handcuffed and taken to jail for having a temper tantrum. Even when seven of nine witnesses recanted, Troy Davis was refused another trial and executed for the murder of a police officer.[2] Trayvon Martin was simply walking home with tea and Skittles when self-appointed crime watcher George Zimmerman followed him and killed him. Crime is at historic lows, but the effort to criminalize our children through zero tolerance in the schools is up.[3] Zero tolerance fuels the cradle-to-prison pipeline ensuring that vulnerable poor and minority children begin school in kindergarten and finish school in the prison system.

Although this court proceeding in the book of John is followed by Jesus' sentencing and death, we are not interested in Jesus' tragic end. We are not too concerned about Pilate's role in the whole affair. Instead, we take a close look at Jesus' accusers—people fed up with Jesus the *criminal*. Yes, we are going to take a look at the angry, middle-class, religious folk who saw Jesus as nothing more than a common criminal, a first-century felon.

If there were such a thing as the six o'clock newscast in the first century, Jesus the felon would appear walking down a street escorted by the police of his day—handcuffed, if you will. The announcer would tell us that the vandal who destroyed Temple property, who repeatedly broke the Jewish laws, the welfare king who relied on the generosity of unsuspecting middle-class women to promote his suspicious doctrine, the man who hung out with tax collectors and prostitutes and claimed to be God, finally had been apprehended and was waiting for sentencing. Yes, in the minds of this first-century felon's accusers, he was little more than a common criminal.

So we are going to point our fingers at Jesus' accusers in this message. But more importantly, we are going to notice that three fingers point back to the Black Church. And when those fingers are aimed in our direction, we may find that we have a lot more in common with Jesus' accusers than we would like.

If we take a close look at this first-century felon's accusers, we observe at least three behaviors. First, they were *hiding from the truth*; second, they were *privileged stone throwers*; and third, they were a *mob looking for easy solutions*. We will examine each of these behaviors closely. As we contemplate the integrity of black churches and black theology, we note that the attitudes of many black believers toward today's felons are chillingly similar to the attitudes of Jesus' accusers.

They were hiding from the truth. Our first-century felon's accusers hid from the truth of what was really happening by describing him as a demon and a violent threat. He destroyed Temple property when he turned over the temple tables. He aided and abetted adulterers by mocking religious laws. He said, "Anyone who is without sin, cast the first stone."[4] As a result, he interfered with official *religious* police business. He stopped the stoning of a woman caught in adultery. And so he became an accomplice in her escape from a death sentence.

The rap that he rapped was a gangsta rap. He was constantly making drive-by threats against the status quo keepers. He predicted their fall and ruin. He claimed to be the real Light. He resisted arrest.[5] Whatever must be the truth about this first-century felon, he was a threat to civilized Jewish existence and had to be dealt with to the maximum extent of the law. The felon's accusers could continue with business as usual from their hiding places, charging that the felon was just getting what he deserved. After all, the system was fair, they reasoned. This is what we see when we read Scripture and point the finger at Jesus' accusers; but then, three fingers point back at us.

Consider our context today and how we view felons. Although disparities in arrest and imprisonment are obvious to most, the average black Christian also finds comfort in knowing that the people we lock up, the *black* people we lock up, are violent threats that must be taken off our streets. Notwithstanding five to ten people in the prison ministry, congregations usually follow the lead of the general population on how to handle the demons in our midst who break the law and threaten the status quo. It is comforting to believe that "these criminals are only getting what they deserve." After all, on the whole, the system is fair. But is that the truth?

According to the 1996 report of the National Criminal Justice Commission, "The vast majority of crime in America is *not* violent and the vast majority of people filling our prisons are non-violent property and drug offenders."[6] It further states, "American incarceration rates are not higher because of high crime rates. American rates of incarceration are higher because of our exceedingly harsh treatment of people convicted of *lesser* crimes."[7] Nonviolent criminals account for *84 percent* of the increase in prison admissions since 1980.[8] The follow-up assertion usually goes like this: "But surely, these nonviolent criminals are still evil and malicious people. They are the parasites of our culture, perhaps even demon possessed. Surely, they deserve the maximum penalty for their crimes." In August 2012, Massachusetts passed its three-strikes law, one of the harshest in the country. The result is automatic life imprisonment. We must ask: Are people really getting what they deserve? Are we as black Christians so consumed with our own lives that we are hiding from the truth?

In states like California where these three-strike laws have been in effect since 1994, 70 percent of all second- and third-strike inmates were *nonviolent* criminals.[9] According to the National Criminal Justice Commission, that means we are paying to keep nonviolent criminals like Michael Garcia in jail. Garcia was a heroin addict who stole five dollars worth of meat to feed his mother, retarded brother, and himself. With a third strike, he is spending life in prison (twenty-four years) without parole. His parole officer reported that he was not a bad guy. He continued stealing because there were no slots available for Garcia in the drug treatment programs.[10]

At the very least, we reason that the system is fair. Everyone knows the consequences, and they all get *equally* what they deserve. Not so, according to the *Harvard Law Review*. In its 1988 review of race, the journal makes the case that discrimination exists against African Americans at almost every stage of the criminal justice process.[11] Most of us do not realize that "tough-on-crime" legislation was designed to contain already disliked people—black people. According to the commission,

> The new drug laws focused almost exclusively on low-level dealers in minority neighborhoods. Police found more drugs in minority communities because that is where they looked for them. Had they pointed the drug war at college campuses our jails would now be filled overwhelmingly with *university* students.[12]

Let's face the reported facts! We can no longer afford to hide from the truth.

Within the Black Church, some of us know firsthand that the system is unfair. Yet, in discussions of crime and punishment we also mimic Jesus' accusers when we assume the position of *privileged stone throwers.*

The chief priests were the ones who wrote and interpreted the law—a class of middle-class priestly legislators, if you will. As a privileged stone thrower, the sins of your group or class and the sins of those who live in your neighborhood—your *hanging* partners—are not really bad sins. My ten-year-old child thinks that we live in a good neighborhood. I told her that our neighborhood was just as bad as any other. We live among unarmed robbers, commonly known as bankers, who get big bonuses at year's end. Those who behave unethically are rewarded for using financial skills to lure into "flexible" mortgage contracts people who trust their financial expertise.[13] They are rewarded for maintaining high interest rates on credit card purchases that cripple the average consumer. We live in a bad neighborhood. When the mortgage crisis hit, economists living in neighborhoods like my own blamed borrowers for their losses. Due to so-called overreaching, many economists now maintain that homeowners caused the financial crisis of 2008.[14] A greedy, responsibility-shirking, collective amnesia often seizes a few financial gurus in my neighborhood. We overlook the fact that in its 2012 National Financial Capability Study, the Financial Industry Regulatory Authority (FINRA) found that 86 percent of the twenty-five thousand adults surveyed were incapable of correctly answering all five basic financial questions.[15] The vast majority of Americans are financially illiterate; if the financial doctor at our local bank reviews an application and decides that we are credit worthy, who are we to argue? When we place blame on borrowers, we know that our rationalizations will be enshrined in policies that protect the banks that participated in predatory lending schemes. In other words, it will be legal to defraud borrowers and steal their homes from under them.

Yet, if you are associated with the privileged stone throwers, your crimes are not considered threatening to the welfare of the group, the city, the state, or the nation. The sins of people *outside* your group, the sins of common folk, are a burden to the establishment. Then, the stones fly! As a privileged stone thrower, you have influence with the Romans. Like our first-century felon's accusers, you are able to call on the ruling party to execute your tough-on-crime judgments. Have we become privileged stone throwers?

Indeed, if we point the finger at the chief priests in Jesus' trial, three fingers point back at us. The race and class of those in jail do not tell us who commits the most crime. Yet, it does reveal who is in control. *We* are in control—middle-class, blue- and white-collar, somewhat educated and somewhat religious folk—the chief priests of our day. One can travel to any prison in the world. The only thing we will learn about criminal activity is *who defines it.* A glance at Germany in the 1940s, and we would be remiss to conclude that Jews were criminals; however, we would be correct to identify the control of Nazis who hated Jews. A glance at South African prisons in the late 1980s, and we would be *incorrect* to conclude that black South Africans were the real criminals in that country; yet, we would be *correct* to conclude that the apartheid party was in control. A look at Chinese prisons today would tell us nothing about who commits the most crimes in China and everything about a government in control of defining criminal activity. Yes, Jesus' accusers were privileged stone throwers. While we do not cast stones, we do cast votes for people who name criminals on our behalf and who represent our beliefs about how criminals should be treated. Even when we do not support tough-on-crime legislators, too many of us secretly and maliciously distance ourselves from the targets of their genocidal policies—our own kin and community.

One must wonder, "Who would be in jail if America's *current* prison population took over lawmaking for the next 10 years?" If current inmates, America's most poor and oppressed population, had a chance to make the laws, we would have new chief priests on the block. We would be put in jail. All of us!

We all would be in jail because we are guilty of first-degree child abuse when we allow legislators to pass laws that take youth from their families, lock them in small cells, deny them an education, deny them regular contact with family for five years—for smoking a plant. Our tacit support of such legislators would constitute criminal activity. If today's inmates were in control, we would get strike one for supporting laws that help the middle class and rich but limit possibilities for the poor. According to the biblical canon, the protection of the poor, the widow, and the orphan are paramount in the administration of justice. Stealing to eat because you were drug addicted and jobless would become a *misdemeanor*; however, walking past a hungry homeless person without offering food or assistance would constitute strike two. Investing in a mutual fund that holds stock in a company that produces high-fashion shoes with cheap foreign labor would constitute strike three because the new government of former inmates knows that it is immoral to subsidize slavery. Creating jobs by paying *share-cropper* minimum wages that have not been adjusted for inflation in over thirty years is unlikely to be considered a mitigating circumstance by this new group of ex-con lawmakers. With three strikes, we all would be doing life without parole.

Oh, it is good to be a member of the privileged stone throwers because as long as we are members, we can create the illusion that our sins are really not that costly to the world. Laws will favor the weaknesses of our group. Cheat the government? We will give you time to pay it back. Ruin working-class people's savings institutions with junk bonds and high-risk mortgages? We will bail out the banks. Buy cocaine or weed downtown and take it back to the suburbs and universities? We will not even look in your neighborhood.

Lastly, this first-century felon's accusers were a *mob looking for easy solutions.* You see, they did not ask what kind of parents Jesus had. They did not want to know who the critical figures were in his life that might account for his antisocial behavior. They were not interested in what led him to destroy the Temple property. They were not concerned about his sense of justice or injustice. They did not evaluate how fleeing from zero tolerance for Jewish boys in Roman society may have triggered his gangsta-like disdain for the privileged stone throwers and their hypocritical laws. All that Jesus' accusers knew was that he broke their laws—the laws of the priestly ruling elite. Since he was not one of them, he was an embarrassment and a threat to their way of life. The easiest solution, then, was the fastest and most punitive—hand him over to the Romans for death by crucifixion. Although priding themselves for being among the most learned of all men, they were really nothing more than a mob.

Are we just a mob, looking for easy solutions to criminal activity today? Of all people, why are so many black Christians supporting punishment as a solution to mental health issues in the community? Let's wake up, beloved. As Michelle Alexander explains in *The New Jim Crow,* we are creating a permanent undercaste of people with records who are never forgiven even after they pay their dues.[16] This criminal justice system, from the time of our emancipation, has been a system used to control and oppress racial minorities and poor white people. Our families are being torn apart and decimated. Wake up! Like the house slave that did not use his favored status to liberate himself and his less favored kin, we are "shuck'n" and "jiv'n" for the master's home while a holocaust occurs in the field right before our eyes.

We preach about the tragic circumstances of this first-century felon's arrest and crucifixion, but we've missed an important message. This criminal proceeding gets played out every single day in courts all over America. After we point the finger at Jesus' accusers, we must be willing to examine how we too stand as accusers in our day. This first-century criminal proceeding ought to make us question our behavior toward those in our nation whom *we* call criminals.

In John 18:37b, Jesus said, "Everyone who *belongs to truth, listens to my voice.*" This felon's accusers neither belonged to truth nor listened to the felon's voice. It is very difficult to belong to truth when you are *hiding from it, casting stones at it from a place of privilege, or converging on it like a mob* in order to avoid the complexities that truth brings. Only Pilate had the moral fiber to stop in the middle of a judicial mess and raise a deep and probing question about this felon's identity. Pilate asked, "What is truth?" So, let us tell the truth about this felon.

His name is Jesus. He was born under what the chief priests would have called "suspicious circumstances." He grew up in a town called Nazareth. Like an urban ghetto, a rural shanty town, or a secluded mountain enclave, there were people who thought that nothing good could come from Nazareth. But, Jesus was from Nazareth. According to the deposition of one witness, he was a homeless man who had no place to lay his head. According to another witness, he used to hang around Samaritans—the dirty people that everyone hated.

But the only thing that really matters about this first-century felon named Jesus is that he specialized in saving people with a record. Did I just suggest, "he *specialized*"? I meant he *specializes*, this very day, in saving people with a record. As far as Jesus was concerned, *everyone* had a criminal record. Jesus was drawn to people with the worst records. Unlike *his* accusers, he did not hide from the truth about people's circumstances; he did not throw stones from a place of privilege; he did not have his disciples surround sinners like an angry mob waiting to lock them up and throw away the key. Jesus loved people who had records. He asked Matthew, a dreaded and despised tax collector, to be a disciple.[17] He let a lady caught in adultery go free.[18] He forgave Peter for committing perjury when he denied knowing him.[19] He talked to a woman with five husbands. Without condemnation, he showed her the way to true worship.[20] He welcomed an armed robber into the kingdom while he was still on the cross.[21] Yes, Jesus is a savior for people with a record. I do not know about you, but I am glad that Jesus specializes in saving people with a record. For, if truth be told, we all have records! In all likelihood, we have a long and extended criminal record with that Judge on high.

But every time our case comes before the Most High Judge, a first-century felon stands up and says, "Your honor, I would like to have a word with you." Just then, the bailiff begins to read a list of your offenses in a stern voice: "Neglecting the poor, STRIKE ONE; stealing, STRIKE TWO; premarital sex, STRIKE THREE; adultery, STRIKE FOUR; getting drunk and high, STRIKE FIVE; lying, STRIKE SIX." The bailiff turns and looks at you, knowing that your time is up. But quick and in a hurry, a first-century felon *turned* public defender approaches the bench, "Your Honor," he says, "I would like to offer my life for the life of the defendant."

So, every time we feel that finger getting ready to point, every time we become frustrated with the criminals of our day and we want to throw everybody in jail, we need to remember the mistakes of Jesus' accusers. *They were people who were hiding from the truth, throwing stones from a place of privilege, acting like an angry mob.* Whenever we start to feel this way, let us not forget what Jesus said to *us* after he returned from representing us at the bench of the Most High Court. That felon *turned* public defender looked at you and said lovingly and with compassion, "I'm a Savior for *anybody* with a record. And the Most High Judge declared . . . 'CASE . . . DISMISSED.' "

* * *

BECOME AN ABOLITIONIST

If we embrace the analysis and insights provided in the preceding sermon, then what happens now? Black pastors and lay leaders must sound the alarm directly within their congregations by reconnecting the Black Church to her own theology while casting out the theologies of foreign gods that have commanded her to be silent so as not to "spook"[22] white Christians. With respect to mass incarceration, Raphael Warnock has adroitly explained the silences in the Black Church and black theology as a consequence of (1) an emphasis on private piety, (2) stigmatization of the issues around crime and punishment and those who have been in contact with the criminal justice system, and (3) the estrangement of black churches from black theology. The first two of Warnock's factors contributing to our silence may be attributed to the third. The fundamental gift of the Black Church and black theology was their refusal to be silenced in the midst of oppression. Each heard from God. Each had something to say about God in a way that differed from the God who spoke to our oppressors. Each knew that it was authentic in a way that the white Church and white theology was not, and according to Warnock white theology is still lacking. It is no wonder that one frustrated reviewer of *Uncle Tom's Cabin* begs the question, "Are there two Christs?":

Talk not of servants being obedient to their masters—let the blood of tyrants flow! How is this to be explained or reconciled? Is there one law of submission and non-resistance for the Black man, and another of rebellion and conflict for the white man? When it is the whites who are trodden in the dust, does Christ justify them in taking up arms to vindicate their rights? And when it is the blacks who are thus treated, does Christ require them to be patient, harmless, long-suffering, and forgiving? Are there two Christs?[23]

Indeed, even today, there are two Christs. One of those Christs has been relegated to a secondary status within many black churches in favor of the one that lied to her and told her that she was born to be enslaved—cursed from birth. Although the original white Christ's lie has been largely dismantled in black churches, the lying Christ's continual influence has led too many black church members to adopt a privatistic theology to the exclusion of the inherent social-justice focus of Jesus of Nazareth. This has resulted in a weak appreciation and support for everything black, from black educational institutions and black businesses to black-led charities and now black boys. Holiness and piety are of utmost importance to the Christian journey but cannot be achieved in the absence of a strong, social moral center. Personal piety and social justice are impossible without each other. The lying Christ separated those two concepts and conflated evil, crime, poverty, and blackness.[24] When we have reconnected to the truth-telling Christ, we have no choice but to reject an exaggerated emphasis on private faith and piety, to reject all embarrassment associated with black institutions and with the criminalization of blackness, and to embrace the truth-telling Christ, son of—the God of the Exodus, major and minor prophets, Christian zealots, abolitionists, liberationists, and priestly social-justice activists.[25]

I am blessed daily to interact with pastors and their congregations who follow the truth-telling Christ. As president and founder of Exodus Foundation.org, it is my mission and that of the staff to stop the flow of African Americans to prisons nationwide through our mentoring and scholarship program. We provide practical assistance to pastors who hear the voice of God as She reveals that heaven is ready to finish the unfinished business of ending slavery locally—and globally.[26]

Heaven is calling us to continue the work of our abolitionist predecessors. In our context, an abolitionist is a person who (1) believes that prisons have failed, (2) advocates for the abolition of prisons, and (3) seeks to build the beloved community.[27] The marching order for the twenty-first-century Black Church is simple: We must become abolitionists. We must put an end to the network of prison plantations that sprang up to put in check our liberation.

We must keep in mind that an abolitionist reform is one that does not strengthen or legitimate the prevailing prison system. A Christian abolitionist works to reform and ultimately to replace the criminal justice system with a restorative justice system based on an informed understanding of the Judeo-Christian tradition and other helpful restorative traditions, led by abolitionist clinical psychologists, judges and attorneys, church elders, prison guards, and probation officers *retrained* as restorative justice advocates and personnel.[28] Retooled with a new ideology, they will be concerned about economic and social justice for all victims who suffer from collective social and economic violence or individual acts of violence. Reconciliation within a caring community will be our aim, not punishment.[29] Punishment is wasteful and does not increase public safety, victim advocacy, or rehabilitation for the inmate. Unlike criminal justice, restorative justice will be curative in the vast majority of civil and criminal cases.

Michael Battle clarifies that mutuality is the goal of the theological teacher. So must it be for abolitionists. We must hear the cries of victims and transgressors in mutually respectful ways inasmuch as we are all victims. Ideally, pastors, priests, and other clergy are the first line of defense in this battle for the physical salvation of black flesh. Both Battle and Warnock mentioned death in their articles. Battle spoke of dying to self, while Warnock spoke of white and black churches that deserve to die if they fail to address the prison holocaust. Given that masses of followers of Christ have soaked in a sense of entitlement to material wealth, we must all die to all material blessings; forsake these blessings as often as possible to do the next good deed; exceed each other in sacrificing income and financial security to align ourselves more closely with the truth-telling Christ; and come out of the ivory tower and the church tower to fight with those on the ground in urban and rural communities. When we take on this charge, our community will be resuscitated.

The criminal justice system, however, cannot be resuscitated. Its cancers have spread throughout the entire body politic. We must dismantle harsh sentencing and improve the living conditions of inmates while we fight, but palliative reform efforts must be abandoned. The Black Church is authorized to make the call. It is time for all of us to note the time of the death of the prison industrial complex, and that time is NOW. Declare with me: The prison industrial complex was dead on arrival. May it return to the depths of hell from which it sprang!

In the restorative justice system, when a youth curses at his teacher and threatens to harm another for the first time, he will not be arrested, taken to jail, and placed in the prison pipeline. Parents and teachers will engage in creative and restorative acts of atonement to make amends and to help restore the peace. We have the technology to monitor the movements of those under supervision without the cost or the inhumanity of the cage. Therapeutic interventions are known to work. For even the most recalcitrant youth, grown-ups must allocate the resources and time to implement the best practices. There is nothing wrong with our youth. Parents and grown-ups have lost their minds. What caring parents after finding their young adult child with several ounces of marijuana would lock him in the basement for five years, offer him little more than a GED while caged, limit family contact, and legalize discrimination against him for the rest of his life? Yet, this is exactly how we are treating our youth and young adults. What could be more demonstrative of mental illness than spending $30,000 a year for ten years to cage a known nonviolent[30] drug addict for stealing to buy drugs while depleting educational funding of the next generation to do so?

Fear, *misptochomy,*[31] and racism have driven the system. Rational thought is absent when these states of mind are present. Indeed, the grown-ups have lost their minds—both those who created the policies and those of us who believed the lies told to justify those policies. Let us begin our mental tune-up: the cage is no place for a youth or adult to prepare for freedom unless we want them to behave like animals when they are released. If a so-called criminal must be contained in a locked facility, it should be a *locked mental health and counseling center.* If he exits, he should exit better equipped to live in his environment and *without* a criminal record. Did he steal a car? When apprehended, he (not the police) must physically return the car and work to pay the owner for his troubles. Did she kill a violent lover? All other things being equal, she likely killed in self-defense. She should not be jailed at all. Was the offense date rape? Incest? These are serious capital crimes. Our sentencing structure is lenient toward sexual violence. According to Scripture, the toranic punishment is death.[32] The lifelong injury to victims of all ages can be irreversible. The Church has dirty hands for its failure to preach against these specific acts of violence. In fact, too often we leave predators in positions of authority and look the other way despite mounting evidence of abuse.[33] Although the testimonies of those who have been resurrected after such trauma are instructive and bring hope to us all, one could argue that the perpetrators deserve to die nonetheless. An execution would be as close to justice as we can get for the victim. Yet, Jesus died for these perpetrators, too. Grace—that is, unmerited favor—is an alternative response to death by execution. Even if we do not utilize executions, atonement will still be impossible or only partial in cases like these. Justice or grace is our only option. We need survivors of violent crimes and their trained caregivers to guide us in shaping a restorative justice response for sexual assaults. Some perpetrators suffer from untreatable mental illness. They will need to be kept indefinitely in a locked mental health facility, but not a cage. The vast majority of such offenders, however, have been influenced by the rape culture in which we live. It authorizes misogyny, condones the use of brute force, and condemns women who fight back. Offenders influenced by this culture and judged to be capable of rational thought are also capable of remorse and reform. Most are released after five to ten years under current law. Too many were overcharged, as in the case of an eighteen-year-old who had consensual sex with a sixteen-year-old and was charged with statutory rape. It is indeed complicated, and we need to keep it that way. Our restorative justice responses must consider the complexities of each individual case.

To prepare to adopt a restorative justice system, *we must divest ourselves of the notion that all the bad guys are in prison.* We must give up the notion that we are actually safer with the current system. In actuality, most of those who have raped and molested live among us—now. They come to our family reunions each year. Some of our churches are run by people who committed date rape when they were youth. They were never charged or reported. Our pews, schools, and businesses are filled with "criminals" of all kinds who were never caught. In fact, as the sermon illustrated, are not we all criminals anyway? The fornicator and adulterer are registered sex offenders according to biblical law books. Many of us are undergoing self-programmed penance for the sins that haunt us. No one knows our turmoil until we have a safe place to confess and atone. From a crime-and-punishment perspective, the unsolved murders and rapes alone make it clear that close to half of perpetrators get away with it. The illusion that the criminals are locked up is a total fiction. The prison system in the United States is designed for social control—not justice or fairness or public safety.

At this moment, no one has adequately sought justice for the hundreds of thousands of homeowners who have already lost their homes. Little has been done to increase the public safety of those about to lose their homes to thuggish mortgage contracts approved by college-educated people. These college-educated criminals walk freely among us. For generations, bank managers have destroyed wealth in the families that they robbed. They have injured more people than all the armed thugs combined.[34] So-called gang bangers, prostitutes, pimps, and drug dealers hold the door for us at Walmart and change our tires at Goodyear; they too walk freely among us. We are mentoring them at Exodus Foundation.org, but we do not see them as the sum of their worst moments in life. The serial killers and predators that we have caught must remain in locked mental health facilities; the other 97 percent are coming home regardless. Most important, in the biblical witness, the divine wisdom refrained from instructing Yahweh's covenantal people to build prisons. There are no Hebrew-built prisons in Hebrew-Israelite society. The prisons we read about in the text belong to conquering peoples or Israel's neighbors.[35] The remedy for crime is simple in the Pentateuch: Make right what you did wrong. In the Holiness Code, holiness is not just about doing the right thing at all times. A holy person is one who makes things right after doing the wrong thing.[36]

We must become abolitionists because our criminal justice system is itself criminal. As one former inmate and activist observed, Black people are convicted in the womb.[37] In the conclusion of *The New Jim Crow*, civil rights attorney Michelle Alexander explains the operation of this pernicious violation of the constitutional and human rights of poor and black people:

> This, in brief, is how the system works: The War on Drugs is the vehicle through which extraordinary numbers of black men are forced into the cage. The entrapment occurs in three distinct phases, each of which has been explored earlier, but a brief review is useful here. The first stage is the roundup. Vast numbers of people are swept into the criminal justice system by the police, who conduct drug operations primarily in poor communities of color. They are rewarded in cash—through drug forfeiture laws and federal grant programs—for rounding up as many people as possible, and they operate unconstrained by constitutional rules of procedure that were once considered inviolate. Police can stop, interrogate, and search anyone they choose for drug investigations, provided they get "consent." Because there is no meaningful check on the exercise of police discretion, racial biases are granted free reign. In fact, police are allowed to RELY on race as a factor in selecting whom to stop and search (even though people of color are no more likely to be guilty of drug crimes than whites)—effectively guaranteeing that those who are swept into the system are primarily black and brown.
>
> The conviction marks the beginning of the second phase: the period of formal control. Once arrested, defendants are generally *denied*

meaningful representation and pressured to plead guilty whether they are or not. Prosecutors are free to "load up" defendants with extra charges, and their decisions *cannot be challenged for racial bias*. Once convicted, due to the drug war's harsh sentencing laws, drug offenders in the United States spend more time under the criminal justice system's formal control—in jail or prison, on probation or parole—than drug offenders anywhere else in the world. While under formal control, virtually every aspect of one's life is regulated and monitored by the system, and any form of resistance or disobedience is subject to swift sanction. This period of control may last a lifetime, even for those convicted of extremely minor, nonviolent offenses, but the vast majority of those swept into the system are eventually released. They are transferred from their prison cells to a much *larger invisible cage*.

The final stage has been dubbed by some advocates as the period of invisible punishment. This term . . . is meant to describe the unique set of criminal sanctions that are imposed *after* someone leaves the prison gates, a form of punishment that operates outside of public view and takes effect outside of the sentencing framework. These sanctions are imposed by operation of law rather than a sentencing judge, . . . to ensure that the vast majority of convicted offenders . . . will be discriminated against LEGALLY for the rest of their lives—denied employment, housing, education and public benefits. Unable to surmount these obstacles, most will eventually return to prison and then be released again, caught in a closed circuit of perpetual marginality.

. . . They become members of an undercaste—an enormous population of black and brown people who because of the drug war are denied basic rights and privileges of American citizenship and relegated to an inferior status. This is the final stage and there is no going back.[38]

Alexander further notes that this system of social control has continually reinvented itself to replace its predecessor and its predecessor before it. Until we, as a society, agree that all people are equally deserving of our compassion, resources, justice, and constitutional protections, it is not enough to tinker with the system in order to reform or refine it. It will merely reemerge in another form. Crime is at historic lows today, as was drug use when Nixon launched the War on Drugs in 1971. The system does not seem rational. Why? Because it is not, nor has it ever been, a war on drugs.

We must reframe the conversation in the public square to accurately reflect truth and educate the saints. The so-called War on Drugs is actually a "War on Black, Brown, and Poor People." We should refer to it as such. When have we ever seen a bag of crack enter a plea agreement? How many times have blunts or prescription drugs been imprisoned? The term "drug" is code for already disliked people. We must abolish this system not only for our own liberation but also for the liberation of all of our kinfolk in the human race and any potentially disliked groups in the future.

The current War on Drugs is nothing more than a strategy of rejection. As anthropologist Mary Douglas notes, strategies of rejection follow four distinct phases in almost every culture around the world. In each case, the target is an individual or group that was already disliked. First, the target is accused of a moral weakness; second, the accusation progresses to a charge of filthy living; third, the target is seen as causing insidious harm that can be neither defended nor denied by the target; and finally, actions are taken to remove the target from the community by death or excommunication.[39]

The prison plantation has replaced the cotton plantation, and the New Jim Crow has replaced the old Jim Crow to disenfranchise already disliked groups. As one white pastor noted in a sermon on this subject, "If what is happening to black youth were happening to white youth, we would have solved this problem a long time ago."[40] The backlash to the Civil Rights movement is that the felon is the new nigger. No one has to say the n-word. In fact, bury the n-word. White supremacy no longer needs it to accomplish the same goals. It has the War on "Drugs."

Upon accepting the call to abolish the prison system and to halt the war on black, brown, and poor people, we must not simply denounce miscarriages of justice against innocent people; rather, it is *foremost and primarily* our duty to stand against the tsunami of miscarriages of justice affecting *guilty* people. Jesus loved and protected guilty people. The abolitionist continues the work of Jesus by offering his or her life for the life of the defendant. As I have stated elsewhere, we have inherited the suffering of Christ. White, black, or brown, we are here, in this lifetime, to continue the redemptive work of Christ, an ex-convict who survived death row. He urged each of us, "Take up your cross and follow me." Riches may come to us so that we may bless others; yet, our reward for following Christ is not riches. It is a cross. We must not get it twisted.[41]

> *Benediction:* As Jesus has done for us, may we go forth now to
> offer our lives for the lives of the defendants in our criminal
> justice system.

VIII

Conclusion

<< 20 >>

GRAPHING THE CONTOURS OF BLACK PRACTICAL THEOLOGY

Dale P. Andrews and Robert London Smith Jr.

The central effort of this project to graph the contours of black practical theology tests the definitions and methodology proposed in the introduction. And the concurrent journey has been illuminating! With this project, we have tried not only to begin the critical work of identifying the requisite terms for defining and constructing black practical theology, complete with its distinguishing rationale and methodology, but also to elicit what we believe is the necessary interdisciplinary work in the theological academy to span the gulf with black churches, faith practices, and the critical needs of black communities and black life. We understand the needed praxis as reflexive engagement within interdisciplinary exchange to feed ecclesial and personal faith practices, which, in turn, should feed back upon the criteria and methods of black practical theology.

For practical theology, the desired interdisciplinary exchange does not occur outside of critical dialogue with persons' faith practices and ecclesial practices in black communities. Still, the interdisciplinary work cannot adequately be sustained within narrowly conceived notions of the applied disciplines commonly known as the clerical paradigm of practical theology. While aspects of the clerical paradigm must remain components of practical theology, the range of practical theology must be interdisciplinary, extending across the theological disciplines and our curricula of human sciences. Therefore, to restate our earlier case, we find it critically important to cultivate black practical theology among scholars who work within the constructive, biblical, historical, and ethical disciplines of black theology and those black scholars who work within practical theology and its customary subdisciplines. This interdisciplinary effort in the research methods and interests of practical theology provided the fulcrum of our trialogues with ecclesial and community practitioners. Perhaps, it may be for the first time that some of these scholars from black theology and practical theology together have engaged in such a thoroughly deliberate and focused theoretical and analytical exchange with black pastors concerning the issues and events that impact black communities.

The overall process has been both provocative and trying. Our respective inquiries have sought to deepen, clarify, and explore through a theological lens the identified issues that shape black consciousness and ecclesial practices. This concluding chapter attempts to extract from these trialogues the salient arguments and points of methodological engagement that sketch the broad contours of a black practical theology.

We have been inspired by the generativity of interest between scholars and church leaders around critical challenges facing black congregations and the black community at large. We have also been struck by just how difficult it has been for some to conduct their research around questions determined by our church leaders within those various, albeit challenging, parameters of community and systemic struggles. We even had a few scholars withdraw from the project long after entering the struggles of writing to address the faith communities' efforts, points of neglect, or depictions of their identified crises in community. Two confessed that they discovered well into their engagement with this project that practical theological methodology required just too much of an adjustment to how they predominately conduct research and publishing efforts. The irony was not lost on us that this chasm actually drove the conceptual development of this project from the onset!

Others struggled deeply with how to redress the insurmountable realities of some of these struggles, both systemically and personally. For nearly all involved, the work moved so close to home that writing outside of the constructs of our respective disciplines made addressing highly contextualized issues rather disorienting. Some of this disorientation likely grew out of the unfamiliarity with the methodology of practical theology in general.

Some authors initially entered their work on the project by leaving behind the methodology we, as the editors, designed to help guide them through the wilderness of praxis-oriented research. Only when challenged by the struggle to redress effectively the questions initially raised by the church practitioners did some participants then reconsider more directly the praxiological methodology designed for the project. After some initial reviews, we asked these few contributors to reconceptualize their respective chapters' focus or goals. These requests required them to step back and reconsider how, or even if, they employed practical theological methodology in an interdisciplinary fashion with the dominant paradigms or methods from their home disciplines.

The payoff of this project is twofold: First, the opportunity to engage one another over the many crises that continue to strangle black communities and congregations has pressed our own interdisciplinary understanding of research, teaching, and ministry. Second, the project has been life-giving in mutually calling our churches to task by showing some ways forward in our efforts to saw through the chains that bind. As we reflect back on the process and outcomes of the project, we try here to draw out the potentially defining contours of black practical theology that emerged from the six trialogues. We also seek to identify ways we might hone further the suggested model of praxiological methodology for black practical theology proffered by this effort.

To begin, then, among the pressing issues with which parishioners in black churches must deal on a daily basis are the high costs associated with health care and health maintenance, particularly neglected care for those who cannot afford health insurance coverage. This issue is nowhere more apparent than in the lives of those suffering from HIV/ AIDS. Dominant practices in our culture and health-care systems operate to pathologize ailing people, especially those already dismissed on the basis of race. The effect is that whole communities are negated. Sadly, our churches often become blindly complicit in such racist assaults by virtue of their spiritualized marginalization of the "sinfully" ill. How different, then, are our church practices from those of the health-care industry, policy makers, or general populace that treat the black community as pathological? Alternatively, when black scholars conduct theological studies that do not deliberately address these consequences, we divorce "doing theology" from how our churches conduct faithful practices to make sense of their worlds of encounter and struggle. The exchange between scholars and pastors regarding health care and HIV/AIDS dramatically underscores this insight.

Edward Antonio argues that black practical theology seeks to understand the world as it is. The effort to seek understanding involves how people of faith understand the world and engage or respond to it. What are our perceived needs and to what extent are such needs-based inventories central to conducting theology? Antonio's theological analysis of the health-care crises of HIV/AIDS questions how theology operates in relation to the world between humanity and God. The challenge Antonio raises for liberation scholars is one of empowerment and capacity-building to interrupt and transform both immediate practices and systems of injustice that assail black bodies and life, as in health care. It is this agency that he regards as praxis.

Theology contributes to marginalization not simply when it operates to empower dominant cultures of privilege and preservation but also when it fails to empower resistance to and transformation of these systems and cultures of marginalization and injustice, whether willful or by consequence. Hence, Antonio offers a remarkable analysis of HIV/AIDS and black health care as social and theological disease. Black practical theology, therefore, must be a theology of engagement in "theodices of care," which seek to understand our needs and suffering, along with God's intervention, without some distorted salvation of righteousness and theological moralizing.

Emmanuel Lartey, writing from a pastoral theologian's perspective, turns to liberation theologies to empower our direct attention to communal care for human well-being and social justice. This turn is an ecclesiological one that does not rest in doctrinal understandings of the Church but instead asks the question, what do folk say the Church is? Lartey is instructive here in that he extends Antonio's notion of faith seeking understanding of the world as it is to how we understand the church in the world. Community care is his focus. What, he asks, are saving acts for the Church and of the Church?

The task, then, for black churches to become or recover as communities of care involves questioning their embedded theologies in practices of various areas of ministry, such as preaching and biblical hermeneutics, particularly as they engage in health-care discourse around HIV/AIDS and poverty. Lartey makes a critically helpful move to redirect the questions of sin away from distorted biblical misappropriations or misconceptualizations of sexuality and human well-being between body and soul in general and toward the exigencies of life-giving community care. Lartey thereby reframes communal care in terms of inclusivity, communal thriving, liberation, activism, and transformation to comprise what he seeks in a Black-Church practical theology.

Gina Stewart, in her pastoral response to Antonio and Lartey, picks up on how both call for a significant reframing of the ways we do theology in the face of a pandemic like HIV/AIDs, which wreaks havoc on black communities, complicated dramatically by the poverty that deepens its strangling hold. Stewart echoes that the theological tenets she finds in the pews reflect embedded theologies based in the "language of witness." The issues of "oughtness" loom large. Our churches face the destructive distortions of a silencing stigma and a pathologizing Otherness when redressing embedded theologies that shape much church practice. Theological malpractice often views suffering as divine punishment, if not by direct divine action, then certainly by divine design. Stewart therefore embraces Antonio's and Lartey's campaigns for reframing how we do theology. For her, practical theology requires rethinking our theology's conflicted values and practices and deliberately engaging with the spiritual force of compassion that drives us into advocacy and agency in community.

Similar efforts to rethink our values drive Phillis Sheppard's vision of transforming our cultural symbols and practices in religion and society regarding oppression on the bases of gender and sexual orientation. Sheppard argues that an important function of black practical theology is to hold up a critically reflexive mirror to black life to reveal how we perpetuate or become duplicitous in gendered and sexualized violence, including the passive violence that assaults the psyche, soul, and bodies of black women and lesbian, gay, bisexual, transgender, queer, and intersexed (LGBTQI) individuals. This concern regarding what Sheppard calls cultural violence should focus our attention on communal ethics of relationality and mutual responsibility. Sheppard's challenge to peer into communal ethics is in dialectic with the beauty of createdness as black women and LGBTQI individuals. The task of practical theology here is to identify, evaluate, and transform traumatic or marginalizing operational theologies at play in our communities and church practices that actually form resistance to transformation.

For constructive theologian Diana Hayes, part of the transformation required involves the "protected space" in our churches for transgressions against black women and sexuality broadly. Hayes exposes the great hypocrisies in our churches' work to deconstruct the racist ideologies that drive biblical hermeneutics while failing to deconstruct similarly the sexist and heterosexist ideologies that function in kind. Hayes sees that black churches remain captive to white Christianity in false pieties that perpetuate power dynamics and privilege, well within the capitalistic and narcissistic individualism of Western culture. Black practical theology may best respond with efforts that contend thoroughly with both the African diaspora and the dramatically diverse religious voices at play. Hayes quite helpfully proposes that womanist theology, as liberation theology, offers the bridge we need for constructing or doing black practical theology along these important lines. This work involves breaking open the hegemonic constraints and silencing sanctuaries that black churches have thus far adopted rather uncritically.

Our pastoral leaders in this trialogue on gender and sexuality, Dennis and Christine Wiley, affirm Hayes' attention to the internalized forms of oppression that reproduce themselves toward other groups or subgroups. Likewise, they concur with Sheppard's focus on the replication of cultural violence among black churches, wherein racism becomes merely a template for the oppression of black women and LGBTQI persons. The Wileys underscore how black churches have been slow to amass leadership in civil rights that challenge society's structures of power and privilege. In considering black practical theology, these pastors ask the driving question of how successful practical theology will be defined or measured for black churches and communities. When it comes to race, gender, or sexual orientation, the dialectics between individualism and communalism loom large culturally and institutionally for our churches. When considering how we contend with oppressive practices and systems, the Wileys challenge black practical theology to weigh together *koinonia* between civil rights and religious rights. In short, how might black practical theology help churches to redirect their morality and faith practices toward radical inclusivity?

The focus on black church practices in community cannot but delve intentionally into expanding questions of ecclesiology. In speaking to global issues of religion among diasporan communities and the challenges of immigration, both Esther Acolatse and Willie Jennings make important correlations to the human gifts of speech and vision, respectively, and draw our attention to the problems we face with each capacity.

Acolatse observes the deep divide between African American churches and African churches—even African churches in the United States. She refers to this divide as intraracial segregation. While the divide between these ethnic identities may have some divergence between slave and colonial narratives, it holds great sway in how we interpret Scripture and theologize. In her practical-theological response, Acolatse appeals to a "care-full" hospitality of encounter that embraces the African as oneself. Such encounters engage cultural and religious difference that allows for Otherness to inculcate one's own space to the ends of mutuality. Acolatse wants to revisit ecclesiology and pastoral care to shape bilingual pastoral practice. This bilingual practice turns upon the natal or primal language of the soul that, theologically, translates our understanding of faith and our faith traditions. She considers this practical theological method to be a pastoral care of hospitality that negotiates multiple "signifiers" to make space for cross-cultural currency intraculturally and globally.

In turning from speech to visioning, Jennings tackles the racial aesthetics of Western life and Christian theology. Visions of beauty have not escaped the universalizing tactics of whiteness. These universalized racial and classist visions of beauty make claims upon the true, the good, the intelligent, and the noble. For our theological understanding, these tastes and desires revolve around claims of divine sanction and racial veneration. Jennings artistically breaks down the capacities of veneration that drive the imitation of white aesthetics. He argues that these imitations push us into reflections (or, perhaps, deflections) that claim cultural authenticity for ourselves and ultimately result in worldviews that evaluate personhood and our possibilities of becoming. Jennings therefore calls for intervention that challenges racial veneration. He finds practical theological answers in our being created in communion with God. God desires this communion, as evidenced in the incarnation, and it is the source of our desire in kind. The aesthetics of our ecclesial life thus becomes the expression of God's saving impulse. Our practical theological intervention then begins with our "creative critique" and questioning, ultimately enabling us to cultivate an artistic witness of the divine. This intervention requires our pursuit of intimate life understood through God's pursuit (the incarnation), but in the intimate life of community.

Delroy Reid-Salmon centers his responses amid the risks and vulnerabilities of diasporan people moving internationally and struggling to thrive. In short, he ponders how practical theology approaches might help address issues of diasporan differences and migrant life. Reid-Salmon feels that diasporan life globally challenges the character of Christianity. This pastoral respondent takes on his conversation partners by pressing the ways diasporan black life—as in Caribbean immigrant communities—contends with their prospects for practical theology. Like Acolatse, he wants to root black practical theology in pastoral care, but more intentionally and thoroughly in the pastoral intervention of diasporan black churches' in current "internal spaces" or narratives. While Reid-Salmon considers this form of intervention also to be a challenge to Jennings' historical theological analysis, the risks of embedded racial veneration that

Jennings already underscores remain rather heightened. Notwithstanding, Reid-Salmon presses further Acolatse's practical theology of hospitality in an effort to flush out her ecclesial turn. He seeks a more embodied theology; that is, he sees lived faith as the place for understanding doctrinal practices of the diasporan experience. Reid-Salmon wants black practical theology to engage the systemic and structural issues, including the public policies and cultural isolation that condition diasporan immigrant life. Along with Acolatse and Jennings, he sees the Church as embodied theology centered in ecclesial communities that seek to offer redemptive care (intervention) for black diasporan people who struggle under poverty and public polices.

Poverty also impacts how our practitioners and scholars contend with issues of education and class. To begin with our practitioner's dialogical responses, Jeremiah Wright cultivates a black practical theology from the cultural strengths of black peoples; he is not content with deficit analyses. Wright argues for more than efforts at "relating" to black congregations and communities. He underscores that critical thinking begins with everyday life. Our tasks therefore involve translating between the worlds of everyday black life and the service of the theological academy—that is, keeping both worlds in critical dialogue.

Wright finds cultural strength in Madipoane Masenya's biblical theological approaches to translating proverbial wisdom. Masenya translates material dialogically between nonliteracy culture and the theological academy. She understands practical theology to pursue prophetic transformation of the status quo of cultural structures and systemic injustice within the contexts of marginalized lives. Masenya sees education and class struggles as core factors in both the apartheid and the postapartheid societies and black churches in South Africa. She demonstrates that the economy in South Africa remains in the constraining hands of the privileged, which she considers the primary condition of their struggles. The systemic and uncritical effects of nonliteracy and poverty breed theological fundamentalism and cultural individualism. The needs identified by the marginalized, as well as their identities and wisdom, determine the efforts of black practical theology. Educators seek to join with the marginalized to transform society in ways that do not impose universalized "one-size-fits-all" solutions to stale bifurcations between society and church.

Wright also draws heavily upon Anthony Reddie's concept of participative black theology. Reddie seeks to cultivate black liberation theology through practical theological methodology. As with Masenya, Wright zeros in on Reddie's collaborative focus on lived experience with so-called ordinary people. Reddie suggests that such an approach is key to transforming popular education with theoretical tools for social change. More specifically, he argues that practical theological methodology is critical to the development of alternative pedagogical approaches to doing theology, including reassessing alleged truth claims and the intellectual objectivity of scholasticism. The transformation of learning itself and the motivation of ordinary folk to social agency entail their critical questions and epistemological insights. Education suffers under the constraints of Western cultural hegemonies and economic systems that exploit the racially marginalized as pawns or even commodities. Reddie's focus on pedagogy, which entails participative experiential models in teaching practices that raise conscientious theological reflection on critical action, turns the tables of educational structures and lack. This move shifts justice beyond the misguided limits of such concepts as fairness. Justice requires systemic analyses of equity for structural and cultural changes. Education can create epistemological frameworks for transforming learning and agency in order to overcome inequities generated by racism and poverty.

The convergence of racism and poverty (or classism) looms equally large in the extreme inequities that undergird the mass incarceration of black citizens. The deployment of harsh penalties, including capital punishment, continues despite the well-documented evidence of wrongful convictions and the exposure of discriminatory policing and prosecuting practices. Our practical theological scholar in spirituality, Michael Battle, returned to church practice from the academy. His attention to the penal and legal justice systems at large involves deconstructing the retributive culture driving these systems. Battle asks profound questions about how we regard and engage the disenfranchised in the communities that our churches serve. He sees the work of black practical theology as cultivating the "inculturation" of spirituality that deals with the reinvented racial caste system of the penal and legal systems. Battle explains that a restorative model of justice will contend with the misguided theories or myths of racial threat that drive our society's policing and prosecuting practices. What has been lost in this incriminating culture is the sense of responsibility for the welfare of others. Battle contends the practical theological turn to spirituality will guide churches to look beyond themselves to living our responsibilities to victims and offenders alike. Forgiveness does not require us to overlook victims; rather, it seeks to build the responsibility of care for the other not simply *to* the offender but *among* offenders.

Battle focuses practical theology on community and restorative models of care that build mutuality between the individual and the community living conscious of its communion with God.

Like Battle, Raphael Warnock serves primarily as a pastor and has been involved with pastoral and public protest against capital punishment and dehumanizing penal practices. Warnock's practical theological redress is directed intentionally to black and womanist theologians and black churches. He argues that black liberationist scholars have lost their inherited revolutionary drive under the interests of academia and professional investments. Black churches do not fare much better in his view, as the drive of a privatistic, inward piety causes them to become self-absorbed theologically and to leave political exigencies unexamined. The consequence is a stigmatizing caste system that criminalizes blackness; he points to Troy Davis' capital execution despite retracted evidence and Trayvon Martin's "in-the-wrong-neighborhood" execution as examples of this system. The culture of dehumanized blackness reconstitutes white supremacy, especially when Whites are the victims of black offenders, alleged or real. What we glean from Warnock is that practical theology holds our feet to the fire of transforming ourselves and our world, interdependently. He presses us to ask always, what is our functioning self-understanding in our liberationist claims?

Consistent with the unusual trialogue on this critical issue, Madeline McClenney, a biblical theological scholar and director of a nonprofit foundation addressing capital punishment and mass incarceration, began this exchange as the black theological scholar (from biblical studies). But in the course of her work on the project, she felt compelled instead to give voice to the practitioner's perspective through a sermon. Here, McClenney embraces what we have called "praxiological intent," through which she insightfully regards sermons as the peer-reviewed journals of the church. With her sermon, McClenney names some of the glaring conditions that underlie the criminalization of otherness: deafness to the fullness of truth-telling; central accusers charging from places of privilege; and the impulsion toward absolving solutions. It is difficult to understand mass incarceration as the end result of simply getting tough on crime when a disproportionate number of the offenses that land people in jail are nonviolent and prosecuted most heavily among marginalized black citizens. McClenney seeks to overturn the prison "plantations" of today's enslavement through the work of a practical, theological reinterpretation of biblical and faith traditions within historical contexts. She calls, in turn, for social and ecclesial transformation, both culturally and systemically. This preaching effort is a form of the praxiological response criticism to which our methodology for black practical theology beckons.

If preaching serves as an archetypical effort in ecclesial praxis of practical theology, it seems fitting that our attention to intergenerational relations directs us to how church ministries may shape a constructive theological enterprise. James Evans, through his approach to constructive and systemic theology, is guided by an epistemological question W.E.B. Du Bois raised—namely, "How does it feel to be a problem?" Evans argues that practical theology's point of departure must be social problems. He sees practical theology as redressing our failure to hold social and theological problems in productive tension. Evans suggests that the issues emerging from our communities and churches should cause black theologians to reexamine the theistic ideas about life with God and one another that are already culturally embedded in patriarchal and racial hegemonies. He therefore begins to outline constructive theological approaches to black childhood, family, and elders. The practical theological turn for Evans begins with excavating the questions at stake for our youth. He considers this practice to be the genesis of rap music and Hip Hop culture, a genesis shared with the blues and early black worship music. The driving questions for church leaders and theologians therefore concern how different generations within the Black Church can take seriously one another's questions. To continue with his practical theological method of questioning, Evans also asks how we might measure black family life and strengths using the "metrics" of our nurtured cultural values and practices, rather than relying on those imposed by mainstream culture. The wisdom of our elders likewise contributes deeply to how we respond to challenging questions of black life, theological reflection, and efforts to stem intergenerational erosion. Our elders deal with the realities of maturing in a culture that valorizes the extension of youth, only to face increasing economic insecurity in their senior years and for their families. In the end the practical theological challenge for black theology comes full circle to ask, how do we engage the past in a way that holds relevance for the present and future of black life?

This engagement between the past and the present for the sake of future intergenerational possibilities constitutes Evelyn Parker's attention to practical theology for the intergenerational formation of community where community has effectively been lost. Parker's attempts to bridge the struggles between the disparate worldviews held by the Hip Hop generation and the Civil Rights generation. While the social problems of segregation and economic constraints on employability persist across the generations, they have also shifted and intensified in different ways. The disparate worldviews reflect disparate responses to mutating but shared struggles. Parker helpfully identifies these different worldviews as the impulse toward communal uplift that characterizes the Civil Rights generation and toward personal uplift that characterizes the Hip Hop generation. Her analysis demonstrates an integral facet of practical theological methods that explore the struggles and perspectives of the participants. Here Parker not only utilizes these methods but also proposes that they drive her practical theology. Her suggested framework requires covenanted space to nurture trust-building encounters for intergenerational listening built on teaching intergenerational sharing. Listening therefore requires learning practices as well as practices that cultivate *leaning* on intergenerational partnerships to transform insights and values, all with the intention to increase mutual accountability and self-interrogation. Parker's practical theology instructs our communities in how we may begin to implement reflexive praxis.

Perhaps more directly than other pastoral respondents to this project, Donna Allen employs the suggested frameworks offered in this trialogue from our black theologian James Evans and practical theologian Evelyn Parker. Allen's work to develop ritual for ecclesial practices out of this trialogue illustrates dramatically the potential offered by the methodology of practical theology between scholars and practitioners alike. Allen begins with practical theologians holding themselves accountable for their practices, on the one hand, and their espoused and theological values and social morals, on the other. She seeks to develop womanist rituals of resistance that can shape ecclesial practices that engage intergenerational struggles. In this effort, Allen employs a womanist lens to overcome or resist asymmetrical, androcentric leadership. She understands that womanist practices emphasize collaboration, communal decision making, and attention to race, class, gender, and sexuality. Allen draws on Evans' suggestions to disentangle the challenges of intergenerational relations to create meaningful dialogue through theological reflection. She also draws on Parker's framework of practices to facilitate this direct engagement. Allen's womanist ritual employs practices both outside and inside the church—namely, around rituals of meal sharing and Holy Communion. The dialogue of the meal outside the church finds its way into the liturgical dialogue of Holy Communion inside the church. With attention to womanist worship, this ritual is intentionally integrative, family inducing, and resistant of oppression, assault, exclusion, and derision. As Allen underscores, this practical theological ritual employs a womanist soteriology in that it shapes ecclesial practices in the ethos of a relational, salvific-seeking ministry.

At the heart of all six trialogues lie various emphases from the methodology of *praxiological response criticism* that we proposed at the onset of this project. The narrativity of this methodology calls for descriptive analysis within critical dialogue that breaks into the already twirling whirlwind of praxis and its all-too-prevalent devolution into despondency.

The faith doctrines and values of tradition are fair game for reflexive transformation, as are the social struggles involved. The response criticism that these trialogues involve entails a heuristic engagement with supposed foundations of the faith, along with the historical contexts and worldviews at work in the theories and lives of our congregants and community members. Of course, praxis itself often requires its own reformation, which, in turn, becomes part of the praxiological intent of this methodology. Ultimately, we are encouraged that our partners in this project turn to transformative agency and strategies, in both personally spiritual and communally ecclesial practices, for the sake of changing lives, society, and faith and never accept the deceitful bifurcation between meaning-making and justice-making.

NOTES

CHAPTER 1: ANDREWS AND SMITH

1   See Dale P. Andrews, *Practical Theology for Black Churches: Bridging Black Theology and African American Folk Religion* (Louisville, Ky.: Westminster John Knox, 2002).

2   See Edgar V. McKnight, *Post-modern Use of the Bible: The Emergence of Reader-Oriented Criticism* (Nashville: Abingdon, 1988); and McKnight, "Reader-Response Criticism," in *To Each Its Own Meaning: An Introduction to Biblical Criticisms and Their Application*, ed. Steven L. McKenzie and Stephen R. Haynes (Louisville, Ky.: Westminster John Knox, 1999).

3   See Robert London Smith, *From Strength to Strength: Shaping a Black Practical Theology for the Twentieth Century* (London: Peter Lang, 2007); for earlier development on this praxiological concept, see James H. Evans Jr., *We Have Been Believers: An African-American Systematic Theology* (Minneapolis: Fortress, 1992).

4   See Paulo Freire, *Pedagogy of the Oppressed*, trans. Myra Bergman Ramos (New York: Continuum, 1970).

CHAPTER 2: PARKER

1   For details of the song "Jesus Walks," by Kanye West, see the song's entry on Wikipedia.

2   Alton B. Pollard III, "From Civil Rights to Hip Hop: A Meditation," in *The Black Church and Hip Hop Culture: Toward Bridging the Generational Divide*, ed. Emmett G. Price III (Lanham, Md.: Scarecrow, 2012), 10.

3   Pollard, "From Civil Rights to Hip Hop," in Price, *Black Church and Hip Hop Culture*, 10. Also, for a history of Hip Hop, see Ralph Basui Watkins, "I Said a Hip-Hop: A Snapshot of Hip-Hop History," in *Hip-Hop Redemption: Finding God in the Rhythm and the Rhyme* (Grand Rapids: Baker Academic, 2011); and S. Craig Watkins, "Introduction: Back in the Day," in *Hip Hop Matters: Politics, Pop Culture, and the Struggle for the Soul of a Movement* (Boston: Beacon, 2005).

4   Bakari Kitwana, *The Hip Hop Generation: Young Blacks and the Crisis in African-American Culture* (New York: Basic, 2002), 28.

5   Kitwana, *Hip Hop Generation*, 8.

6   Kitwana, *Hip Hop Generation*, 9–24.

7   Kitwana, *Hip Hop Generation*, 9.

8   Kitwana, *Hip Hop Generation*, 11.

9   Kitwana, *Hip Hop Generation*, 12.

10   Kitwana, *Hip Hop Generation*, 12.

11   Kitwana, *Hip Hop Generation*, 13.

12   Kitwana, *Hip Hop Generation*, 14–18.

13   Kitwana, *Hip Hop Generation*, 18–19.

14   Kitwana, *Hip Hop Generation*, 20–22.

15   Kitwana, *Hip Hop Generation*, 22.

16   Judith Greene and Kevin Pranis, Justice Strategies, Institute on Women and Criminal Justice, Women's Prison Association, "Part I: Growth Trends and Recent Research," in *The Punitiveness Report—HARD HIT: The Growth in Imprisonment of Women, 1977–2004*, http://66.29.139.159/institute/hardhit/part1.htm (accessed February 12, 2015), 17.

17   Joshua Hutchinson, "Dissed-Enfranchised: The Black Church under the Steeple," in Price, *Black Church and Hip Hop Culture*.

18   Some scholars have called the Hip Hop generation the "post–Civil Rights generation." See *Tie That Binds: Identity and Political Attitudes in the Post–Civil Rights Generation* by Andrea J. Simpson.

19   Emmett G. Price III, "Chasing a Dream Deferred: From Movement to Culture," in Price, *Black Church and Hip Hop Culture*, 24.

20   Price, "Chasing a Dream Deferred," in Price, *Black Church and Hip Hop Culture*, 24.

21   Emmett G. Price III, "Introduction," in Price, *Black Church and Hip Hop Culture*, xv.

22   Rice N Peas Films (http://ricenpeas.com, now online in archive format only) is one reputable source that discusses the rise of Hip Hop in the United Kingdom. See in particular Jemma Desai, "The Rise and Tribulations of British Hip Hop," http://ricenpeas.com/docs/british_hip_hop.html.

23   See Rice N Peas Film, http://ricenpeas.com.

24   Mike Phillips and Trevor Phillips, *Windrush: The Irresistible Rise of Multi-racial Britain* (San Francisco: HarperCollins, 1998), 4.

25   Phillips and Phillips, *Windrush*, 158–263.

26   Kai Wright, "Hip-Hop Kids These Days," *Progressive* 68, no. 10 (2004): 40.

27   Wright, "Hip-Hop Kids These Days," 40; emphasis added.

28   Wright, "Hip-Hop Kids These Days," 41.

29   This list of practices was inspired by Shawn A. Ginwright, "On Urban Ground: Understanding African-American Intergenerational Partnerships in Urban Communities," *Journal of Community Psychology* 33, no. 1 (2005): 103. While Ginwright does not list these actions as I have, he randomly mentions them in his essay on youth and adult partnerships.

30   Evelyn L. Parker, "Sanctified Rage: Practicing Holy Indignation with Teenagers in the Black Church," in *Children, Youth, and Spirituality in a Troubling World*, ed. Mary Elizabeth Moore and Almeda M. Wright (Atlanta: Chalice, 2008).

31   Parker, "Sanctified Rage," in Moore and Wright, *Children, Youth, and Spirituality*.

32   Suzanne G. Franham, Joseph P. Gill, R. Taylor McLean, and Susan M. Ward, *Listening Hearts: Discerning Call in Community* (Harrisburg, Pa.: Morehouse Publishing, 1991), 79.
33   Ginwright, "On Urban Ground," 103.
34   Ginwright, "On Urban Ground," 103.
35   Ginwright, "On Urban Ground," 103.
36   Ginwright, "On Urban Ground," 104.
37   Ginwright, "On Urban Ground," 105.
38   Ginwright, "On Urban Ground," 104. Regarding adult development, Ginwright's discussion is "a strategy to build strong intergenerational relationships by focusing the psychosocial need of adults to partner more effectively with youth in community-change efforts."
39   Ginwright, "On Urban Ground." Ginwright argues for the adoption of worldview by adults, while I argue it is necessary for both youth and adults.
40   Stephen B. Oates, *Let the Trumpet Sound: The Life of Martin Luther King Jr.* (New York: HarperPerennial, 1982).
41   Pollard, "From Civil Rights to Hip Hop," in Price, *Black Church and Hip Hop Culture*, 12.
42   Wright, "Hip-Hop Kids These Days," 41.
43   Pollard, "From Civil Rights to Hip Hop," in Price, *Black Church and Hip Hop Culture*, 12. Pollard indicates his embellishment of bell hooks' well-known phrase "imperialist white-supremacist capitalist patriarchy."

CHAPTER 3: EVANS JR.

1   See the introduction, this volume, 13.
2   See W.E.B. Du Bois Jr., *The Souls of Black Folk* (New York: Tribeca, 2011).
3   James H. Evans Jr., *We Shall All Be Changed: Social Problems and Theological Renewal* (Minneapolis: Augsburg Fortress, 1997), 4.
4   See section II introduction, this volume, 17.
5   See section II introduction, this volume, 18.
6   J. Deotis Roberts, *Black Theology Today* (Lewiston, N.Y.: Edwin Mellen, 1983), 204.
7   J. Deotis Roberts, *The Prophethood of Black Believers: An African American Political Theology for Ministry* (Louisville, Ky.: Westminster John Knox, 1994), 56.
8   George Abasto and Yvonne Abasto, *How to Equip the African American Family: Issues and Guidelines for Building Strong Families* (Chicago: Urban Outreach, 1991).
9   See section II introduction, this volume, 18.
10   Gwendolyn Y. Fortune, "African Americans," in *Encyclopedia of Ageism*, ed. Erdman B. Palmore, Laurence Branch, and Diana K. Harris (Binghamton, N.Y.: Haworth, 2005), 6.
11   Fortune, "African Americans," in Palmore, Branch, and Harris, *Encyclopedia of Ageism*, 7.
12   Fortune, "African Americans," in Palmore, Branch, and Harris, *Encyclopedia of Ageism*, 7.
13   Fortune, "African Americans," in Palmore, Branch, and Harris, *Encyclopedia of Ageism*, 8.
14   See Tatjana Meschede, Laura Sullivan, and Thomas Shapiro, "The Crisis of Economic Insecurity for African-American and Latino Seniors," Demos.org, http://www

.demos.org/sites/default/files/publications/IASP%20Demos%20Senior%20of%20
Color%20Brief%20September%202011.pdf (accessed August 16, 2014).

15 Bobby Joe Saucer, with Jean Alicia Elster, *Our Help in Ages Past: The Black Church's Ministry among the Elderly* (Valley Forge: Judson Press, 2005), xi.

CHAPTER 4: ALLEN

1 Stacey Floyd-Thomas and Anthony Pinn, *Liberation Theologies in the United States: An Introduction* (New York: New York University Press, 2008), 9.

2 New Revelation Community Church (NRCC) is a nondenominational church based in Oakland, California, that I founded in 2004. It is a radically inclusive church; that is, it welcomes all persons to be in faith covenant with the community. The church makes the statement every week that NRCC is a radically inclusive church that welcomes all persons and makes no distinctions based on race, gender, sexual orientation or affection, socioeconomic location, physical or mental ability, or spiritual journey. The racial demographic of the church is 96 percent African American. Denominationally, 95 percent come from historically black denominations and 5 percent have no denomination affiliation.

3 James Evans, see preceding chapter, 36.

4 Evans, see preceding chapter, 36.

5 Evans, see preceding chapter, 38.

6 Evans, see preceding chapter, 39.

7 Evans, see preceding chapter, 39.

8 Evans, see preceding chapter, 42.

9 Delores S. Williams, "Rituals of Resistance in Womanist Worship," in *Women at Worship: Interpretations of North American Diversity*, ed. Marjorie Proctor-Smith and Janet R. Walton (Louisville, Ky.: Westminster John Knox, 1993), 215.

10 Williams, "Rituals of Resistance," in Proctor-Smith and Walton, *Women at Worship*, 220.

11 Williams, "Rituals of Resistance," in Proctor-Smith and Walton, *Women at Worship*, 215.

12 Williams, "Rituals of Resistance," in Proctor-Smith and Walton, *Women at Worship*, 221.

13 Williams, "Rituals of Resistance," in Proctor-Smith and Walton, *Women at Worship*, 221.

14 Williams, "Rituals of Resistance," in Proctor-Smith and Walton, *Women at Worship*, 221.

15 Evelyn Parker, this volume, 27.

16 Parker, this volume, 29. Parker's six actions are as follows: sanctify the space; pray continuously without uttering sound; practice reflective listening; practice appropriate touching; listen to silence; and prepare for potential emergencies.

17 I need to say a word about the broad understanding of prosperity that I am proposing. Although it certainly could include good economic practices, it is not limited to prosperity as it relates to materialism. Rather, it is more like prospering in a faith-informed lifestyle that includes financial "success" as well as also other pearls of wisdom that parents and grandparents pass on to children, such as how to save money and life lessons that shape one's morals and values.

18 Delores Williams is clear that the African American woman's historical experience of acts of sexual terrorism and forced surrogacy against her body renders traditional theology of atonement unacceptable. For Williams, Jesus conquers not sin on the cross but rather in the wilderness; she therefore proposes: "Jesus, then, does not conquer sin through death on the cross. Rather, Jesus conquers the sin of temptation in the wilderness (Matt 4:1-11) by resistance—by resisting the temptation to value the material over the spiritual ('Man shall not live by bread alone'); by resisting death (not attempting suicide that tests God: 'If you are the Son of God, throw yourself down'); by resisting the greedy urge of monopolistic ownership ('He showed him all the kingdoms of the world and the glory of them; and he said to him, all these I will give you, if you will fall down and worship me'). Jesus therefore conquered sin in life, not in death. In the wilderness he refused to allow evil forces to defile the balanced relation between the material and the spiritual, between life and death, between power and the exertion of it." See Williams, *Sisters in the Wilderness* (Maryknoll, N.Y.: Orbis, 1995), 166.

CHAPTER 5: REDDIE

1 See Dwight N. Hopkins, *Introducing Black Theology of Liberation* (Maryknoll, N.Y.: Orbis, 1999), 43–44. See also C. Eric Lincoln and Lawrence H. Mamiya, *The Black Church in the African American Experience* (Durham, N.C.: Duke University Press, 1990); Peter J. Paris, *The Social Teaching of the Black Churches* (Minneapolis: Fortress, 1985); and Anne H. Pinn and Anthony B. Pinn, *Black Church History* (Minneapolis: Fortress, 2002).

2 See Robert Beckford, *Dread and Pentecostal* (London: SPCK, 2000). See also Nicole Rodriguez Toulis, *Believing Identity* (Oxford: Berg, 1997).

3 See James H. Harris, *Pastoral Theology: A Black-Church Perspective* (Minneapolis: Fortress, 1991). See also Dale P. Andrews, *Practical Theology for Black Churches: Bridging Black Theology and African American Folk Religion* (Louisville, Ky.: Westminster John Knox, 2002).

4 Jeff Astley, Leslie J. Francis, and Colin Crowder, eds., *Theological Perspectives on Christian Formation* (Grand Rapids: Gracewings & Eerdmans, 1996), x.

5 See Anthony G. Reddie, *Dramatizing Theologies: A Participative Approach to Black God Talk* (London: Equinox 2006); Reddie, *Working against the Grain: Re-imaging Black Theology in the 21st Century* (London: Equinox, 2008); and Reddie, *Is God Colour Blind? Insights from Black Theology for Christian Ministry* (London: SPCK, 2009).

6 For an exploration of the Black Church as a source for transformative popular education, see Anthony G. Reddie, *Nobodies to Somebodies: A Practical Theology for Education and Liberation* (Peterborough, U.K.: Epworth, 2003), 37–73. This point, however, should not be taken to mean that the Church has not been an important contributor to the development of formal, assessed education in the form of "day schools." It is simply that for the purposes of this discussion the focus is on informal, nonassessed forms of education that have often proved the most ideal framework for the pedagogical developments of transformative popular education.

7 For a helpful summary of the history and development of Sunday schools and the Christian formation and nurture particularly of children and young people, see John Sutcliffe, *Tuesday's Child: A Reader for Christian Educators* (Birmingham: Christian

Education Publishing, 2001). For the wider developments of the church as a source for education, learning, and the creation of a distinctly Christian form of epistemology, see David Willows, *Divine Knowledge: A Kierkegaardian Perspective on Christian Education* (Aldershot: Ashgate, 2001).

8   See Paulo Freire, *Pedagogy of the Oppressed* (New York: Herder and Herder, 1972).

9   See bell hooks, *Teaching to Transgress: Education as the Practice of Freedom* (New York: Routledge, 1994).

10 See Ira Shor, *Empowering Education: Critical Teaching for Social Change* (Chicago: University of Chicago Press, 1992).

11 James A. Banks, *Race, Culture, and Education: The Selected Works of James A. Banks* (New York: Routledge, 2006).

12 James A. Banks, ed., *Multicultural Education, Transformative Knowledge and Action: Historical and Contemporary Perspectives* (New York: Teachers College Press, 1996), 9.

13 See Jurgen Habermas, *Knowledge and Human Interests* (Boston: Beacon, 1971).

14 Banks, *Race, Culture and Education*, 148.

15 Thomas H. Groome challenges aspects of authority-bound notions of knowledge construction in his excellent study that combines practical theology with liberation theology. See Groome, *Sharing Faith: A Comprehensive Approach to Religious Education and Pastoral Ministry* (San Francisco: Haper SanFrancisco, 1991), 36–84. See also his equally influential *Christian Religious Education: Sharing Our Story and Vision* (San Francisco: Jossey-Bass, 1999).

16 For an excellent transformative popular educational resource that critiques "top-down" forms of knowledge construction (including that which is clothed in the costume of "Church Dogmatics"), see Anne Hope, Sally Timmel, and Chris Hodzi, *Teaching for Transformation: A Handbook for Community Workers*, Books 1–3 (Gweru, Zimbabwe: Mambo, 1994); and Hope, Timmel, and Hodzi, *Teaching for Transformation: A Handbook for Community Workers*, Book 4 (London: Intermediate Technology Publication, 1999).

17 See Emmanuel C. Eze, *Race and the Enlightenment: A Reader* (Oxford: Blackwell, 1997).

18 Gayraud S. Wilmore, *Pragmatic Spirituality: The Christian Faith through an Africentric Lens* (New York: New York University Press, 2004), 142–43.

19 See hooks, *Teaching to Transgress*, 93–128.

20 This work is best exemplified in two books: Reddie, *Dramatizing Theologies*; and Reddie, *Working against the Grain*.

21 See Jose Irizarry, "The Religious Educator as Cultural Spec-Actor: Researching Self in Intercultural Pedagogy," *Religious Education [The Vocation of the Religious Educator]* 98, no. 3 (2003): 365–81. See also Clark C. Apt, *Serious Games* (New York: Viking, 1970).

22 The use of comedy is explored in several of my books. As Colin Morris has been known to remark, "The opposite of funny, is unfunny, not serious." Hence, there is no oxymoron in juxtaposing "funny" and "serious" in any approach to theological reflection.

23 See Groome, *Sharing Faith*; and Groome, *Christian Religious Education*.

24 Jerome W. Berryman, *Godly Play: An Imaginative Approach to Religious Education* (1991; Minneapolis: Augsburg, 1995).

25 Jacqueline Bussie has written an award-winning study on the relationship between oppression, laughter, and resistance. The pointed use of laughter and comedy

becomes a means of effecting resistance in the face of oppression and marginalization. See Bussie, *Laughter of the Oppressed: Ethical and Theological Resistance in
Wiesel, Morrison and Endo* (New York: T&T Clark, 2006).

26 For one of the most incisive black theology–inspired critical analyses of the links
between Western capitalism and black poverty, see Itumeleng J. Mosala, *Biblical
Hermeneutics and Black Theology in South Africa* (Grand Rapids: Eerdmans, 1989).

27 See Munyaradzi Feliz Murove, "Perceptions of Greed in Western Economic and
Religious Traditions: An African Communitarian Response," *Black Theology: An
International Journal* 5, no. 2 (2007): 220–43.

28 See Mosala, *Biblical Hermeneutics.* See also Itumeleng J. Mosala and Buti Tlhagale,
eds., *The Unquestionable Right to Be Free* (Maryknoll, N.Y.: Orbis, 1986).

29 See Mokgethi Mothlabi, *African Theology/Black Theology in South Africa: Looking
Back, Moving On* (Pretoria: University of South Africa Press, 2008), 42–49.

30 Arguably, the most persuasive black theologian on this issue has been Dwight
N. Hopkins. See Hopkins, "Theologies in the USA," in *Another Possible World*,
ed. Marcella Althaus-Reid, Ivan Petrella, and Luiz Carlos Susin (London: SCM
Press, 2007), 98–100; and Hopkins, "The Religion of Globalization," in *Religions/
Globalizations: Theories and Cases*, ed. Dwight N. Hopkins, Lois Ann Lorentzen,
Eduardo Mendieta, and David Batstone (Durham, N.C.: Duke University Press,
2001), 7–32. See also Keri Day, "Global Economics and U.S. Public Policy: Human
Liberation for the Global Poor," *Black Theology: An International Journal* 9, no. 1
(2011): 9–33; and Tissa Balasuriya, "Liberation of the Affluent," *Black Theology: An
International Journal* 1, no. 1 (2001): 83–113.

31 Birmingham is in the West Midlands of Britain and is generally understood as the
second city of the nation after London. I have lived in this city since 1984.

32 Details of the game can be found on Wikipedia.

33 This comparative study seeks to outline the ways in which predominantly darker-
skinned people are invariably the ones most impacted by the dominant model of
economic laissez-faire neoliberalism, and in turn attempt to resist and challenge it
by means of liberative models of faith. See Dwight N. Hopkins and Marjorie Lewis,
eds., *Another World Is Possible: Spiritualities and Religions of Global Darker Peoples*
(Oakwood: Equinox, 2009).

34 This term refers to a group of sociopolitical theologies that seek to reinterpret the
central meaning of the God event within history, particularly in terms of the life,
death, and resurrection of Jesus Christ. They provide a politicized, radical, and
socially transformative understanding of the Christian faith in light of the lived
realities and experiences of the poor, the marginalized, and the oppressed. For an
important text that delineates the comparative developments in "theologies of liberation," see Marcella Althaus-Reid, Ivan Patrella, and Luis Carlos Susin, eds., *Another
Possible World* (London: SCM Press, 2007).

35 See Wilf Wilde, *Crossing the River of Fire: Mark's Gospel and Global Capitalism*
(Peterborough, U.K.: Epworth, 2006) for an excellent account of this point.

36 One of the dominant voices arguing for a radical, prophetic form of black theology has been Cornel West. See West, "Black Theology of Liberation as Critique of
Capitalist Civilization," in *Black Theology: A Documentary History, Volume Two:
1980–1992*, ed. James H. Cone and Gayraud S. Wilmore (Maryknoll, N.Y.: Orbis,

1993), 410–25; and West, *Prophesy Deliverance! An Afro-American Revolutionary Christianity* (Philadelphia: Westminster, 2003).

37 James H. Cone, *A Black Theology of Liberation* (Maryknoll, N.Y.: Orbis, 1990), 6.

38 In March 2011, in Sydney, Australia, I employed this method with Aboriginal and Torres Strait Islander people—the indigenous and most oppressed peoples in that island continent. Details of my work can be found on the Christ and Culture Conference 2011 page of the National Council of Churches in Australia, http://www.ncca.org.au/departments/natsiec/583-christ-and-culture-conference-2011. For details on the extant spirituality and theology of aboriginal peoples, see Anne Pattel-Gray, "Australia: Spirituality," in Hopkins and Lewis, *Another World Is Possible*, 64–74.

39 For a helpful text in discerning the similarities and disparities between pastoral and practical theology, see James Woodward and Stephen Pattison, eds., *The Blackwell Reader in Pastoral and Practical Theology* (Oxford: Blackwell, 2000).

40 A number of black pastoral and practical theologians have explored the issues of black self-negation. See Harris, *Pastoral Theology*; Carroll A. Watkins Ali, *Survival and Liberation: Pastoral Theology in African American Context* (St. Louis: Chalice, 1999); Homer U. Ashby Jr., *Our Home Is over Jordan: A Black Pastoral Theology* (St. Louis: Chalice, 2003); Archie Smith Jr., *Navigating the Deep Waters: Spirituality in African American Families* (Cleveland: United Church, 1997).

41 Wilmore, *Pragmatic Spirituality*, 155–66.

42 Emmanuel Y. Lartey offers a brilliant and concise exposition of the praxis mode of theological reflection that underpins all forms of "liberative praxis."; See Lartey, "Practical Theology as a Theological Form," in Woodward and Pattison, *Blackwell Reader*, 128–34.

CHAPTER 6: MASENYA

1 I belong to the International Assemblies of God (IAG) Church in South Africa. It is an offshoot of the Assemblies of God Church, which originated in the United States of America.

2 One pastor of the Apostolic Faith Mission Church—who was interviewed by a student, E. M. K. Mathole, in his master's research regarding how his church responded to the challenge of poverty alleviation—noted that the church had a responsibility to the poor as it was not a club. In Rev. Dr. Burger's view, a club exists solely to serve its members' interests. He found it tragic that, right through the church's history, the church basically tended to develop a "club mentality." In his view, "the church should not be 'distant' and aloof from the community; the church ought to exist in close proximity to the people—right there in the marketplace. That was where Jesus was to be found during His earthly ministry—where it hurt the most." Mathole, "The Christian Witness in the Context of Poverty with Special Reference to South African Charismatic Evangelicals" (doctoral thesis, University of Pretoria, 2005), 257.

3 Danal Dorr, *Spirituality and Justice* (Maryknoll, N.Y.: Orbis, 1984), 79.

4 J. Cochrane, J. de Gruchy, and R. Peterson, *In Word and in Deed: Towards a Practical Theology of Social Transformation: A Framework for Reflection and Training* (Pietermaritzburg, South Africa: Cluster Publications, 1991), 57.

5 Madipoane Masenya (ngwan'a Mphahlele), "'For Better or Worse?': The (Christian) Bible and Africana Women," *Old Testament Essays* 22, no. 1 (2009): 140.

6   Cochrane, de Gruchy, and Peterson, *In Word and in Deed*, 57.
7   The word "nonliteracy" in this essay will refer to a lack of education in its Western mode—that is, "education" as it was introduced to African–South Africans from Britain, for example. It is therefore acknowledged that in precolonial Africa, and up to this day, education has always taken place in various African contexts. In an aural culture, for example, to designate as uneducated the elderly woman who suggested that English not be used as the medium of communication at the women's conference (see one of the opening narratives) would not be accurate. In a culture in which the word of mouth is foregrounded, rather than the written word, the elderly woman who suggested praying that the conference speeches not be delivered in English cannot be regarded as nonliterate.
8   G. E. Dames, "The Dilemma of Traditional and 21st Century Pastoral Ministry: Ministering to Families and Communities Faced with Socioeconomic Pathologies," *HTS Teologiese Studies/Theological Studies* 66, no. 2 (2010): 1–7; emphasis in original.
9   Cochrane, de Gruchy, and Peterson, *In Word and in Deed*, 9.
10   Madipoane Masenya (ngwan'a Mphahlele), "'But You Shall Let Every Girl Live': Reading Exodus 1:1–2:10 the Bosadi (Womanhood) Way," *Old Testament Essays* 15, no. 1 (2002): 99.
11   In article 7 of the Accra Confession, we read: "The annual income of the richest 1% is equal to that of the poorest 57%. Some 24,000 die each day from poverty and malnutrition. The debt of poor countries continues to increase despite having repaid the principal on their loans several times over. Wars over resources such as oil and gold are on the rise and claim the lives of millions, while millions more die of preventable diseases. The HIV/AIDS pandemic afflicts life in all parts of the world but especially in the impoverished global South where anti-retroviral drugs are too expensive to buy. The majority of those living in poverty are women and children, and the number of people living in absolute poverty (less than one U.S. dollar/day) continues to increase." As quoted by Puleng LenkaBula, *Choose Life, Act in Hope: African Churches Living Out the Accra Confession; A Study Resource on the Accra Confession; Covenanting for Justice in the Economy and Earth* (Geneva: World Alliance of Reformed Churches, 2009), 13.
12   World Council of Churches, "Commission on the Churches' Participation in Development," 1980; as quoted by Cochrane, de Gruchy, and Peterson, *In Word and in Deed*, 61.
13   Mathole, "Christian Witness in the Context of Poverty," 249.
14   T. Mofokeng, "The Evaluation of the Black Struggle and the Role of the Black Theology," in *The Unquestionable Right to Be Free: Black Theology from South Africa*, ed. I. J. Mosala and B. Tlhagale (Braamfontein: Skotaville, 1986), 113–28.
15   LenkaBula, *Choose Life, Act in Hope*, 12, 14.
16   LenkaBula, *Choose Life, Act in Hope*, 14.
17   T. Okure, "Invitation to African Women's Hermeneutical Concerns," *African Journal of Biblical Studies* 19, no. 2 (2003): 74.

CHAPTER 7: WRIGHT JR.

1   Dwight Hopkins, *Introducing Black Theology of Liberation* (Maryknoll, N.Y.: Orbis, 1999), 87–124.
2   Hopkins, *Introducing Black Theology of Liberation*, 87–124.

3 Paulo Freire, *Pedagogy of the Oppressed: 30th Anniversary Edition* (New York: Continuum, 2000).

4 Donaldo P. Macedo, *Literacies of Power: What Americans Are Not Allowed to Know* (Boulder, Colo.: Perseus Group, 2006).

5 Geneva Smitherman, *Talkin and Testifyin: The Language of Black America* (Boston: Houghton Mifflin, 1977).

6 Samy H. Alim and Geneva Smitherman, *Articulate while Black: Barack Obama, Language, and Race in the U.S.* (New York: Oxford University Press, 2012).

7 Brandee J. Mimitzraiem, "Too Young to Be Black: The Intergenerational Capability of Black Theology," in *Walk Together Children: Black and Womanist Theologies, Church, and Theological Education*, ed. Dwight N. Hopkins and Linda E. Thomas (Eugene, Ore.: Cascade, 2010).

8 See the section III introduction, this volume, XXX.

9 Janice Hale, *Black Children: Their Roots, Culture, and Learning Styles* (Baltimore, Md.: Johns Hopkins University Press, 2012); Hale, *Learning while Black: Creating Educational Excellence for African-American Children* (Baltimore, Md.: Johns Hopkins University Press, 2001).

10 Asa Hilliard, "AEMP/Closing the Achievement Gap Branch—Instructional Strategies: Facilitating Language and Learning in Standard English Learners (SELs)," Building on Learning Styles and Strengths of SELs, San Diego City College, http://www.sdcity.edu/Portals/0/CollegeServices/StudentServices/Learning Communities/Inst.Strat.CRR.PDF (accessed June 1, 2013).

11 See the section entitled "Learning Styles Valued by the Traditional School Culture," in Hilliard, "AEMP/Closing the Achievement Gap Branch," 5.

12 Macedo, *Literacies of Power.*

13 Smitherman, *Talkin and Testifyin.*

14 See the Center for African American Theological Studies (CAATS) page on the Seminary Consortium for Urban Pastoral Education (SCUPE) website, http://scupe .org/caats/ (accessed June 1, 2013).

15 See a specific list of Garrett-Evangelical Theological Seminary programs at http:// www.garrett.edu/student-life (accessed February 17, 2015).

16 See http://scupe.org/caats/.

17 Urban Theological Institute (UTI), Lutheran Theological Seminary at Philadelphia, http://ltsp.edu/uti (accessed June 1, 2013).

18 Hale, *Black Children*; and *Learning while Black.*

19 Hilliard, "AEMP/Closing the Achievement Gap Branch."

20 Macedo, *Literacies of Power.*

21 Henry A. Giroux, *On Critical Pedagogy* (New York: Continuum, 2011).

22 Chris Hedges and Joe Sacco, *Days of Destruction, Days of Revolt* (New York: Nation, 2012).

23 Obery M. Hendricks, *The Universe Bends toward Justice: Radical Reflections on the Bible, the Church, and the Body Politic* (Maryknoll, N.Y.: Orbis, 2011); Hendricks Jr., *The Politics of Jesus: Rediscovering the True Revolutionary Nature of Jesus' Teachings and How They Have Been Corrupted* (New York: Doubleday, 2006).

24 Allan Boesak, *The Tenderness of Conscience: African Renaissance and the Spirituality of Politics* (Cleveland: Sun, 2005); Allan Aubrey Boesak and Curtiss Paul DeYoung,

Radical Reconciliation: Beyond Political Pietism and Christian Quietism (Maryknoll, N.Y.: Orbis, 2012).

CHAPTER 8: SHEPPARD

1 Johan Galtung, "Cultural Violence," *Journal of Peace Research* 27, no. 3 (1990): 291–92.

2 Emilie M. Townes, *Womanist Ethics and the Cultural Production of Evil* (New York: Palgrave Macmillan, 2006), 45.

3 Audre Lorde, *Undersong: Chosen Poems Old and New* (New York: W. W. Norton, 1992), 85.

4 *The Edge of Each Other's Battles: The Vision of Audre Lorde,* directed by Jennifer Abod (Women Make Movies, 2002), DVD. Documentary based on footage from the 1990 conference "I Am Your Sisters: Connections across Difference" held in Boston.

5 Gloria Anzaldúa, *Borderlands/La frontera* (San Francisco: Spinster/Aunt Lute, 1987), 87.

6 Nikol Alexander-Floyd, "Critical Race Pedagogy: Teaching about Race and Racism through Legal Learning Strategies," *Political Science & Politics* 41, no. 1 (2008): 183.

7 Cheryl A. Kirk-Duggan, "What's Uncivil about Civil War? A Womanist Perspective on Pedagogical Issues in Ancient Biblical Battle Texts," *Society of Biblical Literature Forum* (July 2005), http://www.sbl-site.org/Article.aspx?ArticleID=428 (accessed April 10, 2013); emphasis in original.

8 See "Bishop Eddie Long Preaching on Gays/Homosexuals," www.youtube.com/watch?v=UItGijdsCf8 (accessed June 12, 2012).

9 Pamela R. Lightsey, "The Eddie Long Scandal: It *Is* about Anti-homosexuality," *Religion Dispatches,* October 5, 2010, http://www.religiondispatches.org/dispatches/sexandgender/3444/the_eddie_long_scandal%3A_it_is_about_anti-homosexuality (accessed April 10, 2013).

10 "Daughter of Creflo Dollar, Megachurch Pastor, Says Alleged Abuse 'Was not the first time' during 911 Call," CBSNews.com, June 12, 2012, http://www.cbsnews.com/8301-504083_162-57451441-504083/daughter-of-creflo-dollar-megachurch-pastor-says-alleged-abuse-was-not-the-first-time-during-911-call/ (accessed June 12, 2012).

11 "Daughter of Creflo Dollar, Megachurch Pastor," CBSNews.com.

12 Phillis Isabella Sheppard, *Self, Culture and Others in Womanist Practical Theology* (New York: Palgrave Macmillan, 2011), 25.

13 Sheppard, *Self, Culture and Others,* 26.

14 Sheppard, *Self, Culture and Others,* 26.

15 Sheppard, *Self, Culture and Others,* 26.

16 Sheppard, *Self, Culture and Others,* 187–89.

17 Aurelius Augustine, *Confessions* (New York: Sheed & Ward, 1943), 1:9.

18 Augustine, *Confessions,* 1:9.

19 Aurelius Augustine, *City of God,* trans. Marcus Dodds (New York: Random House, 1950), 14:3.

20 Peter Brown, *The Body and Society: Men, Women, and Sexual Renunciation in Early Christianity* (New York: Columbia University Press, 1988), 399.

21 Augustine, *City of God,* 22:8. This text and those cited below are available online at the Christian Classics Ethereal Library, http://www.ccel.org.

22 Augustine, *City of God*, 16:34.
23 Augustine, *City of God*, 15:2.
24 Barbara Smith, as quoted in Rose M. Brewer, "Theorizing Race, Class and Gender: The New Scholarship of Black Feminist Intellectuals and Black Women's Labor," in *Theorizing Black Feminisms: The Visionary Pragmatism of Black Women*, ed. Stanlie M. James and Abena P. A. Busia (New York: Routledge, 1993), 15.

CHAPTER 9: HAYES

1   Howard Thurman, *Jesus and the Disinherited* (Boston: Beacon, 1996), 7.
2   Dale P. Andrews, *Practical Theology for Black Churches: Bridging Black Theology and African American Folk Religion* (Louisville, Ky.: Westminster John Knox, 2002), 1.
3   Andrews, *Practical Theology for Black Churches*, 1.
4   Bryan Massingale, *Racial Justice and the Catholic Church* (Maryknoll, N.Y.: Orbis, 2010), 13.
5   Massingale, *Racial Justice and the Catholic Church*, 42.
6   Massingale, *Racial Justice and the Catholic Church*, 8.
7   Dale P. Andrews, "Race and Racism," in *The Wiley-Blackwell Companion to Practical Theology*, ed. Bonnie J. Miller-McLemore (New York: Blackwell, 2012), 406.
8   Andrews, "Race and Racism," in Miller-McLemore, *Wiley-Blackwell Companion*, 402.
9   Martin Luther King Jr., "Letter from a Birmingham Jail," in *Walkin' the Talk: An Anthology of African American Studies*, ed. Vernon D. Johnson and Bill Lyne (Upper Saddle River, N.J.: Prentice Hall, 2003), 401.
10 Black Catholic Bishops of the United States, *What We Have Seen and Heard: A Pastoral Letter on Evangelization from the Black Bishops of the United States* (Cincinnati: St. Anthony Messenger, 1984), 7.
11 Kelly Brown Douglas, *What's Faith Got to Do with It? Black Bodies/Christian Souls* (Maryknoll, N.Y.: Orbis, 2005), 189.
12 Marcia Riggs, as cited in Douglas, *What's Faith?*, 189.
13 Douglas, *What's Faith?*, 190.
14 Horace L. Griffin, *Their Own Receive Them Not: African American Lesbians and Gays in Black Churches* (Cleveland: Pilgrim, 2006), 37.
15 Griffin, *Their Own Receive Them Not*, 56.
16 Douglas, *What's Faith?*, 5.
17 Douglas, *What's Faith?*, 9; emphasis in original.
18 Douglas, *What's Faith?*, xv; emphasis in original.
19 Douglas, *What's Faith?*, 31.
20 Douglas, *What's Faith?*, 31.
21 Douglas, *What's Faith?*, xviii; emphasis in original.
22 Griffin, *Their own receive them not*, 57.
23 Andrews, *Practical Theology for Black Churches*, 1–11.
24 Andrews, *Practical Theology for Black Churches*, 3–4.
25 Delores Williams, *Sisters in the Wilderness: The Challenge of Womanist God-Talk*, 20th anniv. ed. (Maryknoll, N.Y.: Orbis, 2013), 21.
26 Forrest Harris, "The Children Have Come to Birth: A Theological Response for Survival and Quality of Life," in *Walk Together Children: Black and Womanist*

Theologies, Church, and Theological Education, ed. Dwight N. Hopkins and Linda E. Thomas (Eugene, Ore.: Cascade, 2010), 36.

27 Harris, "Children Have Come to Birth," in Hopkins and Thomas, *Walk Together Children*, 31.

28 Audre Lorde, "A Litany for Survival," in *The Black Unicorn: Poems* (New York: W. W. Norton, 1978), 32.

29 Stewart Carlyle Fielding, as cited in Harris, "Children Have Come to Birth," in Hopkins and Thomas, *Walk Together Children*, 31.

30 Harris, "Children Have Come to Birth," in Hopkins and Thomas, *Walk Together Children*, 32.

31 Harris, "Children Have Come to Birth," in Hopkins and Thomas, *Walk Together Children*, 37.

32 James H. Cone, *The Cross and the Lynching Tree* (Maryknoll, N.Y.: Orbis, 2012), 160.

33 Cone, *Cross and the Lynching Tree*, 160.

34 Cone, *Cross and the Lynching Tree*, 161.

CHAPTER 10: WILEY AND WILEY

1 Howard Thurman, *Jesus and the Disinherited* (Boston: Beacon, 1976), 7.

2 We define "external oppression" as a sustained attack on any group of people that emanates from an outside group whose members consider themselves different from, and/or superior to, those attacked. "Internal oppression," on the other hand, is a similarly motivated, sustained attack on members of a subgroup of people that stems from other members within the larger group.

3 Phillis Isabella Sheppard, this volume, 98.

4 Sheppard, this volume, 98.

5 Kelly Brown Douglas, *What's Faith Got to Do with It? Black Bodies/Christian Souls* (Maryknoll, N.Y.: Orbis, 2005), 5; see Diana Hayes' discussion of Kelly Brown Douglas in this volume, 119.

6 Mark L. Chapman, *Christianity on Trial: African-American Religious Thought before and after Black Power* (Maryknoll, N.Y.: Orbis, 1996), 3.

7 Chapman, *Christianity on Trial*, 3.

8 Chapman, *Christianity on Trial*, 3. Emphasis added.

9 Archie Smith Jr., *The Relational Self: Ethics and Therapy from a Black Church Perspective* (Nashville: Abingdon, 1982), 15.

10 Smith, *Relational Self*, 15; Thurman, *Jesus and the Disinherited*, 7.

11 Thurman, *Jesus and the Disinherited*, 7–8. Emphasis added.

12 W.E.B. Du Bois, *The Souls of Black Folk* (New York: Barnes & Noble Classics, 2003), 16.

13 See Randall Kennedy, *The Persistence of the Color Line: Racial Politics and the Obama Presidency* (New York: Pantheon, 2011).

14 See Michelle Alexander, *The New Jim Crow: Mass Incarceration in the Age of Colorblindness* (New York: New Press, 2010).

15 We understand that Jackson's opposition to King did not necessarily mean that he was conservative. Malcolm X, who was generally considered to be much more radical than King was, also opposed him. However, if we consider radicalism to be the opposite of conservatism, then it would appear that, even though both King and Jackson attacked racism, Jackson was somewhere to the right of King just as King

was somewhere to the right of Malcolm. Jackson objected to civil disobedience and other disruptive protest strategies that King employed. According to Gayraud S. Wilmore, one characteristic of black religious radicalism is "the acceptance of protest and agitation as theological prerequisites for black liberation and the liberation of all oppressed peoples." See Wilmore, *Black Religion and Black Radicalism: An Interpretation of the Religious History of African Americans*, 3rd ed. (Maryknoll, N.Y.: Orbis, 1998), ix.

16   Some would argue that even King's nonviolent approach to social transformation was relatively conservative. Compared to the fiery rhetoric and more militant style of his contemporary, Minister Malcolm X of the Nation of Islam, King was widely viewed as a more palatable adversary—"the lesser of two evils," if you will—in the eyes of his racist opponents. Wilmore, however, reminds us that black radicalism has been "somewhat less committed to violence as a revolutionary strategy"; basically, "it was an attack on institutional racism without calling into question the permanent, underlying structures of American society"; see Wilmore, *Black Religion and Black Radicalism*, 197.

17   C. Eric Lincoln and Lawrence H. Mamiya, *The Black Church and the African American Experience* (Durham, N.C.: Duke University Press, 1990), 10–16.

18   The vision statement of the Covenant Baptist United Church of Christ, available at http://www.covenantdc.org, reads as follows: "Affirming our African heritage, our vision is to build an inclusive body of biblical believers who continue to grow in Christ as we love, serve, and fellowship with the community and each other."

19   Sheppard, this volume, 100; emphasis in original.

20   Hayes, this volume, 125–26.

21   Hayes, this volume, 124.

22   See Wright's personal account of these aspects of his background and experiences, in Jeremiah A. Wright Jr., "Black Theology/Womanist Theology in Dialogue," in *Walk Together Children: Black and Womanist Theologies, Church, and Theological Education*, ed. Dwight N. Hopkins and Linda E. Thomas (Eugene, Ore.: Cascade, 2010), 251–64.

23   Hayes, this volume, 123.

24   Hayes, this volume, 126.

25   Hayes, this volume, 126.

26   See the online definition at Dictionary.com, http://dictionary.com (accessed August 22, 2014).

27   See the online definition at Dictionary.com, http://dictionary.com (accessed August 22, 2014).

28   Obery M. Hendricks Jr., *The Universe Bends toward Justice: Radical Reflections on the Bible, the Church, and the Body Politic* (Maryknoll, N.Y.: Orbis, 2011), 1–39.

29   Hendricks, *Universe Bends toward Justice*, 18; emphasis in original.

30   Hendricks, *Universe Bends toward Justice*, 20–21.

31   Sheppard, this volume, 98.

32   Sheppard, this volume, 101.

33   Sheppard, this volume, 100; emphasis in original.

34   See James H. Cone and Gayraud S. Wilmore, eds., *Black Theology: A Documentary History, Volume One: 1966–1979* (Maryknoll, N.Y.: Orbis, 1993), 19–26.

35   James H. Cone, *Black Theology and Black Power* (Maryknoll, N.Y.: Orbis, 1997), x.

36 Cone is to be commended for the fact that, when he awakened to his patriarchal blind spot, he encouraged black women scholars, many of whom studied under him and became pioneering womanist theologians, to find and develop their own theological voices. For more on this, see Cone and Wilmore, *Black Theology*, 279–346; James H. Cone, *For My People: Black Theology and the Black Church* (Maryknoll, N.Y.: Orbis, 1984), 122–39; and Delores S. Williams, "James Cone's Liberation: Twenty Years Later," in *A Black Theology of Liberation: Twentieth Anniversary Edition*, ed. James H. Cone (Maryknoll, N.Y.: Orbis, 1990), 189–95.

37 Jacquelyn Grant, "Black Theology and the Black Woman," in Cone and Wilmore, *Black Theology*, 328.

38 See Acts 2:42.

39 James Strong, *Strong's Exhaustive Concordance of the Bible* (Peabody, Mass.: Hendrickson, 2007), Strong's no. 2842.

40 Acts 2:44-45.

41 Jeremiah Wright concurs that "in the black church we have many deeply homophobic members. You can talk all the profound theory you want to talk, but there is a deep homophobia in the church that is still real"; see Jeremiah A. Wright Jr., "Doing Black Theology in the Black Church," in *Living Stones in the Household of God: The Legacy and Future of Black Theology*, ed. Linda E. Thomas (Minneapolis: Fortress, 2004), 18.

42 Sheppard, this volume, 98.

43 Martin Luther King Jr., "Remaining Awake through a Great Revolution," an address delivered at the Washington National Cathedral, March 31, 1968, in *A Testament of Hope: The Essential Writings of Martin Luther King, Jr.*, ed. James Melvin Washington (New York: Harper & Row, 1986), 268–78; quotation, 276.

44 Martin Luther King Jr., *Why We Can't Wait* (New York: New American Library, 1964), 80–81.

45 Sheppard, this volume, 98.

46 Sheppard, this volume, 98.

47 Sheppard, this volume, 101.

48 Sheppard, this volume, 101; emphasis in original.

CHAPTER 11: ACOLATSE

1 Jacques Derrida and Anne Dufourmantelle, *Of Hospitality* (Stanford, Calif.: Stanford University Press, 2000), 73–77. See also Tomi Oredein, "Hospitality and Domesticity: Where Can These Black Women Live?," theotherjournal.com, October 6, 2014, http://theotherjournal.com/2014/10/06/hospitality-and-domesticity-where-can -these-black-women-live/ (accessed January 27, 2015).

2 Hugh R. Page, ed., *The Africana Bible: Reading Israel's Scriptures from Africa and the African Diaspora* (Minneapolis: Fortress, 2010).

3 Consider the numerous surrounding nations and Kings (Cyrus, Is. 45; Nebuchadnezzar–Daniel) used to discipline Israel and individuals like Rahab, Joshua 2, and above all Moses' father-in law, Jethro, and his advice on leadership.

4 The influence of Gentiles and the Gentile mission in general fill the New Testament pages. Individuals include Cornelius (Acts 10:1–11:18) and Jairus the centurion, who affords Jesus a chance to teach about faith and authority (Mark 5:35-43). In addition are the numerous times Jesus points to an outsider/foreigner, even a religious other,

as being one from whom his own people, the Jews, could learn about right attitude and living. A good example is the parable of the Good Samaritan (Luke 10:25-37).

5   Dale P. Andrews, *Practical Theology for Black Churches: Bridging Black Theology and African American Folk Religion* (Louisville, Ky.: Westminster John Knox, 2002).

6   See the section V introduction, this volume, 149.

7   The ongoing projects in religious pluralism and the continuing debates in the theology of religions indicate that these are matters pressing on the church and on the diversity of Christian perspectives to attend to faithful listening not only to Christian voices other than their own but to what people of other faiths might help Christians understand about the triune God. See the range of opinions in John Sanders, ed., *What about Those Who Have Never Heard? Three Views on the Destiny of the Unevangelized* (Downers Grove, Ill.: InterVarsity, 1995). See also Lesslie Newbigin, *Proper Confidence: Faith, Doubt and Certainty in Christian Discipleship* (Grand Rapids: Eerdmans, 1995).

8   See Peter Paris, *Black Leaders in Conflict: Joseph H. Jackson, Martin Luther King, Jr., Malcolm X, Adam Clayton Powell, Jr.*, 2nd ed. (Louisville, Ky.: Westminster John Knox, 1991).

9   Edward Farley, *Theologia: The Fragmentation and Unity of Theological Education* (Philadelphia: Fortress, 1983).

10   Don Browning, *A Fundamental Practical Theology: Descriptive and Strategic Proposals* (Minneapolis: Fortress, 1991).

11   Ray Anderson, *The Shape of Practical Theology: Empowering Ministry with Theological Praxis* (Downers Grove, Ill.: InterVarsity, 2001).

12   J. Kameron Carter, *Race: A Theological Account* (New York: Oxford University Press, 2008).

13   Esther E. Acolatse, "What Is Theological about Practical Theology? Toward a Pastoral Hermeneutic of Primal Speech," *Practical Theology* 7, no 3 (2014): 205–20.

14   Deborah van Deusen Hunsinger, *Theology and Pastoral Counseling: A New Interdisciplinary Approach* (Grand Rapids: Eerdmans, 1995).

15   Acolatse, "What Is Theological?," 212.

16   Acolatse, "What Is Theological?," 213.

17   Acolatse, "What Is Theological?," 213.

18   Acolatse, "What Is Theological?," 213–14.

19   Acolatse, "What Is Theological about Practical Theology?," 214–15; see Lamin Sanneh, *Translating the Message: The Missionary Impact on Culture* (Maryknoll, N.Y.: Orbis, 1989), 50–84, 214–16.

20   Acolatse, "What Is Theological?," 215–16.

21   Acolatse, "What Is Theological?," 216.

22   Acolatse, "What Is Theological?," 217.

23   Acolatse, "What Is Theological?," 217.

CHAPTER 12: JENNINGS

1   There are a number of interesting accounts of the aesthetic intervention within the history of black struggle in the United States and other postcolonial sites. See Richard J. Powell, *Black Art and Culture in the 20th Century* (New York: Thames & Hudson, 1997); Samuel A. Floyd Jr., *The Power of Black Music: Interpreting Its History from Africa to the United States* (New York: Oxford, 1995); Gerald Early,

One Nation under a Groove: Motown and American Culture (Ann Arbor: University of Michigan Press, 2007); Clyde R. Taylor, *The Mask of Art: Breaking the Aesthetic Contract; Film and Literature* (Bloomington: Indiana University Press, 1998).

2 John L. Comaroff and Jean Comaroff, *Ethnicity, Inc.* (Chicago: University of Chicago Press, 2009); Vijay Prashad, *The Karma of Brown Folk* (Minneapolis: University of Minnesota Press, 2000); Deborah Poole, *Vision, Race, and Modernity: A Visual Economy of the Andean Image World* (Princeton, N.J.: Princeton University Press, 1997).

3 St. John of Damascus, *Three Treatises on the Divine Image*, trans. Andrew Louth (New York: St. Vladimir's, 2003), Kindle edition.

4 Walter Wink, *The Powers That Be: Theology for a New Millennium* (New York: Random House, 1998); Wink, *Naming the Powers* (Minneapolis: Fortress, 1984).

5 See Greg Tate, ed., *Everything but the Burden: What White People Are Taking from Black Culture* (New York: Random House, 2003).

6 Two notable exceptions are Peg Zeglin Brand, ed., *Beauty Matters* (Bloomington: Indiana University Press, 2000); and Taylor, *Mask of Art*.

7 Elaine Scarry, *On Beauty and Being Just* (Princeton, N.J.: Princeton University Press, 1999), 58.

8 Scarry, *On Beauty and Being Just*, 114.

9 Scarry, *On Beauty and Being Just*, 114.

10 Scarry, *On Beauty and Being Just*, 114; emphasis added.

11 Thorstein Veblen, *The Theory of the Leisure Class* (New York: Dover Publications, 2004), 223–44; Meg Armstrong, "'The Effects of Blackness': Gender, Race, and the Sublime in Aesthetic Theories of Burke and Kant," *Journal of Aesthetics and Art Criticism* 54, no. 3 (1996): 213–36; Arthur C. Danto, "Beauty and Beautification," in Brand, *Beauty Matters*, 65–83.

12 Scarry, *On Beauty and Being Just*, 88–89.

13 Scarry, *On Beauty and Being Just*, 90.

14 Terry Eagleton, *The Ideology of the Aesthetic* (Cambridge: Blackwell, 1990), 75.

15 Eagleton, *Ideology of the Aesthetic*, 75.

16 Christine Hünefeldt, *Paying the Price of Freedom: Family and Labor among Lima's Slaves, 1800–1854* (Berkeley: University of California Press, 1994); Jennifer L. Morgan, *Laboring Women: Reproduction and Gender in New World Slavery* (Philadelphia: University of Pennsylvania Press, 2004).

17 Lois Parkinson Zamora and Monika Kaup, eds., *Baroque New Worlds: Representation, Transculturation, Counterconquest* (Durham, N.C.: Duke University Press, 2010); Serge Gruzinski, *The Mestizo Mind: The Intellectual Dynamics of Colonization and Globalization* (New York: Routledge, 2002); Sabine MacCormack, *On the Wings of Time: Rome, the Incas, Spain, and Peru* (Princeton, N.J.: Princeton University Press, 2007).

18 Timothy Ware, *The Orthodox Church* (New York: Penguin, 1985); John Baggley, *Doors of Perception: Icons and Their Spiritual Significance* (New York: St. Vladimir's, 1995); Marie-José Mondzain, *Image, Icon, Economy: The Byzantine Origins of the Contemporary Imaginary* (Stanford, Calif.: Stanford University Press, 2005); Paul Evdokimov, *The Art of the Icon: A Theology of Beauty* (Knob Hill, Calif.: Oakwood, 1996).

19 Andrew Louth, "Introduction" to John of Damascus, *Three Treatises on the Divine Image*, 54.

20 Friedrich Schleiermacher, *On Religion: Speeches to Its Cultured Despisers* (Cambridge: Cambridge University Press, 1996); Jacqueline Mariña, ed., *The Cambridge Companion to Friedrich Schleiermacher* (Cambridge: Cambridge University Press, 2005).

21 Readers can find images such as these through almost any online search using the keywords "Tommy Hilfiger ads." I accessed such images on April 25, 2013.

22 Johann Gottfried Herder, *Another Philosophy of History and Selected Political Writings* (Indianapolis: Hackett, 2004); Immanuel Kant, *Observations on the Feeling of the Beautiful and Sublime* (Berkeley: University of California Press, 1960); John H. Zammito, *Kant, Herder and the Birth of Anthropology* (Chicago: University of Chicago Press, 2002).

23 Walter Benn Michaels, *Our America: Nativism, Modernism and Pluralism* (Durham, N.C.: Duke University Press, 1995); Michaels, *The Shape of the Signifier: 1967 to the End of History* (Princeton, N.J.: Princeton University Press, 2004); James Clifford, *The Predicament of Culture: 20th Century Ethnography, Literature, and Art* (Cambridge, Mass.: Harvard University Press, 1998); Adam Kuper, *Culture: The Anthropologists' Account* (Cambridge, Mass.: Harvard University Press, 1999).

24 T. J. Gorringe, *Furthering Humanity: A Theology of Culture* (Farnham, U.K.: Ashgate, 2004); Kathryn Tanner, *Theories of Culture: A New Agenda for Theology* (Minneapolis: Fortress, 1997).

25 Magnus Mörner, *Race Mixture in the History of Latin America* (Boston: Little, Brown, 1967); Margaret R. Greer, Walter D. Mignolo, and Maureen Quilligan, eds., *Rereading the Black Legend: The Discourses of Religious and Racial Difference in the Renaissance Empires* (Chicago: University of Chicago Press, 2007).

26 Amy Chua, *World on Fire: How Exporting Free Market Democracy Breeds Ethnic Hatred and Global Instability* (New York: Anchor, 2004), Kindle edition; Edward E. Telles, *Race in Another America: The Significance of Skin Color in Brazil* (Princeton, N.J.: Princeton University Press, 2004); Eduardo Bonilla-Silva, *Racism without Racists: Color-Blind Racism and the Persistence of Racial Inequality in the United States* (Lanham, Md.: Rowman & Littlefield, 2006); Erynn Masi de Casanova, "'No Ugly Women': Concepts of Race and Beauty among Adolescent Women in Ecuador," *Gender and Society* 18, no. 3 (2004): 287–308; Gargi Bhattacharyya, John Gabriel, and Stephen Small, *Race and Power: Global Racism in the Twenty-First Century* (London: Routledge, 2002).

27 Emmanuel Chukwudi Eze, *Achieving Our Humanity: The Idea of the Postracial Future* (New York: Routledge, 2001); Eze, *Race and the Enlightenment: A Reader* (Cambridge: Blackwell, 1997).

28 Cited in Eze, *Race and the Enlightenment*, 29. Emphasis added.

29 Molly Rogers, *Delia's Tears: Race, Science, and Photography in Nineteenth-Century America* (New Haven, Conn.: Yale University Press, 2010); Saul Dubow, *Scientific Racism in Modern South Africa* (Cambridge: Cambridge University Press, 1995).

30 Sander L. Gilman, *Smart Jews: The Construction of the Image of Jewish Superior Intelligence* (Lincoln: University of Nebraska Press, 1996).

31 Casanova, "No Ugly Women," 287–308; Anne Anlin Cheng, "Wounded Beauty: An Exploratory Essay on Race, Feminism, and the Aesthetic Question," *Tulsa Studies*

in Women's Literature 19, no. 2 (2000): 191–217; Mimi Thi Nguyen, "The Biopower of Beauty: Humanitarian Imperialisms and Global Feminisms in an Age of Terror," *Signs* 36, no. 2 (2011): 359–83; Markus M. Mobius and Tanya S. Rosenblat, "Why Beauty Matters," *American Economic Review* 96, no. 1 (2006): 222–35.

32 St. John of Damascus, *Three Treatises on the Divine Image*, Kindle, L239.

33 St. John of Damascus, *Three Treatises on the Divine Image*, Kindle, L350.

34 St. John of Damascus, *Three Treatises on the Divine Image*, Kindle, L586.

35 James C. Scott, *Domination and the Arts of Resistance: Hidden Transcripts* (New Haven, Conn.: Yale University Press, 1990); Scott, *Weapons of the Weak: Everyday Forms of Peasant Resistance* (New Haven, Conn.: Yale University Press, 1985).

36 Cheng, "Wounded Beauty," 209.

37 Cheng, "Wounded Beauty," 209.

CHAPTER 13: REID-SALMON

1 See section V introduction, this volume, 149.

2 Percy C. Hintzen, "Diaspora, Globalization and the Politics of Identity," in *Culture, Politics, Race and Diaspora: The Thought of Stuart Hall*, ed. Brian Meeks (Kingston, Jamaica: Ian Randle Publishers, 2007), 249–68.

3 Irma Watkins-Owens, *Blood Relations: Caribbean Immigrants and the Harlem Community, 1900–1930* (Bloomington: Indiana University Press, 1996), 56–74.

4 Willie James Jennings, this volume, 163.

5 Jennings, this volume, 161–64.

6 Jennings, this volume, 164.

7 Jennings, this volume, 165.

8 Jennings, this volume, 173. My concern here is to what extent has Jennings taken into account the black religious worldview of the wholeness and interrelatedness of life where there is no separation between the secular and the sacred. The biblical understanding Jennings expresses comes close to this cosmology. For a detailed discussion, see John S. Mbiti, *African Religions and Philosophy* (London: Heinemann, 1969). Consult also Dale P. Andrews, *Practical Theology for Black Churches: Bridging Black Theology and African American Folk Religion* (Louisville, Ky.: Westminster John Knox, 2002), 24.

9 Jennings, this volume, 174–75. For a discussion on the mythical roots of racial prejudice, see Robert E. Hood, *Begrimed and Black: Christian Traditions and Blackness* (Minneapolis: Fortress, 1994); Sylvester A. Johnson, *The Myth of Ham in Nineteenth-Century American Christianity* (New York: Palgrave Macmillan, 2004). A major text on the constituents and rationale of the black diaspora can be found in Michelle M. Wright, *Becoming Black: Creating Identity in the African Diaspora* (Durham, N.C.: Duke University Press, 2004).

10 Kelly Brown Douglas, *What's Faith Got to Do with It? Black Bodies/Christian Souls* (Maryknoll, N.Y.: Orbis, 2005).

11 Jennings, this volume, 164.

12 Jennings, this volume, 164.

13 Jennings, this volume, 180.

14 Barbara Dianne Savage, *Your Spirits Walk beside Us: The Politics of Black Religion* (Cambridge, Mass.: Harvard University Press, 2008); Anthony B. Pinn, *The Black Church in the Post-Civil Rights Era* (Maryknoll, N.Y.: Orbis, 2002); C. Eric Lincoln

and Lawrence H. Mamiya, *The Black Church in the African American Experience* (Durham, N.C.: Duke University Press, 1990); Henry H. Mitchell, *Black Church Beginnings: The Long-Hidden Realities of the First Years* (Grand Rapids: Eerdmans, 2004).

15 Samuel K. Roberts, *African American Christian Ethics* (Cleveland: Pilgrim, 2001); Cheryl J. Sanders, *Empowerment Ethics for a Liberated People* (Minneapolis: Fortress, 1995); Peter J. Paris, *The Spirituality of African People: The Search for a Common Moral Discourse Ground* (Minneapolis: Fortress, 1995); Paris, *The Social Teaching of the Black Churches* (Philadelphia: Fortress, 1985).

16 Homer U. Ashby Jr., *Our Home Is over Jordon: A Black Pastoral Theology* (St. Louis: Chalice, 2003); Andrews, *Practical Theology for Black Churches*; James H. Harris, *Pastoral Theology: A Black-Church Perspective* (Minneapolis: Fortress, 1991).

17 See Willie Jennings, *The Christian Imagination: Theology and the Origins of Race* (New Haven, Conn.: Yale University Press, 2010); J. Kameron Carter, *Race: A Theological Account* (New York: Oxford University Press, 2008).

18 For a representative study of this issue, consult Dwight N. Hopkins, *Shoes That Fit Our Feet: Sources for a Constructive Black Theology* (Maryknoll, N.Y.: Orbis, 1993); Noel Erskine Erskine, *Decolonizing Theology: A Caribbean Perspective* (Maryknoll, N.Y.: Orbis, 1981).

19 Jennings, this volume, 165.

20 See, for example, James Cone, *Spirituals and the Blues* (Maryknoll, N.Y.: Orbis, 1992).

21 This intellectual framework and hermeneutic are delineated in the following works: Anthony G. Reddie, *Is God Colour-Blind? Insights from Black Theology for Christian Ministry* (London: SPCK, 2009); J. Deotis Roberts, *Africentric Christianity: A Theological Appraisal For Ministry* (Valley Forge, Pa.: Judson, 2000); Molefi Kete Asante, *Afrocentricity* (Trenton, N.J.: African World, 1988).

22 For an informative exploration of the subject, see Dwight N. Hopkins, *Being Human: Race, Culture, and Religion* (Minneapolis: Fortress, 2005).

23 Randall C. Bailey and Jacquelyn Grant, eds., *The Recovery of Black Presence: An Interdisciplinary Exploration* (Nashville: Abingdon, 1995).

24 Bob Marley, *Redemption Song* (Kingston, Jamaica: Island Records, 1973).

25 See Esther E. Acolatse, this volume, 151. For an alternative perspective of theology of pastoral care, see Andrews, *Practical Theology for Black Churches*, 24–30.

26 This is a very important idea in light of the general theories about the origins of the African American church traditions—namely, in response to rejection by the white church, in forms of African survivals and indigenous development. Dale Andrews offers an additional perspective, suggesting that the origin of the Black Church was in an intentional act by black Christians to establish their own space and community for worship; see Andrews, *Practical Theology for Black Churches*, 32. Acolatse departs from these general theories of the origin of the Black Church; her theory could be regarded as that of the origin of the black diasporan church.

27 Acolatse, this volume, 152.

28 Acolatse, this volume, 156.

29 Acolatse, this volume, 158.

30 Acolatse, this volume, 158.

31 Acolatse, this volume, 158.

32 Acolatse, this volume, 158.

33 Acolatse, this volume, 159–60.

34 Arthur Sunderland, *I Was a Stranger: Christian Theology of Hospitality* (Nashville: Abingdon, 2006); Amos Yong, *Hospitality and the Other: Pentecost, Christian Practices and the Neighbor* (Maryknoll, N.Y.: Orbis, 2008); Christine D. Pohl, *Making Room: Recovering Hospitality as a Christian Tradition* (Grand Rapids: Eerdmans, 1999).

35 Black theology has not given this issue the attention it deserves. For examples of theological treatment of this issue, consult Ched Myers and Matthew Colwell, *Our God Is Undocumented: Biblical Faith and Immigrant Justice* (Maryknoll, N.Y.: Orbis, 2012); Jean-Pierre Ruiz, *Readings from the Edges: The Bible on the Move* (Maryknoll, N.Y.: Orbis, 2011); Miguel A. De La Torre, *Trails of Hope and Terror: Testimonies on Immigration* (Maryknoll, N.Y.: Orbis, 2009). The moral and ethical basis of this practice is delineated in Dan W. Wilbanks, *Re-creating America: The Ethics of U.S. Immigration and Refugee Policy in a Christian Perspective* (Nashville: Abingdon, 1996).

36 Paula Allen-Meares and Sondra Burman, "The Engagement of African American Me: An Appeal for Social Work Action," *Journal of National Association of Social Workers* 40, no. 2 (1955): 5. See also Tom Feelings, *The Middle Passage* (New York: Dial, 1995).

37 Archie Smith Jr. and Ursula Riedel-Pfaefflin, *Siblings by Choice: Race, Gender, and Violence* (St. Louis: Chalice, 2004), 53–74.

38 My concern is to show that a significant sector of black Christian faith is under-represented in black theology. This project is an attempt to remedy this defect. The following works on this subject may be consulted: Delroy A. Reid-Salmon, *Home Away from Home: The Caribbean Diasporan Church in the Black Atlantic Tradition* (Oakville, Conn.: Equinox, 2008); John F. Sensbach, *Rebecca's Revival: Creating Black Christianity in the Atlantic World* (Cambridge, Mass.: Harvard University Press, 2005).

39 For suggested correctives to this problem, see Christine Chivallon, *The Black Diaspora of the Americas* (Kingston, Jamaica: Ian Randle Publishers, 2011); Gwendolyn Midlo Hall, *Slavery and African Ethnicities in the Americas* (Kingston, Jamaica: Ian Randle Publishers, 2006).

40 Katie Geneva Cannon, "Homecoming in the Hinterland," in *Ethics That Matters: African, Caribbean, and African American Sources*, ed. Marcia Y. Riggs and James Samuel Logan (Minneapolis: Fortress, 2012), 26.

41 Cannon, "Homecoming in the Hinterland," in Riggs and Logan, *Ethics That Matter*, 28–29. See also J. Deotis Roberts, *The Prophethood of Black Believers: An African American Political Theology for Ministry* (Louisville, Ky.: Westminster John Knox, 1994).

42 James Wm. McClendon Jr., *Systematic Theology, Volume 1: Ethics* (Nashville: Abingdon, 1986), 79–84.

43 Cannon, "Homecoming in the Hinterland," in Riggs and Logan, *Ethics That Matter*, 32–35.

44 Cannon, "Homecoming in the Hinterland," in Riggs and Logan, *Ethics That Matter*, 33. See also Obery M. Hendricks Jr., *The Universe Bends toward Justice: Radical Reflections on the Bible, the Church, and Body Politic* (Maryknoll, N.Y.: Orbis, 2011).

45   McClendon, *Systematic Theology, Volume 1: Ethics*, 83.

46   James Cone, *God of the Oppressed* (New York: Seabury, 1975), 217.

47   For further study on this subject, consult Albert Raboteau, *Slave Religion: The "Invisible Religion" in the Antebellum South* (New York: Oxford University Press, 1978); Gayraud Wilmore, *Black Religion and Black Radicalism: An Interpretation of the Religious History of Afro-American People* (Maryknoll, N.Y.: Orbis, 1984), 1–28, 238–41.

48   Russell R. McLeod, *Providing a Health-Care Sanctuary: Meeting the Needs of the Undocumented Alien* (Madison, N.J.: Drew University, 2003). Although McLeod's study lacks scholarly rigor, it provides useful information and serves as an important resource for study on the Caribbean Diasporan Church.

49   McLeod, *Providing a Health-Care Sanctuary*, 41–47.

50   For an informative discussion on the meaning of the term "diaspora," consult Hintzen, "Diaspora, Globalization and the Politics of Identity," in Meeks, *Culture, Politics, Race and Diaspora*, 249–68.

51   McLeod, *Providing a Health-Care Sanctuary*, 48.

52   McLeod, *Providing a Health-Care Sanctuary*, 50–51.

53   McLeod, *Providing a Health-Care Sanctuary*, 51.

54   Jack Nelson-Pallmeyer, *The Politics of Compassion* (Maryknoll, N.Y.: Orbis, 1988), 115.

55   Cannon, "Homecoming in the Hinterland," in Riggs and Logan, *Ethics That Matter*, 29.

56   Cannon, "Homecoming in the Hinterland," in Riggs and Logan, *Ethics That Matter*, 29.

CHAPTER 14: AMUGI LARTEY

1   Leonardo Boff, quoted in Rosino Gibellini, *The Liberation Theology Debate* (London: SCM Press, 1987), 4.

2   Dwight Hopkins, "Black Consciousness," in *Dictionary of Third World Theologies*, ed. Virginia Fabella and R. S. Sugirtharajah (Maryknoll, N.Y.: Orbis, 2000), 32.

3   Leonardo Boff and Clodovis Boff, *Introducing Liberation Theology* (Maryknoll, N.Y.: Orbis, 1987), 3.

4   See Dale P. Andrews, *Practical Theology for Black Churches: Bridging Black Theology and African American Folk Religion* (Louisville, Ky.: Westminster John Knox, 2002).

5   Boff and Boff, *Introducing Liberation Theology*, 5.

6   Tavis Smiley, *The Covenant with Black America* (Chicago: Third World, 2006), 11.

CHAPTER 15: ANTONIO

1   Thomas R. Frieden, Foreword, *CDC Health Disparities and Inequalities Report— United States (2011)*, Centers for Disease Control and Prevention, 1. The website for the report is online at http://www.cdc.gov/minorityhealth/CHDIR/2011/CHDIR2011.html#CHDIR, and the report is available in PDF format at http://www.cdc.gov/mmwr/pdf/other/su6001.pdf (accessed February 20, 2015).

2   "Disparities," HealthyPeople.gov, http://healthypeople.gov/2020/about/Disparities About.aspx (accessed August 25, 2014). Healthy People is a government program

that supports prevention efforts through the U.S. Department of Health and Human Services.

3   Centers for Disease Control and Prevention, "Racial/Ethnic Disparities among Children with Diagnoses of Perinatal HIV Infection—34 States, 2004–2007," *Morbidity and Mortality Weekly Report (MMWR)* 59, no. 4 (2010): 97–101, http://www .cdc.gov/mmwr/preview/mmwrhtml/mm5904a2.htm (accessed January 29, 2013).

4   All of this data is available from the U.S. Department of Health and Human Services Office of Minority Health: http://minorityhealth.hhs.gov/omh/browse .aspx?lvl=4&lvlID=21 (accessed August 25, 2014); and http://minorityhealth.hhs .gov (accessed January 29, 2013).

5   Gloria L. Beckles and Benedict I. Truman, "Education and Income—United States, 2005 and 2009," *CDC Health Disparities and Inequalities Report—United States (2011)*, 13.

6   Jaime Raymond, William Wheeler, and Mary Jean Brown, "Inadequate and Unhealthy Housing, 2007 and 2009," *CDC Health Disparities and Inequalities Report—United States (2011)*, 21–27.

7   Ramal Moonesinghe, Julia Zhu, and Benedict I. Truman, "Health Insurance Coverage—United States, 2004 and 2008," *CDC Health Disparities and Inequalities Report—United States (2011)*, 35–37.

8   Fuyuen Y. Yip, Jeffrey N. Pearcy, Paul L. Garbe, and Benedict I. Truman, "Unhealthy Air Quality—United States, 2006–2009," in *CDC Health Disparities and Inequalities Report—United States (2011)*, 28–32.

9   I recognize that the violence of the cross can and has been a stumbling block and that for communities of suffering, theology must not invoke so-called redemptive suffering without anguish.

10   "Neurological Complications of AIDS Fact Sheet," National Institute of Neurological Disorders and Stroke, http://www.ninds.nih.gov/disorders/aids/detail_aids.htm (accessed August 25, 2014); see also "Signs and Symptoms," http://www.aids.gov/ hiv-aids-basics/hiv-aids-101/signs-and-symptoms/ (accessed January 15, 2013).

11   Centers for Disease Control and Prevention, "Racial/Ethnic Disparities," 97–101.

12   Mindy Thompson Fullilove and Robert E. Fullilove III, "Stigma as an Obstacle to AIDS Action: The Case of the African American Community," *American Behavioral Scientist* 42, no. 7 (1999): 1121.

13   Edward V. Morse, Patricia M. Morse, Kendra E. Klebba, Mary R. Stock, Rex Forehand, and Evelina Panayotova, "The Use of Religion among HIV-Infected African American Women," *Journal of Religion and Health* 39, no. 3 (2000): 261–76.

14   For example, Timothy W. Sloan of St. Luke's Missionary Baptist Church (Humble, Tex.), Joseph Smith, assistant pastor at Alfred Street Baptist Church (Alexandria, Va.), Sheridan Todd Yeary (Baltimore, Md.), and Charles Coleman of Fisher Street United Methodist Church (Jonesboro, Ark.); see "NAACP Tries to Help Black Churches Fight HIV/AIDS," kait8.com, July 23, 2012, http://www.kait8.com/story/19093950/ naacp-tries-to-help-black-churches-fight-hivaids (accessed January 31, 2013).

15   See Sabin Russell, "Black Leaders Call for More HIV Testing: Disease Dispro-portionately Affects African American Women," SFGate.com, August 15, 2006, http://www.sfgate.com/health/article/Black-leaders-call-for-more-HIV-testing -Disease-2491165.php (accessed January 31, 2013).

16   See Jessica Gresko, "NAACP Develops HIV Manual for Black Churches," *Seattle Times*, July 21, 2012. Cf. http://www.blackhealthzone.com/naacp-develops-hiv-churches.

17   Riley C. Snorton, *No One Is Supposed to Know: Black Sexuality on the Down Low* (Minneapolis: University of Minnesota Press, 2014). The phrase "on the down low" describes black men who have sexual intercourse with both men and women but do not describe themselves as gay or queer; see Cathy J. Jones, *The Boundaries of Blackness: AIDS and the Breakdown of Black Politics* (Chicago: University of Chicago Press, 1999).

18   See Gerhard Falk, *Stigma: How We Treat Outsiders* (New York: Prometheus, 2001).

19   Balm in Gilead, http://www.balmingilead.org/index.php/about/about-the-balm .html (accessed August 25, 2014).

20   Edward P. Antonio, "Answering Tough Questions: Tragedy and the Justice of God," *Circuit Rider* (Aug/Sept/Oct 2012), http://www.ministrymatters.com/all/entry/ 3084/article-answering-tough-questions-tragedy-and-the-justice-of-god (accessed August 23, 2014).

21   Antonio, "Answering Tough Questions."

CHAPTER 16: STEWART

1   Howard W. Stone and James O. Duke, *How to Think Theologically* (Minneapolis: Fortress, 2006), v–vi.

2   Stone and Duke, *How to Think Theologically*, 15.

3   Stone and Duke, *How to Think Theologically*, 16.

4   Jimmy Allen, *Burden of a Secret: A Story of Truth and Mercy in the Face of AIDS* (Nashville: Moorings, 1995), 207.

5   Mbwambo, Kilonzo, et al. (2004), cited in Jessica Ogden and Laura Nyblade, "Common at Its Core: HIV-Related Stigma across Contexts," International Center for Research on Women–ICRW (2005), 33, http://www.icrw.org/files/publications/ Common-at-its-Core-HIV-Related-Stigma-Across-Contexts.pdf (accessed November 30, 2013).

6   Tom Charlier, "Memphis 'a Perfect Storm for HIV,'" *Commercial Appeal*, July 29, 2012, http://www.commercialappeal.com/news/local-news/hiv-rampant-among -african-americans-as-memphis (accessed August 22, 2014).

7   Emmanuel Y. Amugi Lartey, this volume, 204–5.

8   Lartey, this volume, 206; emphasis in original.

9   Centers for Disease Control and Prevention, http://www.cdc.gov/hiv/statistics/ surveillance/incidence/ (accessed August 22, 2014).

10   Lartey, this volume, 206.

11   Lartey, this volume, 212.

12   Sara Doughton, "Raphael Warnock's Piety and Protest: Saving Bodies and Souls," Yale University Notes from the Quad (March 2013), http://notesfromthequad .yale.edu/notes/2013-03-05-000000/raphael-warnocks-piety-and-protest-saving -bodies-and-souls (accessed August 22, 2014).

13   Cheryl A. Sanders, *Ministry at the Margins: The Prophetic Mission of Women, Youth and the Poor* (Downers Grove, Ill.: InterVarsity, 1997), 28.

14   LaShieka Purvis Hunter, "HIV/AIDS at 30: Edwin Sanders Ministers to 'Whosoever They May Be,'" Colorlines.com, March 28, 2011, http://colorlines.com/

archives/2011/03/hivaids_at_30_edwin_sanders_ministers_to_whosoever_they
_may_be.html (accessed November 30, 2013).

15 Robert Balint and Kristen Meinzer, producers, "Fighting AIDS from the Pulpit, Beginning with the Pastor Himself," Takeaway, July 25, 2012, http://www.the takeaway.org/2012/jul/25/fighting-aids-pulpit-beginning-pastor-himself/ (accessed November 30, 2013).

16 J. Deotis Roberts, *The Prophethood of Black Believers* (Louisville, Ky.: Westminster John Knox, 1994), 90.

17 Lartey, this volume, 210.

18 Robert S. Harvey, "Restoring the Social Justice Identity of the Black Church," *Student Pulse* 2, no. 2 (2010), http://www.studentpulse.com/articles/162/restoring -the-social-justice-identity-of-the-black-church (accessed November 30, 2013).

19 Lartey, this volume, 210–11.

20 Brad R. Braxton, "The Holy Spirit, Jesus and Social Justice in Black Churches: Making Noise or Making a Difference?" *Huffington Post*, March 5, 2011, http://www .huffingtonpost.com/brad-r-braxton/the-spirit-jesus-and-soci_b_829665.html (accessed November 30, 2013).

PART VII INTRODUCTION

1 See the 2003 University of Maryland study and the 2007 Yale University School of Law study cited on the Amnesty International website entitled "Death Penalty and Race," http://www.amnestyusa.org/our-work/issues/death-penalty/us-death-penalty -facts/death-penalty-and-race (accessed January 11, 2015). Amnesty International's full report, "United States of America: Death by Discrimination—The Continuing Role of Race in Capital Cases," April 23, 2003, can be found here: http://www .amnesty.org/en/library/info/AMR51/046/2003/en (accessed January 11, 2015).

CHAPTER 17: BATTLE

1 E. A. Wallis Budge, trans., *The Paradise of the Holy Fathers* (Seattle: St. Nectarious, 1984), 2:332–33.

2 Jess Mawhirt, "Segregation and Incarceration: How Life in the Ghetto Leads to Life in Prisons for Young Black Men," *Colgate Academic Review* 7, art. 9 (2012): 153, http://commons.colgate.edu/car/vol7/iss1/9 (accessed March 4, 2013).

3 Michelle Alexander, *The New Jim Crow: Mass Incarceration in the Age of Color-blindness* (2010; New York: New Press, 2012).

4 Amnesty International, "United States of America: Death by Discrimination—The Continuing Role of Race in Capital Cases," *AMR* 51, no. 46 (2003): 1–60, http:// www.amnesty.org/en/library/info/AMR51/046/2003/en (accessed March 4, 2013); see also University of Maryland Study, January 2003, "An Empirical Analysis of Maryland's Death Sentencing System with Respect to the Influence of Race and Legal Jurisdiction," http://www.aclu-md.org/uploaded_files/0000/0376/md_death _penalty_race_study.pdf (accessed February 26, 2015); see also the Yale University Study, December 2007, available online via the Death Penalty Information Center website, http://www.deathpenaltyinfo.org/node/2245 (accessed March 4, 2013).

5 Wandera-Chagenda, "Zero Hour," in *African Christian Spirituality*, ed. Aylward Shorter (Maryknoll, N.Y.: Orbis, 1980), 57.

6   Lamin Sanneh, *Translating the Message* (Maryknoll, N.Y.: Orbis, 1989).

7   Sanneh, *Translating the Message*, 167.

8   Rowan Williams, Archbishop of Canterbury, "Criminal Justice—Building Responsibility," Prison Reform Trust Lecture, press release February 1, 2007, http://rowanwilliams.archbishopofcanterbury.org/articles.php/1446/commission -of-inquiry-needed-into-failing-penal-system-lecture-criminal-justice-building -responsibil (accessed August 23, 2014).

9   Sanneh, *Translating the Message*, 172.

10 Sanneh, *Translating the Message*, 203.

11 Sanneh, *Translating the Message*, 173.

12 Frederick Buechner, *Wishful Thinking: A Seeker's ABC* (San Francisco: Harper-SanFrancisco, 1993), 119.

13 This mutuality also reflects a presupposition in secular theories of education that the authentic teacher makes words and behavior congruent; see Stephen D. Brookfield, *The Skillful Teacher* (San Francisco: Jossey-Bass, 1990).

CHAPTER 18: WARNOCK

1   James H. Cone, "Theology's Great Sin: Silence in the Face of White Supremacy," *Union Seminary Quarterly Review* 55, nos. 3–4 (2001): 3.

2   Helmut Gollwitzer, "Why Black Theology?" in *Black Theology: A Documentary History, Volume One: 1966–1979*, ed. James H. Cone and Gayraud S. Wilmore (Maryknoll, N.Y.: Orbis, 1979), 159. See also John Patrick Daly, *When Slavery Was Called Freedom: Evangelicalism, Proslavery, and the Causes of the Civil War* (Lexington: University Press of Kentucky, 2002); and H. Shelton Smith, *In His Image, but . . . : Racism in Southern Religion, 1780–1910* (Durham, N.C.: Duke University Press, 1972).

3   See Douglas A. Blackmon, *Slavery by Another Name: The Re-enslavement of Black Americans from the Civil War to World War II* (New York: Doubleday, 2008).

4   Martin Luther King Jr., "Letter from Birmingham Jail," in *Why We Can't Wait* (New York: Harper & Row, 1964), 90–91. Emphasis added.

5   James H. Cone, *God of the Oppressed* (San Francisco: Harper, 1975), 52–53.

6   See Joseph Johnson, "Jesus, the Liberator," in *Quest for a Black Theology*, ed. James J. Gardiner and J. Deotis Roberts (Philadelphia: Pilgrim, 1971), 97–111; and Johnson, "The Need for a Black Christian Theology," *Journal of the Interdenominational Theological Center* 2, no. 2 (1974): 19–29. See also Lawrence E. Lucas, *Black Priest/ White Church: Catholics and Racism* (New York: Random House, 1970); Leon Watts, "The Black Church Yes! COCU No!" *Renewal* 10, no. 3 (1970): 10–11; and Gilbert Caldwell, "Black Folk in White Churches," *Christian Century*, February 12, 1969, 209–11. See also J. Alfred Smith Sr.'s reflections on the impact of this revolutionary period on his pastoral ministry and the significance of black theology in the context of urban uprisings and challenges by black youth to his Christian identity in the context of Oakland, California. Smith, "Black Theology and the Parish Ministry," in *Black Faith and Public Talk*, ed. Dwight Hopkins (Maryknoll, N.Y.: Orbis, 1999), 89–95; and J. Smith, *On the Jericho Road: A Memoir of Racial Justice, Social Action and Prophetic Ministry* (Downers Grove, Ill.: InterVarsity, 2004).

7   See Dwight N. Hopkins and George C. L. Cummings, *Cut Loose Your Stammering Tongue: Black Theology in the Slave Narratives*, 2nd ed. (Louisville, Ky.: Westminster John Knox, 2003).

8   Michelle Alexander, *The New Jim Crow: Mass Incarceration in the Age of Color-blindness* (New York: New Press, 2010).

9   Alexander, *New Jim Crow*, 16.

10 See David P. Wright's and Hans Hubner's discussions of "Unclean and Clean" in the Old Testament and the New Testament, respectively, in *The Anchor Bible Dictionary*, vol. 6, ed. David Noel Freedman (New York: Doubleday, 1992), 729–45. Among the many examples of Jesus' radical confrontation with the religion and politics of uncleanness are Mark 2:15-17 and Luke 15:1-2.

11 See Gayraud Wilmore, *Black Religion and Black Radicalism: An Interpretation of the Religious History of Afro-American People*, 3rd ed. (Maryknoll, N.Y.: Orbis, 1983), 163–95.

12 See Glorya Askew and Gayraud Wilmore, eds., *Reclamation of Black Prisoners: A Challenge to the African American Church; A Book for Individual and Congregational Study* (Atlanta: ITC, 1992).

13 Raphael Warnock, *The Divided Mind of the Black Church: Theology, Piety, and Public Witness* (New York: New York University Press, 2014), 190.

14 Exod 3:8.

15 Rev 21:1.

16 Letter dated Saturday, May 10, 1740. See Frank Lambert, "I Saw the Book Talk: Slave Readings of the First Great Awakening," *Journal of Negro History* 77, no. 4 (1992): 185–98.

17 Martin Luther King Jr., *Stride toward Freedom: The Montgomery Story* (San Francisco: Harper & Row, 1958), 44.

18 See Dale S. Recinella, *The Biblical Truth about America's Death Penalty* (Boston: Northeastern University Press, 2004), 247–73.

19 Jen Marlowe and Martina Davis-Correia, with Troy Anthony Davis, *I Am Troy Davis* (Chicago: Haymarket, 2013).

20 Gunnar Myrdal, *An American Dilemma: The Negro Problem and Modern Democracy* (New Brunswick, N.J.: Transaction, 1996).

CHAPTER 19: MCCLENNEY

1   Madeline McClenney-Sadler, *A Savior for People with a Record* (Durham, N.C., March 27, 1997; rev. 2012); all rights reserved.

2   Officer Mark MacPhail was murdered while protecting a homeless man from an assault. Although the weapon was not recovered, the prosecution reportedly called eyewitnesses. Seven of the nine witnesses began recanting within five years of the time a jury unanimously found Mr. Davis guilty and sentenced him to death.

3   Zero-tolerance policies provide for immediate punishment of an infraction and limit authority figures in their use of discretionary measures to curb misconduct.

4   John 8:2-11.

5   John 7:30; John 10:39.

6   Steven Donziger, ed., *The Real War on Crime* (New York: HarperCollins, 1996), 9.

7   Donziger, *Real War on Crime*, 10.

8   Donziger, *Real War on Crime*, 16.

9 Proposition 36 was passed in 2012. California's three-strikes law now requires the third offense to be serious or violent.

10 Donziger, *Real War on Crime*, 19.

11 "Developments in the Law: Race and the Criminal Process," *Harvard Law Review* 101, no. 7 (1988): 1473–1641.

12 Donziger, *Real War on Crime*, 115; emphasis added.

13 Jack Guttentag, "Another View of Predatory Lending," Wharton Financial Institutions Center, revised August 21, 2000, 5, http://fic.wharton.upenn.edu/fic/papers/01/0123.pdf (accessed August 21, 2014).

14 See William Emmons, "The Foreclosure Crisis in 2008: Predatory Lending or Household Overreaching?" *Regional Economist* (July 2011): 12–15.

15 Annamaria Lusardi, Chris Bumcrot, Judy Lin, and Tippy Ulicny, "Financial Capability in the U.S.: Report of Findings from the 2012 National Financial Capability Study," May 2013, http://www.usfinancialcapability.org/about.php (accessed August 21, 2014); prepared by the Financial Industry Regulatory Authority (FINRA) Investor Education Foundation.

16 Michelle Alexander, *The New Jim Crow: Mass Incarceration in the Age of Colorblindness* (New York: New Press, 2012), 182.

17 Matt 9:9-13.

18 John 8:10-11.

19 Mark 14:66-72.

20 John 4:16-18.

21 Luke 23:43.

22 An outdated and derogatory reference to the frightening appearance of a person of African descent.

23 Debra Rosenthal, *Harriet Beecher Stowe's "Uncle Tom's Cabin": A Routledge Study Guide and Sourcebook* (New York: Routledge, 2004), 35.

24 "Whites have used Christ to 'order' and maintain the status quo and Blacks have used Christ to overturn the status quo and 're-order' society," says Dr. Rodney Sadler in "Do We Worship the Same God?" (unpublished speech for Mecklenburg Ministries in Charlotte, N.C., 2008). See James Cone, "The Terrible Beauty of the Cross and the Tragedy of the Lynching Tree," in *The Cross and the Lynching Tree* (Maryknoll, N.Y.: Orbis, 2011), 30–64. See also H. Shelton Smith, *In His Image, but . . . : Racism in Southern Religion 1780–1910* (Durham, N.C.: Duke University Press, 1972); and Robert E. Hood, *Begrimed and Black: Christian Traditions on Blacks and Blackness* (Minneapolis: Fortress, 1994), 18–19.

25 I add the descriptor "priestly" to indicate that social justice is indeed a matter of personal piety and priestly duty for a community that upholds the directive to be a "nation of priests," as found in Exod 19:6.

26 See the Exodus Foundation website, www.exodusfoundation.org.

27 Mark Morris, ed., *Instead of Prisons: A Handbook for Abolitionists* (New York: Prison Research Education Project, 1976), 10.

28 See Lev 5–6; Howard Zehr, *The Little Book of Restorative Justice* (Intercourse, Pa.: Good Books, 2002); and James Samuel Logan, *Good Punishment? Christian Moral Practice and U.S. Imprisonment* (Grand Rapids: Eerdmans, 2008).

29 Logan, *Good Punishment?* 10.

30 "Unviolent" connotes that no physical injury occurred, whereas "nonviolent" connotes a purposeful effort toward reconciliation. See Morris, *Instead of Prisons*, 10.

31 A term I coined to denote hatred of the poor using the Greek prefix "mis," to hate, and "ptoxos," the poor or bent over.

32 Deut 22:25-26.

33 Consider cases like that of Pastor Eddie Long where the questionable appropriateness of admitted contact is enough for congregational leaders to take investigative action. See the case of God calling me to minister to a young girl whose preacher-father was charged with indecent behavior with a minor. Madeline McClenney-Sadler, "For God's Sake, Mommie Help!" in *Mother Goose, Mother Jones, Mommie Dearest: Biblical Mothers and Their Children*, ed. Cheryl A. Kirk-Duggan and Tina Pippin (Atlanta: SBL Series, 2009), 9–22.

34 The cost of theft is estimated at $10 billion annually, and the cost of foreclosures at $2.2 trillion over the five-year period from 2007 to 2012. Compare $50 billion in theft to $2.2 trillion in foreclosures.

35 See forthcoming article tentatively titled "Believers Unchained."

36 Lev 17–26.

37 See Carl Upchurch, *Convicted in the Womb* (New York: Bantam, 1997).

38 Alexander, *New Jim Crow*, 180–82; emphasis added.

39 Mary Douglas, "Witchcraft and Leprosy: Two Strategies of Exclusion," *Man*, new series, vol. 26, no. 4 (1991): 723–36.

40 Pastor Russ Dean, Myers Park Baptist Church, Charlotte, N.C.

41 Madeline McClenney-Sadler, "A Letter to African-American Churches concerning the Saints Coming Home from Prison," in *Ministry with Prisoners and Families: The Way Forward*, ed. W. Wilson Goode Sr., Charles E. Lewis Jr., and Harold Dean Trulear (Valley Forge, Pa.: Judson, 2011).

LIST OF CONTRIBUTORS

ESTHER E. ACOLATSE is Assistant Professor of the Practice of Pastoral Theology and World Christianity in The Divinity School at Duke University, Durham, N.C.

DONNA E. ALLEN is Pastor at New Revelation Community Church, Oakland, Calif.

DALE P. ANDREWS is Distinguished Professor of Homiletics, Social Justice, and Practical Theology in The Divinity School at Vanderbilt University, Nashville, Tenn.

EDWARD P. ANTONIO is Harvey H. Potthoff Associate Professor of Christian Theology, Associate Dean of Diversities, and Director of Justice & Peace at Iliff School of Theology, Denver, Colo.

MICHAEL BATTLE is President of PeaceBattle Institute, Raleigh, N.C., and Interim Dean of Students and Community Life, Episcopal Divinity School, Cambridge, Mass.

JAMES H. EVANS JR. is Robert K. Davies Professor of Systematic Theology at Colgate Rochester Crozer Divinity School, Rochester, N.Y.

DIANA L. HAYES is Emerita Professor of Systematic Theology at Georgetown University, Washington, D.C.

WILLIE JAMES JENNINGS is Associate Professor of Theology and Black Church Studies in The Divinity School at Duke University, Durham, N.C.

EMMANUEL Y. AMUGI LARTEY is L. Bevel Jones III Professor of Pastoral Theology, Care, and Counseling in the Candler School of Theology at Emory University, Atlanta, Ga.

MADIPOANE MASENYA (NGWAN'A MPHAHLELE) is Professor of Old Testament Studies in the Department of Biblical and Ancient Studies at the University of South Africa, Pretoria, and an ordained minister in the International Assemblies of God Church in South Africa.

MADELINE MCCLENNEY is President at Exodus Foundation.org, Huntersville, N.C.

EVELYN L. PARKER is Professor of Practical Theology and Associate Dean for Academic Affairs in the Perkins School of Theology at Southern Methodist University, Dallas, Tex.

ANTHONY G. REDDIE is Coordinator of Community Education at Bristol Baptist College, Bristol, U.K.

DELROY A. REID-SALMON is Pastor at Grace Baptist Chapel, Bronx, N.Y., and research fellow at Oxford Centre for Christianity and Culture, Regent's Park College, U.K.

PHILLIS ISABELLA SHEPPARD is Associate Professor of Religion, Psychology, and Culture in The Divinity School at Vanderbilt University, Nashville, Tenn.

ROBERT LONDON SMITH JR. is Pastor at Rubislaw Parish Church, Aberdeen, U.K., and honorary researcher in King's College at University of Aberdeen, U.K.

GINA M. STEWART is Pastor at Christ Missionary Baptist Church, Memphis, Tenn.

RAPHAEL WARNOCK is Pastor at Ebenezer Baptist Church, Atlanta, Ga.

DENNIS W. WILEY and CHRISTINE Y. WILEY are Co-pastors at Covenant Baptist United Church of Christ, Washington, D.C.

JEREMIAH A. WRIGHT JR. is Pastor Emeritus at Trinity United Church of Christ, Chicago, Ill.

Index

2012 National Financial Capability Study, 285

abolitionist, 289–91, 294, 296
Academic English Mastery Program, 90
aesthetic regime, 163–64, 166, 171, 179–80, 188–89
aesthetics of whiteness, 164
Africana Bible, 153
ageism, 14, 17–18, 27, 30, 36, 41, 48–49, 51–53, 55, 213
AIDS Foundation, 231
Alexander, Michelle, 92, 251, 256, 272, 278, 287, 294
Alim, Samy, 86
Allen, Jimmy, 235
American Academy of Religion, 278
Antony, St., 255, 257
artistic ecclesiology, 182, 184, 190
Astley, Jeff, 60
Augustine, St., 106; *City of God*, 107, 323–24; *Confessions*, 106–7

Balm in Gilead, 231
Banks, James, 61

Barr, Bob, 277
Barth, Karl, 45
bell hooks, 33, 61, 63
bilingual: analysis, 160; pastoral practice, 305; skills, 156, 158, 160; theological speech, 156
Black Church, 6, 9, 20, 24, 27, 39–41, 44, 48–53, 55, 59, 76–77, 98, 113–14, 122, 124, 126–27, 132, 150–54, 187–90, 204–6, 208–9, 227–28, 237–38, 248–49, 257–58, 271, 273–74, 278–79, 289
black church conservatism, 134
black consciousness, 3, 203, 300
black diaspora, 191, 193–95, 197
Black Power, 124, 130, 140, 142, 164, 269
black practical theology, 3–10, 12–15, 60–61, 110, 114–15, 22, 193–95, 197–98, 217–18, 226–27, 229–30, 248, 299–311; liberative, 60; *see also* practical black theology; theology, black
black thematic universe, 8–9
black theological anthropology, 106